THE MARK OF SHAME

Stigma of Mental Illness and an Agenda for Change

Stephen P. Hinshaw

OXFORD
UNIVERSITY PRESS
2007

OXFORD
UNIVERSITY PRESS

Oxford University Press, Inc., publishes works that further
Oxford University's objective of excellence
in research, scholarship, and education.

Oxford   New York
Auckland   Cape Town   Dar es Salaam   Hong Kong   Karachi
Kuala Lumpur   Madrid   Melbourne   Mexico City   Nairobi
New Delhi   Shanghai   Taipei   Toronto

With offices in
Argentina   Austria   Brazil   Chile   Czech Republic   France   Greece
Guatemala   Hungary   Italy   Japan   Poland   Portugal   Singapore
South Korea   Switzerland   Thailand   Turkey   Ukraine   Vietnam

Published by Oxford University Press, Inc.
198 Madison Avenue, New York, New York 10016

www.oup.com

Oxford is a registered trademark of Oxford University Press

Library of Congress Cataloging-in-Publication Data
Hinshaw, Stephen P.
The mark of shame : stigma of mental illness and an agenda for
change / Stephen P. Hinshaw.
    p. cm.
Includes bibliographical references.
ISBN 978-0-19-530844-0
1. Mental illness—Social aspects.   2. Mental illness—Public opinion.
3. Stigma (Social psychology).   I. Title.
RC455.2.P83H56 2006
616.89—dc22   2006019106

9 8 7 6 5 4 3
Printed in the United States of America
on acid-free paper

Acknowledgments

Writing a book of this sort is a labor of love. Throughout my work, I have learned a wide array of concepts, I have read diverse scientific literatures, and I have scoured references from works of history to articles in current magazines and newspapers. Without support, I couldn't have done it.

Dante Cicchetti encouraged me to contribute an article on stigma and mental illness for a special issue of his journal, *Development and Psychopathology*, a number of years ago. At that time he knew of the writing I was doing on my father's lifelong mental illness and of my growing interest in the shame and silence that too often accompany mental disorders. After we wrote that article together, both Dante and Sheree Toth were to have been my coauthors for this book. Yet my own momentum on the project and their increasing involvement in numerous other activities prevented this collaboration from coming to fruition. Still, several of the vignettes about children in these pages emanate from them, as do some of the key thoughts about resilience and developmental issues. I thank them heartily for their efforts and support.

A number of people who study stigma have been instrumental in guiding my ideas. I express my deep admiration for these pioneers: Patrick Corrigan, Jennifer Crocker, John Dovidio, Amerigo Farina, Susan Fiske, Samuel Gaertner, Erving Goffman, Nick Haslam, Bruce Link, Brenda Major, David Penn, Jo Phelan, Norman Sartorius, Otto Wahl, and many others. I have ridden on their shoulders; the next generation of scholars and activists owes them a major debt of gratitude.

For careful and thoughtful reading of chapter drafts, I express my great appreciation to Andrea Stier and Rudy Mendoza-Denton, whose critiques were sharp and insightful. For perceptive comments on selected chapters, I thank David Donovan, Joelle LeMoult, and Lynn O'Connor. For ideas, encouragement, and general support, I express my appreciation to Mario Aceves, Brian Bohn, Jessica Borelli, Whitney Brechwald, John Guerry, and Liz Owens. Two anonymous reviewers made cogent comments on a penultimate draft. For mentorship when I was an intern at UCLA's Neuropsychiatric Institute, as well as sensitization to issues related to stigma, I deeply thank Kay Redfield Jamison. For masterful editorial assistance, I express my appreciation to Catherine Fan.

My editor at Oxford University Press, Catharine Carlin, has been entirely encouraging from the moment we discussed the possibility of this book. As any writer knows, such support and encouragement are essential during the many times that the author begins to wonder whether things will ever really come together. She has a keen eye and ear for conveying essential messages.

In many ways, a book like this has been a lifetime in the planning. If it weren't for the experiences in which I grew up, including my father's lifelong mental disorder and his gradual opening up to me as I attained adulthood, I would not have become interested in mental illness and the stigma that surrounds it. And if it weren't for the support of my mother, no one in our family could have made it through. Both of them are the ultimate sources of this work.

My wife, Kelly Campbell Hinshaw, has been a constant support, emotionally and intellectually. She is embarking on her own book project at present in order to give children everywhere the gifts of her artistic eye. My love and gratitude are endless, Kel. My oldest son, Jeffrey Wyn Hinshaw, is embarking on adulthood, and my hopes are that he can blend science and compassion in his life work. It is for our youngest, Evan Robert Hinshaw, that I have my most fervent hopes—that he can grow up in a world that is far less prone to dehumanizing and stigmatizing mental illness.

Many authors say it, but it nonetheless true here: All of these people deserve my deep accolades, but any errors or misstatements are fully my own.

Although I have great hopes that this work will help to provide a surge of interest, enthusiasm, and rigor in an area that is continuing to rise in importance, I will be pleased if these words help even one beginning research investigator, one budding clinician, or one frustrated yet hopeful individual or family member who is dealing with mental disorder. I dedicate this book to all persons with mental illness, along with their caregivers and support systems. All we are asking for is a fighting chance.

Contents

Introduction   ix

1 What Is Mental Disorder and What Is Stigma?   3

2 Perspectives From Social Psychology, Sociology,
  and Evolutionary Psychology   28

3 Historical Perspectives on Mental Illness and Stigma   53

4 Modern Conceptions of Mental Disorder   73

5 Evidence From Scientific Investigations   93

6 Indicators of Stigma From Everyday Life   115

7 Stigma of Mental Illness: An Integration   140

8 Research Directions and Priorities   157

9 Overcoming Stigma I: Legislation, Policy, and Community Efforts   176

10 Overcoming Stigma II: Media and Mental Health Professionals   202

11 Overcoming Stigma III: Families and Individuals   217

12 Concluding Issues   232

Notes   245

References   285

Index   317

Introduction

Mental illness has been part of the human condition for as long as our species has existed, affecting countless individuals, families, and communities. Major advances regarding mental disorders are now appearing with regularity, particularly with respect to treatment options. Yet emotional reactions to mental disorder are still dominated by fear, pity, and scorn; societal responses continue to be characterized by banishment, punishment, and neglect. Although the very nature of mental illness makes it understandable that empathy is difficult to sustain, the lack of respect and fairness signals deeper currents.

At one level, things appear to be changing. People with mental disorders are "coming out of the closet" with increasing frequency. Celebrities and authors now openly disclose their stories of substance abuse, mood disorder and treatment with electroconvulsive therapy (Kitty Dukakis), postpartum depression (Brooke Shields), bipolar disorder (Jane Pauley), or suicidality (William Styron); star athletes are coming forward with their experiences in therapy (for example, Alex Rodríguez, the New York Yankee and American League Most Valuable Player in 2005).[1] Even those without celebrity status are more open and increasingly likely to admit that they see a therapist or take psychoactive medications such as Prozac or similar compounds. Have we in fact entered a new era of openness and tolerance?

In 1999 President Bill Clinton and Tipper Gore sponsored the first-ever White House Conference on Mental Health.[2] This conference made public the importance of mental disorder and stated explicitly that people with mental disorders must be accorded the same respect as those with physical illnesses. During that same year the Surgeon General of the United States, Dr. David Satcher, released a report on mental disorder, the first such report ever to emanate from that high office. Noteworthy in this landmark document was the contention that stigma is the "most formidable obstacle to future progress in the arena of mental illness and mental health."[3] Both events gave hope that public discussion would become commonplace. With less fanfare, the New Freedom Commission on Mental Health reiterated, in the summer of 2003, that the current system of mental health care in the United States is "in shambles" and that core elements for change include greater public understanding of mental health issues, early detection of mental illness, elimination of disparities in access to care, enhanced scientific research, and a family- and consumer-driven approach to service provision.[4] At the same time, other nations are actively promoting national-level public-awareness campaigns.[5]

These are indeed encouraging signs. But it is also important to examine the other side of the coin. For instance, harsh counterattacks by other celebrities have gained notoriety—for example, the berating of Brooke Shields by actor Tom Cruise, whose headline views in 2005 included the belief that mental illness portrays weakness and that medication treatment poisons the body. At a larger level, research funds on the causes of and treatments for mental illness still lag well behind expenditures for physical illnesses, and insurance coverage for mental disorders does not have parity with coverage for other conditions. Even professionals and scientists in the mental health fields must contend with stigma, as the study and treatment of mental disorder rank low in terms of prestige.

People with mental illness continue to suffer discrimination, including a lack of viable opportunities for housing and employment, as well as restrictions on the right to vote, obtain a driver's license, or maintain child custody. These kinds of discrimination are often triggered simply by a history of mental disorder rather than by any documented disability. Media stereotypes emphasize the high rates of violence among those with mental illness and treat the entire topic with misinformation and even ridicule. The truth is that only a small subgroup of people with mental illness are likely to be violent—but the risk of being *victimized* by violent crime is far greater in people with serious mental disorders than in the general population. This fact conveys the marginal existence of far too many people who experience mental illness.[6]

Throughout history, people with mental disorders have been the victims of punitive, cruel, and even genocidal practices. Today, well-intended deinstitutionalization strategies, which have virtually emptied most mental hospitals, have lacked sufficient funding for community treatments. As a result, urban streets are flooded with individuals who quickly become homeless or who must live in facilities that can be as degrading as those of the large state hospitals of a few decades ago. In the remaining public hospitals, conditions are marked by understaffing, patient assaults, drug trafficking, dangerously high levels of psychotropic medications, and suicides.[7] Such circumstances apply across the world; neglect and abandonment do not recognize national or cultural boundaries.

Given the negative perceptions of mental illness, and given the ignorance that is still rampant, it is not surprising that a great many people with mental disorders delay seeking help for years, even decades.[8] Concealment remains a major means of coping, as a history of mental illness is near the bottom of the list of life experiences most people would ever wish to divulge. Family members are strongly affected, experiencing guilt, self-blame, closed doors, and a clear sense of psychological burden. Stigma toward relatives is fueled by the prevailing view that mental illness is caused by faulty upbringing—which until recently was the dominant perspective of the mental health professions.

Stigma

How can those interested in mental illness understand this state of affairs? *Stigma* is a term conveying a deep, shameful mark or flaw related to being a member of a group that is devalued by the societal mainstream. Racial minorities have been stigmatized throughout history, as have many other outgroups. My contention, increasingly shared by almost everyone who does serious research on this topic, is that individuals with mental illness receive extreme stigma.

What, for example, is the worst thing that one can be called in modern society? Think of the following terms: crazy, nuts, loco, wacko, psycho, off your rocker, out of your mind, mental case, schizo, deranged—just a few of the synonyms and slang phrases for mental illness, which rival ethnic, racial, and sexual epithets as sources of ridicule. Some of these words are among the first used by young children to discount and dismiss disliked peers, signaling that stigmatization permeates our language throughout the lifespan. Although current standards prevent most of us from using the kinds of racial and ethnic slurs that were common a generation ago, there are few restrictions on terms of ridicule to denote mental disorder. It is not only permissible but also quite common to brand persons showing ignorance as "retards," individuals with aberrant behavior as "psychos," and unpopular ideas as "crazy" or "insane."

Think also of the words used throughout history to describe mental illness: insanity, madness, and lunacy, to name just three. These imply a permanent loss of the capacity for reason, which often justifies placing restrictions of the rights of those who are afflicted. The pain engendered by mental illness is searing enough, but the devastation of being invisible, shameful, and toxic can make the situation practically unlivable.

Many aspects of mental illness are difficult for relatives or members of society to contend with. Indeed, despairing, angry, irrational, or out-of-control behavior patterns can raise fears over safety and may threaten a fundamental sense of stability and mental control. Creating distance from the person in question, and even putting that person down, can preserve self-esteem and ward off the threat, at least in the short run. Yet the distancing and rejection serve to magnify fear and ignorance, creating a vicious cycle.

Once the castigation begins, perceivers come to view those with mental illness as lacking the fundamental qualities of humanity. History shows that when subhuman status is assumed, harsh consequences typically follow. It is difficult to put into words the plight of people with mental disorders throughout history, but the following examples may give at least a flavor:[9]

- Early human skulls, dating from many thousands of years ago, show evidence of circular holes bored into them, holes that could have been created only from other humans' having pierced them with sharp, round instruments, presumably to aid in the release of evil spirits from inside their heads.
- Throughout history, societies have tended to banish persons with mental disorders from the mainstream, leaving them on the utter margins of society. "The insane were pariahs who wandered over the countryside in the manner of werewolves, seeking shelter in stables and pigsties . . . people mocked at them, beat, tortured, or burned them."[10]
- Hundreds of thousands of women in Europe were branded as witches from the late 1400s through the next several centuries. Many appear to have been suffering from mental disorder, yet in accordance with official church regulations outlined in the infamous *Malleus Maleficarum* [Witches' Hammer], they were tortured and burned at the stake in order to expel the devil from their bodies and save their souls.
- Within the asylums created for the mentally ill in Europe following the Renaissance, forms of "care" included chains and stocks, as well as whippings and beatings, with unspeakably filthy, overcrowded conditions the norm. Such practices were justified by the belief that afflicted individuals had lost their reason and therefore could not feel pain as acutely as other humans.
- The nobility and general public of the eighteenth and nineteenth centuries made tours of mental asylums in Europe and the United States to observe the chained and raving people housed there in the manner of animals at a zoo. Such observations were not a trivial pastime but instead constituted a frequent excursion for many affluent members of society.
- In the past century, Hitler's policies of compulsory sterilization, and then genocide, were designed for people with mental illness and mental retardation, as well as Jews, gypsies, and gay and lesbian persons. Years before Hitler attained power, however, scientists and mental health professionals throughout Europe and the United States were promoting legislation mandating sterilization of those with mental illness, under the banner of the eugenics movement. These restrictions provided a model for the Nazis.
- Currently, homelessness is fueled by a mental health system that fails to provide even rudimentary care for those formerly housed in institutions. A third or more of the homeless population suffers from severe mental illness,[11] and a lack of systematic care plagues people with

mental disorders even if they do find shelter. Isolated in inner-city settings, many current "community" residences rival earlier institutions as sources of despair and even premature death.

- Jails and prisons have become the largest mental facilities in the United States, fueled by the increasing tendency to criminalize mental illness and the closure of most public mental hospitals. Psychological and psychiatric care is woefully inadequate in prisons, and exposure to violent conditions can only worsen the prognosis.[12] Training of police and law enforcement officials is almost nonexistent.
- Media portrayals of people with mental disorder continue to feature stereotypes and ridicule, equating mental disorder with incompetence and violence. These depictions shape the attitudes and emotional responses of the general public by permeating advertisements, newspaper articles, television and radio programs, and films.
- Stigma occurs worldwide. In India people with mental disorder may be left outside and chained to stakes as they become progressively more demented. In Japan, sufferers are relegated to lifetimes of silence, given the general code of never disclosing personal weakness; surveys in China also reveal great stigmatization. Abuses have been recently uncovered in Turkish mental hospitals, where electroshock treatments are used without anesthesia as punishment, even for children. Half of those with mental disorders in Western nations fail to seek treatment or cannot get care, but in the Third World the rate is closer to 90%.[13]
- In the United States, knowledge of mental illness has improved over the past decades, but stigmatization of the most severe forms of mental disorder has actually *increased*.[14] In addition, diagnostic rates for conditions such as depression, attention-deficit/hyperactivity disorder (ADHD), and autism have multiplied, providing both hope and potential stigmatization for increasing numbers of children, adolescents, and adults.

In short, despite greater awareness and communication, the plight of those with mental disorders continues to be precarious. Because mental disorder is often banished from mainstream discussion, the conditions and experiences of most people who live with mental illness are rendered invisible, making change efforts difficult to mount.

Objectives

I address two key questions in this book. The first pertains to why, particularly in a society as modern and secular as the United States, people with mental illness continue to receive such stigmatization. In other words, given the major shifts in conceptions of human behavior and leaps in scientific knowledge that have occurred in recent decades, along with the increasing recognition that mental illness is not rare,[15] why is stigma still so rampant? How does mental illness elicit a "switching off" of compassion rather than a promotion of empathic responding, when empathy and support are so desperately needed?

I draw on many different perspectives to address this question. One scientific view comes from social psychology, the study of intergroup relations and the mental processes through which humans quickly make distinctions between those they perceive as their close contacts (ingroups) and those they view as foreign (outgroups). Another emanates from sociology, which brings the perspective of labeling theory—which deals with the power of labels to shape responses to disenfranchised persons. Yet another stems from evolutionary psychology, featuring discussion of naturally selected mechanisms through which people may be programmed to detect particular differences and deviancies in fellow humans. I also examine historical trends, tracing themes of human reactions and responses to mental disturbance throughout past epochs. This analysis reveals that societal attitudes toward mental disorder have been cyclic throughout the millennia, with periods of progress followed by retrenchment into fear, exclusion, and cruelty.

The overall conclusion is that, despite recent advances, individuals with mental disorder continue to suffer from discrimination and stigmatization at alarming rates. The ensuing neglect and exclusion impede adequate research funding and clinical care, fueling the myth that mental illness is lifelong, hopeless, and deserving of revulsion. Consequences for individuals, families, communities, and society at large are widespread.

The second fundamental question relates to what can be done about this long-standing predicament. Are there insights that can guide efforts to combat the stigma related to mental disorder? My discussion draws on fields as disparate as clinical and social psychology, psychiatry, molecular genetics, public health, legislative policy, and public relations. I consider, for example, whether a conception of mental disorder as "brain disease" will help or hinder efforts toward clear thinking and reduction of stigmatizing attitudes. I also explore the kinds of public awareness campaigns and societal changes that stand the greatest chances of success, along with what can be done at more personal levels. Although I do not contend that progress will be rapid, openness is emerging and progress is real. Personal disclosure of narrative accounts is an essential tool for change, given its potential to humanize mental illness.

Organization

Chapter 1 provides definitions of the elusive concept of mental disorder and illustrates several key forms of mental illness. My objective is to portray the kinds of symptoms and impairments involved and to ponder the ways in which scientists and the public have attempted to understand the nature of deviant behavior. I also define the related concepts of stereotyping, prejudice, discrimination, and stigma, providing a needed foundation for all of the material that follows. Because stigma is a strong, even violent term, originally connoting physical marks or brands and today associated with deep psychological "stains" that mark the individual as deeply flawed, there should be ample justification before it is asserted that mental disorders are truly stigmatized.[16]

Chapter 2 deals with perspectives related to stigma and discrimination from social psychology, sociology, and evolutionary psychology. I draw on research findings from a wide array of fascinating investigations. This chapter reveals that, although stigma processes are quite pervasive in all social groups, they can still be modulated and overcome.

Chapter 3 provides a history of views on and responses to mental disorder, beginning with prehistoric times and continuing until the end of the nineteenth century. Because of the incredible advances in scientific understanding during the past hundred years, I devote Chapter 4 to twentieth-century perspectives. Although a complete discussion of these recent trends could, in and of itself, result in book-length coverage, I highlight the most important themes related to the stigmatization of mental illness in modern times.

Chapter 5 looks at scientific data on the knowledge, attitudes, and behavioral responses of the general public toward mental illness and addresses the question of whether persons with mental disorders actually continue to receive stigma. Also included are the perspectives of family members, mental health professionals, and individuals with mental disorders themselves. The question of whether stigmatization continues to exist is not simply rhetorical: Several decades ago, influential scholars and commentators concluded that stigma regarding mental disorder had become a thing of the past. I strive to weigh the evidence carefully and objectively. Although information about developmental issues is quite limited, data on children and stigma are brought into the mix.

Chapter 6 shifts focus to broader forms of evidence for stigmatization, through indicators such as linguistic practices, accounts in public media, attitudes displayed by the mental health profession, discriminatory policies, and views found in personal and family narratives. These types of data are highly influential—in fact, the evidence from these less overtly scientific sources may be even more compelling than the results of formal scientific studies.

Chapter 7 synthesizes material from the preceding chapters to provide a brief, integrative account of the stigma of mental illness. Central to this chapter is the concept of threat, related to both perceivers and victims. In fact, the legacy of harsh responses to mental disorders can be explained largely by the real and symbolic threat posed to members of society from the behavior patterns in question—and from the label itself. The point here is not to blame society at large for negative responses to mental illness but to understand the roots of the strong tendencies toward fear, exclusion, and blame. Chapter 8 features suggestions and strategies for further research on the stigmatization of mental illness. My hope is that this material may be of use not only to the public at large but also to the next generation of investigators of this fascinating and troubling topic.

In the final chapters I explicitly consider what can be done to combat the stigma and discrimination of mental illness. Chapter 9 deals with strategies at the levels of legislation, policy, and community-wide efforts, with the potential for broad impact across society. The focus of Chapter 10 is public media, as well as attitudes and practices in the mental health professions. Chapter 11 considers families and individuals with mental disorder themselves, including the importance of involvement in treatment and in advocacy groups. Although it cannot be the sole strategy, access to responsive treatment may be a particularly important means of countering stigma. Finally, Chapter 12 features speculations about future concerns and challenges for those interested in stigma.

Personal Background and Final Goals

The nature of mental disorder and the reasons for its stigma are complex, troubling, and intensely interesting, fully deserving of thorough elucidation. The thorny history of the topic and the sheer volume of research findings require an objective review of the evidence. At the same time, the legacy of neglect, discrimination, and cruelty regarding mental illness makes it difficult to remain dispassionate, particularly in terms of recommendations for change. I therefore aim to strike a balance. On the one hand, I do not want the urgency of the topic to cloud my ability to weigh evidence thoughtfully and scientifically, but on the other hand I also wish to go beyond a purely objective stance and make clear and practical suggestions for overcoming stigma.

My background may help to provide a unique perspective on the topics under discussion. First, I work in the area of developmental psychopathology, which features research on the origins of mental disorders among children, adolescents, and adults. I am interested in both general scientific principles and the unique, dynamic patterns of change that exist within every individual's life. This dual perspective is important for a topic like stigma, which follows general rules but is also played out in specific, individualized ways for each affected person and family.

Second, as a clinical psychologist, I have considerable experience in assessment procedures and treatment programs. For example, I have conducted many summer camp programs for children with attention and learning problems, and I have performed treatment studies since the time of my doctoral dissertation. This background has given me a firsthand view of stigma and its consequences among children, adults, and family members. At the same time, my training as an academic researcher gives me considerable experience in evaluating scientific evidence.

Third, I have a history of family experiences with mental illness. Most notably, my father had lifelong, misdiagnosed bipolar disorder, and a number of relatives have experienced other conditions. Although my father was in many respects resilient, the condition—and the stigma he experienced—took a major toll on him and the whole family. My experiences can, I hope, help in my effort to blend objective coverage with the perspective of an insider.[17]

Overall, my aims are to promote understanding of mental illness and the human responses it evokes; to promote additional research efforts on mental disorder and its stigmatization; to foster empathy for those who suffer from the disorganization and despair that frequently accompany mental illness (while simultaneously realizing the real difficulties that emerge from mental disorder); and to emphasize the types of personal, family, and social action that can reduce discrimination and stigmatization at local, national, and international levels. Despite major advances in treatment and research in recent years, mental disorder will remain part of the human condition for the foreseeable future, spawning impairment, disability, and even tragedy. Stigma will not disappear overnight. Still, we cannot allow those with mental disorder to continue to receive the levels of degradation and ridicule that have permeated far too much of human history. A far brighter future can and will emerge when knowledge replaces ignorance, when effective treatments supplant custodial care and inadequate community intervention, when legislation mandates equality, and when contact with the realities (rather than the stereotypes) of mental disorder taps people's empathy. Those who experience mental disorder, along with their families and communities, deserve no less.

THE MARK OF SHAME

1

What Is Mental Disorder and What Is Stigma?

Following an adolescence marked by average school achievement and a few friends, Carl began to isolate himself from others after his high school graduation. Ten months later, he now mutters to himself in his bedroom throughout the day and night, hardly leaving this room. Incomprehensible ideas have crowded his mind. Some months back he believed that signals were being sent to him by strangers on the street, conveying threats that he could not specify. Now, when he does leave his room to appear in front of his increasingly worried family, he often places his hands over his ears in an attempt to stop the voices he hears, which tell him that he is despicable and that he is a conduit for radio transmissions. His thoughts have increasingly coalesced around the idea that he is the victim of a massive plot and that the rest of the house is bugged. He is convinced that his very thoughts can be transmitted to the FBI.

Smoking cigarettes and listening to the same CDs over and over appear to be his main activities. His few remaining contacts have stopped calling, as he was prone to inundate them with rants about the plots with which he is obsessed. Occasionally, when the voices in his head get too frightening, he storms from the house, agitated and yelling, causing his family great fear over what the neighbors will think. As this pattern has intensified, Carl refuses to be seen by any kind of doctor or professional. Indeed, for him, the problems are located out there in the world, not at all in his own mind. Now panicked, his family wonders how and why their 19-year-old son has sunk so far into irrationality and isolation. What can they tell their relatives and neighbors, who have already begun to voice curiosity, fear, and derision?

At age 25, Alice started waking up at 4 A.M., bursting with energy and ideas. From home, she would start making telephone calls and sending e-mails to national and international business contacts, who were startled by her messages of plans for a series of new inventions, some of which appeared initially to be creative but soon started to sound unrealistic. During the day, she played loud music on her car radio as she sped from appointment to appointment, worrying and then angering her clients with her irrelevant speeches on the value of her new investment plans and her ultimate design to take over the company. Her boyfriend became alarmed at the amounts of money she began spending on clothes and books— sometimes thousands of dollars at a time. Yet Alice responded with righteous anger when he or anyone else confronted her, stating that they were standing in the way of a great career move that was soon to come about, if only everyone would permit her to have new wardrobes and freedom. At the same time, her appetite for alcohol and drugs like cocaine appeared insatiable.

In the midst of her energy and euphoria, however, she began to have thoughts of despair and occasional bursts of rage, wondering why the rest of the world couldn't keep pace with her heightened speed and refused to understand her ascending trajectory as a world-class financier. Soon her judgment began to deteriorate. In one incident, for example, she hired a design consultant for the entire office without checking with the head of the firm, promising a small fortune for a complete makeover of the physical space.

Increasingly angry at being confronted, she then "crashed," withdrawing from work and sinking into a deep period of despondency during which she became slowed, brittle, and vulnerable, wondering at first silently and then out loud whether her life was really worth living. Alone in her apartment, she has unplugged the phone and sleeps throughout the day, the memories of her grand plans to become an international investment guru a faded memory. Her chief emotion is now one of drained exhaustion and despair. Puzzling over the dramatic shift in her personality, her boyfriend is wondering how to get her to a psychiatric hospital.

Initially, there would be just mild feelings of dread, as José, aged 41, took walks in his neighborhood to the grocery store, a half mile from his home. He was bothered by the feeling that all was not right—a little hole in the pit of his stomach, a message in his mind to get back home to safety as soon as possible. A few days later, as he pushed the shopping cart into the store, the dread permeated his whole body, and he felt, as never before, that he was going to suffocate. Sensing the blood coursing through his veins and feeling that he would pass out and die, he ran from the store toward home, desperately trying to catch his breath. He felt somehow apart from his body, as if witnessing the catastrophe from afar. Collapsing several times but then pulling himself back up, he made it back to his own block. Gradually his heart slowed. Once inside the safety of his living room, he almost cried from the relief he felt.

From that day forward, he limited himself to walking only a block from home. Even at that distance, however, he could feel the initial pinpricks of fear tingling beneath his skin. Little wonder that he now refuses to venture out at all. He calls in sick to work, begging his boss to let him telecommute and work exclusively at home. The contrast between the safety of his house and the world outside has become vast; he will do anything to avoid that feeling of having a suffocating heart attack he experienced at the store.

José's world is ever diminishing: He won't go out to dinner or to a movie but stays in with delivered meals and rented films brought over by friends. Safety is his chief concern at this point. He will do anything to prevent another episode of terror.

When Betty thinks of food these days, it is with disdain and disgust. True, she is still really hungry a lot of the time, but what she needs, she is certain, is to stay in control. At age 17, she has realized that too much of her life has been out of control—trying to please her family with grades, trying to please boys with looks, gaining more weight than she wanted during early adolescence. Her strong belief now is that if she can restrict her caloric intake to 600 calories per day, she will obtain an ideal body shape and be in complete control of her emotions and her hunger. Her fear of being fat has, in fact, taken on a messianic fervor; all other goals pale in comparison. Always something of a perfectionist, she now has the sole goal of trying to achieve a perfect, boyish figure. But it is an objective that seems always unattainable, as she always finds another flaw, another sign of fat.

Her weight has crept down to 93 pounds on her 5 foot 6 inch frame. Although she is sometimes dizzy and it is increasingly difficult for her to keep up her intensive exercise regimen because of weakness, she pushes on, restricting her intake to a minimum diet of low-fat foods. To others, she looks gaunt, even cadaverous, but she still notices a slight roundness to her stomach that she simply must eliminate. She is furious when others dare to tell her to eat more at meals. Don't they realize how urgently she needs to control her appetite and prevent the return of her former, indulgent, overweight state?

After the first few months of Brian's life, his parents began to notice that Brian didn't respond to his name the way their other children did. For a time, they even thought that he might be deaf. As much as his family tried to show their love for him, he wasn't responsive to others. He resisted being held in his mother's arms, stiffening and turning away.

During his toddler years, he seemed much more interested in lining up blocks and then dolls and other toys in rigid straight lines than in making eye contact or playing with nearby peers. When his parents pointed at toys or other objects across the room, he didn't seem to follow or even notice their excitement in sharing their interest with him. His early language was basically an echo of words he had just heard; spontaneous speech was nonexistent. By age 3, if his daily routine became interrupted with even the slightest deviation, he would throw a tantrum that soon exhausted his parents.

Month by month, he now appears to be living increasingly in his own world. His main pleasure seems to emanate from viewing shiny objects, particularly those that he can make spin around, or from listening to music. In fact, he can imitate some pieces of music quite precisely by humming.

His parents increasingly wonder what they could possibly have done wrong: Why is our son so different from the rest of the kids in the neighborhood? Will he ever learn to speak normally or play in a group and have fun? How do we bring him back into a world of people? In fact, when he has a major outburst, the looks they receive in the grocery store or on the streets where they live have been enough to convince them not to take him out in public.

Their friends have told them about an intensive early intervention program for children with developmental disorders, in which therapists come into the home and teach the family how to promote eye contact and speech through rewards and lots of one-on-one time. But Brian's parents are almost too exhausted to consider looking into it and are unable to escape the feeling that they must have done something wrong during those early months.

Mental illness afflicts hundreds of millions of people around the world. Recent surveys in the United States reveal that mental illness in all its varieties is quite prevalent and that more serious, debilitating forms are experienced by about 6% of the population. Consequences can be severe: More than 30,000 Americans commit suicide every year—with most of these related to serious mental disorder—almost double the number who die in homicides.[1] The preceding case studies provide a sampling of the behavioral aberrations, emotional suffering, social isolation, active (though often frustrated) coping attempts by individuals and their family members to get help, and deep pain that constitute the common accompaniments of mental disturbance.

The subject of the first vignette, Carl, has been diagnosed with the disorder called schizophrenia, as a result of his paranoid ideas, his hallucinations, his disordered thinking, and his increasingly unmotivated and apathetic state. Alice's manic high, followed by an increasingly severe depression, resulted in a diagnosis of bipolar disorder. José suffers from panic disorder plus agoraphobia, which signifies an extreme fear of being in the world outside his home that is motivated by his utter desire to escape any more panic attacks. Betty's preoccupation with thinness and her markedly decreased body weight led to a diagnosis of anorexia nervosa. Brian is afflicted with autistic disorder (often known as autism), related to his social isolation, need for sameness, and marked language delays.

Even these brief descriptions capture the clear impairment associated with these conditions. Other, more common types of mental afflictions—such as depression, attention-deficit/hyperactivity disorder (ADHD), and learning disorders—also produce considerable pain and disability. Furthermore, personality disorders, which are marked by the existence of long-standing and extreme traits (e.g., anger, dependency, obsessiveness) that permeate a person's inner world and behavioral style, can be particularly disruptive to social encounters and inner well-being.

How can scientists, clinicians, and the general public account for such behavioral and emotional patterns? Although many different definitions and explanations have been invoked across human history, most of the current models lie within a medical classification system, with "mental illness" assumed to be the underlying entity. However, defining this concept is an extremely complex task. In fact, the nature of mental disorder is one of the most difficult and controversial topics in all of human science. Part of the difficulty relates to the huge gaps in knowledge that still exist about the brain, particularly how it and the environment work together to create behavior, emotion, and self-awareness. Another issue pertains to the great varieties of human cultures, along with the realization that the kinds of social transgressions and behavioral problems considered deviant in one society may be viewed as normative in another. A third issue pertains to the mysterious nature of many symptoms of mental illness, which are often irrational and self-defeating and, in many instances, cause threat to other people, who may fear for their own tenuous hold on stability and control.

Attempts to delineate and define mental illness have filled articles, chapters, and books written from clinical, philosophical, and scientific perspectives for centuries. Massive debate continues to this day as to the precise nature of mental disorder and even, in some accounts, as to whether it exists.[2] Although a comprehensive account is not possible in these pages, given the sheer volume of debate, rhetoric, and evidence on the topic, my objective is to present several models that have been used to define mental illness.

But why is this discussion needed in a book on stigma? Wouldn't it be better to simply cut to the chase and discuss the nature of stigmatizing responses to various forms of mental disorder? I think not, because of the crucial fact that the way in which mental disorder is defined has major implications for social responses. In other words, reactions from members of society depend heavily on their understanding of mental illness.

In fact, there are at least two core layers of societal reactions to the behaviors that characterize mental disorder. First, certain behavioral and emotional patterns may elicit fearful responses that are nearly automatic in nature, particularly if the patterns are highly deviant or frightening. In other words, when disturbed behavior is perceived as sufficiently threatening, observers tend to avoid or even punish the person in question without much deliberation.

Second, however, all humans show a strong tendency to search for causes of unexpected events. Put in more academic terms, we make *attributions* for unusual occurrences.[3] People are particularly likely to seek explanations for aberrant behavior displays that violate everyday social norms and often promote unease. These explanations are closely related to the models we use to help ourselves understand and account for deviant behavior in a given culture and historical period. For this reason, it is essential to consider the ways in which our society defines and understands mental disorder. Definitions of disturbing behavior patterns may, in fact, either amplify or diminish the initial, automatic patterns of response. Even if a social perceiver has yet to encounter an individual so designated, the social meanings of the term *mental illness* or *mental disorder* and the expectations it creates for social interchange are highly likely to shape reactions and responses.

For example, if deviance is believed to result from possession by evil spirits, a certain set of responses is likely to occur over and above the initial automatic reactions such behaviors may elicit. Responses in this case are quite likely to be punitive, in accordance with ethical and religious strictures. Alternatively, if the behaviors are believed to constitute weak will or moral fiber, then other types of social reactions might be predictable (e.g., blame and castigation or perhaps attempts to bolster the moral standing of the individual in question). Still other responses might be expected when aberrant behavioral patterns are linked to poor parenting, and another set may attend to an ascription to faulty genes. Given that many of these explanations coexist, a complex mixture of responses can result.

Overall, the meanings ascribed to the term *mental disorder* serve as the primary filters through which expectations and final judgments regarding deviant behavior are likely to be processed. I now review some of the key ways in which scientists and clinicians, as well as the general public, have defined such behavioral patterns.

Definitions of Mental Disorder

Statistical Rarity

An often-used definition today—but one that has doubtless been important at a more intuitive level throughout history—involves the *statistical model*. Here, abnormality and mental disorder are defined by deviance from statistical norms. Many traits of a biological nature (e.g., height, blood pressure) and of a psychological or behavioral nature (e.g., depression, hyperactivity) are distributed throughout the population in the shape of a normal curve, whereby the majority of the population clusters near the middle of the distribution and many fewer individuals show either very high or very low evidence of the trait or feature. From this perspective, deviance is viewed as statistical rarity, constituting extremes of behavior that seldom occur in the general population. Those who are at the extreme ends of the distribution are literally 'ab-normal'—that is, far from the statistical norm or average value of the population.

Many conditions in the domain of mental disorder are defined in this way. For instance, those persons scoring in the top few percentage points in terms of sad mood, pessimism, low energy, and decreased self-worth are typically considered depressed. Similarly, those in the upper realms of inattentive, impulsive, and hyperactive behaviors are diagnosed as having ADHD.

Two issues are immediately apparent. First, the score that tells us where normality ends and abnormality begins is almost always arbitrary. If the underlying distribution is truly normal, the curve is smooth as it subsides into its extremes, lacking any natural markers that signify a qualitatively distinct segment of the population. As a result, there is a great deal of dispute regarding basic questions such as how many adults are depressed or how many children have ADHD (or, for that matter, how many people suffer from high blood pressure, or hypertension). The statistical model often suffers from the arbitrary nature of the cutoffs for abnormality.

Second, although each end of a normal distribution is equally unlikely in a statistical sense, in practice societies tend to label or diagnose only those individuals on one side of the curve (e.g., those with excessive depression as opposed to the absence of depression, or those with greater numbers of ADHD-related symptoms rather than those with highly focused attention). In the real world, the statistical model is supplemented by social norms and values.

Overall, the statistical model can be a useful starting place, but statistical deviance alone does not necessarily signify underlying impairment, dysfunction, or mental disorder. In addition, traits or conditions that are clearly "normal" in a statistical sense may still be impairing. For instance, tooth decay is present in the vast majority of children who live in communities that lack fluoridation, but it makes no sense to argue that cavities and resultant gum disease are healthy.[4] From a more psychological standpoint, abusive parenting has been found to be more far prevalent than was formerly believed or admitted, but its rate of occurrence does not negate its harmful effects or the need for preventive intervention related to child abuse.[5] In general, despite the utility of the statistical model, other criteria are needed to define behavior as abnormal or disordered.

Social Norms and Social Deviance

Perhaps the main standard used throughout the world for defining abnormality, particularly in the form of mental disorder, has to do with the social rather than the statistical deviance of the behavior patterns in question. In order to cohere as a social unit, a group of individuals must establish guides or norms for behavior. Actions that violate these norms and threaten the coherence of the group are branded as unhelpful and atypical, with strong social pressure to identify the offenders and relegate them to the subgroup of individuals who do not belong in the mainstream. The resultant punishment and isolation serve to reinforce the majority for their rule-abiding behavior, which preserves social cohesion.[6]

When the deviant behaviors are particularly threatening to the group, there is added temptation to label the person in question as having an underlying mental condition. The reason is that the behavior is now ascribed to irrational, out-of-control forces within the individual rather than to anything related to the norms or standards themselves. From this vantage point, no one in his or her "right mind" could have chosen to violate the group code so egregiously; such behavior must be the product of aberrant internal processes that are fundamentally disturbed. The violated norms and strictures are upheld.

On the whole, this sociological perspective emphasizes the relativistic, culture-bound nature of deviant behavior. With regard to social deviance, there would not necessarily be any particular behavior pattern that would universally be branded as deviant, as the values and norms of the culture define what is acceptable. Yet the labeling of at least *some* types of behavior as deviant is inevitable and universal, given the need for social groups to indicate and enforce their norms.

As a result, this perspective presents a conundrum for those who wish to define abnormal behavior or mental disorder in an objective fashion. After all, if mental disorder is simply a substitute term for social deviance or social transgressions, then the objective, scientific status of the study of mental illness is extremely questionable, as the social relativism of the deviance model is at odds with attempts to have a more objective, universal basis for defining mental disorder. Also, when social or political deviance is automatically defined as mental disturbance, the implications for social control are alarming. Witness, for example, the former Soviet Union's labeling of certain political beliefs as indicative of an underlying psychiatric condition or the fact that the official classification of mental disorders in the United States listed homosexuality as a mental disorder until the early 1970s.[7] The danger is that, when any form of behavior that fails to conform to social or political mores or when any form of protest against existing social conditions is ascribed to an internal flaw or underlying psychopathology, the system against which it is directed becomes absolved. Extreme caution must be used when invoking social deviance models as the sole basis for defining mentally disordered behavior.

Moral Transgression

This model is an extension of the social norms/social deviance model. Here, behaviors that violate not only social rules but also ethical and moral codes are branded as disturbed or disordered. From this perspective, aberrant behavior is not just statistically rare or socially deviant but also fundamentally evil or bad.

For most of human history, moral perspectives have served as the predominant means of perceiving, defining, and responding to aberrant behavior (see Chapter 3). Because the behavior patterns in question are viewed, from this perspective, as depraved and morally unsound and because the individual is typically blamed for showing inadequate moral character, the kinds of retribution reserved for such violations are likely to be severe. Indeed, in order to set an example for the rest of the social group regarding expected consequences for the moral transgressions, punishment is often extremely harsh.

Throughout history and continuing to this day in some cultures, the moral model has incorporated the contention that the source of immoral behavior is one's possession by entities such as evil spirits or the devil. Yet such "infestation" does not often absolve the afflicted individuals of responsibility or blame. Rather, because of the perception that these people must not have utilized their free will or moral strength to stop the possession, extremely high levels of retribution can be expected. In other words, the ascription to possession by outside forces typically does not absolve these individuals of blame.

Importantly, the moral model is not simply a relic of the historic past, nor is it found exclusively in non-Western societies. Members of contemporary society tend to believe that a considerable amount of abnormal behavior is immoral. The earlier example of the branding of homosexuality as a mental disorder as recently as three decades ago—and the current debate about gay marriage—reveal the moral terms by which such behavior is viewed. Consider as well the kinds of attitudes and attributions made about the homeless population, with a great deal of antipathy evidenced toward those who cannot provide basic shelter for themselves. Because behavior and emotion are typically believed to be under volitional control, behavioral and emotional deviance is still frequently attributed to ethical lapses. Moral frameworks for abnormal behavior are alive and well.

A key question is whether efforts to account for mental disorder in nonmoral terms—in particular, the ascription of abnormal behavior to biological frameworks and medical models—can succeed in reducing stigma. I have much to say in this regard in later chapters but highlight for now the fact that such efforts and campaigns face a major uphill struggle. That is, the unknown, frightening, and threatening aspects of many forms of deviant behavior tend to elicit ascriptions to moral weakness or depravity almost as a default position. The strong tendency to make moral judgments about emotional and behavioral responses is a key consideration regarding any efforts to combat stigma.

Personal Impairment and Ecological Views

A relatively recent perspective on defining mental disorder is related to the impairment caused by the deviant behavior patterns. The crux of the argument is that it is not statistical rarity, social deviance, or moral transgression that should define mentally disturbed behavior but rather the impairing or handicapping nature of the behaviors in question. The question becomes the following: Does the behavioral pattern cause significant problems for the person's social or occupational functioning, academic attainment, close relationships, or general well-being? If so, then mental disorder may be inferred; if not, the behavioral pattern may be abnormal in one or more respects but does not qualify as mental illness.

For example, although developmentally extreme levels of impulsive and hyperactive behavior may be statistically rare and considered socially (or even morally) deviant, for some people they may constitute an adaptive, energetic behavioral style that fuels productivity, so long as personal adjustment and the rights of others are not compromised. On the other hand, if these behaviors cause major problems at school—or, for an adult, at the workplace—and disrupt relationships with caregivers and peers, then the ascription to the underlying mental disorder of ADHD may be warranted.[8] From this perspective it is the impairing or handicapping nature of the problematic behavior that yields a designation of mental or behavioral disturbance.

Although intuitively appealing, this definition is far from perfect. For one thing, there is considerable clinical judgment involved in appraising the extent of impairment an individual is experiencing. One person's "adaptation" may well be another's considerable struggle. Relatedly, whose perspective defines the designation of impairment—that of the individuals, their caregivers, or society at large? Differences across such sources are highly likely. Furthermore, it is possible to envision a situation in which two people who are equally disordered in a psychological or behavioral sense encounter two different social environments, one supportive and accommodating and the other harsh and unyielding. Impairment may be minimal for the first individual but substantial for the second, even though the behaviors and dysfunctions in question are initially identical. Is it logical to infer that only the second person has a mental disorder? This is a major question for those who view mental illness as a sole function of biological causes or other factors residing solely within the individual.

The notion of personal impairment or handicap is, of necessity, *ecological* in nature, taking into consideration the fit between (a) the traits and attributes of the affected individuals and (b) the characteristics of their environment or niche. From this view, pathology or mental disturbance is located neither in the person nor in the social context but rather in the interface between the two. This framework has interesting implications for how mental disorder, as well as the stigma that pertains to it, could be reduced. Specifically, it may take changing the nature of the fit rather than altering the nature of the individuals to produce meaningful improvements. This could occur via school or workplace accommodations as opposed to—or in addition to—individual treatment. In short, a more accepting classroom, workplace, family, or society at large may be crucial in helping to overcome impairment and stigma.

The definition of mental disorder based on personal impairment or handicap is appealing because it considers the ramifications of aberrant behavior for personal well-being and adjustment. It also raises a host of challenging issues regarding the interplay between individual traits and behaviors on the one hand and social and cultural contexts on the other. Although certain forms of disturbed behavior are severe enough to cause maladaptation in nearly any social context—for example, the flagrantly irrational behavior indicative of psychosis—the core of the ecological model is that the person's context and setting are essential to ascertaining the presence of pathology.

Medical Models

A counterpoint to the preceding conceptions is found in models based on medical perspectives. Beginning with the views of Hippocrates, who believed that mental states and afflictions emanated from imbalances in essential bodily fluids (humors), medical models have constituted an attempt to establish an expressly scientific viewpoint, in which abnormal behavior is considered a sign of bodily or brain deficiencies or excesses. In the highly medical, scientifically oriented twentieth century, various medical conceptions of abnormal behavior came to predominate in many Western societies (see Chapter 4), and because of brain imaging and other technological advances, these perspectives have gained further ascendancy.

What is meant by a medical model of mental disorder? In brief, an analogy is made to medical illnesses, in which various organs or organ systems are infected or diseased, lacking the ability to function properly. In the realm of mental disorder, the problems are behavioral and mental in nature, and the afflicted organ is the brain. At the first stage, the diagnostician asks about *symptoms* (reported problems) or *signs* (objective indicators) that may signal underlying conditions. Because, however, symptoms and signs are not specific (for example, a fever could indicate influenza or meningitis; poor concentration might signal ADHD, depression, Alzheimer's disease, or just boredom), the diagnostician looks for clusters of symptoms that appear together, which are termed *syndromes*. The ultimate objective is to discover a syndrome with an underlying cause, called a *disorder* or *disease*.[9] Overall, the clear intention is to take abnormal behavior out of the realm of cultural or moral standards and into the scientific domain of disease states, which are objective and universal (although culture-specific manifestations may still exist).

Key problems with the medical analogy are apparent at practical and conceptual levels. First, the types of behavioral or emotional "disturbance" to which a medical model may be applied must still be based on judgments of statistical abnormality, social deviance, moral transgressions, or personal impairment. In other words, a completely objective perspective on abnormal behavior is not possible. Indeed, attempts to define a "pure" medical model tend to ignore the social contexts in which judgments of disturbed or maladaptive behavior arise; they also run the risk of searching for underlying biological aberrations for what are actually issues related to unfair or inhumane social norms. A chilling example from the eighteenth and nineteenth centuries is the mental illness of *draepetomania*, which referred to the underlying dysfunctions motivating some slaves to run away from their masters.[10] Unthinking application of medical models can lead to misguided or even repressive consequences.

Second, the medical model of physical illnesses links biological symptoms and signs such as stomach pain or prolonged fever to objective, physiological markers of disease, such as aberrant X-rays, lab tests, or blood levels. These hard criterion measures are used to validate the symptoms. For mental dysfunction, however, the symptoms are of a psychological nature—for instance, a persistently sad mood, excessive activity levels, or hearing voices in the absence of actual auditory stimuli—and objective indicators are typically lacking to corroborate them. Part of the reason for the continuing stigmatization of mental disorders may well be that they are perceived as less real than physical illnesses, given the lack of hard biological indicators underlying their presence. Technological advances in neuroscience, such as high-resolution brain imaging, have provided startling new evidence of the neural and neurophysiological underpinnings of several forms of mental disorder.[11] As a result, there is hope for a greater recognition of serious mental illness as observable, objective, and brain based.

I quickly point out, however, that *all* mental experiences are based in brain neurochemistry and that observing neural images related to serious psychopathology does not necessarily assert that genes, brain structures, or biological processes caused the symptoms in question—or that biologically based interventions are the only appropriate avenues for treatment. The brain is quite plastic, meaning that experience shapes its architecture and the pathways and firing patterns of its neurons. Medical models must be extended to incorporate processes that span biology and experience, which work in concert.

There is no single medical model. Infectious diseases are often viewed as the prototype, in which an infectious agent (e.g., a virus) operates within the host to create a state of disease. Even here, however, certain properties of the host organism may slow or stop the disease from taking hold; the pathways to disease are not always straightforward. Also, because of improvements in sanitation and public health, the diseases that are currently the most lethal in Western societies are no longer infectious illnesses but problems such as cardiovascular disease or cancer. Each of these is a multifaceted class of illnesses that is likely to be spurred by multiple processes (such as genetic risk, environmental toxins, or even lifestyles in the case of cardiovascular disease) and can lead to common pathways of illness. In addition, genetic predispositions for nearly all mental disorders are not single genes but rather combinations of genes, interacting with one another and with the environment.[12] Unless medical models expand to incorporate context, culture, and development, the chance for reductionism is great.

Harmful Dysfunction

A relatively new paradigm for understanding the nature of mental disorder was conceived by Jerome Wakefield in the 1990s.[13] His integrative definition takes into account both social norms and personal impairment on the one hand and an explicitly scientific, evolutionary perspective on the other. This formulation has spurred a renewal of scientific efforts to define mental disorder.

Regarding the harmful dysfunction (HD) model, Wakefield first contends that aberrant behavior cannot be considered as mentally disordered unless it explicitly violates social norms or induces substantial impairment to the individual in question. That is, the first component of the definition involves *harm*.

As with all definitions incorporating such socially normative perspectives, this component is culturally relative: What might be considered harmful or impairing in one society or culture may not in another. The key point is that social and personal judgments are a *necessary* component of defining behavior patterns as mentally disordered.

In fact, without harm, there is no need to go further. Wakefield gives a provocative example from medicine: A small number of people are born with six toes. Because having a sixth toe causes no real harm to the individual (i.e., it does not impede locomotion or promote injury to the foot), there is no need for medical referral, and the condition is not typically considered to be a disorder. Absent any evidence of harm, from this perspective, there is no disorder.

Yet this criterion alone is far too relative to constitute a viable definition. Indeed, designations of harm could easily constitute cases of social deviance per se, without the presence of a deeper level of medical or neural problem. The behavior pattern in question must also be *dysfunctional* in an evolutionary sense to qualify as a mental disorder. In other words, there must be an aberration in a naturally selected mental mechanism that is not working as intended (in other words, as naturally selected).

The meaning here is more complicated. Just as natural selection has led to organ systems with certain natural functions that promote survival in a given ecological niche—for example, the visual system, with the purpose of perceiving the world in terms of pictorial representation—it has also led to the development of brains and central nervous systems with other, more complex natural functions. Natural functions are those that evolution has guided and that are essential for a thriving individual.

To give an example of what is meant by a natural function, I point out Wakefield's example of noses. One function of these organs is to hold up glasses, but this is clearly not their naturally selected function, which is the process of olfaction. The brain's complex systems have a number of apparent natural functions, including (a) appraisal of the world in order to gauge responses to threatening stimuli; (b) memory, toward the end of recalling the location of food supplies or predators or potential mates; and (c) in the case of humans, extensive planning and reasoning to prepare for future contingencies. Although teleological arguments—that is, those positing that such mechanisms were created or designed with a goal in mind—must be avoided, Wakefield is attempting to place his argument into the accepted language of evolutionary theory, from which natural functions of physical or mental mechanisms can be inferred from their design and their workings in the world.

Crucially, the HD model asserts that a mental disorder is present only if the behavioral patterns signify an underlying *dysfunction* in the mental mechanisms in question. To be specific, exhibiting unpopular religious beliefs may be construed as socially or morally deviant in a given culture and therefore harmful, but there is, in all likelihood, no dysfunction. Accordingly, it is not an instance of mental disorder. On the other hand, if a person continually displays hallucinations or delusions, it can be argued that such behavior is not only personally and socially harmful but also dysfunctional, in that there is an aberration in the natural functions of visual and auditory processing systems (i.e., hallucinations) or in the mind's ability to sort obvious truth from fantasy (i.e., delusional beliefs). The same could be said of chronic levels of depressed mood leading to social withdrawal and suicidal ideation or for the extreme isolation and lack of empathy of autism. Not only is the person in question harmed, but the systems underlying behavioral activation, motivation, and mood regulation (or social approach and empathy in the case of autism) are surely dysfunctional as well.

Despite its appeal, HD suffers from the field's lack of full knowledge of healthy mental and emotional mechanisms and their natural functions. If we are not positive as to the nature of functional minds and mental mechanisms, how can we know what is inherently *dys*functional? Also, critics have argued that mentally disordered behavior could reflect the actions of perfectly sound mental mechanisms—with respect to the environments for which they were naturally selected many generations ago—in the context of our modern environments, which may be ill suited to these evolved mental systems. For instance, anxiety in the presence of snakes or spiders may cause personal suffering or harm, but these reactions may be understandable and adaptive (rather than dysfunctional) in the context of the survival advantage conferred by such responses in the early phases of human history. As is well known in evolutionary biology, traits that are adaptive in their environment of origination may be quite maladaptive when contexts change.[14]

Overall, HD is a recent attempt to place definitions of mental disorder on a dual foundation of (a) social/cultural norms and personal harm plus (b) scientific understanding of natural selection and evolution. Along with future models that will inevitably follow from it, HD must rely on expanding knowledge in a number of domains, ranging from neuroscience and evolutionary theory to the influences of sociocultural context on behavior.

Developmental Psychopathology

None of the models so far has addressed a key fact: Mentally disordered behavior, just like typical behavior, is not static but rather dynamic and fluid. Such behavioral patterns wax and wane over time and change in relation to social context. Furthermore, mental disturbance does not simply emerge de novo (except perhaps in the case of sudden accidental brain injury) but rather reveals itself in phases and stages. Utilizing guidelines from diverse scientific fields such as embryology, developmental psychology, and systems theory, proponents of developmental psychopathology (DP) attempt to explain mental disturbance as a complex, interactive array of personal and environmental influences that unfold across development to produce both healthy and adaptive functioning.[15] The DP model incorporates elements of personal impairment/ecological perspectives, medical models, and harmful dysfunction, but it does so with more explicit consideration of the emergence of mental disturbance from prior developmental states while emphasizing the continuous interplay of biological underpinnings and environmental contexts in such behavior.

One DP principle pertains to the linkage between normal and atypical behavior patterns. As just noted, abnormal behavior does not emerge suddenly or unexpectedly but rather results from processes whereby normal development has become arrested or sidetracked. For instance, well before the severe symptoms of schizophrenia emerge in adolescence or adulthood, subtle motor and language disturbances and emotional problems often appear during early childhood.[16]

Second, mental disorder is not a static entity. Persons with mental disorders often shift from phases of relatively normal and healthy functioning to psychopathology and then back. Such relapses and remissions serve as reminders that mental health and mental disorder result from dynamic processes; they are not as distinct from normal functioning as might be believed from reductionistic models, either biological or social.

Third, although underlying biological predispositions for psychopathology clearly exist, the contexts that surround the individual exert great influence over symptoms and impairments. As with the ecological model, proponents of the DP perspective believe that the person and the environment are inextricably linked in any expression of mental disorder. The DP model expands upon the ecological view by positing that people and environments influence each other reciprocally. For instance, early in development, a given child's withdrawn, inhibited temperament may elicit certain types of parental response (e.g., overprotection), which further shape the child's unfolding behavior patterns. Such processes tend to repeat and expand across development, exemplifying *transaction*.[17]

In short, DP emphasizes the rich array of multilevel influences—spanning genes and biological factors, families, and cultures—that interact and transact throughout development to produce both healthy and disordered functioning. This model serves as an antidote to simplistic conceptions that emphasize exclusive biomedical or environmental influences. The utter complexity of the brain, the huge variety of social and cultural environments, and the staggering potential for their interactions during development mean that mental disorder is multifaceted and complex rather than simple and straightforward.

Summary

This tour of various conceptions and definitions of mental disorder has spanned a diverse set of perspectives. The statistical model can be a useful starting point, but there is no automatic assumption that rare traits or attributes are inherently harmful or that frequently displayed features are always adaptive. Definitions based on social deviance or moral transgressions suffer from the problem of extreme cultural relativism, with the potential for those in social or political power to utilize the label of mental disorder for social control. Still, social norms and ethics provide a key basis for decisions about mentally disturbed versus mentally healthy functioning. The criterion of personal impairment or handicap leads to the inescapable contention that the impairment that results from problematic behavior is highly dependent on social context and ecological fit between such behavior and the environment in which it occurs. Medical models have regained ascendancy in Western societies during the last century, but precise parallels between physical and mental signs and symptoms are not always easy to make, and complete understanding of neural substrates of consciousness, personality, and psychopathology is not yet a reality. HD is an explicit attempt to blend a criterion relating to personal harm/ impairment with one pertaining to dysfunction in naturally selected mental systems. Although promising, it runs the potential risk of confusing dysfunction in an evolutionary sense with fully functional mental mechanisms that are ill suited to our current environments. Finally, DP models involve complex transactional processes of genetic predispositions, biological substrates, environmental inputs, and social/cultural context in shaping both healthy and maladaptive functioning. From this perspective, simple and unidirectional models of mental disorder are not possible, pointing toward the interdisciplinary efforts needed to understand the development of abnormal behavior.

In all, there is no satisfactory or simple definition of mental disorder. If there were, the nature of its stigmatization would be far easier to address. There will always be some degree of social judgment in defining mental disturbance, but this fact should not allow us to succumb to the irrational conclusion that mental disorder is mythical or nonexistent. Although biological and medical paradigms are becoming predominant, reductionistic medical-model accounts are not accurate. The reciprocal interplay between biology and environment in shaping behavior is the rule rather than the exception, particularly for mental disorder. Because the locus of mental disorder is the enormously complex human brain, which interacts with social environments in complex, nonlinear ways, it is hard to imagine any simple definition of mental illness.[18]

Official Conceptions of Mental Disorder

What, then, are the official conceptions and definitions of mental disorder in the current era? The criteria offered in most textbooks typically include some combination of statistical abnormality, social deviance, and personal impairment or handicap as the key features. Moral models are not currently emphasized, given the secular tone of contemporary society and science. Medical models and, in some instances, DP perspectives have become ascendant.[19]

The fourth edition of the *Diagnostic and Statistical Manual of Mental Disorders (DSM-IV)* is the official classification system in the United States. Published in 1994 and updated in 2000, it provides a definition of mental disorder that reflects Wakefield's HD model, stating that mental illness includes personal/social maladjustment plus dysfunction. After a cautionary note regarding the impossibility of finding a coherent definition covering all of the forms of mental disturbance, the authors state the following:

> Each of the disorders is conceptualized as a significant behavioral or psychological syndrome or pattern that occurs in an individual and that is associated with present distress (e.g., a painful symptom) or disability (i.e., impairment in one or more important areas of functioning) or with a significantly increased risk of suffering, death, pain, disability, or an important loss of freedom. In addition, this syndrome or pattern must not be merely an expectable and culturally sanctioned response to a particular event, for example, the death of a loved one. Whatever its original cause, it must currently be considered a manifestation of a behavioral, psychological, or biological dysfunction in the individual. Neither deviant behavior . . . nor conflicts that are primarily between the individual and society are mental disorders unless the deviance or conflict is a symptom of a dysfunction in the individual.[20]

The influence of HD is unmistakable here. Yet the meaning of the term *dysfunction* is not specified, reflecting the incomplete knowledge base regarding brain function at present. Still, the intent is to reserve psychiatric classification for truly dysfunctional behaviors and not just those that are socially deviant or personally troublesome.

An important critique is that the *DSM-IV* categories are static, consisting of symptom lists and commonly associated features but lacking a true appreciation of the dynamic, fluid nature of mental disorder. In other words, mentally disordered behavior exists in tandem with a person's coping strategies, adaptive strengths, and social networks, but categorical classification systems have trouble providing such a multifaceted depiction through single-word diagnoses. The potential for stereotyping also exists: A person can too easily be reduced to a label, inasmuch as the cross-sectional descriptions are not effective in conveying the transactional processes that may have led, during the person's development, to the constellation of behaviors now warranting diagnosis. Finally, it is quite possible that several distinct developmental pathways can lead to the same *DSM* diagnosis—a process referred to as "equifinality"—revealing the limitations of a completely symptom-based, descriptive classification.[21]

A major issue for scientists and clinicians alike is whether mental disorders represent true categories—that is, conditions with clear boundaries from other disorders and from nondisturbed functioning—or reflect instead the imposition of yes-no classifications on continuous measures of the symptoms in question. Most experts concur that few conditions listed in the *DSM-IV* are real categories; they instead reflect cutoffs imposed on underlying dimensions of behavior. Such categorical designations can still be useful and practical, given the clinical need to make treatment decisions. Indeed, cutoff points can be selected on the basis of data; they need not be completely arbitrary.[22] Because of the stigma that is associated with categorical designations, however, clinicians must weigh the pros and cons of assigning a diagnosis when there may in fact be a negligible distinction between individuals just above and just below the cutoff point.[23]

What kinds of conditions are listed in the *DSM-IV?* All of the examples at the beginning of this chapter are included, plus a great many more.[24] The variety of diagnostic categories reflects the rapid expansion of the boundaries of psychopathology. In fact, over the last half-century, the domain of mental disturbance has stretched markedly, with a huge expansion of *DSM* from the first edition (published in 1952) to the present. The implications for stigmatization are provocative. On the one hand, the greater numbers of disorders and the increased numbers of people who develop them could result in enhanced public identification with mental illness. On the other hand, the potential for the mental illness label to be applied to ever-larger segments of the populace may lead to (a) greater stigma for increasing numbers, to the extent that the very label of mental illness is denigrated, and (b) a trivialization of the entire concept, as mental illness comes to be seen to encompass more and more of what was formerly considered to entail normal-range functioning. Critics view the expanding domain of mental illness with cynicism, claiming that the widening boundaries reflect not only an increased medicalization of many aspects of current life but also an explicit attempt on the part of pharmaceutical firms to create new markets for psychotropic medications.[25]

Given the wide range of conditions considered to reflect mental illness, the question arises as to the right kind of coverage for this book. That is, should only the most severe and debilitating forms of mental disorder be considered—that is, those (like schizophrenia, severe depression, bipolar disorder, obsessive compulsive disorder, agoraphobia/panic, and autism) that reveal evidence for moderate-to-strong genetic liability, clear neurobiological underpinnings, cross-cultural manifestations, and serious impairment?[26] Indeed, these are the categories that might be expected to show the greatest evidence for stigmatization. Yet less severe forms of mental disorder have the potential to receive stigma as well. In particular, observers may come to attribute deviance of a milder variety—which may become salient only in certain settings—to personal weakness or, in the case of children and adolescents, ineffective parenting as the main cause. I therefore take an inclusive rather than a narrow perspective on mental disorder, but I highlight the need for specifying the particular types of mental disturbance that receive stigma and discrimination. In fact, unless the particular form of disturbance is specified, attributing stigma to "mental disorder" may be feeding into a key stereotype—namely, that all mental illness is alike.[27]

Finally, what is the personal and economic impact of mental disorder? A groundbreaking report was issued in the mid-1990s regarding the "global burden of disease," which refers to the types of personal, vocational, and economic impairment and disability associated with various illnesses worldwide. This authoritative statement concluded that four of the top ten diseases around the world in terms of impairment and disability were mental disorders: depression, schizophrenia, bipolar disorder, and obsessive compulsive disorder. Furthermore, within the next decade, depression is projected to become the most impairing disease on earth, related to its high prevalence (more than 10% of the population will suffer from major depression in their lifetime, with women at particularly high risk) and its severe effects on employment, relationships, and even mortality, in the form of suicide and additional health risks. Indeed, during the 1990s, it was noted that within the United States "mental disorders collectively account for more than 15 percent of the overall burden of disease from *all* causes and slightly more than the burden associated with all forms of cancer."[28] Clearly, the impact of mental disorders is both real and ever increasing.

In sum, a definition of mental disorder that is fully satisfying at clinical, scientific, and philosophical levels continues to be elusive. Yet the same lack of certainty applies to many physical illnesses, for which definitions continue to lack complete precision and clear boundaries with healthy functioning are not obvious. When the symptoms in question are thoughts, feelings, and behaviors—and when the nature of the relationships among the mind, the brain, and behavior is still under exploration—it is hardly surprising that absolute definitions are hard to come up with. Mental illness is a harsh reality for many individuals and families, with up to 6% of the population currently affected by serious forms that markedly affect personal attainment, safety and health, personal judgment, and close relationships, and many more suffering from moderately severe conditions.[29] The question now turns to the nature of social responses to mental disorders, requiring a definition of the concept of stigma.

Stereotyping, Prejudice, Discrimination, and Stigma

What is meant by the stigmatization of mental disorder—or of any trait or feature? In formulating an answer, we must first distinguish the concept of stigma from the related processes of stereotyping, prejudice, and discrimination. Although overlap clearly exists, emphasis on their distinctiveness may help to clarify the rest of the material.

Stereotypes, Prejudice, and Discrimination

First, *stereotypes* are beliefs about social groups that are made in an all-or-none fashion, characterizing a group as a whole while dismissing individual differences or the unique characteristics of persons within the group. For example, one may assert that academic types are conceited, members of the neighboring town are overbearing, a certain ethnic group is overly constricted emotionally (or lazy, hostile, territorial, etc.), or persons with physical disabilities are dependent and sad.

Because we all deal with a complex social world every day, stereotyping is a prevalent human response to the need to conserve our cognitive resources by making mental categories. Being able to categorize and predict behavioral reactions on the basis of group characteristics facilitates quick decision making. Using current terminology, stereotypes are viewed as cognitive *schemas*, mental templates through which people organize their worlds. Although stereotypes may be based in factual information, they often involve overgeneralization from what may be only a germ of truth. They can also be blatantly false.[30]

When stereotypes become rigid, and particularly when they overlook any specific data regarding the person or group in question, they tend to acquire a negative, pejorative flavor. They are now *prejudices*, defined as unreasoning, unjustifiable, overgeneralized, and negatively tinged attitudes toward others related to their group membership. The term literally connotes prejudgment, reflecting ascriptions made about members of a social group in the absence of evidence. Beyond stereotypes, which pertain to blanket descriptions of members of a particular group, prejudice connotes a darker, affect-laden tone. Prejudice regarding ethnic/racial differences is a frequently studied topic in social psychology.[31]

The term *discrimination* pertains to the unfair treatment of others or harmful actions toward them, based on their membership in a specific group. Discrimination may be instigated by individuals, families, or communities—or by cultures or nations as a whole. When it occurs, the rights of the targeted group are limited. Discriminatory practices may be unofficial or officially sanctioned by law or judicial ruling.

A useful perspective is as follows. Stereotyping conveys the *cognitive* aspect of group differentiation, in which members of foreign or unfamiliar social groups are viewed in highly categorical ways that distinguish them from members of one's primary group. Prejudice, in contrast, connotes the *affective* or emotional aspect of such differentiation, by which the outgroup members are devalued. Discrimination pertains to *behavioral* responses, particularly those actions that delimit the rights of others or overtly harm them. Although some investigators use prejudice as the overarching term, with recognition given to its cognitive, affective, and behavioral manifestations, viewing these concepts as separable may help to clarify linkages between social cognition, emotion, and interpersonal behavior.

At first glance, it would be logical to assume that stereotypes, prejudices, and discrimination are associated in a linear way: Stereotypes lead inevitably to prejudicial attitudes, which in turn promote discriminatory practices. Yet the actual associations among attitudes, emotions, and behavior are far from perfect, reflecting complex processes.[32] It is possible for someone to voice stereotyped beliefs ("People with mental disorders are unpredictable") or prejudicial attitudes ("Such individuals are morally reprehensible") but simultaneously to maintain close contact with certain members of this disparaged group (e.g., having a particular colleague or friend with mental disorder). In other words, beliefs or feelings about a group as a whole may not pertain to individual members of that group. Complicating matters further are the forces in modern society that prohibit or at least diminish the overt expression of prejudicial attitudes, making it difficult to detect prejudice through traditional attitude scales. I will have more to say about these forms of indirect or even unconscious prejudice later on.

Furthermore, a history of discrimination against a minority group can foster stereotyping and prejudice, even in those who may never have encountered a representative of that group. The prejudicial attitudes can, in fact, serve to perpetuate the discriminatory practices by blaming the victims for their own plight. In other words, prejudice may result from unwitting "system justification," with biases and prejudices leading to a mindset that perpetuates the inequality. Institutional policies (e.g., discriminatory laws) can actually produce stigmatization against outgroup members without any display of individual-level prejudice by a perceiver. [33]

Stigma

What, then, is meant by the concept of *stigma?* The term is a harsh one, emanating from historical practices of literally branding members of castigated groups in order that they carry a visible sign of disgrace. The resultant brands or marks signaled the flawed, deviant nature of their bearers; all of the members of the society therefore knew of the individual's degraded status.

Dictionary definitions state that stigma is a "mark of infamy, disgrace, or reproach" or "a mark of shame, a strain on a person's good reputation"; the *Random House Thesaurus* includes the synonyms *reproach, taint, tarnish, disgrace, infamy,* and *disrepute.*[34] Stigma refers to a global devaluation of certain individuals on the basis of some characteristic they possess, related to membership in a group that is disfavored, devalued, or disgraced by the general society. Its connotations imply harsh moral judgments placed on those who are linked with the group in question.

In the early 1960s sociologist Erving Goffman wrote a classic work on this concept, titled *Stigma: Notes on the Management of Spoiled Identity.* Through this work he chronicled the intricate patterns of social interactions and self-perceptions pertaining to individuals with conditions or attributes that are devalued in a given culture. According to Goffman, the term had its origins in ancient Greece, referring to "bodily signs designed to expose something unusual and bad about the moral status of the signifier: The signs were cut or burnt into the body and advertised that the bearer was a slave, a criminal, or a traitor—a blemished person, ritually polluted, to be avoided, especially in public places."[35]

Since antiquity, the plural term, *stigmata,* has referred to the marks on the body of Jesus from the nails and spears of the crucifixion, visible signs of humiliation and pain. Another intriguing use emanates from the fifteenth, sixteenth, and seventeenth centuries, when much of Europe was preoccupied with identifying, torturing, and executing witches (see Chapter 3). Stigmata were the numb, insensitive portions of the skin of the accused, signifying that the Devil had taken possession of the body and soul. Identifying stigmata was therefore a crucial aspect of the "diagnosis" of witches.

The modern usage of the term connotes the underlying disgrace and shame rather than the bodily signs per se. Indeed, Goffman contended the following:

> By definition . . . we believe the person with a stigma is not quite human. On this assumption we exercise varieties of discrimination, through which we effectively, if often unthinkingly, reduce his life chances. We construct a stigma-theory, an ideology to explain his inferiority and account for the danger he represents. . . . We tend to impute a wide range of imperfections on the basis of the original one. . . . Further, we may perceive his defensive response to his situation as a direct expression of his defect, and then see both defect and response as just retribution for something he or his parents or tribe did, and hence a justification for how we treat him.[36]

As we can see, stigma incorporates elements of stereotyping: An individual is perceived as a member of a group with certain characteristics, with the group identity taking precedence over any individual qualities that person may possess. It also involves prejudice, given that the perceptions are negatively tinged, often to an extreme. It incorporates discrimination as well, as perceivers, communities, and societies engage in shunning, exclusion, and punishment.

But stigma is more than the sum of its parts. From its very definition, it connotes an internal "mark" of deep degradation to the individual who carries it and a license to the social majority to perpetuate and escalate their judgmental attitudes and responses. It therefore goes beyond the presence of negative attitudes or prejudices per se. Stigmatization may also be extended to those who are merely associated with stigmatized subgroups, such as family members, workmates, or other associates, a process Goffman branded as "courtesy stigma." Stigma casts a long shadow.

In current thinking on the topic, stigmatization is viewed as a set of social processes (comparison, identification, devaluation) that lead to continuing denigration. Perceivers first recognize a difference that signals membership in an outgroup; intense devaluation of that characteristic (and of the group identity it reflects) propels such recognition into stigmatization. A crucial process in this regard involves the global attribution of negative traits to the individual's devalued characteristic—that is, the person is viewed as intrinsically flawed. Another process includes self-fulfilling prophecies, whereby the perceiver's expectation of deeply dysfunctional behavior and the stigmatized person's expectation of social rejection serve to shape encounters negatively. The castigated individual's behavior may begin to conform to the initial stereotype, setting in motion a vicious cycle of interactions. Finally, current theories of stigma pay particular attention to effects on those who are stigmatized, emphasizing the dynamic interplay of societal stereotypes with personal characteristics and the coping abilities of recipients of stigma.[37]

There has been an explosive growth of research and theorizing about stigma in the decades since Goffman's conceptualization. In fact, stigma processes are now analyzed with respect to conditions such as gay and lesbian status, HIV/AIDS, urinary incontinence, step-parenting, physical disabilities, a wide range of physical illnesses, receipt of welfare, old age, obesity, left-handedness, and many more. There are thousands of citations of stigma in the psychological research literature, with the number still growing.[38]

In an important review of the topic, Link and Phelan made the key point that social power is a necessary component of stigma. That is, many differences occur between people, but only some are stigmatized. For stigmatization to occur, perceivers must be in a position of social power, such that their worldviews of what is right versus wrong or healthy versus sick are influential.[39] Indeed, when low-status individuals within a society gossip or verbally degrade those of higher status, there are typically no important social consequences; it is only when those in power devalue others that stigma occurs. As power shifts, however, formerly stigmatized traits and attributes may be upgraded in status, signaling that there is malleability in stigma processes.

Does stigma lie in the eyes of the perceiver or in the response of the deviant individual? Goffman responds as follows:

> The stigmatized individual tends to hold the same beliefs about identity that we do; this is a pivotal fact. . . . The standards he has incorporated from the wider society equip him to be intimately alive to what others see as his failing. . . . Shame becomes a central possibility, arising from the individual's perception of one of his own attributes as being a defiling thing to possess.[40]

In other words, the demeaning attitudes of perceivers may well come to be internalized by the possessor of the devalued attribute in question.[41]

Current formulations, however, emphasize that lowered self-esteem is not an inevitable reaction to being stigmatized. In fact, there is great variability in psychological and behavioral responses among persons in outgroups, and many people from stigmatized groups show *higher* levels of self-esteem than do members of nonstigmatized groups. They may use cognitive, behavioral, or emotion-related strategies to cope with stigma and prejudice, such that a sense of self-worth is not always compromised.[42]

There is an insidious and global quality to stigmatization. Once individuals are stigmatized, they are likely to be discriminated against and excluded from many forms of social interchange. Furthermore, perceivers are likely to interpret all aspects of the functioning of stigmatized people in terms of the discredited attribute, exemplifying the global nature of the categorical thinking involved in the process of stigmatization.[43] Through stigma processes, the flaw is magnified until it comes to reduce the individuality and even the humanity of the targeted person.

Stigma is both universal and specific to individual cultures. All societies and cultures are motivated to find outgroups to degrade and stigmatize, but the specific forms of what constitutes deviance vary across cultures and over time. Take, for example, thin versus heavier female body size, the acceptance of which has alternated throughout history and across various societies.[44] The hopeful sign here is that, as particular attributes come to be valued positively in a given culture, the stigma that surrounds them can decline both for the perceiver and the perceived.

An immediate question arises: Can being branded as mentally disordered lead to a more favorable social status in the foreseeable future, fostering major reductions in its stigmatization? In some cultures, historically as well as currently, signs of aberrant, even psychotic, behavior in shamans or religious leaders have led to reverence on the part of beholders. Even today in industrialized nations, there is a tendency to equate at least some forms of "madness" with creative genius. Yet mental illness tends to receive extremes of social perceptions, fluctuating between utter repulsion on the one hand and fascination, awe, or reverence on the other. The normalization of mental illness—that is, its perception as a difficult but accepted part of everyday life—has been a far more elusive goal.

The reduction of *individuality* that accrues from stigmatization may lead to perceptions of a person's reduced *humanity* as well. When perceivers begin to view a devalued, marked, and stigmatized person as less than fully human, the potential for punitive and even deadly responses is not far behind. Perceptions of subhumanity will come to justify exclusionary and, at times, lethal responses on the part of those with social power, in that the victim is seen to lack the fundamental attributes that would mandate any form of respect.[45]

In summary, the term *stigma* connotes a deep mark of shame and degradation carried by a person as a function of being a member of a devalued social group. Stigmatization encompasses those interpersonal processes whereby other members of society come to devalue the group or characteristics in question and begin to interpret all of the person's attributes and characteristics in terms of this flawed identity. It incorporates the social and institutional structures and policies that emphasize the views of the majority, even to the detriment of the devalued subgroup. Aspects of stereotyping, prejudice, and discrimination are clearly involved in stigmatization, yet the latter term captures more fundamentally the deep sense of external and internal devaluation of the individuals in question, the global nature of the ascriptions made to their flawed nature, and the tendency in perceivers to automatically invoke stereotypes in relation to those people. Stigma processes also involve self-stigmatization, whereby members of stigmatized groups are prone to internalize the negative messages they receive and to use the coping responses of secrecy and concealment.[46] Finally, stigmatization can lead to dehumanization, with perceptions of less-than-human status justifying extreme responses.

The central question for the following chapters is how and why persons with mental disorder are so stigmatized. This account will lead into the social psychology and sociology of exclusion, the areas of natural selection and evolution, historical accounts of attitudes toward mental disorder, and various research methodologies used to document stigma and discrimination.

2

Perspectives From Social Psychology, Sociology, and Evolutionary Psychology

For many decades, sociologists and social psychologists have made important contributions to our understanding of prejudice, discrimination, and stigma. In addition, evolutionary psychology, which utilizes principles of natural selection to comprehend human behavior patterns, has surged in explanatory power and popularity in recent years and has led to provocative insights. My goal in this chapter is to discuss the fundamental tenets of these accounts in order to provide a clear perspective on the mechanisms underlying the pervasive tendencies for humans to socially devalue and stigmatize their peers. Much of the work covered herein pertains to racial prejudice, which has been the subject of a large body of research, fueled in part by the school desegregation and civil rights movements of the latter half of the twentieth century. Because applicability of this work to mental disorders is not always clear, I show parallels with and lessons for mental illness when possible. The sheer volume of research on stigma processes means that this review is necessarily selective.

Stigmatization is an interpersonal process requiring both perceivers (i.e., those who stigmatize) and recipients or victims of degradation. Because of the importance of uncovering the roots of stigmatization, much of the analysis pertains to perceivers and the mechanisms underlying their tendencies to stigmatize others. Yet because of the inherently relational nature of stigma and the need to understand the ways in which stigmatization influences its victims, material on these individuals' responses to rejection is also featured.

The Social Psychology and Sociology of Stigma

Social psychologists investigate, among other topics, (a) social cognition, referring to the cognitive structures and processes related to perceiving others, and (b) intergroup conflict and hostility (as well as the flip side of these processes, empathy and altruism). Sociology is concerned with the social structures and social processes that permeate all cultures, with particular focus on social power. A key premise of all such work is that humans are extremely interpersonal beings, with extensive social comparison processes present in every culture. Furthermore, whereas people are active perceivers of their social worlds, many of the messages about social values in a given culture are so pervasive and overlearned that a considerable amount of processing goes on in an automatic, unconscious manner. In fact, overcoming stigma may well require the overriding of automatic processing that takes place.

Half a century ago, most research and theorizing was based on the premise that prejudice and stigma stem from deep-seated personal tendencies, such as authoritarian personality styles or other forms of psychopathology within the perceiver. The perspective has now shifted radically to a view emphasizing the universality of social comparisons, the ubiquity of stigmatization processes, and the clear association between social power and stigma. In other words, stigmatization is embedded in everyday psychological functions (e.g., tendencies to categorize), social processes (e.g., ingroup versus outgroup identification), and structural variables (e.g., unequal social power and justice). Although some personality types may be particularly vehement in their tendencies to show prejudice and to stigmatize others, stigma processes are part of the everyday landscape. Still, they are malleable and changeable. That is, although stereotyping and stigma are omnipresent, their automatic activation can be controlled by conscious thought, and changes in social policies can facilitate "downstream" alterations in individual attitudes and behavior.

At a basic level, for humans everywhere the formation of social groups was (and still is) necessary for survival. There is a fundamental tendency to identify with *ingroups,* those social clusters of which one is a member by birth or community, and to distinguish the members of one's ingroup from those in *outgroups*—which refer to those clans, tribes, or communities viewed as foreign, who may pose a threat to survival, particularly when resources are scarce.[1] Ingroup identification is linked to perceptions of similarity, proximity, and familiarity; to shared family or cultural ties; or to more visible attributes such as skin color. It requires very little justification for individuals to begin to differentiate ingroup from outgroup members. In other words, there is a strong urge for people to begin the process of separating "their own kind" from others.

There are a number of social psychological considerations to make regarding the tendency toward the denigration of outgroups. I first consider the kinds of characteristics that tend to receive such negative attention, as well as the key dimensions on which such processes may be based. I then take up several important properties related to stigmatization, as well as the functions that stigma serves for ingroup members who devalue outsiders. From the perspective of sociology's labeling theory, I briefly note the power of social labels to fuel stigmatization, and I close by integrating the psychological, social, and institutional levels that are related to the formation, development, and maintenance of stigma.[2]

Recipients of Stigma: Types and Dimensions

Goffman's landmark book on stigma identified three groups of characteristics that are likely to receive stigmatization. The first involves physical deformities, or what he termed "abominations of the body." These include excessive body weight, facial or bodily disfigurements, or physical disabilities or handicaps. (The origin of the term *handicap* emanated from a disabled individual's having "cap in hand" to beg for crumbs or change; it is a word that itself reflects stigmatization.) The second category includes "tribal" characteristics (i.e., familial and intergenerational traits and cultural markers such as racial, religious, or national status that differ from those of the individuals who are in power). The third category concerns blemishes of character, which involve looked-down-upon personality or behavioral configurations "perceived as weak will, domineering or unnatural passions, treacherous and rigid beliefs, and dishonesty, these being inferred from a known record of, for example, mental disorder, imprisonment, addiction, alcoholism, homosexuality, unemployment, suicidal attempts, and radical political behavior."[3] Goffman's contention is that the character flaws in this category may be inferred entirely from stereotyped associations to the outgroup in question. That is, to be influenced by the *reputation* of those with such traits, perceivers may never have to encounter the behavior patterns directly. In fact, a history of mental disorder may incur stigmatization before social perceivers have actually met or interacted with the person in question.

Since the time of Goffman's writing, much of the literature on stigma has essentially ignored these three types. Indeed, this typology is not mutually exclusive: Obese individuals may be perceived as possessing a physical deformity (i.e., the overweight character of their body) and evidencing a blemish of character (i.e., the lack of willpower that led to this condition in the first place). The categories are not exhaustive, either; women have received discrimination and stigmatization throughout history, but the female sex does not fit into any of these three designations. Finally, each category may mask key subdistinctions: Under "blemishes of character," stigmatization of adopted children may differ in important ways from the stigma of violent crime, and both may differ from the stigma of depression. Yet evolutionary accounts have resurrected this typology of stigmatized conditions, as discussed at the end of the chapter.

Another tradition has focused on dimensional factors that shape stigma responses. The most elaborated model emanates from Edward Jones and colleagues, who posited six fundamental dimensions: (a) concealability—the extent to which a devalued condition is either visible or able to be hidden; (b) course—the development of the condition or trait over time; (c) disruptiveness—the extent to which it strains interpersonal interactions; (d) aesthetics—the types of bodily or facial deviation from the norm that it incorporates; (e) origin—a crucial dimension related to the ways in which the devalued condition came into being and to its perceived controllability; and (f) peril—the danger or threat that it poses.[4] I highlight the applications of these dimensions to mental disorders.

First, *concealability* pertains to a continuum of stigmatized attributes ranging from visible features, such as racial characteristics or clear disfigurements, to hidden "marks," such as a history of imprisonment or mental disorder. Although stigma might at first glance appear to be stronger with respect to overt, visible, and nonconcealable marks, there are special dilemmas for those with attributes that can be hidden. Consider, for instance, the issues for individuals with personal or family histories of mental illness: Should this fact be disclosed? Can behavior and self-presentation be adjusted to prevent the "leakage"? What if the perceiver eventually finds out anyway—will any chance of positive interactions be ruined? Persons with concealable stigmas (as well as their relatives) are often quite vigilant about the possibility that interaction partners may find them out, prompting stress and role conflict.[5] The resultant tension can spread to perceivers, who may begin to suspect the hidden stigma and may themselves become anxious about how to react if a disclosure is made. Interestingly, because less severe forms of mental illness are likely to be more concealable than overt, flagrant patterns, stigma can be strong in such cases, as perceivers may blame the individual for inadequate volitional control.

Second, the *course* of a stigmatized attribute affects interpersonal relations. With other factors equal, a long-term course is associated with lowered acceptance. Chronic illnesses (e.g., paralysis, AIDS) tend to receive far more stigmatization than acute conditions. In terms of mental disorder, the strong belief is that serious mental illnesses are inevitably chronic and unremitting; this perspective plays a key role in the large degree of stigmatization related to mental illness. As it becomes increasingly recognized that mental disorders are treatable and that adaptive, resilient functioning is a real possibility, stigma could decrease accordingly.

Third, mental disorder is likely to be perceived as extremely *disruptive* to social encounters, given the irrational, inconsistent nature of its most severe symptomatology and the negative associations with the very label. The view that mentally disordered individuals are unpredictable is likely to fuel apprehension and fear on the part of the perceiver, leading to both avoidance and interpersonal rejection. Although the specific kinds of disruption and threat vary greatly across different forms of mental disorder—for example, severely depressed mood differs markedly from agitated paranoia, and both of these differ from obsessive-compulsive patterns or substance abuse—expectations surrounding the general label of mental illness may themselves trigger stigma because of the implied potential for disruption of social encounters.

Fourth, with respect to *aesthetics,* a large literature has developed on humans' tastes and preferences in terms of the appearance and attractiveness of their peers, revealing strong tendencies to reject those who fail to meet standards of beauty.[6] Deep-seated emotional reactions may attend to the perceptions of those with noteworthy disfigurements. With regard to mental disorder, a disheveled person with severely irrational behavior will tend to elicit disgust. Furthermore, some of the psychoactive medications used to treat psychoses and schizophrenia can induce side effects that influence motor movements and facial musculature, including the disfiguring and potentially permanent syndrome known as tardive dyskinesia, in which drooling and facial grimacing are salient.[7] Certain interventions for mental disorder have the potential to fuel stigmatization in the form of reduced aesthetic properties of the treated individual.

Fifth, regarding *peril,* conditions appear to be stigmatized in direct proportion to their propensity to result in danger and overt threat. A key example is the brutally stigmatized condition of leprosy (now termed Hansen's disease), a contagious bacterial illness for which leper colonies were built in many areas of the world for much of recorded history. Indeed, the very term "leper" connotes degradation, isolation, and stigma. The isolation of such facilities portrays the lengths to which societies will go to banish afflicted individuals in the service of delimiting contamination. In relation to mental disorder, the most salient theme is one of dangerousness, an image promoted heavily by stereotypes of violence, including media depictions that exaggerate both unpredictability and tendencies toward aggressive behavior. Other forms of threat are more symbolic, to the extent that mentally disturbed behavior forces perceivers to confront fears of a disrupted social fabric—or anxiety over their own mental stability.

Finally, the dimension of *origin* (referring to how the trait took form) is of great theoretical and clinical significance. I start with attribution theory, a key topic in social psychology.[8] Attributions are causal explanations for behavior, which are especially likely to be invoked when unexpected or socially deviant behavior occurs. (If behavior is predictable, little motivation exists for understanding its origins.) Causes array themselves on several dimensions (e.g., internal versus external; stable versus unstable), each of which has implications for emotional and behavioral responses.

A crucial attributional dimension of great relevance to stigma and closely linked to the concept of origin pertains to the *controllability* of a causal factor. Specifically, when negative traits and characteristics are believed to emanate from sources over which an individual can exert personal control, blame and castigation are the typical reactions from perceivers, often leading to rejection and punishment. On the other hand, ascription of negative behaviors to uncontrollable causal forces should lead not only to a lack of blame but also to increased compassion and sympathy. Weiner and colleagues present experimental evidence in this regard: When perceivers believe that deviant behavior emanates from conditions outside of one's control (i.e., physical deformities), sympathy and compassion are likely, but aberrant behavior linked to volitional control (i.e., behavioral or mental problems) generates rejection and hostility.[9]

A core assumption is that mentally disturbed behavior is viewed as the product of weak will or other indicators of controllable causes. As a result, inappropriate and socially deviant behavior patterns linked to mental illness are likely to encounter hostile rather than empathic responses. On the other hand, because of their underlying assumption that mental illness emanates from naturalistic processes outside of personal control, medical model attributions would be expected to reduce blame and fuel acceptance and sympathy. Given the cyclic history of medical perspectives on mental disorder throughout history and their resurgence within the last several decades, this is a crucial topic, which I discuss at length subsequently.[10]

I pause to present another relevant social psychological construct with important linkages to perceptions of origin and control: the "just world" hypothesis.[11] The key premise here is that individuals often find it extremely distressing to witness some of humanity's striking examples of suffering, including poverty, illness, and severe behavioral deviance. Although perceivers may feel guilty when confronted with such tragedy and even potentially responsible for ameliorating such problems, they may also experience powerlessness and even despair. As a self-protective mechanism, they are motivated to cling to the belief that the world is, in fact, just and fair rather than random and cruel, to ward off the perception that such afflictions could potentially befall them personally.

Yet belief in a just world prompts the contention that the afflicted persons in question must actually have been responsible for their plight. In other words, if the world is truly fair, then misfortune is likely to be deserved. The attribution of negative events to personal control "may not only wipe away both the guilt and the disagreeable prospect of having to give time and money, but it provides a comforting illustration of how evil will get its just desserts."[12] In short, when perceivers operate with the belief in a just world, they are motivated to make personally controllable attributions for threatening, disturbing, or distressing behavior patterns, providing the comforting view that the social system is indeed fair and serving to fuel harsh responses toward those who display deviant behavior. Implications for stigma related to mental illness are clear.

Key Features of Stigma and Stigmatization

I now address several features of stigma, each of which has clear relevance to people with mental disorders.

Pervasiveness   The most marked conditions in a given society or culture tend to produce strong consensus regarding their devalued status. In other words, stereotypes about devalued groups are extremely *pervasive*. Especially given the huge impact of print and visual media in modern societies, but also through storytelling, literature, and folklore in less Westernized cultures, there is usually a great deal of agreement about the racial, religious, and behavioral subgroups that are devalued and shunned. The very creation of a social fabric within a community emanates in part from the boundaries that separate acceptable from unacceptable attributes, traits, and behaviors—in other words, ingroups from outgroups.[13]

Societal views related to a given outgroup are typically perceived as factual rather than mythical or stereotypic. Children learn of such stereotypes as early as the preschool years, attesting to the strength of such perspectives. Even those persons in a culture who disavow the stereotypic depictions of certain subgroups, including those with the stigmatized condition themselves, are highly likely to know of the existence of these portrayals.[14]

An important upshot is that societal stereotypes of outgroup members are so overlearned by most people in a given culture as to be automatically induced when a member of a devalued group is encountered. Even if the perceiver is not consciously aware of such reactions, the automatic induction of the negative stereotype produces strongly conditioned emotional and behavioral responses.[15] *Implicit* stereotypes and prejudices are those that are unconscious as opposed to consciously and overtly expressed. In the domain of race, a wealth of current research relates to implicit stereotyping and prejudice, which is done without conscious introspection. Little is known, however, about implicit attitudes toward individuals with mental disorder.[16]

Ambivalence   A second key feature of stigmatizing reactions is the *ambivalence* inherent in their display. The argument starts from the premise that reactions to disturbing behavior are inherently complex, balancing compassion on the one hand with harsh judgment on the other. Many if not most members of modern society hold two often-conflicting values: (a) egalitarianism, the belief in the equal worth of all humans and the equal opportunities that should be available to all members of society; and (b) individualism, the belief that individual efforts determine personal advancement. To the extent that egalitarian views are salient, the perception of stigmatized groups should elicit identification, sympathy, and efforts to correct the social injustices that led to the social and behavioral problems. On the other hand, if individualistic views predominate, members of stigmatized groups will tend to receive blame for insufficient efforts on their own behalf.[17]

The implication is that members of stigmatized groups may be perceived as both disadvantaged, through no fault of their own, and deviant, with primary responsibility for their problematic behavior or traits. Because these perceptions can occur together, ambivalence is likely, resulting in both sympathy and rejection. As a result, reactions to stigmatized persons are prone to be unstable, shifting between empathy and revulsion. In addition, it may take only a small stimulus—for example, witnessing one additional member of a stigmatized group—to shift an initially positive response to a negative one (or vice versa).[18] Such complexity makes for difficulties in investigating stigma, much less in reducing it. Still, the presence of initial compassion for stigmatized individuals gives hope, as it provides a starting place for intervention efforts.[19]

Complicating matters is the fact that, with respect to racial and ethnic prejudice, as well as discrimination against women, social processes in the last half-century have fostered a changing set of standards for what is acceptable in terms of publicly displayed attitudes. Expressions of racism or sexism may therefore be more masked than the overt, bigoted forms that were formerly commonplace. Via "modern" or "symbolic" prejudice, biased attitudes may be expressed through conservative political views emphasizing individual responsibility rather than direct antipathy toward the outgroup in question.[20] Such expressions reflect the deep, even unconscious ambivalence in members of modern society regarding prejudicial attitudes and emotions.

Although social standards have changed in recent decades with regard to the overt display of racial and sexual attitudes and biases, it is not at all clear that standards with respect to mental disorder have undergone a parallel shift, given the overtness of many indicators of bias and stigma toward mental illness. In the future, as social mores change and overt disparaging of mental disorder is frowned upon, attitudes may be increasingly expressed in terms of masked and "modern" forms of stigmatization, as well as through implicit bias.

Anxiety   Interactions between perceivers and stigmatized individuals are likely to result in *anxiety* for both. If perceivers are overtly prejudiced, they may expect hostility when dealing with an outgroup member, fueling their own apprehension and anxiety. Even people without overt prejudice may be genuinely concerned with the potential peril and threat of interacting with stigmatized individuals, whom they have been conditioned to fear and avoid. Hence, anxiety as well as antipathy may result.[21] It is also possible that perceivers may genuinely wish to behave in accepting, nondiscriminatory fashion but remain unsure of how to act, especially if there is a lack of prior experience with members of stigmatized groups. If perceivers attempt to suppress stereotyped images of stigmatized partners, in an honest attempt to behave in egalitarian or empathic fashion, such suppression may result in a "rebound" of the very thoughts and stereotypes that are being pushed underground.[22] Again, anxiety may result.

From the perspective of the stigmatized individuals, particularly if they carry a hidden or concealed stigma, anxiety is likely to accompany many forms of social encounter, including conversations, social outings, or job interviews. This anxiety will relate to both the potential for the interaction partner's "uncovering" of the devalued condition and the fear of subsequent rejection. In fact, being a recipient of discrimination is likely to generate vigilance to the possibility of further rejection in new encounters, fueling tension and wariness. Such anxiety can cumulate in terms of marked personal stress and even risks to health.[23] Overall, anxiety characterizes the reactions of both perceivers and recipients of stigma, and it is likely to be particularly strong when the "mark" is concealable, as is often the case regarding mental disorder.

For those who receive stigma, the concept of *rejection sensitivity* is relevant. It reflects the proneness to anticipate hurt and rejection when interacting with social partners. Heightened rejection sensitivity on the part of devalued individuals may prompt avoidant behaviors or even hostility, further disrupting the behavioral interchange. A related concept is *stigma consciousness*, reflecting the expectation that stigmatization exists and may well occur during social interchange.[24] These ideas have not been applied systematically to persons with mental disorder, but their adoption could be fruitful.

Self-Denigration and Shame   Does stigmatization inevitably predict lowered self-esteem and shame for the devalued individual? Classic literature on the topic answered in the affirmative, under the assumption that the experience of chronic rejection and discrimination (sometimes termed *enacted stigma*) would inevitably lead to an internalization of the negative ascriptions, with resultant shame (known as *felt stigma*).[25] Defined as "a painful mental feeling aroused by a sense of having done something wrong or dishonorable or improper,"[26] shame is fueled by the intensely social nature of life and by humans' self-reflective tendencies, which result in internalized devaluation when one does not live up to social or moral standards.

Current research, however, reveals that those in outgroups do not invariably show shame or lowered self-esteem. In fact, as opposed to the perspective that stigmatization is a process propagated by deeply prejudiced perceivers with inevitable psychological damage for its recipients, social psychologists now conceptualize stigma as related to everyday social cognitive and interpersonal processes, which are followed by a wide range of responses in victims. Several mechanisms may help to preserve self-esteem in those who are stigmatized—for example, attribution of negative feedback to prejudice rather than personal flaws, discounting of attributes that are denigrated as relatively unimportant to oneself, and identification with and activism on behalf of the stigmatized group.[27]

In the case of mental disorder, however, lowered self-esteem and the development of shame are particularly likely. For one thing, the very symptoms of many forms of mental illness include sad mood, social isolation, and tendencies toward self-blame. In major depression, for example, core features include guilt and the overattribution of personal responsibility for negative events. Shame may be part of the syndrome itself. Also, many forms of mental illness incur major life disruption—for example, hospitalization, ruined relationships, and financial loss. Deep shame might well be expected in the wake of such events. In short, when one's own mind and personality are the "marked" conditions, shame is likely.

Although solidarity with other group members has been a powerful source of positive identification for individuals in ethnic and racial minorities, until quite recently there has been little impetus for identification with the amorphous "group" of fellow individuals with mental disorders—who have nearly always been politically disenfranchised and largely invisible. Self-help groups and advocacy movements for persons with mental disorders are a potentially powerful means of overcoming stigma (see Chapter 11).

Mechanisms Underlying Stigma and Stigmatization

What are the mechanisms that motivate and fuel stigma? In other words, what are the potential benefits or gains for social perceivers who engage in the stigmatization of others, especially those with mental illnss?[28]

(1) Promotion of Social Identity and Outgroup Derogation   Clear benefits accrue from being a member of a strong primary group: resources, status, and even survival. The formation of social identity with ingroup members is therefore highly motivated. In fact, humans appear to be almost wired to form ingroup identifications. "Minimal group" research reveals that it takes extremely little justification to promote ingroup identification. That is, the totally arbitrary designation of others as ingroup members—through sitting near one another, wearing similarly colored shirts, or even the flipping of a coin—can promote strong identification.[29]

A number of consequences result from ingroup identity. At a cognitive level, people come to believe that ingroup members are similar to themselves; affectively, positive emotion toward and empathic concern for ingroup members increase; behaviorally, there is increased likelihood of approach, cooperation, and helping.[30] Developing a strong ingroup identity is also likely to fuel contrasts with outgroup members, prompting their devaluation through what social psychologists call "downward comparison." In other words, a strong identification with the ingroup promotes sharp differentiation from those who are not in the group.

But does ingroup membership necessitate the downgrading of outgroup members? Research in this area is complex, but the bottom line is that, whereas such tendencies are likely, ingroup favoritism does not mandate outgroup denigration. In the words of Allport, who pioneered relevant work during the middle of the last century:

> although we could not perceive our in-groups excepting as they contrast to out-groups, still the in-groups are psychologically primary. We live in them, by them, and, sometimes, for them. Hostility toward out-groups helps strengthen our sense of belonging, but it is not required.[31]

Overall, it should not be concluded that prejudice and stigmatization are inevitable results of the formation of strong ties with members of the ingroup.

Even though ingroups and outgroups may solidify under minimal conditions, the presence of competition, particularly amidst scarce resources, is likely to accentuate these processes. According to "realistic group conflict theory," subgroups that threaten the economic or political viability of a social grouping or community (or who jeopardize its core values) are particularly likely to be stigmatized. In other words, competition and threat push ingroup identification to new heights and outgroup derogation to new depths.[32] A clear implication is that when persons with mental illness are perceived as helpless and needy—that is, as a group likely to provide a drain on social resources—their stigmatization is likely to increase. In addition, when political leaders or media accounts emphasize that the presence of mental illness is a threat to a community's economic or social well-being, prejudice should similarly rise.

(2) Enhancement of Self-Esteem   Clear evidence exists that putting down members of the outgroup serves not only to bolster social identity with the ingroup but also to lift one's self-esteem. In other words, downward comparisons with those lower in status can enhance the self-perceptions of the perceiver.[33]

Fein and Spencer showed that people who had received information damaging to their self-esteem were likely to make disparaging characterizations of members of stereotyped outgroups. Such negative evaluations served, in turn, to restore and bolster their own self-images.[34] Particularly alarming is the fact that the existence of stereotypes provides a convenient and viable tool through which self-esteem enhancement can occur when individuals have suffered a blow to their self-worth. Indeed, because of the pervasiveness and cultural acceptance of stereotypes, their use to denigrate an outgroup member does not arouse much guilt or remorse. Castigation of outgroup members appears to constitute a safe and easy mechanism through which perceivers may bolster their self-perceptions.

Yet self-esteem enhancement is not a full explanation of stigmatization. For one thing, it does not explain the strong consensus that develops within most cultures about the recipients of denigration; other social processes must also be at work to shape the consistency of stigma targets. Moreover, it does not deal well with the tendencies for outgroup members to believe stereotypes foisted on them and, at times, to go along with the denigration they experience. In addition, enhancement of self-esteem cannot, in and of itself, explain the types of structural discrimination and stigma fueled by social institutions. Still, enhanced self-esteem may well be a motivator for at least some ingroup members to participate in putting down the outgroup.[35]

(3) System Justification   Every society on earth displays a hierarchical structure with respect to status, access to resources, and power. Given this fundamental social tendency, putting down of the have-nots may well serve to justify the existing social structure on the part of the haves. In other words, because of the pervasiveness of hierarchical divisions of power and resources, those on the top rungs downgrade less-enfranchised members of the hierarchy to fuel the perspective that their higher status is justified and fair.

Note the parallel here with the "just world" hypothesis described earlier, through which belief in fairness can motivate the blaming of less-fortunate individuals for their afflictions. Several types of "legitimating myths"—for example, beliefs in a merit-based society or an impartial world—bolster the status quo and ease the minds of high-status perceivers, so that their privileged status is seen as the result of effort and sacrifice rather than emanating from a discriminatory system.[36]

From this vantage point, stigmatization is a consequence rather than a cause of social injustice—a consequence that maintains the hierarchical status of ingroup-outgroup relations. System justification provides a top-down view of prejudice and stigma; it motivates the perspective that programs to address stigma must deal with social policies of discrimination. The system justification perspective also helps to explain the strong consensus across most societies about the targets of discrimination—who are likely, by definition, to be those on the lower rungs of the social hierarchy.

(4) Management of Anxiety and Terror Regarding Mortality Another function of stigmatization is that it may facilitate the attempts of perceivers to manage strong anxiety in the face of thoughts about life and death. That is, all humans face existential anxiety related to the arbitrariness and brevity of life and the presence of tragic circumstances throughout the world. Because awareness of such misfortune and mortality can be debilitating, people are motivated to adopt a worldview that upholds some degree of order and stability in order to preserve basic personal equilibrium. Yet the presence of outgroup members, particularly those signaling personal or social threat, may challenge a perceiver's fundamental belief systems and stability. Under the perspective known as *terror management theory,* people manage such threat and even terror by engaging in the stigmatization of outgroup members, which helps to preserve stability.[37]

In fact, experimental evidence reveals that harsh judgments against outgroup members are intensified when thoughts of death or mortality are primed. This tendency may be particularly strong when the outgroup suffers from physical deformities or extreme disorders of behavior, which can remind perceivers of life's fragile and transitory nature. This provocative idea moves perspectives on stigma from structural and intergroup processes to existential, meaning-based views of the kinds of scenarios likely to elicit psychological threat and prompt harsh reactions against marked individuals in order to ward off such threat. Stigma has deep psychological functions, as well as ones embedded in social structures.

Labeling Theory and Its Modifications

Labeling theory emerged from sociological and philosophical views emphasizing the socially constructed nature of reality—in other words, the belief that identity is strongly shaped by social processes. The idea is that when those with social power (or those sanctioned by society, like professionals) place labels on deviant behavior in order to begin to control or treat it, individuals who are assigned the labels take on attributes and role identities consistent with the label. This process forces a fundamentally changed identity for the labeled person, and a new social role emerges.

Consider the following argument: Although there is a great deal of deviant behavior in society—termed *residual deviance*—much of it is viewed as transitory or otherwise excused by the majority. If, however, such behavior is frequently displayed and highly visible, it is likely to become officially branded and diagnosed. Through this latter process the labeled individual is now expected to perform in accordance with the new role. Indeed, the expectations set in motion a chain of events that lead to a changed self-image, as well as reinforcement for the continuing display of deviance. Only a subset of those exhibiting such behavior get classified and labeled, but when they do, the label propels them into a career earmarked by the deviant role.[38]

Regarding juvenile delinquency, for example, many adolescents commit antisocial acts (especially boys), but only some are caught and adjudicated. The official labeling of such actions as delinquent sets in motion a host of social processes, such as detention, probation, collection of official records, and social/personal identification as a delinquent. Those adjudicated take on this delinquent role, with clear implications for their identities and their futures. Similarly, in the case of mental illness, the argument is that many forms of deviant behavior are expressed by members of society, but the identification, branding, and labeling of such actions as evidence of mental disorder coalesce to launch a "career" that reflects the mental illness role.

This formulation, termed *primary labeling theory,* was quite radical, given its denial of an independent entity termed mental illness and its direct implication that such mental disorders are created by labeling processes. Labeling theory served as a cautionary note, prompting great hesitancy to utilize psychological and psychiatric labels (see also Chapter 4 with respect to the antipsychiatry movement of the 1960s and 1970s).[39]

Critics soon pointed out, however, that the behaviors receiving such labels have a fully independent existence, whether or not diagnosis and labeling occur. Scientific advances of the last few decades have, in fact, made it extremely difficult to deny the psychobiological reality of serious mental illness. At the same time, clinical research increasingly demonstrates the helpful (rather than inherently harmful) effects of many forms of treatment. From this perspective, receiving an accurate diagnosis or label may be quite positive: It can potentially reduce self-blame, it provides a framework for comprehending the distressing and impairing features of mental disorder, and it constitutes a means of receiving needed intervention. In short, enthusiasm for the tenets of primary labeling theory—namely, that the label is fully responsible for creating the condition—eroded quickly in most quarters.[40]

Yet evidence continues to reveal that, even if labeling does not itself create dysfunction, it can have extremely deleterious consequences for people with mental disorders because of the negative connotations carried by the label. In fact, regarding what is termed *secondary labeling theory* or *modified labeling theory:*

Its basic premise is that although labels may not "cause" sustained mental illness, the stigma associated with treatment for mental disorder affects the course of illness by lowering a person's self-esteem, constricting their interpersonal networks, and reducing their chances for employment and income, all of which increase stress. These stressors, in turn, place persons at risk for increased symptoms.[41]

In other words, a label of mental illness, a history of mental hospitalization, or identification as a treated patient can all produce stigmatizing responses on the part of perceivers, as well as internalization of such negative reactions on the part of the individual. Secondary labeling theory holds that labels can produce demoralization, concealment, and a constriction of social networks over and above the disabilities related to the mental disorder itself.[42] Current conceptions of stigma owe much to the tenets of secondary labeling theory.

Origins and Functions of Stigma at Multiple Levels

I now provide a synthesis of the preceding material through a three-level conceptualization encompassing psychological, social, and structural factors pertinent to stigmatization. Because these levels are inherently interconnected, it is impossible to posit stigma as existing expressly within the person, as exclusively social, or as solely structural/institutional. Stigmatization is embedded in dynamic and interconnected processes that include cognitions, attitudes, and identity formation at the individual level; a host of intergroup phenomena at the social level; and institutional and economic conditions and factors at the structural level.[43] Biologically based, naturally selected propensities related to the stigmatization of outgroup members have also gained ascendancy, and I discuss evolutionary views on stigma in a separate section following this synthesis.

(1) Individual/Psychological Processes   Humans have strong tendencies to categorize their social worlds. Our interpersonal environments are quite complex, quickly resulting in information overload; as a result, we have highly developed cognitive structures for handling and managing this barrage of social information. That is, we "sort" the social world through mental templates or schemas. Without such guideposts and shortcuts, no one could navigate the myriad of social stimuli encountered each day. People therefore make quick judgments about individuals from different towns, those with different hair color, or those who are of higher or lower social status on the basis of the schemas formed about such groups. These ways of perceiving the world, which can quickly become stereotypes, preserve cognitive resources when perceivers are tired, pressed for time, or engaged with other stimuli or decisions.[44]

Such categorizing leads people to see those from foreign social groups as "all the same," exemplifying what is termed the *outgroup homogeneity* effect.

At the same time, ingroup members are perceived as relatively diverse, distinct, and individualized. Perceivers are also likely to form associations between relatively rare, negative events (e.g., violence, aggression) and other rare categories (e.g., ethnic minority groups; persons with mental disorder) because of the distinctiveness of both.[45] It becomes easy to see how stereotyping could quickly result.

Additional consequences proceed from such categorization. Perceivers favor ingroup members for rewards; they evaluate the efforts of ingroup members more positively than those of outgroup members; and they code *positive* attributes of ingroup members and *negative* attributes of outgroup members at abstract levels, facilitating the recall of such attributes and promoting further stereotypes. In short, when others are categorized into ingroups versus outgroups, amplification processes emerge that perpetuate the initial ingroup favoritism and outgroup derogation.[46] From this perspective, stigmatization does not require major social injustices or structural inequalities to emerge; it begins with entirely normal patterns of everyday social cognition in any society.

Perhaps the most noteworthy feature of these sociocognitive processes is their automatic and almost immediate nature. That is, schemas become quickly and unconsciously activated when an individual is confronted with the image of another person, particularly an outgroup member. The resultant cognitive processing is automatic, preserving cognitive resources. This sobering view provides a warning that tendencies to label and stereotype are a fundamental, perhaps inevitable part of the human condition.

At the same time, the stigmatization and discrimination that result from these tendencies are not completely hardwired or unchangeable. People can invest the cognitive and emotional energy necessary for more deliberate social processing, through which complex information about individuals is integrated into balanced, thoughtful judgments rather than quick stereotypes. Through effort and practice, people can overcome stereotypic thoughts and reactions and substitute them with stereotype-breaking beliefs. Considerable practice of such nonbiased responding is required to overcome the automatic nature of stereotyping: In Devine's words, it requires "intention, attention, and time."[47] I return to means of promoting such acceptance and compassion in the final chapters.

Another psychological construct relates to *individual differences* in perceivers. That is, certain types of people may be more likely than others to display stereotyping, prejudice, and discrimination against outgroup members. In the 1940s and 1950s, considerable interest emerged in the "authoritarian personality," signifying a type of individual who was prone to exhibit extremely conservative political views and to show hostility toward multiple ethnic and racial groups.[48] Although the idea that the roots of prejudice and stigma lie in the authoritarian personality—or any particular personality configuration—has largely fallen out of favor, evidence does exist that certain types of authoritarian beliefs, including the view that persons with mental disorder are inferior (and require coercive forms of intervention), are associated with the desire for social distance from those with mental illness.[49]

A more recent individual-difference phenomenon is the social dominance orientation (SDO), which reflects the propensity to believe that hierarchical, competitive social structures are just and fair. Persons with high levels of SDO do, in fact, show higher levels of racial bias and prejudice than do those with lower levels.[50] It is still an open question as to whether such individual differences are predictive of the tendency to display stigmatizing attitudes toward people with mental disorders.

(2) Social Processes   Social-level analyses of stigma relate to the themes of *social identity* (the sense of group identification with an ingroup), *ingroup enhancement* (the processes used to bolster one's ingroup), and *outgroup denigration* (the downgrading of outgroup members). These processes appear in humans across all cultures and nations, signaling a strong likelihood of species-wide functions related to ingroup versus outgroup processes.

An important corollary relates to the *self-fulfilling prophecy*. When people devalue those who are members of an outgroup, they often set in motion a chain of expectancies for awkward or unpleasant social interchanges that are communicated to the interaction partner. Furthermore, even if perceivers do not operate with such explicit biases, stigmatized individuals may believe that such beliefs are present, given the pervasiveness of stereotypes regarding marked conditions such as mental illness. As a result, they may behave in hesitant, restrained fashion—while believing that perceivers are judging them more harshly than is actually the case. In the ensuing vicious cycle, even originally fair-minded perceivers may begin to respond with distance, estrangement, or hostility, completing the self-fulfilling prophecy.[51]

A crucial topic in social accounts of stigma involves the work of Steele and colleagues on *stereotype threat*. Their premise is that cultural stereotypes are pervasive in society: For example, females are poor at mathematics, or African Americans have low scholastic aptitude. When stigmatized individuals are confronted with a performance situation in which the stereotype is salient, their performance is likely to suffer. This tendency would be particularly likely to hold up when the outgroup members exhibit high levels of *stigma consciousness*— that is, when they show great awareness of stigmatization.

In a series of now-classic investigations, members of underrepresented minority groups show decrements on tests of mental abilities, controlling for their own initial test performance, when they are led to believe that the tests are diagnostic of cognitive ability—in other words, when the stereotype threat is raised. Performance does not suffer, however, if the same tests are labeled in more neutral terms (for example, as sample items). The same is true for women regarding tests of mathematical ability.[52] In terms of underlying processes, one view holds that the stereotype raises anxiety in the outgroup members, who now fear that their poor performance may, in fact, validate the stereotype. The resultant apprehension—and preoccupation with the stereotype instead of the test itself—can lead to reduced performance.

Although research from this perspective on ethnic minority groups and women is now established, almost completely unknown is the extent to which the same phenomenon may be at work with respect to persons with mental disorders.[53] For example, when such individuals participate in social interactions or job interviews, it is quite possible that they perceive a stereotype threat that is related to being awkward or incompetent, which could, in turn, negatively influence their performance. This area constitutes an important topic for future investigations.

Finally, other forms of threat play a large role in social theories related to stigma. Perceivers may experience *social threat* in the form of apprehension over the potential for outgroup members (particularly those with mental disorders) to challenge their own propriety, morals, and stability. This phenomenon is emphasized in (a) realistic group conflict theory, which posits that competition for scarce resources may heighten stigma; and (b) terror management theory, which emphasizes the symbolic threats posed by those outgroup members who invoke primal fears.[54] Recipients of prejudice or stigma may experience *identity threat,* whereby certain types of stigmatizing messages from society may threaten the outgroup members' entire social identity. The recipients' *appraisals* of such messages—and of their coping abilities with respect to dealing with these messages—are crucial in predicting ultimate responses to stigma.[55] I focus on these threat theories in the integrative model of stigma presented in Chapter 7.

(3) Structural Processes   Hierarchical structures are endemic in human societies, all of which feature haves and have-nots. From this perspective, stigmatization comprises a system-justifying set of processes related to supporting fundamental inequities. Indeed, those on the lowest rungs of the hierarchy are quite likely to be stigmatized; prejudice serves to "blame the victims" for their plight, absolving the perceiver (and the system) from responsibility.[56]

A related issue is the set of *institutional supports* for discrimination in a given culture or society (i.e., those cultural practices that maintain the status quo). For example, the crayons labeled "flesh" in young children's supplies are light tan or pink in hue, consistent with the coloring of European Americans but not of other ethnic groups. In prior decades, dolls for children were largely white in color, and even children of color preferred such dolls to those closer to their own skin tones.[57] For mental illness, consider that, in 2005, a New England toy manufacturer produced a special Valentine gift: a teddy bear titled "Crazy for You," dressed in a straightjacket and holding commitment papers (those resembling legal documents forcing individuals into a mental hospital against their will).[58] This mocking portrayal of "craziness" exemplifies the institutional and cultural messages conveyed about mental illness.

At a larger level, cultural beliefs and social institutions are mutually reinforcing. For example, the Protestant ethic fuels the formation of meritocratic societies, which themselves perpetuate the belief that hard work receives rewards. Regarding people with mental illness, a belief in their incompetence perpetuates job discrimination, which, in turn, promotes a lack of skills and competence, reinforcing the initial belief.[59] Overall, stereotyping and stigmatization may be driven to a large extent by processes that operate at the level of social institutions and the general culture.

Another macrovariable relates to economics. A key hypothesis here is that more societal attention is paid to deviance—and that harsher responses to such deviance take place—during periods of difficult economic circumstances than in economically stable times. In other words, "during economic hard times, there should be a heightening of intolerance and a greater hostility toward marginal people, and with it a greater tendency to mark with stigma those who were previously accepted or whose behavior had hitherto been accepted."[60] The mediating variable is presumed to be the heightened level of stress in social perceivers, associated with economic hardship. This scenario exemplifies realistic group conflict theory, in which competition for scarce resources motivates high levels of outgroup prejudice.

A classic example is given in the work of Hovland and Sears, who found evidence for a statistical association in the early 1900s between the price of cotton in the Deep South and the number of lynchings of African Americans. Specifically, lower prices, reflecting economic hardship for farmers, were associated with an increase in such murders.[61] Regardless of whether this specific assertion is completely valid, note that society provides sizable amounts of money and resources for individuals with serious mental illness, as well as mental retardation (although not to the extent of parallel expenditures regarding physical illness). During times of economic hardship, the willingness to provide such support may wane, as evidenced by slashes in budgets for mental health and welfare during recessionary periods. In short, economic factors may influence levels of tolerance for those with mental disturbance both directly and indirectly.

Overall, responses to those who are devalued take place at psychological, social, and structural/institutional levels, which are highly intertwined. A key question is whether a deeper source of stigmatization exists—that of internal programming at the level of naturally selected tendencies to exclude other humans with certain characteristics. The recent resurgence of evolutionary accounts of human behavior includes stigma processes, which I now discuss.

Evolutionary Psychology and Stigma

Over the past three decades, the field initially known as sociobiology and later termed evolutionary psychology has made important, if sometimes controversial, inroads into the explanation of complex human behavior in terms of naturally selected, biologically based processes.[62] Applying such principles to human social behavior marks a major shift from the views that predominated throughout much of the last century, which focused almost exclusively on the cultural and social origins of human behavior. Although the surge of evolutionary accounts has raised hackles, through the potential for resurrecting the unscientific and racist perspectives of social Darwinism of the late nineteenth and early twentieth centuries and the potential for reducing complex, contextualized social behaviors to simplistic notions of biological adaptations, sophisticated analyses from an evolutionary perspective have reopened discussion of the real possibility that patterns of human social behavior arise from naturally selected mechanisms.

From an evolutionary perspective, natural selection leads to adaptations that solve problems of survival for a species. At a psychological level, the mind is assumed to contain a host of domain-specific "modules," each designed to work out specific adaptive problems.[63] Regarding social interactions, the contention is that there exists an intricate web of benefits, as well as costs, related to forming coalitions with social partners and social groups. In the words of Neuberg and colleagues:

> Humans are, and have always been, social creatures. . . . Individuals who work well within the group structures should be more likely to transmit their genes into future generations. . . . Over long periods of time, then, sociality could become a biologically based human characteristic. This is not to say, of course, that humans are fully prosocial in their aims and actions. Interestingly, a cooperative group context itself provides particularly rich opportunities for individuals to behave in selfishly exploitative ways. . . . There must be mechanisms to identify individuals who threaten or hinder successful group functioning, to label them as such, to motivate group members to withhold group benefits from them, and to separate such individuals from the group if necessary. . . . We propose that stigmatization is such a mechanism.[64]

In other words, whereas humans have always needed other humans for procreation, coparenting, and cooperation, there are still costs to close social interactions, including competition over shelter, economic resources, and mating partners; the potential for aggression and violence; and the contraction of contagious diseases. People need to be intricately attuned to the characteristics of fellow humans that invite social approach, as well as those that suggest social distancing and rejection, with such attunement based on a complex, specific set of evolved mechanisms. The assumption is that ancestors encompassing a balance of approach and avoidance were those most likely to survive and procreate, exemplifying natural selection.

Some of the motivation for pursuing evolutionary models stems from problems with the classic social psychological models of stigmatization—which have not always been successful in predicting which characteristics are likely to be stigmatized in various cultures and societies. In other words, these models are not particularly adept at explaining the consistency and universality of stigmatization. Such consistencies, in fact, beg for a more fundamental set of principles.

Kurzban and Leary have put forth the most elaborated evolutionary view of stigma. I rely heavily on their analysis, also taking into account the synthesis of Neuberg and colleagues.[65] It is important to keep in mind that naturally selected mechanisms and adaptations are operating in environments that are substantially different from those in which they emerged tens or hundreds of thousands of years ago. Indeed, many forms of maladaptive behavior may relate to just such mismatches between genes and current environmental contexts. As Neuberg and colleagues have stated, "Just because certain stigmas were adapted for the social and physical environments of our evolutionary past, this does not imply that they are adaptive today."[66] Still, the legacy of naturally selected tendencies is likely to be strong and deep.

Adaptations for Social Exclusion

A key assumption is that humans have been selected not only for social approach strategies but also for guarding against indiscriminate social contacts. Indeed, an individual who chose to "socialize in any way with every other creature it encountered would be a strange one indeed and clearly at a selective disadvantage."[67] Regarding circumstantial evidence for mechanisms that put appropriate "brakes" on sociality, Kurzban and Leary cite examples of social exclusion among nonhuman species, particularly primates but also including a number of other species whose members avoid or directly punish other individuals that threaten disease or invade social groupings. For humans, three particular adaptations are deemed salient: those related to (a) *dyadic cooperation*—avoidance and punishment of persons who are suspect as partners in social exchange because of tendencies to "cheat" or because of a lack of resources with which to reciprocate; (b) *parasite avoidance*—shunning of those likely to harbor communicable diseases or transmittable parasites; and (c) *coalitional exploitation*—domination of subordinate subgroups based on different skin color or nationality.

Dyadic Cooperation   In the complex arena of how and why humans select peers for exchange and cooperation, individuals must weigh the potential risks of being exploited by potential interaction partners. That is, the possible benefits of sharing and cooperating must be judged carefully against the possibility that the partner may not reciprocate or have sufficient resources to be a viable collaborator in the future.

In *reciprocal altruism,* fitness benefits may accrue from sharing key resources, but only to the extent that there is the likelihood of a later payoff when the partner reciprocates. Kurzban and Leary provide the example of early human hunters who shared excess food with less successful hunters in anticipation of later reciprocation during hunts on which they were less successful themselves. Yet if the choice of partners for such reciprocal altruism is not selective, the initiator of the interchange may become exploited, clearly reducing survival probabilities. Evolution of "cheating detection" modules is hypothesized to have been necessary for survival, comprising cognitive processes that are exquisitely sensitive to the tendencies of fellow humans to fail to reciprocate.

In *mutual enhancement,* humans come to value others with skills that complement and supplement their own. Friendships are likely to form on the basis of such reciprocal systems of mutual valuation of skills. If, however, the potential interaction partner actually possesses few resources (showing low "social capital"), there would be cost to the first person in terms of wasted investment. Hence, selection should favor those perceivers able to appraise the potential for friendship and subsequent reciprocation.

With these concepts in mind, Kurzban and Leary hypothesize that three features of potential interaction partners should serve as red flags: (a) unpredictability of behavior, making it difficult to assess the partner's potential to reciprocate or share skills; (b) possession of minimal social or economic resources (e.g., signals of poverty or infirmity), producing the judgment that few benefits may accrue from cooperating with or befriending this individual; and (c) evidence of cheating, that is, exploitation of the provider's resources without subsequent exchange or reciprocation. How can this analysis relate to mental disorder?

First, I have already discussed how behavioral unpredictability may be quite pertinent to the potential stigmatization of those with mental disorders, given that many such conditions lead to a lack of consistency and regularity of emotional and behavioral displays. Unexpected, erratic, and unpredictable behavior may serve as a cue for the perceiver that the potential partner may not be trustworthy regarding later exchange—thereby yielding social threat. Second, debilitating and/or chronic forms of mental disorder do not enhance economic productivity or social engagement. In fact, clear evidence points to the negative long-term economic consequences of several forms of mental illness.[68] Perceptions could understandably develop that the individual in question has few social resources worthy of exchange. Third, the most blatant form of unreciprocated social exchange, cheating, appears directly linked to Goffman's type involving character blemishes, including dishonesty.[69] Erratic, inconsistent, or irrationally rigid behavior patterns in people with mental disorders may well signal that they will not reciprocate.

From the evolutionary psychology perspective, then, persons with mental illness are likely to be perceived by potential exchange partners as unpredictable, as lacking in important social capital, and in some cases as poor bets for social reciprocation. These perceptions are likely to fuel naturally selected modules that involve rejection.

Parasite Avoidance   A growing area of work on evolution involves the effects of parasites. Comprising viruses, bacteria, insects, or other organisms, parasites can cause serious illness and even death to the host organism. Importantly, these parasites are most readily transmitted to "victims" from hosts who are biologically similar to them. From an evolutionary point of view, there will be competing tendencies and pressures for the formation of social bonds versus the avoidance of peers who might be carrying parasites. Indeed, failure to avoid disease-carrying hosts could place individuals at a severe adaptive disadvantage.

Across many different species, hosts have evolved complex defenses against parasites, which include biochemical and immune defenses, grooming rituals, and avoidance patterns toward those fellow creatures perceived as likely carriers. However, there are no perfect detection systems to signal potential risks for infestation; inferences are made from observation of behavior. The evolutionary perspective is that humans have been selected for careful vigilance regarding potential indicators of disease or parasitic infection in others because failures to detect potential parasite carriers (false negative errors) are a far worse problem than overdetection and exclusion of harmless individuals (false positive errors).

What are the markers that might lead to defensive, avoidant maneuvers?

First, parasites can cause damage that disrupts an individual's symmetry; creates marks, lesions, or discoloration of body parts; and causes behavioral anomalies as a consequence of damage to muscles or muscle control systems. . . . Second, the presence of parasites might activate antiparasite systems. . . . For example, birds infested with lice court less and groom more than parasite-free ones. . . . Last, some parasites manipulate their hosts in order to increase their spread by inducing coughing, sneezing, the excretion of fluids, and so forth.[70]

Aesthetic values (including the preference for symmetry in facial features) may therefore protect the individual from potential parasitic infection.[71] Human illness and disability, potentially signaling the effects of infestation or infection, would be included as targets of the detection systems. It is possible, then, that blemished, less attractive individuals or those with deviations in terms of posture or motor behavior (such as overzealous grooming related to obsessive-compulsive disorder) could serve as triggers for exclusion.

The expected type of response toward a potentially infected or infested person would be avoidance, particularly of close physical contact. Unlike the strong motivation for punishment of dyadic cheaters, the primary response to disfigurement, disease, and/or lack of attractiveness is behavioral shunning and distancing. From this perspective, humans will be motivated to avoid close contact with fellow humans who have disfigurement, aberrant movements, or attributes that do not adhere to cultural standards of beauty. This mechanism appears relevant to the stigmatization of physical disabilities and certain mental disorders.

Coalitional Exploitation   This category refers to the long-standing human tendency to shun "tribes" unfamiliar to the individual or members of foreign communities or nations, in accordance with principles based on ingroup versus outgroup differentiation. Kurzban and Leary contend that this naturally selected process of ingroup identification includes punishment, domination, and even exploitation of outgroup members, given that such tendencies on the part of perceivers would place them at a selective advantage. The hypothesis is that there has been an evolutionary trend toward (a) identification of those groups that are different from the ingroup, (b) competition with and punishment of vanquished outgroup members, and even (c) sexual exploitation of females in the conquered outgroup. Although the complex mechanisms that drive such adaptive strategies are important to consider—and although it is tempting to invoke them because of the chronic and depressing human history of intergroup conflict and war—these points would appear to relate to tribal stigmas based on ethnic, national, or religious criteria rather than to mental disorders. Yet I return to this topic later, raising the possibility that under some circumstances the stigmas usually reserved for individuals of different ethnicity or nationality may become pertinent for mental illness.

Specificity of Predictions   A key feature of the evolutionary perspective is how specific its predictions are. For one thing, Goffman's three-category model, which appeared to have little relevance for social psychological accounts of stigma and stigmatization, is strikingly parallel to Kurzban and Leary's three detection modules. In other words, cheaters or those with low social capital in dyadic social interactions are clearly linked to "blemishes of character," the detection of parasitic infestation risk ties in closely with Goffman's physical deformities and "abominations of the body" (as well as the types of unpredictable motor behavior associated with certain forms of mental disturbance), and the coalitional exploitation model is highly associated with tribal stigmas that relate to domination of those with national and ethnic/racial differences.

In addition, the evolutionary model makes specific predictions regarding *emotional responses* that are related to the three detection mechanisms. That is, violators of dyadic exchange or those believed to possess low social capital are predicted to evoke anger related to the violation of the implicit or explicit social contract. Those suspected of spreading infectious disease should elicit disgust as well as fear, and members of tribal outgroups should prompt not only fear but also hatred as a function of their threat to the "home" group or nation.

Finally, as highlighted earlier with respect to *behavioral responses*, the clear expectation is that dyadic violators and cheaters will be punished; those believed to be infectious will be avoided or shunned; and members of outgroup "tribes" will be dominated and exploited or even annihilated. In terms of mental disorder, which is presumably linked to both social contract violations and some types of parasitic infection avoidance, the expected social responses would range from avoidance to punishment but not typically to the types of group-level exploitation and extermination reserved for national or ethnic groups who are in conflict with the ingroup or home tribe. Again, however, there may be some conditions under which people with mental disorders might provoke these latter responses, a point to which I return in Chapter 4.

As with evolutionary psychological accounts of other social interaction patterns, supportive evidence is difficult to establish, given the absence of fossil records of human behavior. Still, evolutionary models provide a note of caution to those who conceptualize stigma as entirely social and cultural, and arguments in favor of the evolutionary models are accruing. This perspective provides a means of understanding the universality of stigma with regard to mental illness.

Concluding Issues

Much research has been conducted with respect to social psychological and sociological aspects of prejudice, discrimination, and stigmatization. Furthermore, evolutionary psychological models are gaining explanatory power. Discussion of these perspectives has emphasized individually based response tendencies (e.g., categorization and stereotyping, detection modules related to exclusion), social mechanisms (e.g., ingroup biases, self-fulfilling prophecies, stereotype threats), and institutional processes and structures (e.g., economic and political practices, system justification, cultural supports) that are related to stigma. Because stigmatization is quite likely to derive from multiple sources, it cannot be well understood with reference to any particular level or any specific subsystem alone.

A crucial issue about both social cognitive and evolutionary accounts is not only their propensity for reductionism but also their potential for pessimism with respect to the inevitability of stigma. The presence of (a) inevitable and automatic social cognitive processes related to categorization and stereotyping and (b) naturally selected adaptations for detection and stigmatization of key deviancies gives rise to the suspicion that some tendencies toward exclusion and punishment may be "part of human nature." I reemphasize, however, that humans are malleable. Effortful information processing can occur, and stigma processes are not destined to permeate all human social encounters with outgroups.[72] Despite strongly ingrained tendencies to conserve cognitive resources via schema formation and stereotyping, to notice ingroup versus outgroup status, and to detect and avoid social cheaters or potentially contagious individuals, it does not follow that prejudice or exclusion are inevitable or morally justifiable.

As Oskamp has stated, whereas some forms of prejudice and stigma may have provided an evolutionary advantage in earlier phases of human history, they now pose a major threat to the survival of the species, given the advances in weaponry and technology that undergird both modern warfare and modern reproductive technology.[73] Indeed, Kurzban and Leary remind us that egalitarian rather than punitive ideals can be promoted by governments, that contagious individuals can be cared for by parents and health-care workers, and that rival tribal groups can be united under larger coalitional structures and through the promotion of superordinate, prosocial goals.[74] The key point is that, whereas the roots of stigmatizing processes appear to lie deep within both human nature and the social and political structures that humans have created, the degrading, humiliating, and terrorizing aspects of prejudice and stigma are not predestined. Stigma typically involves deep ambivalence, blending empathy and concern with fear, dread, and hostility. As a result, promoting identification with and sympathy for outgroup members is a worthy goal. Before considering, however, how such promotion might be accomplished, I provide historical, empirical, and general cultural evidence for the stigmatization of mental disorder.

3

Historical Perspectives on Mental Illness and Stigma

How have various societies and cultures conceptualized abnormal behavior throughout human history? In what ways have individuals with mental illness been treated in different eras? Can appreciation of the past inform society's current efforts to understand and destigmatize mental disorder? These are the key questions addressed in this chapter.

The literatures on history, anthropology, and psychiatry contain vivid descriptions of various conceptions of abnormal behavior and the plight of persons with mental disorder throughout the human past.[1] Attempting to probe periods of prehistory is plagued by conjecture, but once humans began to write down narratives of their cultural practices, descriptions of people with atypical behavior patterns became common. Many ancient texts, including the Bible, are rich sources of description; some of these accounts are strikingly close to modern conceptions of mental illness. I cannot provide a comprehensive, detailed overview of historical patterns and trends, as such material could easily fill a book (or multivolume set) in and of itself. Rather, to gain appreciation of the origins of current perspectives and to lay a foundation for the many conceptual frameworks that exist in modern society, I provide a selective review. Although the focus is on adults with mental disorders, I provide brief coverage of historical perspectives on children. Also, because most of the information pertains to Western cultures, they receive emphasis, but when possible I note non-Western perspectives as well.

All too often, historical accounts portray the past in sweeping, almost stereotypic fashion. For example, the naturalistic models of ancient Greece and Rome are contrasted with the chaos and ignorance of the Dark Ages, or the witch-hunting of the 1500s and 1600s is juxtaposed with the humane treatment of the late Enlightenment (i.e., the period coinciding with the French and

American revolutions). The reality, however, is far more complex than these portrayals. All eras contain traces of past views and precursors of subsequent eras.[2] Also, a characterization of history as sequential and progressive, moving inevitably toward more humane and enlightened attitudes, is not accurate. Cyclic processes are far closer to the truth, whereby themes of biological versus environmental causation, attribution to personal control versus lack of such control, and punitive versus humane care can be seen to wax and wane across time. Although real progress has been made in recent years with respect to scientific understanding of mental illness and its treatment, modern viewpoints are incomplete because vast areas of psychology and neuroscience are still uncharted territory. Nor are current perspectives always benign, given that they continue to contain elements of moralism and ignorance. Despite the common view that history proceeds in linear fashion toward an enlightened future, the actual story is circular and messy, and the current situation is far from what it could be.

Initial Dichotomies and Themes

(1) A key dichotomy relates to the classic philosophical split, or dualism, between mind and body. From the time that humans first started to self-reflect, it has undoubtedly been difficult to associate the vivid experience of consciousness with anything bound to bodily functions. The nature of the mind has been one of the great mysteries, with a number of life forces having been invoked to explain human consciousness and free will. A fundamental question is whether conscious experience emanates from physical processes grounded in the body—the brain, in particular—or whether mental life is distinct from chemical, physiological forces, with a source and essence of its own. The latter view, relating to the independence of mental life, is called dualism. Dualistic accounts have been increasingly questioned in recent years, given the explosive growth of knowledge about the brain. Currently, the question concerns how our conscious experience is linked to brain functioning.[3] The entire issue poses key questions for philosophers, neuroscientists, and clinicians.

Consider the very term *mental disorder*. It explicitly communicates that a "mental" disturbance is separate from "physical" illnesses or processes, with several implications. For instance, if mental disturbances are in the mind but not of the body, they may not be seen as real. Perhaps they are imagined, or their sufferers do not exert enough control over their mental lives. Alternatively, if the mind is conceptualized as occupying a higher plane of existence than mere bodily processes, then mental afflictions would be viewed as evidence of a fundamental lack of reason and moral sense. The deepest human qualities would be seen as absent in the person with mental disturbance, who may be perceived by others as less than fully human.

(2) There has also been a split between the ascription of mental disturbance to (a) demons, evil spirits, or other malevolent forces and (b) natural, disease-related

variables and processes. Various historical epochs are, in fact, often character-ized by their adherence to one side of this division or the other. In reality, many opinions about mental disturbance throughout history contain *blends* of de-monologic perspectives with those of a more biomedical nature. For example, throughout much of Europe in the sixteenth, seventeenth, and eighteenth cen-turies, mental disturbance was seen as resulting from imbalances of basic bodily fluids, or humors (extending the view that Hippocrates first promoted approx-imately 2,000 years earlier), which worked together with supernatural forces or spiritual malaise. Given the permanence of both types of causal influence, it is no surprise that pessimism predominated with respect to mental disturbance. Even today, our increasingly sophisticated biomedical perspectives remain laden with value judgments and stereotyped views about the nature of the disturbed behavior.

(3) A third dichotomy exists with respect to the age-old distinction between determinism and free will. Are humans' fates and destinies under the control of external forces, such as the stars and planets, the cycles of nature, or physi-cal laws? Or, uniquely in the world, do humans have the capacity to control their futures and make volitional choices? This is an issue of long-standing philosophical and ethical debate. Implications for disturbed human function-ing are provocative. If human actions are determined completely by outside forces or natural laws, whether demonologic or biomedical, then there would appear to be little hope for the role of personal effort or free will in changing any aspect of behavior. On the other hand, if human action is in fact the prod-uct of volition and effort, then blame is likely to be placed on the individuals in question when outcomes are problematic—for example, when they develop se-rious behavioral and emotional difficulties.

In other words, people with patterns of abnormal behavior have been caught in a double bind. When their disturbed behaviors are viewed as the products of deterministic forces that transcend their personal control, a sense of pessimism or even fatalism is likely to predominate. On the other hand, the attribution to an underlying weakness or lack of resolve fosters harsh, moralis-tic reactions. Either way, responses are unlikely to be benign or empathic.

(4) With regard to treatment and care, a huge dichotomy has centered on punitive versus humane alternatives. Neglect and harsh forms of care have been prevalent throughout history, with many practices so dehumanizing as to defy the imagination. Respectful, therapeutic alternatives have been offered and maintained relatively rarely, at least in the historical record. Even when they have occurred, the reforms driving them have often been short lived. Also, the tendency to banish mentally disordered individuals from the mainstream of society has served to render their plight nearly invisible to most citizens, making change efforts extremely difficult to mount.

(5) A final theme relates to the huge lags in time between general scientific and humanistic advances on the one hand and comparable gains in the un-derstanding of behavior and emotion on the other. Even during the Renais-sance and the Enlightenment, which witnessed many important advances in

human knowledge, progress related to the understanding of mentally disturbed behavior was extremely slow to emerge. Although evidence for compassionate care does exist, such enlightened responses have often emerged late in the chain of humanistic and scientific advances. This legacy is a tremendous burden to overcome.

Ancient Eras Through Greece and Rome

As noted in the introduction, ancient skulls show evidence of trephines—circular holes bored into them—providing circumstantial evidence for attempts to rid humans of evil spirits. In some cases there is evidence of healing around the trephines, indicating that the individuals survived the procedures and revealing that their intended nature was surgical.[4] Whether such trephining was intended explicitly to free the bearer of evil spirits or to perform other kinds of primitive surgery, it is undoubtedly the case that the predominant attribution for severely disordered behavior throughout much of history has been to various sorts of evil spirits possessing the individual in question.

In other words, the main causal model of mental disorder has been demonologic. This fact is not surprising when one considers the tenor and spirit of most human societies and cultures across history: Mysterious forces were believed to rule the earth, and inexplicable events were thought to have their origins in such forces and spirits. Ascriptions to possession have been found in written evidence from ancient Egypt, China, and Greece, as well as the Middle East. For example, in Egypt around 5000 B.C., evidence points to the attempts to cure a princess of demonic possession, which was a more humane alternative to the predominant mode of dealing with such disturbed behavior, namely the killing of the possessed individual.[5] The Bible notes, in fact, that disturbed behavior was punishable by death during the times of the Old Testament.

Throughout various historical epochs, different kinds of spirits—ancestors, animals, heroes, gods—were thought to be capable of possessing a person. Animal spirits have been credited as the apparent source of conditions such as tarantism (dancing manias attributed to possession by tarantulas) or lycanthropy (possession by wolves), and these beliefs have persisted into recent centuries. Other forces, including the stars and moon, have also been invoked. Many cultures adopted worldviews whereby religious and theological perspectives constituted the entire framework for understanding natural and behavioral phenomena. Such perspectives were present in ancient Hindu cultures, revealing that they are not solely Western phenomena.

What are the implications for perceptions of those with aberrant behavior? Belief in possession by demons, spirits, or other supernatural forces has led to a wide variety of exclusionary and punitive practices, including the prescription of death. These responses are not surprising, given the moral cast of such views. In some instances, however, possession has been the source of feelings of reverence or awe toward afflicted individuals. For example, shamans and healers are still revered in certain non-Western cultures, and some of the most creative and influential visionaries in modern societies are considered "mad."[6] There has been little in the way of a middle ground: The behavior patterns have tended to prompt perceptions of either subhumanity (with consequent fear and banishment) or, more rarely, superhuman status (with attendant awe and reverence). Lacking is the belief that people with mental disorder are part of the mainstream.

In Greece at the time of Homer (ca. 800 B.C.), the predominant belief was that people became mentally afflicted because one or more of the gods had taken their minds. Homeric drama contains a number of depictions of disturbed behavior attributed to this cause. Selected temples also began to serve as places of refuge. Named for Aesculapius, the god of healing, these temples imbued treatment with religious overtones. Intervention was predicated on the principles of exercise, occupation, enjoyment, and sanctity of the temples and the tree groves surrounding them.[7] Patients who entered the temples would fast for a period of time and receive purification through bathing and rest; some were even placed into a dreamlike state through narcotics to enhance religious visions and motivate reverence toward the priests, who subsequently began to interpret their visions and prescribe various interventions. It is estimated that hundreds of these kinds of healing temples were established in Greece.

Yet a majority of individuals with symptoms of mental disturbance did not make it to these places of refuge: Large numbers were stoned or murdered instead. Undoubtedly, many of those afflicted were simply kept at home, with whatever resources a family could manage. In all, despite the presence of refugelike temples, mental disturbance in Greece was associated with considerable shame.[8]

As with many other aspects of human thought and culture, a change in conceptions related to mental disorder appeared in the Golden Age of Athens. Shortly before that time, in the sixth century B.C., some of the first dissections of human bodies occurred, as a spirit of naturalism and scientific inquiry began to percolate. Yet mental afflictions were still largely attributed to spiritual conditions or the direct intervention of the gods until the work of Hippocrates took place. His life spanned the fifth to the fourth centuries B.C. A contemporary of luminaries such as Pericles, Thucidides, Sophocles, Socrates, and Aristophanes, Hippocrates was not only the "father of medicine" but also the originator of much of contemporary psychology and psychiatry. He wrote some of the first clinical accounts of melancholia (severe depression), dementias (loss of cognitive functioning), delirium (severe disruption of consciousness), and postpartum psychosis (severely irrational behavior following childbirth). He also constructed the first classification of mental disorders, which included epilepsy, mania, melancholia, and paranoia. Above all, he contended that psychological symptoms have natural causes, just like physical disease states. Moreover, he believed that the brain was the locus of thought, feeling, and action. Given the almost completely supernatural, demonologic accounts of mental symptoms in place, these insights are startling in their originality and modernity.

Yet there was no sound neurological or psychological research on which to make further advances.[9] Hippocrates believed that air, or breath (*pneuma*), was the key life force, similar to the *prana* of Hindu belief. His physiological theories postulated that the bodily fluids, or humors, were the locus of the most salient mental afflictions. An abundance of phlegm yielded the phlegmatic (dull) temperament and personality; accumulations of black bile predisposed one to melancholia (depression); yellow bile was associated with choleric reactions of anxiety, irritability, and troubled dreams; and excess blood was related to mood swings and shifts.

These naturalistic as opposed to spiritual or demonologic views were not fully accepted by contemporaries and their immediate descendants. Plato viewed madness as both physiological and emanating from the gods. Still, like Hippocrates, he advocated for humane family care. His pupil Aristotle believed that the heart rather than the brain was the seat of most human qualities and introduced the concept that nervous states and conditions are related to the warmth and coldness of vapors emanating from the heart.

What were the treatment implications of the Hippocratic views of mental disturbance? A premium was placed on restoring a balance of humors. For melancholia, this was to be achieved through rest, exercise, and abstinence from sex and alcohol. Although Hippocrates himself was not a staunch advocate of bloodletting, the idea that excess blood influenced mood and behavior led to its common practice, which continued for 2,000 years. In addition, emetic substances (those that induce vomiting) were prescribed.

In the years following the death of Hippocrates, the center of Greek civilization moved from Athens to Alexandria. Later, as the Roman Empire dominated the entire Mediterranean region and beyond, the science of psychology and mental disturbance began to slow markedly. Treatment strategies comprised a blend of isolation, bloodletting, various punishments, and emetic herbs. Unfortunately, the optimistic regimen initiated at the Aesculapian temples began to be replaced by harsher forms of intervention, including the jumping upon or beating of patients in order to frighten away "unreason" or demons.

History is replete with nearly forgotten thinkers and practitioners. Around the first century B.C. in Alexandria, a physician named Asclepiades (a) separated the phenomena of hallucinations and delusions; (b) made a clear differentiation between acute and chronic mental disorders; (c) believed that mental diseases could be related exclusively to emotional disturbances (rather than to supernatural forces or bodily humors); and (d) promoted treatment practices such as music, rest, and comfort, countering the practices of bloodletting or placement into prisons or dungeons, which were by then commonplace. Almost as a voice in the wilderness, he presaged a number of beliefs and practices that are quite advanced, but few followers emerged.[10]

More typical, in fact, were the views of Celsus, a Roman who contended, quite strongly, that the optimal treatments for those with mental afflictions were those that emphasized restraints (for example, in "fetters" or chains), states of deprivation and hunger, placement in total darkness, and intentional use of fright, the latter in order to distract the individual from disturbed modes of thinking. The rationale was the belief that mental disturbance afflicted a person's fundamental mental faculties and intellectual functioning. As a result, only fright or terror might restore proper sensibilities because the parts of the mind that emphasized reason were inaccessible. In addition, by the height of the Roman Empire, a great deal of medical and scientific thinking had reverted to superstition and mysticism.

Galen, who lived in the second century A.D., provided a comprehensive account of mental disorders that blended enlightened ideas and confusing speculations. He believed, for example, that the warmth and coldness of the brain promoted mental disorders; he also advanced the notion that organs near the afflicted one would become diseased, a process called "sympathy." As convoluted as they seem today, Galenic ideas constituted the high-water mark of post-Hippocratic conceptions of mental disorders and persisted for more than 1,500 years. As Zilboorg stated, "Political historians divide ancient history from medieval by emphasizing the decisive invasion of Rome by the Barbarians in the latter part of the fifth century . . . [but] the Dark Ages in medical history began with the death of Galen in 200 A.D."[11]

In terms of institutional care for medical conditions, public hospitals did not appear in Rome until the end of the fourth century A.D., but even then, no special provisions were made for those with mental disorder. In fact, the first such facilities appeared in Byzantium and Jerusalem during the fourth and fifth centuries. Arabic and Islamic nations began asylum care well before institutions appeared in Europe, which did not occur for hundreds of years.[12] In the Western world, the main forms of compassionate care emerged in selected monasteries.

What can be learned from this brief tour of Greek and Roman views? First, cycles of scientific advancement versus retrenchment—and of compassion versus cruelty—existed even within the ancient era. Second, both supernatural and biomedical conceptions of mental disturbance were associated with humane care, the former at healing temples and the latter in terms of the naturalistic views of Hippocrates. Yet each perspective also fostered intolerance and harsh treatment, meaning that there is no easy or automatic linkage of underlying conceptual models of mental disorder with treatment practices. Third, consistent with a key theme noted earlier, scientific theorizing about mental disorder lagged well behind advances in "harder" sciences and mathematics even during the golden era of Greece. This trend signifies the uphill battle that those interested in mental health have always needed to fight.

Medieval Period Through the Persecution of Witches

In the waning centuries of the Roman Empire, several trends led to the demise of scientific thinking about mental afflictions. Roman culture embraced diverse views, including superstitious beliefs imported from the far reaches of its empire. Mistrust of Greek ideals and principles became rampant. The rise of Christianity, along with the seeking of deep philosophical and spiritual under-pinnings to explain human nature, promoted a turning away from naturalism to a range of philosophical, religious, and occult beliefs about the nature of disturbed behavior. Over time, the predominant worldview again became moral in nature, with behavioral deviance believed to reflect the results of a perennial struggle between good and evil rather than the influences of psychological or physiological factors. Dissection of corpses was disallowed; religion and morality, rather than humanism and science, were the perspectives through which human behavior was appraised and judged.

Monasteries became the refuges where medical and psychological arts were preserved. At the same time, the spread of Christian doctrine gave license for practices such as exorcisms to remove the offending evil spirits from the afflicted individual. On the other hand, Islamic and Byzantine scholars and physicians did maintain some beliefs of the Greeks. In the ninth century A.D., al-Razi, working in Baghdad, upheld Galenic ideals and created a special wing of a hospital for those with mental illnesses.[13] In Europe, the worldview had become almost exclusively moralistic and religious. Monks and other religious figures replaced physicians as the sources of care, and the struggles of those afflicted with mental disorders (and even physical illnesses) became miniature battlegrounds for grand battles between holy and satanic forces.

Such thinking was not universal, however. The *Encyclopedia of Bartholomaes*, written in the 1200s, stated that both physical and emotional causes could trigger some forms of mental disorder. Yet during this same era the term *lunatic* became official, signaling the belief that phases of the moon were tied to disturbed behavior. Astronomical phenomena were thought to merge with physical triggers and moral failings to allow the forces of evil to overtake the individual in question.

Through religious doctrine, which was now the official source of societal views, mental afflictions indicated that their bearer was a heretic, one whose religious faith was not sufficiently strong to withstand possession by demonic forces. Note a crucial point in this reasoning: The perceived weakness of the sufferer was believed to set the stage for possession, so that ascriptions to demonology were merged with attributions of responsibility and control.

The most renowned center in Europe for the care of those with mental disorder emerged in Gheel, Belgium.[14] Gheel evolved as model of community-based intervention: Persons with mental disorder lived directly in the community, receiving respect emanating from a blend of religious sympathy with the notion that mental disorder was a treatable form of illness. In much of Europe, however, the predominant mode of "care" consisted of banishment to the countryside or confinement in prisons, dungeons, or former monasteries. Special cages, boxes with iron gratings, or even towers located within city walls were used to confine lunatics in these settings. An era of institutionalization had thus begun.

Special asylums designed for those with mental disorder began to appear, with an early example in Metz, Germany, in 1100. The oldest continuously operating hospital in Europe, London's Bethlehem, was opened in 1247 and began to receive "lunatics" during the next century. By the early 1400s, reports began to emanate about the decaying, horrendous conditions there. The contracted form of the hospital's name, Bedlam, made its way into the general discourse as a term signifying utter chaos.

Social historians such as Alldderidge contend that a major reason for the chains and other symbols of cruelty at such facilities was the intractable, often violent behavior of the patients, centuries before any viable treatments were available.[15] Still, outside Europe, records exist of asylums for the mentally ill in Cairo and Baghdad, where far more humane standards of care were put into place. Cruelty was not confined to Europe, however: A large facility in Constantinople featured the confinement of mentally disordered persons by neck chains, with regular and severe beatings given to any sign of agitation or disorder.[16]

During the pre-Renaissance period of the thirteenth and fourteenth centuries, a series of more enlightened ideas about the nature of mental disorder emerged. In England, a form of mental status examination was utilized for determining the competency of people to stand trial for legal offenses. If they were found to be incompetent to stand trial, guardians were appointed to look after their affairs. The record of such practices bespeaks the problems with overgeneralizing about entire historical periods.[17]

Yet on the whole, the science and clinical care of those with mental illness continued to be backward. Medical practice was tied explicitly to astrology, dissections were based on models from pigs rather than humans (the first human dissection since the period of the late Roman Empire did not take place until 1315), alchemy was perhaps the foremost medical science, and numerology was rampant. Treatments included the whipping of afflicted individuals. Bloodletting remained a prevalent form of intervention, although its effects were now timed to various phases of the moon or stars to produce optimal effects.

Throughout, a key means of intervention for those with mental disorders was to eliminate them from the mainstream of society and the community:

> It often happened that the patient's own family would disavow him. Such mentally sick people, most frequently women, were literally thrown out into the streets. Unable to care for themselves, they wandered along the roads and through the woods. They lived in the stable with horses and cattle and would frequently lose all vestiges of their former human appearance.[18]

Countrysides housed barely subsisting individuals who had been cast away because of their extremes of behavior. Institutions for those with mental disorders housed relatively small numbers. Monasteries continued to be an alternative for some, often offering humane care. In the vast majority of cases, persons with mental disorders were either cared for privately at home or banished.

The force of the Catholic Church was gaining increasing power in Europe. Kings reigned with not only political but also religious backing. Devil-sickness was increasingly used as a term to denote mental disorder. Although the Renaissance had begun in earnest in the fifteenth century, with a harkening back to the artistic and scientific ideals of classical Greece and an explosion of creative and scientific advances, there was little resurgence with respect to medicine and psychiatry. Witches (by definition, women) and sorcerers (men) had been assailed by religious authorities for many centuries, but the frenzy against the power of such heretical beings, who were believed to be literally possessed by the devil, rose to a fever pitch.

In 1484 the German professors and Dominican friars Sprenger and Kramer obtained a papal order, or bull, investing them with the power of inquisitors to find, root out, torture, and murder witches. Several years later they published a detailed book that portrayed in great detail the existence of witches, the means of assessing them, and the legal procedures for sentencing and annihilating them. Titled the *Malleus Maleficarum* [Witches' Hammer], it was subsequently published in 19 editions through the 1800s, with the newly invented printing press leading to its widespread use among both clergy and political leaders.

A great deal of deviance became officially attributed to the pernicious efforts of witches, who were thought to alter the natural order of human relations by casting spells on unsuspecting people. In Zilboorg's estimate, hundreds of thousands of witches were tortured and executed in the sixteenth century alone. Indeed, the last official execution of a witch in Europe was recorded in Switzerland in 1782, revealing 300 years of the active practice of witch-hunting and murder. In terms of the relation between witchcraft and mental disorder, it is likely that most of those persecuted in witch hunts and witch trials were not initially mentally disordered, but the extremes of torture used to extract confessions may have led, in some cases, to hallucinations and delusions.[19] On the other hand, it is clear that many women with mental illness were, in fact, branded as witches. Revealing the pervasiveness of this worldview, medical practitioners who professed a naturalistic, rather than demonologic, conception of disturbed behavior were themselves often considered heretics.

What was the goal of witch-hunting? Because the possessed soul had to be set free, it was mandatory that the accused witch be burned to death following detection, inquisition, and torture. Also, recall that one of the diagnostic signs for detecting a witch was the presence of numbed areas of the skin, known as stigmata, which were considered evidence of infestation by the devil.

Humanitarian pleas were made in the sixteenth century. Weyer, a German physician known as the father of modern psychopathology, called for a naturalistic view of mental disorder. He contended that the mind, like the body, could fall prey to illness.[20] In addition, Vives pleaded for humane treatments, as well as a truly empirical science of the human mind. These voices, however, were outweighed by the legal and religious forces of the Inquisition. Indeed, following the Reformation, Protestants joined Catholics in the detection and destruction of witches. Furthermore, the concepts of individual conscience, will, and guilt also fueled stigmatization.[21]

Asylums, Enlightenment, and Liberation

As the European world gradually became less dominated by the church and as the Scientific Revolution developed, challenges to demonologic perspectives began to mount. In the seventeenth century, following from some of the great discoveries in the physical and astronomical sciences, a larger revival of Greek ideals of medicine began to take place. Yet for mental afflictions, the results were not always positive. Harvey's discovery of the circulation of blood led to even greater use of bloodletting (often to extremes) for all kinds of physical and mental afflictions. Willis, who discovered a pair of cranial nerves and classified psychopathology with some accuracy—and who is considered to be one of the fathers of neurology—still held the beliefs that (a) beatings of those with mental disorders were a viable treatment and (b) possession by the devil was a major causal factor. Cruelty coexisted with enlightenment and scholarship.

Tremendous demographic and political forces were at work, prompting a population shift to urban centers and creating a huge rift in the feudal system that had been in place for centuries.[22] Greater numbers of almshouses for the impoverished and dispossessed, hospitals for the sick and infirm, and asylums for those with mental disorders were being created. Conditions were generally dismal, if not appalling. Rats infested many facilities, as did standing water and extremes of temperature. Yet because the plight of those with mental disorders was largely hidden from public view, ignorance bred further distancing and neglect:

> The fact that patients had to live in cells or dungeons with nothing to cover them and only straw to lie upon was due in part to the failure to provide any other means of caring. . . . Neglect of their duties by those in charge of institutions was possible only because of the lack of public interest.[23]

It is estimated that in Paris during the sixteenth century, more than 30% of the population of approximately 100,000 citizens were beggars. The sheer numbers of vagrant individuals, amidst the utter wealth in the hands of a few members of the royalty and nobility, led to a call for institutional means of dealing with the problem. Leprosariums, those asylums for housing people with leprosy that had been in place for centuries, were converted into institutions for indigent individuals. Known as poorhouses or almshouses in English-speaking lands, they began to include mentally disturbed people among their populations. Facilities designed specifically for those with mental disorders were also growing.

A pervasive view was that insane individuals had lost their reason, the cornerstone of the human soul. This perception fueled public views of those with mental disturbances as no more than beasts or children, with their lack of fundamental humanity serving to justify the degradation and humiliation they often experienced. Even at the level of physical sensation and pain, it was believed that beatings, inductions of fright, or subjugation to extremes of cold did not affect the mentally disordered in the same ways they would affect normal people, given that mental illness thwarted fundamental mental capacities.[24]

The Enlightenment is associated with the eighteenth century, during which a host of complex scientific, sociological, and political forces shook Europe. A growing number of scholars and physicians worked to rescue the science and practice of mental disorder from the legacy of witch-hunting and neglect. Biological theories abounded, and classifications of mental afflictions proliferated. Nevertheless, over and above bloodletting, treatments still included abandoning individuals to the countryside, throwing them into water, firing cannons above their heads to frighten them back to sensibility, twirling them to the point of unconsciousness, and chaining them in dungeonlike asylums. Impoverished persons with mental disorder received the worst forms of care, whereas those from upper classes might hold out hope for private settings with better conditions.

Treatment practices based on fear and torture were not restricted to those on the bottom rungs of society. King George III of England, the ruler during and after the American Revolution, was decreed to be insane for many years of his life. His treatments included encasement in a mechanical device that allowed no movement, beatings, near-starvation, and being chained to a stake.[25] The school of thought underlying such treatment was termed crisis theory, which held that creating physical crisis could lift the soul and reason from their afflicted states.

Although the absolute numbers in institutional settings were still quite small, those housed there were increasingly placed on display:

> If apprehended and interned, the mentally sick were placed side by side with murderers and other criminals in chains and in fetters, without hope of redemption. . . . Without sufficient nourishment and covered by their own excreta, they would literally rot in flesh and in spirit. The community thought of them as little as of refuse once it is taken care of by the organization for sewage disposal, unless it was occasionally to come and look at them for a small admission fee and enjoy seeing them rave and perform their "antics."[26]

In London, a mainstay of weekend activities for many citizens was the touring of Bedlam. Parallel practices occurred at Bicetre hospital in Paris and even in the New World at the Pennsylvania Hospital in Philadelphia. The upper classes could amuse themselves by watching the raving, screaming, chained persons with mental disorders, whose conditions had been greatly compounded by the effects of chronic institutionalization. The numbers of visitors vastly outstripped the census of patients: It has been estimated that 19,000 visitors per year toured Bethlehem, which housed only 200 or so patients.[27]

Social philosophers and critics, particularly in France, voiced outrage at the unspeakable conditions of the institutions and the governmental abandonment of those housed there. Pleas for care of the mentally ill began to take on the same political and moral tone as other social causes, such as slavery and poverty. Toward the end of the eighteenth century, revolutionary political forces demanded human liberation, promoted humanistic views of the perfectability of humankind, and advocated for naturalistic (as opposed to demonologic) conceptions of mental disorder. Pussin and Pinel in France, Tuke in England, Rush in the United States, and Chiarugi in Italy independently called for the liberation of the insane from shackles and for a humanitarian approach to care.

Pinel, a learned French physician charged with the administration of Bicetre, was appalled by the conditions there and immediately demanded the removal of the chains. Witnesses recounted the initial unchaining of several long-term patients in moving terms: One man had been chained for 36 years and was dying at the time; another, who had previously murdered a man in the throes of psychosis, calmly witnessed the removal of his chains and saw the sun for the first time in years, remarking on its beauty. The fears that such liberation would create violence were not borne out.[28]

Working in England, Tuke became incensed by the intolerable conditions in asylums. Using influence with the Religious Society of Friends (Quakers), he opened the York Retreat (to counter the practices of the York Asylum) in 1796, so that "a milder and more appropriate system of treatment than that usually practiced might be adopted."[29] The abhorrent conditions in almshouses and asylums for the mentally ill, which the York Retreat intended to redress, were startling: In one report to Parliament, it was found that 13 mentally ill women, naked and filthy with urine and hardened excrement, inhabited a cell that measured 12 feet by 8 feet.

In the New World, during the colonial period of the 1600s and early 1700s, there was no formal policy toward those with mental problems. These people, often termed "distracted," were almost exclusively a private, family matter. North America was so rural that the lack of centralized population gave rise to few public concerns. Notions regarding witchcraft had emigrated from Europe, as indicated by the infamous Salem, Massachusetts, witch trials of 1692. Only with the coming of urbanization was there a need for specific institutions for those with mental disorders. Pennsylvania Hospital, with special provisions for lunatics, opened in 1752. As Morton recounted, patients were placed in the cellar, with the following treatments:

Their scalps were shaved and blistered; they were bled to the point of syncope; purged until the alimentary canal failed to yield anything but mucus, and in the intervals, they were chained by the waist or the ankle to the cell wall. . . . It was not considered improper or unusual for the keeper to carry a whip and use it freely.[30]

By 1789, paralleling the reform movements in Europe, Rush began to model this facility on more enlightened principles. Even the heroes of the Enlightenment were not completely rid of older attitudes regarding care for the mentally ill. Rush believed in the use of purgatives, emetics, and bloodletting; Pinel held that physicians must still approach patients in harsh fashion and that fright and restraints were sometimes necessary for patients from lower social classes. Scientific understanding of the underpinnings of mental disorder was still at the level of the views of Hippocrates, and the range of effective treatments was small. Still, the forces of liberation presented the world with a far more respectful and caring approach to mental disorder.

Moral Treatment, Reform, and State Institutions

By the beginning of the nineteenth century, efforts toward systematic change had taken hold. Pinel introduced the term *traitment moral* [moral treatment] with respect to his conception of humane care, not to connote religious morals but instead incorporating two views. First, he believed that mental disorder affected individuals' moral (i.e., psychological, social) faculties without completely overwhelming their sense of reason. The person suffering from mental disturbance was therefore still fundamentally human. Second, intervention should be based on the promotion of hope, kindness shown by staff, and the cessation of most forms of cruelty. The idea that persons with mental disorder were not beasts deserving of filth, darkness, and humiliation was revolutionary. Moral treatment involved the following principles:

> A kindly interest in the needs of individual patients took the place of wholesale confinement at the least possible expense. . . . Efforts were made to improve the quality of attendants. . . . Until that time, because of the low wages and the occasional unpleasant or dangerous nature of the work, keepers had to be selected from . . . coarse, uneducated persons . . . who otherwise would be unemployed . . . [and] were permitted to rule by terror and force. Now they were instructed in methods of kindly supervision and in the solicitation of more normal interests and habits. The surroundings of patients were made as pleasant and healthful as possible . . . gardens, shaded walks, and ample space for taking systematic exercise. . . . In some asylums, instruction was given in reading, writing, arithmetic, music, and dancing.[31]

During the early 1800s, moral treatment in the United States was established at several facilities, modeled on the practices of the York Retreat in England. Although advocates of moral treatment discounted demonologic views, they had little new to offer in terms of definitive theories of mental disorder. They did, however, hold to the premise that social conditions could influence the life course of those afflicted with even serious levels of mental disturbance.

Moral treatment was not universal. Confinement and care at home, banishment to rural wandering, or placement in almshouses or prisons continued to be the predominant means of dealing with mental illness. Conditions in most asylums were horrific. In the United States, institutions that did not subscribe to moral treatment might effect the sedation of unruly patients by opium or camphor in addition to restraints and beatings.[32]

In the 1840s Dorothea Dix, a retired American schoolteacher, began a personal crusade, convincing local, state, and federal legislators of the inhumane conditions for mentally disturbed people in almshouses and prisons. She advocated passionately for the construction and staffing of hospital facilities specifically designed for the care of those with mental disorders, based on principles of moral treatment. The following is an excerpt of her words to the Massachusetts legislature in 1843:

> I shall be obliged to speak with great plainness, and to reveal many things revolting to the taste. . . . But truth is the highest consideration. . . . If I inflict pain upon you, and move you to horror, it is to acquaint you with sufferings which you have the power to alleviate, and make you hasten to the relief of the victims of legalized barbarity. . . . I come as the advocate of helpless, forgotten, insane, and idiotic men and women; of beings, sunk to a condition from which the most unconcerned would start with a real horror. . . . I proceed, Gentlemen, briefly to call your attention to the *present* state of Insane Persons confined within this Commonwealth, in *cages, closets, cellars, stalls, pens! Chained, naked, beaten with rods,* and *lashed* into obedience. . . . A young woman, a pauper in a distant town . . . was for years a raging maniac. A cage, chains, and *the whip,* were the agents for controlling her, united with harsh tones and profane language. Annually, with others [the town's poor] she was put up at auction, and bid off at the lowest price.[33]

Dix's work continued in Europe. In the United States, her success is reflected especially in the rapid growth of state-supported facilities for persons with mental illness and mental retardation throughout the rest of the nineteenth century. The backdrop of the Industrial Revolution, the increasing urbanization of the population, and the perception of a large increase in the mentally ill population provided additional impetus for states to begin to invest finances in such hospital settings.

State-supported hospitals were initially designed with precision and an eye toward humane care and therapeutic objectives. Several forces, however, conspired to lead this reform effort in a different direction. First, moral treatment, which involved extensive training of staff and mandated smaller facilities, was expensive to implement. State legislatures were initially reluctant to direct any funds for institutional care of the mentally ill; when they did, cost savings could eventually be found in large, centralized institutions. Second, psychiatry in Europe and the United States began to adopt a more hereditarian, pessimistic perspective, fueled by promotion of the views of social Darwinism and genetic determinism. Third, immigrant populations began to flood the United States in the middle of the nineteenth century. Ethnic prejudice was widespread in the society at large, leading to a further downgrading of the status of those with mental disorder, who included a large percentage of impoverished individuals from various ethnic groups.

State hospitals for the insane and state institutions for the "feebleminded"—the term of the era for persons with mental retardation—were typically built a day's carriage ride from metropolitan areas or, in some instances, near the exact center of a state (to provide maximum convenience for all of the state's residents). The distancing of these facilities from large cities amounted to banishment of those housed there; it also cut off ties between institutionalized persons and their families. In conjunction with overcrowding, such isolation reinforced societal fears of the differences between the mentally ill and the rest of society and emphasized the hopelessness of the endeavor: "To the public mind, these fortresses seemed to conceal some dark horror, and the mentally disturbed were once again seen as freakish and dangerous."[34] The kinds of conditions in almshouses and jails that the mental hospitals had been designed to overcome were now amplified in these asylums.

In short, the well-intentioned reform movement initiated by Dix ended up repeating the sins of the past. Unless human tendencies to segregate, isolate, and punish those with aberrant behavior patterns are consciously and strenuously countered and unless reforms are adequately funded and monitored, even the best-intentioned ideas will not live up to their initial conceptions. In fact, the enormous growth of state facilities for persons with mental disorder continued until the middle of the twentieth century, with more than half a million people incarcerated in such facilities in the United States during the 1950s.

Finally, the growth of psychiatry and psychology in the nineteenth century was strong. Included was a major increase in classification systems. Griesinger, for example, published an influential text in which he claimed that mental diseases are brain diseases, espousing a medical-model view.[35] Also, psychological (as opposed to demonologic or biological) causes for mental disorder began to gain prominence, utilizing a number of philosophical doctrines and supporting them with experimental evidence and clinical case documentation. Through the psychological laboratory of Wundt, the study of individual differences by Galton (a cousin of Darwin), and the origins of psychoanalytic theory and therapy via Freud and followers, a secularized psychology was taking hold in the public's mind, leading to new conceptions of the nature of human functioning and mental disorder.

At the same time, biological views on mental disorder were also the focus of increasing interest. The discovery of the bacterium responsible for syphilis—a disease causing psychotic symptoms in advanced stages—served as a call for unified biological accounts of psychiatric symptomatology in the early 1900s. Biological and hereditarian views continued to be pursued.

By the end of the nineteenth century many models of mental disturbance were vying for respectability. As for treatment and care, the overwhelming trend was for persons with the most severe forms of mental illness to be housed in large institutions. Increasing belief in genetic (and deterministic) underpinnings of many forms of severe mental disorder, prejudice against the growing immigrant population, and competition for scarce resources converged to bring on a sense of hopelessness regarding those individuals with mental disorder.

Children With Mental Disturbance

To understand the plight of youth with disturbed behavior across history, it is first necessary to consider the more basic issue of how children have themselves been conceptualized. Many historians and scholars contend that childhood is a relatively recent concept. Indeed, for much of recorded history, children were viewed largely as miniature adults.[36] Whereas childhood was recognized in ancient Greece and Rome—cultures in which strong value was placed on the education of children, at least those of higher social classes—during much of history children were valued chiefly for their abilities to produce economic gain for their families.[37]

A major factor in this regard is the difficulty that many human societies have faced with respect to the basic survival of their youngest members. Viewing children as having a separate, protected status may have been a luxury that most cultures could not afford, as infant and child mortality rates were extremely high until recent times. In the United States and Europe, even as late as the seventeenth and eighteenth centuries, the clear majority of children did not survive past the ages of 4 or 5 years. As a consequence, there was a limited fostering of attachments between children and their parents, as the odds were high that children would simply not be around for long.

Rates of harsh treatment of children, including exploitation, neglect, abandonment, and abuse, have been widespread throughout history. Indeed, a common practice throughout multiple cultures has been the practice of infanticide—the intentional killing of babies and young children—when family size became too large and when providing for yet another mouth to feed was not possible. This practice was much more likely when the child displayed physical or behavioral deviance. Infanticide was also practiced in ancient Greece and Rome, particularly by families whose children showed mental or physical disabilities. Short of being killed, such youth were treated with scorn and derision.[38]

From the periods termed the Dark and Middle Ages (roughly 500–1300 A.D.), no recordings of children's games or children's literature have been found, suggesting strongly that children were viewed primarily as adults of small stature, with no special accommodations made for their developmental status. Even paintings of children from this period show them depicted essentially as small adults. Youth were commonly put to full-time work by the age of 6 years, and marriages were arranged before adolescence in order to ensure the economic well-being of families. It was not atypical for children to be sold into slavery, and beatings were routinely accepted as discipline. As soon as children could work in agrarian cultures, they typically did. With the advent of industry in the past several hundred years, children provided a cheap source of labor until restrictions on this practice became instituted within the last century. Furthermore, practices such as compulsory education or specialized means of providing for the developmental needs of children were virtually nonexistent before the late 1700s and did not become common until a hundred years later.

During the Renaissance, as the witch hunts intensified, children with aberrant behavior were likely to be branded as witches, with public humiliation, incarceration, torture, and burning at the stake the consequences for those youth so judged. As the Renaissance progressed, however, infanticide was officially denounced, and orphanages emerged as institutions for children without parents and for those with mental disorders. Like adult institutions, these soon became overcrowded and abusive: The mortality rates in orphanages in Europe were high, with most children residing in such facilities failing to survive into adolescence.[39]

Phaire is credited with publishing in 1545 the first volume on the special problems and issues of childhood *(The Boke of Chyldren),* including the phenomena of nightmares and bed-wetting. In the sixteenth and seventeenth centuries, several reformers began to kindle the notion that childhood should be a protected period of life and that the education of children was a top societal priority. Yet it was still the norm for children to receive harsh punishment, and education was restricted to a few youth of the privileged classes. By the late 1600s, particularly among wealthier families—who did not require their children to enter the labor force—it was finally considered acceptable for parents to be amused by children's antics and for closer bonds to develop. Philosophical writings (for example, by Locke and Rousseau) promoted the importance of educating children and viewing them as worthy of special care.[40] The Enlightenment and the moral treatment that followed it were movements that also paid careful attention to children's welfare. By this time children had become the focus of explicit study, and investigations of mental problems in children had begun to occur.

Until only the past few decades, parents have held the right to physically and emotionally devastate children, largely because of the views that family matters such as discipline are inherently private and that children are no more than family property. In the American colonies of the seventeenth and eighteenth centuries, "stubborn child laws" gave imprimatur for parents to put children to death if they were not sufficiently compliant with adults' orders and commands.[41] The brutalization of children meant that intergenerational patterns of maltreatment were widespread.[42] In the late nineteenth century, the Society for Prevention of Cruelty to Children was founded in the United States *after* the establishment of the Society for Prevention of Cruelty to Animals.

The campaign of Dorothea Dix included strong advocacy for maltreated and mentally disordered children, and the reform efforts led to the creation of a number of mental hospitals (or units of larger facilities) explicitly designed for children and adolescents. Yet these institutions, intended as places of care and treatment, followed the fate of the adult hospitals of the nineteenth century, becoming overcrowded venues of neglect and maltreatment. Even when the need for treatment of child mental disorders came to be recognized, facilities quickly became dehumanizing.

By late in the nineteenth century, social work had become established to deal with the social and cultural contributors to the problems of impoverished children in inner-city settings. Special education for children with learning problems and mental disorders began, as did reforms geared toward preventing root causes of delinquency. In the early twentieth century, developmental psychology and child psychology became recognized as fields of scientific inquiry, and official scientific policies regarding optimal child rearing as well as treatment of children with mental disorders emerged.

Overall, the development of meaningful conceptions of the unique needs and rights of children has been painfully slow. Exploitation, forced labor, and abuse have been the rule across cultures and throughout history. Such devaluation of children, coupled with the stigmatization of mental disorders, has meant that children displaying aberrant behavior received a double stigma. Recognition of children's rights and awareness of the unique needs of children with mental disorders are relatively recent additions to human affairs.

Conclusions

First, conceptualizations of and attitudes toward mental disorder have shown a cyclic course throughout history. For instance, Greek healing temples shared many attributes (respect, rest, treatment incorporating spiritual enlightenment) with both the Gheel community and the moral treatments of the early nineteenth century. In addition, naturalistic views of mental disorder emerged suddenly through the work of Hippocrates in classical Greece, went largely underground during the Dark and Middle Ages (though never disappearing entirely), and resurfaced during the Renaissance and the Enlightenment. Unwavering linear trends are rare.

Second, views about mental disorder and disturbed behavior have emanated as much from philosophy, history, and cultural mores as from scientific findings.[43] Conceptions of behavior and emotion are largely a function of folk psychology, moral principles, and general cultural worldviews. Even today, views about the nature of mentally disturbed behavior reflect such values. Nowhere is this contention more evident than in the area of childhood, where the core beliefs have long been that children are miniature adults, whose care is the exclusive, private concern of parents and whose labor is essential for family survival. Scientific models and empirical evidence alone are unlikely to be sufficient to promote lasting changes in societal attitudes and behavioral responses.

Third, it is difficult to escape a sense of pessimism when analyzing this history and reflecting on the sheer number of lives across the millennia that have been led in painful silence, if not abject cruelty and punishment. Exclusion and dehumanization of those with mental disorder have been primary responses for far too long. Given the evidence, it becomes tempting to consider that humans are simply destined to exclude or punish those perceived as having mental afflictions. A similar perspective might emerge from a parallel tour of human history regarding racial and ethnic differences, where patterns of slavery, torture, and genocide are omnipresent. Still, reasons for optimism also emerge from a review of historical trends, including many instances of reform, as well as non-Western models of more humane care. Because of the increasingly rapid shifts in scientific, clinical, and popular views of mental illness during the tumultuous twentieth century, these trends require their own chapter.

4

Modern Conceptions of Mental Disorder

The twentieth century witnessed a host of events related to mental illness, each of which had major implications for stigma. Because of the sheer magnitude of scientific discoveries and secular worldviews that emerged and reemerged during this time period, only selected trends can be highlighted. Although much of the focus is on the United States, I provide broader perspectives when possible.

Key Trends of the Twentieth Century

Secularization

Moral and ethical perspectives declined markedly during the last century while psychological, scientific conceptualizations of abnormal behavior became ascendant. Expressly psychological perspectives on topics such as psychopathology, child rearing, and potential for human growth replaced moralistic and demonologic perspectives, as well as the humoral theories that had remained in place as remnants of Greek and Roman theorizing. Although some degree of ethical and moral judgments continue to exert considerable weight regarding beliefs about deviant and disturbed behavior, attributions to demonic possession are by now limited to certain fundamentalist religious sects or some non-Westernized cultures, reflecting the general cultural shift to a "modern" perspective on behavior and pathology. To a degree that would shock observers from past eras, individuals, families, communities, and the media now espouse secular conceptions of psychological functioning that have become embedded in the mainstream culture.

What is meant by a psychological set of explanations for behavior? Haslam posits that psychological reasoning about behavior incorporates ascriptions to causal forces that are mental rather than physical and that rely on mechanistic concepts rather than on "free will." In other words, psychological perspectives lie somewhere in the middle of a continuum between biomedical models on the one hand and expressly volitional accounts of behavior on the other; they are scientific but not linked specifically to brain function per se. The growth of psychology during the past 100 years has permeated nearly all aspects of modern culture, with a cadre of psychological "experts" now recognized as authorities on lifestyles, coping, parenting, and a myriad of other processes believed to be essential for well-being.[1]

A huge influence in this vein was the rise of Freudian theory and psychoanalytic therapies in the early to middle decades of the last century, which quickly spread to the United States following Freud's visit to Clark University in 1909. Through the acceptance of Freudian ideas, a wholly psychological view of development, normal functioning, and abnormal behavior became mainstream. Aside from an initial positing of a largely instinctual basis for human drives, the core ideas place maximum weight on psychological constructs such as parenting styles, internal conflicts, and unconscious motivations to explain the entire spectrum of typical and atypical functioning. The competing school of behaviorism provided an alternative psychosocial view, with its emphasis on laws of conditioning and the environmental shaping of behavior. Other models of abnormal behavior and therapy in the middle of the twentieth century also favored environmental, psychological perspectives—for example, Rogers's client-centered therapy and the wide array of family systems and couples-therapy approaches. In each, explanations focused on psychological processes rather than moral principles or strict biomedical frameworks.

A key offshoot has been the development of a huge industry of outpatient therapy, initially performed by psychiatrists but expanding in the last half of the twentieth century to include a host of mental health professionals. Although psychoanalytic treatment predominated for decades (by the 1950s and 1960s, the chair of nearly every department of psychiatry in the United States had been trained in psychoanalytic principles and therapy), it was replaced by other theoretical models, particularly those based on cognitive-behavioral principles, which emphasize lawful relations between thought processes and behavioral responding.

Yet because of the relative lack of success of nearly all one-on-one, office-based psychosocial treatments for the most severe forms of psychopathology, hospital treatment (and medications, after midcentury) were the core modalities for persons so afflicted. Greater prestige was and still is accorded to those professionals working in outpatient therapy with milder forms of disorder than for those treating more severe diagnoses in institutional settings, signaling that the more serious forms of mental disorder receive greater stigma.[2] In practice, psychological models came to be associated with affluence and the ability to "talk through" modern problems of everyday life, whereas the most serious and disorganized forms of disturbance were relegated to institutional care, with attendant lack of status and prestige for the professionals involved, as well as reliance on biological treatment.

The secularization of abnormal behavior occurred in many forms. For example, the child guidance movement was organized in response to the mental health problems of growing numbers of urban youth. The trend toward "mental hygiene," initiated early in the twentieth century, was initially formed to counter the growing ills of institutional care, instigated in large measure by Clifford Beers, who recounted his experiences with mental disturbance in *A Mind That Found Itself*.[3] Psychological testing became a mammoth undertaking in schools (to predict the need for special education), industry (to aid in employee selection), and wartime efforts (to facilitate placement of personnel in the military enterprises of World War I and II). The artistic, literary, and cultural mores of Western society came to embrace the Freudian values of unconscious motivation, conflict across generations, and struggles between individuals and society.

From this perspective, it is tempting to think that stigma reduction would have been widespread, in that overtly moralistic attitudes toward deviance were now replaced by a more modern and less blaming set of beliefs. First, however, the newer psychological models were laden with a great deal of folk wisdom, which included a strong dose of ethical and moral judgments. Second, many psychological models (including both psychodynamic and behavioral/social learning conceptions) explicitly placed responsibility on the family—and parenting practices, in particular—for the origins of mentally disturbed functioning. In other words, insensitive or inadequate parenting (usually assumed to be mothering) were viewed as the primary causal variable for nearly all forms of mental illness. As a result, stigmatization of family members increased. Third, psychological models presented a stark contrast to the biological and hereditary conceptions of the most severe forms of mental disorder, relegating these latter types of disturbance to a frightening and even subhuman level. In short, psychological and secular views of mental disturbance did not automatically reduce stigma.

Eugenics

An ominous chapter of human responses to mental disorder emerged in the late 1800s and grew rapidly during the first half of the twentieth century. Known as the eugenics movement, it featured scientifically backed views of the dangers of unlimited reproduction among persons viewed as potentially tainting a society's gene pool.[4]

Starting with Galton, who posited hereditary underpinnings of both genius and insanity in the nineteenth century, and Pearson, the statistician who provided data analytic strategies underlying the genetic transmission of various traits and conditions, the movement began to include the views of influential scientists and practitioners in the United States and England. They argued that humanity was becoming infested with genetically inferior "stock," including persons of ethnic minority backgrounds, as well as individuals (and their relatives) with mental illness, criminality, or mental retardation. Eugenic measures were strongly advocated.

These included policies of both *positive eugenics,* involving the encouragement of procreation on the part of healthy parents, and—far more repressively— *negative eugenics,* featuring restrictions on the reproductive rights of persons with mental disorders and mental retardation. Such restrictions initially included the forbidding of marriage or the desanctioning of existing marriage. Forced sterilization soon became a primary tool.

Linked strongly with racist and anti-immigration sentiments in the late nineteenth and early twentieth centuries and driven by social Darwinism, the eugenics movement gained momentum. It became more forceful during the isolationist 1920s and 1930s, during which time the U.S. Congress passed strict anti-immigration laws in order to delimit "inferior" races from populating the nation. Not only were influential scientists vocal advocates of eugenics in both its positive and negative forms, but major private sources (including the Rockefeller and Carnegie foundations) contributed to its promotion.

With regard to mental disorder and mental retardation, the first state sterilization act was passed in 1907 in Indiana. When state legislatures called upon scientific experts to provide evidence for such statutes, a number of biologists, psychologists, sociologists, and superintendents of state hospitals provided testimony in support of both the banning of marriage and mandatory sterilization.

As more and more states followed suit, ethical and legal concerns with the abrogation of civil liberties emerged. A key test case occurred in 1927, when the U.S. Supreme Court upheld a sterilization order for a woman with alleged mental retardation, in the famous case of *Buck v. Bell.* This decision allowed forced sterilization for those placed in state institutional facilities, which housed disproportionate numbers of impoverished and ethnic minority individuals. Among the justices voting in favor of this ruling, which passed 8 to 1, were William H. Taft, Oliver Wendell Holmes, and Louis Brandeis. Clearly, eugenics rulings were not carried out by a radical fringe but instead by the mainstream scientists and jurists of the day.

By 1940, fully 30 states had enacted legislation mandating sterilization for those with various forms of criminality, including rape convictions and violence, the categories of "idiocy" and "imbecility" related to mental retardation, and insanity in the form of serious mental illnesses. Kevles recounts that more than 36,000 such people were sterilized in the United States from 1907 through the early 1940s; Black places estimates at almost double that number.[5] It is hard to imagine a more officially sanctioned and institutionalized form of stigmatization than this: by official decree and forced surgery, persons with serious mental disturbance were forbidden to reproduce.

Far more extreme measures were becoming policy in Europe. Hitler's rise to leadership in Germany in 1933 was soon followed by the passage of the Eugenic Sterilization Law, which made sterilization compulsory for a wide range of physical, mental, and intellectual disabilities, regardless of institutional placement. Within three years, a quarter of a million Germans had been sterilized. Such efforts soon dovetailed with the extreme anti-Semitism of the Nazi government, which promoted and supported massive efforts to isolate, rob, starve, and finally murder the entire Jewish population of Europe, with concentration camps the specific institutions in which the forced labor and annihilation of the Holocaust took place. Less well remembered is that gypsies, gay men, lesbian women, persons with mental retardation, and those with mental disturbance were also included in the official decrees to be annihilated. Documents from Germany in the 1930s reveal that much of the inspiration for such policies emanated from the eugenics movement in the United States. It is unknown how many persons with mental subnormality and mental illness were killed during the Nazi domination, but estimates from the Nuremberg trials placed the numbers at nearly a quarter of a million.[6]

That it had become governmental policy in a major world power not only to sterilize but also to exterminate such individuals is revealing of the lengths to which societies can and will go to exclude those with mental disorder in order to "protect" the majority. The view that persons with mental disorders were genetically inferior, incapable of reason, and likely to contaminate the region's or nation's "stock" reveals the lethal potential of negative eugenics models.[7] With respect to racial and ethnic differences, such beliefs have culminated in the institution of slavery, including justification for the harsh treatment of slaves because they are not capable of true human responses, as well as ethnic cleansing and extermination. For those with mental disturbance, such views have similarly promoted policies intended to rid the earth of the deviant, subhuman people in question. Given the genetic zeitgeist today, we are at a crossroads as to whether future policies will witness a return to such repressive eugenic policies or whether our nation and world can emerge with a different conception of human variability and potential.

Institutional Care

Large state institutions continued to dominate as the primary venue of treatment for those with severe forms of mental disorder during the first half of the twentieth century. Despite a growing movement to promote mental hygiene across the population, these facilities grew ever larger and more crowded, with their physical and geographical isolation continuing to insulate them from the public. Such institutional environments featured fixed rules, complete staff control of the residents' lives, isolation from the mainstream of society, and frequent brutality.[8]

Reform movements were renewed in the 1940s. In the wake of the massive screening of personnel for the efforts of World War II, a social/environmental perspective on mental disorder emerged. Passage of the Federal Mental Health Act of 1940 paved the way for the creation of the National Institute of Mental Health and signaled the beginning of a hugely increased federal presence in mental health research and policy. Reduced state budgets, however, led to a continuing consolidation of funds into the large, centralized facilities that had mushroomed in the nineteenth century. In asylums such as Philadelphia State Hospital (known as Byberry), there were up to 80 patients in a single dormitory room. Photographs from the 1940s reveal a resemblance of this facility to a crowded concentration camp.[9] Squalor and neglect, as well as assaults from patients or staff, plagued twentieth-century asylums. In the words of a reformer of the 1940s:

> The noise and filth, the crying, swearing, laughter and inarticulate mumbling drive the depressed into deeper chasms of oblivion and the maniacs [sic] up ever more dizzy precipices of exaltation. Few are ever helped to break out of the fog of illusion that envelops them and to grasp some little part of the reality which might lead them to mental health again.[10]

History had come full circle, with the state hospitals promoted by Dix in the middle of the nineteenth century as replacements for the degrading conditions of almshouses and prisons now surpassing these latter facilities as places of despair, hopelessness, and degradation.

Biological treatments for those with the most severe forms of mental disorder were on the rise by the 1940s, including insulin shock treatment, electroconvulsive treatment (ECT), and prefrontal lobotomies. These treatments were not, in the main, subject to valid experimental trials, and the initial optimism regarding their reported success rates began to fade.[11] Specific medications for mental afflictions did not yet exist; sedatives were virtually the only type of pharmacologic intervention available. Deutsch wrote *The Shame of the States* in 1948; exposés in major periodicals appeared; and popular books and films such as *The Snake Pit* caught the public eye.[12] It was not, however, until the advent of the first generation of antipsychotic and antidepressant medications during the 1950s that hospital stays became shorter and censuses began to drop. By that time, a strong movement toward community forms of intervention, particularly for seriously disturbed individuals, had begun to emerge.

Community Mental Health and Deinstitutionalization

The reform movement regarding mental health care had many roots: a Scandinavian push toward "normalization" of environments for those with mental retardation and mental disorder, the psychosocial/environmental focus of the psychotherapy and public health movements, a growing federal investment in mental health, and the increasing recognition that prevention (rather than tertiary care efforts for those already afflicted) was essential for the promotion of mental health across the population. Also, the availability of medications to help alleviate the acute symptoms of severe psychoses and depressions provided real enthusiasm regarding the potential for noninstitutional treatment to be provided for a large number of seriously disturbed patients. Parallel to the call for moral treatment in the early nineteenth century, a serious effort toward deinstitutionalization and community-based care had begun.

The federal Community Mental Health Services Act became law in 1954, mandating shifts in funding to facilities located in communities rather than institutions. In California, the Short-Doyle Act of 1957 provided a major impetus for the funding of non-hospital-based mental health facilities. At this time the federal Joint Commission on Mental Health was formulating recommendations to the American public, and members of the commission tended toward a social/environmental, optimistic view regarding mental disorder. The commission's report was finally issued in 1961, shortly after John Kennedy became president.[13] Its four-pronged goals included (a) enhancement of basic research on processes leading to mental disorder, (b) reduction of mental hospital size through the promotion of a variety of community alternatives, (c) dissemination of educational information on mental disorder and mental health to the public, and (d) a doubling of federal expenditures devoted to mental health care. Note that the third goal—public education—was expressly intended to reduce stigmatization.

Over the next two years, the Kennedy administration and bipartisan congressional leaders worked on a crucial piece of domestic legislation, which finally passed in 1963 as the Community Mental Health Centers Construction Act. This law mandated the building of community-based facilities designed to facilitate inpatient care, outpatient therapy, partial hospitalization, emergency services, and consultation and liaison services. State hospital censuses, which had begun to decrease during the mid-1950s because of the availability of psychotropic medications, now plummeted as funding promoted the development of community-based facilities (for example, Title 18 and 19 funds diverted a large proportion of elderly patients with mental disorders from hospitals into nursing home facilities). The growth of state institutions, over a century in the making, had finally been reversed.

Deinstitutionalization gained momentum, initially fueled by the optimism underlying the community mental health movement. As the Johnson administration promoted civil rights and the Great Society, the United States entered a period of optimism over social programs in general. A key offshoot was the surge of judicial rulings and state legislation on mental health issues, beginning in the late 1960s and peaking in the 1970s, which have since been termed a revolution in mental health law.[14] Civil rights were now being granted to individuals with mental disorders and mental retardation.[15] Other court rulings mandated a right to treatment when forced institutional care was implemented.

The optimism, however, gave way to harsh realities. The emptying of large state facilities was not accompanied by adequate provision of the range of needed community supports for job training, social skills intervention, housing assistance, or programs to ensure adherence to medication regimens. In fact, state legislatures came to realize that by drastically reducing the size of public hospital facilities, costs could be cut, particularly in the absence of adequate expenditures for viable outpatient alternatives. In states such as California, which had led the nation during the early reform movement of the 1950s and 1960s, deinstitutionalization was achieved by a series of for-profit "board and care" homes, often situated in abandoned apartment buildings or motels in inner-city areas.

Furthermore, during the Nixon administration of the late 1960s and early 1970s, federal funding for community mental health centers was drastically reduced. Indeed, only 700 or so of the planned 2,000 facilities were constructed. Although the Carter administration did pass a Mental Health Systems Act, it did not take effect until 1980, just before the new Reagan administration almost totally reversed the 30-year pattern of increased federal involvement in mental health by sharply cutting assistance payments for those with mental disorders. With state hospital censuses having dropped precipitously, homelessness became a national issue, with estimates that a third or more of the growing numbers of homeless people in urban areas were suffering from serious mental disorder. This subgroup of the mentally ill became subject to harsh stigmatization, centering on perceptions of their filth, bizarreness, and transient status.[16]

By the end of the twentieth century, community facilities in New York City evidenced the squalor and neglect formerly associated with large state hospitals. A major *New York Times* series documented not only utterly hopeless lives but also early death from the lack of basic shelter and medical care. Individuals were noted to have languished in decrepit rooms and without any medical or even nutritional monitoring for months if not years.[17]

At the same time, prison populations in the United States skyrocketed during the last years of the century, as fears of inner-city crime and violence and calls for "law and order" reemerged, triggering increased criminalization of drug possession and status offenses. Jails and prisons have now replaced mental hospitals as repositories for individuals with mental disturbance who have been involved in drug-related or other criminal activity and whose histories frequently include homelessness and neglect. The Los Angeles County Jail is now considered the largest "mental facility" in the United States, if not the world, with thousands of people with mental disorders incarcerated there each day— but without treatment plans. Overall, more than 150,000 individuals per year with mental illnesses are estimated to be admitted to state and federal prisons; for youth, high rates of incarceration in juvenile detention facilities include large numbers with untreated mental disorders.[18] Jails and prisons may therefore serve as venues of "reinstitutionalization," with high rates of drug trafficking, sexual exploitation, and recidivism.[19] On the whole, community facilities and jails have come to embody the worst aspects of the state institutions they were created to replace, revealing once again the cycles of reform and retrenchment in mental health care.

I hasten to point out that many of the seriously mentally ill individuals in current society have extremely difficult problems. The initial optimism about providing care for them was quickly dampened with the combination of inadequate funding, insufficient treatment, and almost nonexistent support systems.

As Grob explains, some of the blame should go to unrealistic expectations on the part of reformers:

> For too long mental health policies have embodied an elusive dream of magical cures that would eliminate age-old maladies. . . . The public and their elected representatives often accepted without question the illusory belief that good health is always attainable. . . . The result has been periods of prolonged disappointment that have sometimes led to the abandonment of severely incapacitated persons.[20]

In other words, when reform movements fail to deliver on visions of cure, there may be a feeling of justification for the subsequent neglect of the most seriously disturbed individuals, particularly given the fear and exclusionary tendencies they tend to elicit in the first place. One clear antidote is the promotion of a hopeful yet realistic set of attitudes, through which people with serious mental disorder can be deemed worthy of rehabilitation and respect through considerable support—but without the false hope of a panacea.[21]

Children and Mental Disorder

The twentieth century witnessed a surge of interest in children's rights, children's welfare, and children's mental health. Among key trends, I briefly describe these areas.

Child Welfare and Treatment, Mental Hygiene, and Child Guidance   When Lightner Witmer opened the first psychological clinic in the United States in 1896 at the University of Pennsylvania, much of the focus was on the assessment and treatment of children. Shortly thereafter, in 1909, influential psychiatrist Adolf Meyer teamed with Clifford Beers to initiate the National Committee for Mental Hygiene, which incorporated principles of pubic health and prevention in an attempt to improve conditions in mental health facilities for persons of all ages and to educate the general public.[22] In 1910 President Theodore Roosevelt convened the first-ever White House Conference on Children, during which policies of removing children from homes solely on the basis of familial poverty were denounced. Although some aspects of child welfare were slow to emerge—for example, it was not until 1938 that the Wages and Hours Bill was enacted into law, with stipulations that children under 16 years of age could not work in dangerous occupations—research on child development and child welfare was rapidly growing. In terms of treatment, child guidance clinics emerged. Devoted initially to the prevention and treatment of juvenile delinquency, their mandate expanded to include treatment of a variety of child and family problems. In short, the initial decades of the twentieth century witnessed a surge of interest in children's psychological functioning, child welfare, and treatment strategies for children's behavioral and mental problems.[23]

Psychological Models and Blaming of Parents The predominant theoretical orientation regarding child mental disorders was, at this time, psychoanalytic in nature, paralleling similar views regarding adult disturbance. In this view, nearly all psychopathology was attributed to unconscious motivation and to faulty parent-child interactions during the earliest years of life. For child disorders, as well as adult conditions (which were assumed to emerge from patterns established during infancy and toddlerhood), the explicit view was that parents—and mothers, in particular—were the culprits. For example, the discovery of early infantile autism in the 1940s was quickly accompanied by the belief that parents had subjected the children in question to "emotional refrigeration," prompting a retreat into autistic aloneness. Even schizophrenia was attributed to the effects of mothers whose negative and controlling attitudes were held to prompt illogical thinking and identity loss. Given that mental disorder was viewed as the product of faulty parental socialization, the stigmatization of families became official policy.[24] Indeed, a major rationale for the formation of self-help and advocacy groups in the 1970s and 1980s was to counteract such positions of "family blame" through a view of serious mental disorder as biomedical and genetic in origin.

Growth of Child Mental Health and Classifications of Mental Disorders in Children
During the past 50 years, there has been a surge of academic and clinical interest in child and adolescent mental health and mental illness. Although research funding and careful investigations of treatment strategies still lag behind counterpart endeavors for adult conditions, the growth of scholarly and treatment-related activities in relation to child mental disorders is remarkable. For example, the first edition of the American Psychiatric Association's *Diagnostic and Statistical Manual of Mental Disorders, DSM-I,* published in the early 1950s, contained only two major childhood categories: adjustment reactions and schizophrenic reactions of childhood. By the time the fourth edition appeared in 1994 (with revisions in 2000), nearly 100 pages were devoted to mental disorders "usually first diagnosed in infancy, childhood, or adolescence."[25] This rapid accretion of child mental disorders reflects both the great increases in scientific study of mental conditions in children and the psychological and biomedical zeitgeist of recent decades. Clinical psychology and psychiatry began to offer specialty training in child and adolescent research and treatment, leading to a proliferation of professionals and investigators with a developmental focus. Overall, official recognition of child mental disturbance, along with greatly expanded research and clinical attention to this domain, has been a key trend of the last 50 years.

The impact on stigmatization has been mixed. Whereas greater numbers of previously unrecognized children are now being helped, stigmatization may be a consequence of diagnosis and labeling, particularly if evaluations are not evidence based and not carefully performed. It is also the case that the legacy of blaming parents for their children's disturbances has been slow to fade. Moreover, many forms of treatment for children are based on outmoded models, revealing a great need for investigation of the types of procedures that truly work.[26]

Legislative Reforms Beginning in the 1960s, child abuse was formally recognized by the medical profession as a serious problem in distressingly high numbers of children.[27] Within a decade, nearly every state had passed legislation mandating the official reporting of abuse to agencies concerned with child welfare and protection. Also, in 1974 the Juvenile Justice Delinquency Prevention Act was implemented, which provided federal funding for community-based rather than institutional treatment for juvenile status offenders. The following year, in 1975, the federal Education for All Handicapped Children Act (Public Law 94-142) mandated special education services in the "least restrictive alternative" settings for children and adolescents with learning, emotional, behavioral, and mental disorders that affect school achievement. Subsequent reauthorizations of this legislation have expanded the mandate to include broader conceptions of mental and emotional disturbances. In short, protection of the rights of children, along with explicit promotion of the use of preventive services and special education procedures, was increasingly emphasized in the latter half of the twentieth century. One result is that families now have incentives to obtain diagnoses of mental disorders in order to attain rights, protection, and funding for their children.

Summary

This review of key trends in the last century has uncovered the greatly increased secularization of views regarding mental disorder, which are highly psychological at present; the eugenics movement in the United States and the genocide of those with mental disorder in Europe; the rise and fall of mass institutionalization as the primary mode of care for severe mental disorder in the United States; the promise (followed by the distressing realities) of the deinstitutionalization and community mental health movements, as well as the increasing criminalization of mental illness; and the enhanced recognition given to child welfare and to mental disorders in children and adolescents. The past century was therefore laden with cycles of optimism and hope interspersed with pessimism and neglect.

One key conclusion is that there was an increasing split, throughout the twentieth century, between public views of persons with "everyday" psychopathology, treatable through outpatient psychotherapy and increasingly accepted in our postmodern society, and those with the most severe forms of disturbance, whose treatment venues shifted from state hospitals to community facilities and prisons. The latter continue to be linked with views of (a) the permanence of their conditions, (b) exclusively biological treatments, and (c) an aura of dangerousness and societal pessimism. Although all forms of mental illness receive stigma, the most serious and chronic variants are particularly prone to negative perceptions.

Perhaps the most important trend in recent years has been the renewed interest in biological and genetic underpinnings of mental disorder. Because of the key implications for stigma resulting from this perspective, I consider the resurgence of these views in some detail.

Reemergence of a Medical-Genetic Paradigm

During the 1960s, a time of radical social change, a movement directly countering the medical model of mental illness began to emerge. It was fueled by diverse authors (later termed antipsychiatrists) such as Szasz, who contended that mental illness was a complete myth; Laing, who pointed out the existential aspects of psychiatric symptomatology in the face of oppressive families; and Foucault, who described the social and political roots, in European history, of the historical rise of institutions for those with mental disorder.[28] Each contended that mental illness was a social construction used to label socially intolerable behavior (or responses to untenable family or political conditions) and brand it as the product of internal, individual flaws, thereby depriving it of any social or political meaning.

At the same time, psychology and psychiatry were undergoing self-examination. Research was demonstrating that even seasoned clinicians could not agree on the presence of major mental disorders such as schizophrenia and depression in a given patient. How valid was the concept of mental disorder if its most serious manifestations could not be diagnosed reliably? This work spurred a renewed commitment to accurate classification, known as the "neo-Krapelinian" movement of the 1970s, invoking the name of the German psychiatrist who had ushered in modern psychiatric classification in the early 1900s. In *DSM-III* (1980) and *DSM-IV* (1994), vague descriptions of psychopathology came to be replaced with precise symptom lists, requirements for duration and impairment of the symptoms, and decision trees to aid in the diagnostic process.[29] The reliability of psychiatric diagnosis improved substantially, thereby discrediting one major critique raised by the antipsychiatrists.[30]

At the same time, biological and genetic perspectives on mental disorder were reemerging. First, psychotropic medications were proliferating. The early versions of these antipsychotic, antidepressant, and anxiety-reducing agents had been discovered serendipitously, and their initial use fueled rapid decreases in the censuses of public mental facilities. Neuroscientific knowledge accumulated rapidly, such that specific receptors and neural sites of action of these medications became discovered, providing the hope for an increasingly rational, planned, and scientific enterprise of psychopharmacology. Many previously untreatable patients with schizophrenia, severe mood disorders, panic-level anxiety, and child disorders were showing clinically significant symptom relief and improvement in impairment levels as a function of medication treatment. As a result, a renewed appreciation for the biological roots of mental disorder was rapidly emerging.[31]

Second, behavior genetic investigators were uncovering increasingly strong evidence for a genetic basis of many major disorders, with heritability figures shown to be moderate or high. For example, half of the risk for schizophrenia is attributable to genes, with heritabilities for bipolar disorder, ADHD, and autism even higher. With the advent of molecular genetic technologies in recent years, the search for specific genes that confer such risk is proceeding rapidly.[32]

Third, in the last several decades sophisticated neuroimaging techniques have been providing unprecedented views of the brain, revealing anatomical structures and functional processes that are associated with major forms of mental disturbance. Such vivid portrayals of the neurobiological underpinnings of serious psychopathology make it hard to believe that mental illness is either imaginary or the product of weak will.[33]

In general, whereas naturalistic, biological accounts of mental disturbance have been posited for several millennia, the humoral notions of Hippocrates have been replaced by an explosion of knowledge regarding neurotransmission, brain-related substrates, pharmacologic intervention, and genetic liability to psychopathology. The sophistication of current methods has provided unprecedented evidence for biological correlates of severe mental disorder. At the same time, health economists have realized that the most life-impairing illnesses in the world increasingly constitute mental disorders, which cause major impacts on education, employment, economic productivity, life satisfaction, and even physical health.[34] The presence and the importance of mental illness are difficult to escape, and the biological and genetic underpinnings of mental disorder are increasingly accepted.[35] A major question pertains to the ramifications of such a revitalized medical model for the stigmatization of mental illness.

Implications for Stigma

On the basis of such evidence, a number of scientists, as well as advocacy groups composed largely of families of individuals with severe mental illness, have called for the renaming of mental disturbance as *brain disorder* or *brain disease*.[36] The idea is to eliminate the unsatisfying term "mental disorder," with its dubious philosophical underpinnings, its checkered history in terms of public acceptance, and its tendency to blame individuals and their family members (particularly parents) for core symptoms, and replace it with an explicitly medical/biological ascription for the troubling behavioral and emotional patterns. The express hope is that such renaming will reduce stigma by ascribing the symptoms to brain pathology rather than moral turpitude, faulty parental socialization, or other blameworthy causes. Attribution theory tells us, in fact, that ascriptions of deviant behavior to noncontrollable, biogenetic causes should reduce blame and enhance sympathy (see Chapter 2).

At one level, it is hard to argue with the contention that the locus of all behavior, whether normal range or severely disturbed, is the brain. In addition, there is compelling motivation to overthrow the long-standing views that mental disorder is a consequence of moral failings or weak personal will—or that heritable conditions such as schizophrenia, bipolar disorder, and autism are caused by insensitive parenting. So, is there is any downside to the recent attempt to recast mental disorder as brain disease?

There may well be. For one thing, placing the entire onus of mental disturbance on a static conception of brain disease is inaccurate. Graphic images of the biological, brain-related correlates of psychosis or depression (or other forms of serious mental illness) do not automatically imply that the brain-related problems are primary causes. Environmental input is crucial for the shaping of the brain and its unfathomably complex interconnections. The term *plasticity* is used to denote the fluid interplay of biology and experience in the continuous modification of the nervous system throughout development. Recall from Chapter 1 the developmental psychopathology (DP) perspective, which fully acknowledges the importance of genetic and brain-related bases of mental disorder yet incorporates them into a transactional model in which biology and experience work together. Overall, accounts that reduce mental disorder exclusively to aberrant biology and genes are overly simplistic.

In fact, despite the strongly heritable nature of many mental disorders, there is no single gene that appears responsible for any of them. Serious mental disturbances—even those forms known to have high levels of genetic liability—emanate from combinations of multiple, small-effect genes that interact with one another and with the biological and social environment. Social input, whether from parents, schools, or peers, may be crucial in this regard. In other words, the genetic model is not as simple or straightforward as is often portrayed.[37]

More directly related to the topic at hand, what are the implications for stigma if the terminology is changed to brain disorder or brain disease? Does reattributing mental disorder to biomedical and/or genetic factors automatically decrease prejudice and stigmatization? On the affirmative side of this question, helping perceivers to understand that mental illness has biological origins, rather than constituting a willful, chosen condition, can reduce blame, anger, and avoidance. In large, representative samples of the U.S. population, questionnaire responses reveal that attribution of mental disorder to biological and genetic causes is associated with a reduced desire for "social distance" from people with mental disorders.[38] At least some of the principles of attribution theory appear supported in this regard.

On the negative side, however, such an attribution may fuel the notion that the disordered behavior is permanent and chronic. Ascriptions to faulty brains and/or genetic causes are high on the *stability* dimension of attribution theory, with a strong propensity for promoting the view that the condition is inborn and immutable.

Next, experimental research reveals unexpected consequences of a biogenetic attribution. Mehta and Farina had undergraduate research participants interact with a partner who disclosed a history of "nervous breakdowns" and treatment in mental hospitals. The manipulated variable focused on the cause of these problems: Statements allegedly written by the partner disclosed that the condition emanated from either (a) a disease or medical model—here, the individual's statement described a "disease like any other, which affected my biochemistry" and noted the receipt of medication as a treatment; or (b) a psychosocial model, in which the partner disclosed that the behaviors were related to "the way I was raised and the kinds of things that happened to me as a kid" and disclosed receiving talk therapy.

As expected, participants expressed lower levels of blame for the partner in the medical/disease condition than in the psychosocial condition, upholding the contention that ascriptions of deviance to uncontrollable causes (i.e., biological factors) can reduce blame. Yet this investigation went beyond expressed attitudes to include social encounters between the participants and the interaction partners. Here, participants were told that they could punish the partner with electric shock for mistakes the partner made when performing a task. In a striking finding, those participants who had received the biological script from their partners administered *greater* levels of shock than those who had received the psychosocial-causation script.[39] Despite reducing expressions of blame, biological attributions fueled an *increase* in punitive encounters.

Additional research has similarly revealed that biological attributions, particularly those that emphasize a genetic basis for mental disorder, can be associated with harsh responses. For instance, Phelan found that these ascriptions fueled desire for greater social distance from the afflicted individual's biological relatives. Genetic attributions may be particularly likely to increase familial stigma because of the association between genetic liability and the expression of disorder in relatives.[40] In addition, through both survey studies and experimental research, investigators have shown that biological and genetic attributions for mental illness are associated with (a) a desire for *greater* social distance and (b) the perception that mentally ill people are dangerous and unpredictable.[41] Biogenetic attributions may also foster attitudes of "benevolence," the view that individuals with mental disorder are immature and incapable of self-care.[42] Such attitudes reveal pity rather than respect, potentially fueling further stigmatization.

What could help to explain such counterintuitive findings? Although this entire area of research is in great need of additional, sophisticated research efforts, consider the following argument. First, it is quite possible that at least some of the behaviors related to mental disorder generate fear or revulsion at an automatic level, prompting stigmatizing responses well before attributions even come into play. In other words, if behaviors are sufficiently threatening, the search for causal explanations may not be terribly relevant, given that rejection and social distancing can be nearly automatic.

Second, consider attributes such as racial/ethnic status, which are clearly outside one's personal control. These have been among the most consistently and harshly castigated marks throughout human history, despite the clear lack of personal responsibility for such inborn differences. Some attributes, then, appear to circumvent attribution theory. Along with ethnic minority status, mental illness may be a key example.

Third, to the extent that secondary labeling theory is valid, the very diagnosis or label of mental illness can set in motion a chain of stereotypes and prejudicial assumptions that once again trump the perception of whether the afflicted individual was personally responsible for the disorder. Such labeling carries implications of incompetence, even violence and dishevelment; these qualities are likely to be stigmatized regardless of whether the individual was responsible for their display.

Fourth, the typical belief (in most Western societies) is that behavior and emotion are under one's volitional control. As a result, most perceivers would tend to doubt, at least initially, the supposition that disturbed behavior is a function of biological processes rather than a product of personal control and responsibility. It may be a hard sell to convince the public that mentally disturbed behavior is beyond volitional control. Many may, in fact, resist efforts to discount personal responsibility for behavior, dismissing them as modern-day excuses.[43]

Nonetheless, consider the scenario in which a perceiver *does* come to believe in such biological and genetic attributions. Three key consequences are likely to ensue: (1) A biomedical attribution tends to fuel the conviction that the condition is immutable and unchangeable. This belief in permanence and hopelessness is likely to fuel pessimism and despair, thereby increasing stigma. (2) This ascription may also promote pity, related to the completely uncontrollable nature of the genetic and/or biological causation of the core problems. Pity is far from respect, and it may not include a belief in the individual's amenability to treatment. (3) Biogenetic explanations may also directly foster the view that the behavior patterns in question emanate from a deficient, defective, underlying biology—in particular, faulty genes—with the resultant perception that the person is deficient and fundamentally flawed. That is, the genetic attribution may trigger a conception that the person in question is qualitatively distinct from and inferior to other humans.

This point requires elaboration. Recall the evolutionary view of stigmatization discussed in Chapter 2. From this vantage point, the stigma of mentally disordered behavior is thought to emanate from two naturally selected response modules: distancing related to fear of parasitic infestation and shunning with respect to the belief that such persons will offer poor social reciprocation or reveal low social capital. Mental illness stigma does not, however, appear to be linked to the third exclusionary module, which involves the kinds of harsh punishment and exploitation of different "tribes" (i.e., those who are racial minorities).

Yet it could well be that exclusively biological attributions, particularly if they involve notions of defective genes, can promote the view that the mentally ill person is part of a distinct subgroup of genetically deficient individuals, one that is fundamentally subhuman. As a result, this ascription may come to invoke the kinds of harshly punitive and even exploitative responses typically reserved for nationalistic, ethnic, and/or tribal stigmas. In other words, the biogenetic explanation may inadvertently set in motion the response module linking the outgroup member to a distinct, inferior caste or tribe, invoking ideas of fundamental subhumanity.

The harshest responses to mental disorder in recent history occurred when eugenicists portrayed the permanent, negative effects of allowing genetic flaws to taint the gene pool and when Hitler explicitly categorized and branded persons with mental illnesses as a deficient subclass who were despoiling the superior Aryan race (see earlier sections of this chapter). The passage of mandatory sterilization laws, as well as subsequent extermination efforts, were not far behind. In short, biogenetic ascriptions may produce unanticipated stigmatization, given their potential to fuel perceptions of less-than-human status. The behaviors (and the mental illness label) are threatening to observers in and of themselves; furthermore, rather than prompting sympathy, the biogenetic attribution may come to increase the threat and fear value of the behavior patterns because it encourages the idea that people who display them are fundamentally different and deficient, even at the level of their genes.

Imagine a scenario in the not-too-distant future when specific genotypes are established as linked to substantial risk for certain mental disorders (or rather, "brain diseases"). There may be strong medical and societal pressure on the family to eliminate such risk prenatally through preventive abortion, as is the case today for the many (albeit rare) forms of genetic risk for severe mental retardation.[44] Increasingly sophisticated genetic knowledge could make it likely that mental disorder will receive the ultimate stigmatization in the form of its potential elimination.

My objective is not to state that attributing serious mental disorder to biological, genetic vulnerabilities is always wrong minded. In fact, there *is* substantial genetic risk for many forms of mental disorder, and appropriate ascription to such causal factors could help to reduce the blame surrounding traditional views of disturbed behavior. However, the blanket ascription of mental illness to aberrant genes is not only inaccurate scientifically but also potentially predictive of extreme stigmatization.

Haslam points out key problems with the simplistic notion that attributing mental disorder to uncontrollable causes will automatically reduce stigma. He focuses on schizophrenia, but his words have implications for mental disorder in general:

Even if schizophrenia were to become recognized by the lay public as just as much a disease as diabetes, equally grounded in a chemical malfunction of known cause and outside of intentional control, the characteristics that lead it to be stigmatized would remain unchanged. The condition would retain its . . . association with violence, as well as the apparent unpredictability and incomprehensibility that have made madness so unsettling to observers through the ages. . . . The simple point here is that a great deal of the stigma of mental disorder springs from sources other than responsibility attributions, and changing these attributions by an uncritical and vulgarized adoption of the disease model may well leave many sources untouched, as well as spawning new ones.[45]

Indeed, some of these "new" sources may pertain to notions of fundamental difference, irrevocable flaw, and essential subhumanity.

Relevant to this discussion are the eloquent arguments of Susan Sontag, who claimed that that, despite their status as "illnesses," a number of poorly understood diseases throughout history (e.g., leprosy, tuberculosis, cancer, AIDS, and mental disorders) have become metaphors for vulnerability, weakness, and a host of blameworthy personal characteristics. In other words, these conditions—about which knowledge is limited—have come to symbolize personal weakness or moral flaws. They are often viewed as physically and even morally contagious, with the very name of the illness symbolizing danger, culpability, and taboo. Mental disorder is currently loaded with such metaphoric meaning, signaling weakness, violence, lack of control, and shame. The medical/genetic attribution may not only fail to supplant such vivid associations but also fuel the perception that people with mental illness are fundamentally flawed at the level of their underlying, immutable biology.[46]

A counterreaction to the "brain disorder" movement is receiving support. Read and Harre have called for abandoning wholesale tendencies to attribute mental disorders to biological and genetic causes, on the grounds that the public will reject them as overly simplistic and that such models do not foster behavioral contact with persons displaying psychopathology. Watson and Corrigan recently made the important point that biogenetic attributions for mental illness can foster the belief that a lack of control on the part of persons with mental disorders portends violence and irrationality.[47]

It may be that it is the *reductionistic* aspects of biological, genetic depictions that produce these unintended consequences. That is, if such views emphasize that those with mental illness are no more than the product of flawed genes, their essential humanity is likely to be diminished. One antidote could be integrative models. In the 1970s, Engel called for a "biopsychosocial" perspective, in which individual predispositions, psychological influences, and social/cultural context were all deemed necessary to understand psychopathology.[48] Currently, the DP model provides a means of capturing the complex nature of both healthy and atypical human functioning. Such integrative models are inherently complex, however, and not as readily accessible to the public as bullet-pointed headlines to the effect that mental illness emanates exclusively from bad parents or bad genes.

In sum, with our current state of knowledge, denying the genetic bases and neural roots of mental disorder would betray ignorance. Yet emphasizing a reductionistic, genes-are-destiny, dehumanizing viewpoint not only is inaccurate but also potentially fuels punishment and deep stigma. An important task will be to promote integrated, balanced, and human portrayals of mental illness, which can foster understanding, respect, and empathy.

Historical Lessons: Tolerance Versus Stigmatization

What can be learned from the historical accounts in Chapters 3 and 4? Although demonologic views and moralistic stances have been associated with abandonment, punishment, and even the elimination of those with mental disturbance, extremely empathic treatments have emanated from religious and spiritual views (e.g., ancient temples and medieval monasteries; the Gheel community; moral treatment). Similarly, naturalistic, medical models from ancient Greece brought with them the potential for compassion and humane medical care, yet they often deteriorated into bloodletting, sedation, and other punitive forms of intervention. More recently, biological/genetic models have provided untold promise in terms of understanding serious mental illness but have also been associated with institutional care, lobotomies, and forced sterilization (or even genocide). On the whole, there is no automatic, one-to-one linkage between causal models and stigmatization.

Perhaps the key issue pertains to the *kinds* of moral models and biomedical ascriptions that promote intolerance and punishment on the one hand and compassion on the other. As for religious and moral beliefs, it may be that those forms that uphold a harshly punitive deity or offer a worldview of predestination promote more negative responses to deviant behavior than those that posit a more compassionate, tolerant power or promote the view that people can change. A fundamental belief in the capacity for human growth appears crucial in this regard.[49] In other words, it may not be that religious, spiritual, or moral beliefs per se are the determining factor but rather that the underlying assumptions and practices of such models are associated with tolerance versus stigmatization.

Regarding biomedical perspectives, models emphasizing a qualitative difference between the afflicted individual and other humans seem to foster greater stigmatization than those positing a difference in degree or quantity. If the person with mental disorder is perceived as fundamentally distinct from other humans—for example, possessing a distinctly deviant set of genes—this belief may set the stage for exclusion, over and above the automatic tendencies toward distancing prompted by disturbed behavior patterns or labels themselves. On the other hand, if the deviation is viewed as quantitative, such that the behavioral difference is on the same continuum as that of the rest of humanity but simply more extreme, tolerance and compassion may have a greater chance of emerging. Current scientific evidence indicates that most forms of mental illness appear to differ quantitatively but not qualitatively from normal-range functioning.[50] Portrayals of mental disturbance that accentuate the similarities of afflicted individuals to other people, the malleability of psychological disturbance, and the kinds of struggles and triumphs that occur on a daily basis could all serve to highlight the underlying humanity of persons with mental disorders.

Still, what specific evidence exists regarding the extent of mental illness stigma in current society? I take up this important question in the next two chapters.

5

Evidence From Scientific Investigations

Scientific investigations of public attitudes toward mental disorder began in earnest during the 1940s and 1950s, a time of renewed national interest in mental health and community-based alternatives. Early studies included both attitude surveys and evaluations of intentional efforts to educate the public about mental disorder; the attempt was to pave the way for individuals in mental hospitals to return to the community without stigmatization. This work has maintained its momentum through the present day. Although much research in this area has focused on the knowledge, attitudes, and behavioral responses of the general public, I also review studies of the beliefs and responses of persons with mental disorders themselves, the burden on families, and the attitudes of mental health professionals. A near absence of research means that children's attitudes toward mental illness receive only brief coverage.

A key issue in research on stigma involves the relationship between *knowledge* about mental illness, *attitudes* expressed toward those with mental disorders, and *behavioral responses* of social perceivers. Because these three domains are at best imperfectly correlated, I highlight the particular type of response featured in the investigations under review.

The General Public and Stigma: Studies From the 1940s Through the 1960s

Early studies utilized the methodology of presenting participants with case-history vignettes that described one or more mental disorders. Outcome measures typically included factual measures, tapping specific knowledge of mental illnesses; attitude items, indicating overtly expressed feelings; social distance scales, which appraise the degree of desired contact with or distance from an individual so depicted; and semantic differentials involving selection from a pair of adjectives (such as "dirty" versus "clean") to describe the vignette.[1]

The main conclusion was the large degree of stigmatization expressed by the general public toward people with mental illness. Indeed, when respondents identified a pattern of behavior as representing mental disorder, negative, rejecting responses were highly likely, as was desire for social distance. At the same time, knowledge levels were low, as many depictions of mentally disordered behavior were not considered as mental illness by respondents. The investigators' clearest explanations for the stigmatizing attitudes were the unpredictability and the threatening nature of the behavior patterns in question.

In some studies both lack of knowledge and negative attitudes were associated with lower levels of education in respondents. Yet these response patterns were not restricted to members of society with poor educational or occupational backgrounds. Revealing the extent of negative attitudes in such research, in an important review article from the early 1970s Rabkin stated the following: "In a very real sense, mental patients have taken the place of lepers as targets of public disgust, dislike, and rejection."[2]

To give a flavor of these findings, I highlight several pertinent studies. As early as 1943, Allen investigated community attitudes toward mental illness and found that the predominant view was one of fear and stigmatization. Another survey was conducted on a carefully selected and representative sample of adults in Trenton, New Jersey, in the 1940s. Here, respondents from higher ranks of socioeconomic status were less likely to brand mental disorder as sinful and more likely to hold optimistic views for recovery. A far more extensive investigation was conducted during the 1950s by Nunnally, in which the respondents comprised a nationally representative sample of 400 adults who responded to an extensive rating scale, as well as other types of questions. The key conclusions were pessimistic: Although the more educated segments of the sample had greater *knowledge* about mental disorder than did the less educated subgroups, *attitude* differences were small between different educational levels, with all such attitudes decidedly negative. On semantic differential items, for example, respondents characterized those with mental illness as dirty, dangerous, cold, worthless, insincere, unpredictable, undependable, and tense. The respondents also viewed psychiatrists and mental health professionals in a more pejorative light than they did general physicians, with mental hospitals and their staff receiving particularly strong devaluation. Overall, whereas gross misinformation about mental disorder was not always apparent, attitudes were derogatory.[3]

Whatley helped to revitalize the use of social distance scales, which had originally been devised during the 1920s and 1930s to measure racial and ethnic prejudice. He asked more than 2,000 adults from Louisiana to respond to descriptions of persons who had been in mental hospitals or who had seen a psychiatrist. These items included living near, hiring, having as a neighbor, having as a roommate, hiring as a babysitter, or having one's offspring marry the individual in question. Although respondents indicated that living near such a "mental patient" would be acceptable, the overwhelming majority rejected closer degrees of contact, particularly those having to do with an offspring's marriage to such a person or having that person as a babysitter. Younger respondents and those with higher levels of education were somewhat less rejecting and distancing than older respondents or those with lower educational levels, but responses did not vary as a function of having visited a mental hospital or having a relative with mental disorder, suggesting that a mere history of contact with mental disorder is not terribly influential. In sum, respondents did not want close relationships with individuals characterized as mentally ill.[4]

A milestone in the history of research on attitudes toward mental disorder was reached through the work of Shirley Star of the National Opinion Research Center, who wrote a number of vignettes (known as the Star vignettes), each of which depicted a distinct pattern of mentally disturbed behavior. These included two types of schizophrenia, as well as depression, alcoholism, conduct disorder (i.e., aggressive, delinquent behavior), and serious anxiety. Diagnostic labels were typically not included, in order to ascertain whether the public would identify the behavior patterns in question as related to mental disturbance. With her work on this topic cited in the influential report of the Joint Commission on Mental Illness and Health (see Chapter 4), Star found that the public, represented by a sample of more than 3,500 respondents, was extremely reticent to label any of these vignettes as depicting mental illness. In fact, only the description of floridly psychotic, paranoid schizophrenia consistently elicited such a designation. This work set the stage for increased efforts on the part of mental health officials to foster the belief that mental disorder is just as real as physical ailments.

Promoting such awareness had already emerged as a priority. Beginning in 1951, Cumming and Cumming selected two similar rural towns in Canada, an experimental one receiving educational intervention, plus a similar "control" town. The 6-month educational campaign featured group discussions and films intended to promote tolerance and foster the view that mentally disturbed behavior is not completely distinct from the norm. The specific intervention strategies also took the form of appeals in the media (e.g., stories in the town's newspaper; film showings and follow-up discussions). Although this work was far reaching, the results were sobering. Quantitative data revealed little, if any, change in the experimental town as a function of the intervention, with respect to either social distance measures or the community members' perceived responsibility toward mental disorder. In addition, consistent with Americans responding to the Star vignettes, the townspeople reserved the designation of mental illness only for seriously psychotic behavior.[5]

More qualitatively, Cumming and Cumming described the anxiety and even outright hostility shown by the citizens of the experimental town as the months went by. Several key members of the community, including the mayor, distanced themselves considerably from the project. In fact, a rumor circulated during the intervention period that the real rationale for the professionals' interest was the projected building of a mental hospital near the community. Overall, the initial optimism of the intervention team was shaken by the experience of attempting community-wide attitude change, suggesting major resistance on the part of the public toward accepting mental disorder as part of a continuum with normality.

Nearly two decades later, Rootman and Lafave sampled another rural Canadian town and reached different conclusions.[6] More than 70% of the respondents now branded a vignette of an alcoholic as evidencing mental illness, compared to under 30% in Star's work and in the Cumming and Cumming intervention study; similar figures held for a vignette depicting "simple schizophrenia," a condition marked by serious social withdrawal but without psychotic features. The public had apparently learned to recognize several different disturbed behavior patterns as forms of mental illness. Furthermore, with respect to social distance, 78% of the newer Canadian sample stated that they would be willing to be roommates with a person with mental illness, compared to 44% from the earlier study. It appeared that knowledge had increased and social distance had decreased during the 1950s and 1960s.

On the other hand, perhaps respondents had by this time learned to provide more socially desirable responses to formal attitude and social distance scales. Indeed, Rootman and Lafave speculated explicitly whether such informational gains and attitude change were commensurate with actual behavioral tolerance: "It is possible that increasing sophistication about mental illness may not be tantamount to increased tolerance. . . . People may have simply acquired a verbal smoke screen that permits more effective masking of real feelings."[7] Indeed, another investigation conducted during the late 1960s regarding public attitudes revealed that the two conditions most dreaded by respondents were insanity and leprosy.[8]

Such conflicting reports led to a major split in opinion.[9] On the one hand, survey data were revealing a greater tendency for respondents to recognize Star's vignettes as depicting mental disorder, a greater belief that mental disorders require treatment (and that such treatment can be helpful), and a lower level of desire for social distance from those with mental disorder. Reasons for these changes were hypothesized to include federal initiatives and public awareness campaigns (e.g., public service announcements). Indeed, studying urban, lower-class populations in Baltimore during the 1960s, Crocetti and colleagues found more benign attitudes than had been the norm during early work in the field. Their conclusions were clear: "There is evidence that for at least a decade the public has accepted mental illness as illness, that it looks to the medical profession for the treatment of this illness, and that it is optimistic about the outcome of such treatment."[10] A growing consensus was that mental disorder no longer received stigmatization.

Even at the level of attitudes, however, other investigations showed far more pessimistic findings. Lamy asked undergraduate students make "snap judgments" of two groups: ex-mental patients and ex-convicts. The participants were more pessimistic about the ex-mental patients, perceiving them to be less reliable in emergencies, believing them to be greater risks in jobs requiring high responsibility, and stating that a mother requiring child care for a weekend should choose an ex-convict.[11] Furthermore, across several different samples, Tringo found that, among 21 different disability groups under investigation, mental disorder was ranked dead last—that is, it invoked the greatest social distance desired on the part of respondents. Individuals with mental disorder were more rejected than ex-convicts, dwarfs, hunchbacks, or persons with mental retardation.[12] In vignette-based research, Phillips also showed that as a hypothetical individual moved on a continuum from being treated by a clergyman, physician, or psychiatrist to being cared for in a mental hospital, social rejection and social distance increased. This work directly highlighted the stigmatization related to treatment seeking on the part of people with mental disorders.[13]

Additional research by Phillips pointed to important effects of the *label* of mental disorder on the perceptions and attitudes of the public. He found that when normal-range behavioral descriptions were paired with the depiction "never having sought professional help," social distance was minimal: Nearly all of the respondents would have these people as neighbors, rent them a room, work with them, or let their child marry one. Yet when the same description of normal-level behavior was accompanied by the label of "ex-mental patient," only a minority stated that they would rent the person a room, and fewer than 20% reported that they would let their daughter or son marry such a person.[14] In other words, the label of mental illness and the designation of mental patient status were associated with high levels of stigmatization and social distance, even when no problematic behavior was noted. This finding was used to support primary labeling theory, the radical version emphasizing the power of labels to create deviant careers (see Chapter 2).

Who was correct: those optimistic experts who attested that stigma was declining, or those who contended that fundamental attitudes were still rejecting and stigmatizing? It took additional studies to provide a more definitive answer.

The General Public and Stigma: Studies From the 1970s to the Present

Improved Attitudes?

Echoing strongly the optimistic perspective from their earlier work, Crocetti and colleagues published a book-length account of their extensive surveys in 1974, in which they contended that public attitudes toward mental illness had become extremely accepting. Their belief was that stigmatization and discrimination against those with mental disorders no longer existed.[15] Supporting this view, Gove contended that stigma was a mild, transitory problem for persons with mental disorder: Negative social effects might emanate directly from disturbed behavior, but labeling effects per se were minimal.[16] In fact, by 1980 a workshop convened by the National Institute of Mental Health on attitudes toward mental disorder eliminated the word *stigma* from its title, in response to the perception that improved attitudes and reduced prejudice were now the norm.[17] The strong sense, promoted by respected investigators and recognized at the level of governmental mental health agencies, was that stigma toward mental disorder was fast disappearing, if not gone altogether.

Critics of this perspective, however, were continuing to assert a different view. For one thing, they pointed out that the optimists were still basing their assertions on evidence provided from vignettes of behavioral patterns, with attitude and social distance scales as dependent measures. Such attitudes, it was claimed, may reflect "what to say" more than what is actually felt and may not be matched by covert attitudes or discriminatory responses to persons with mental illness.

In addition, other data revealed that mental disorder continued to elicit extremely negative reactions. Olmstead and Durham performed semantic differential studies in the early 1960s and again in the 1970s and found that attitudes had remained virtually unchanged during that time. Typical descriptions involved the terms *dirty, weak, dangerous, cold,* and *ignorant.* And in studies featuring explicit comparisons between persons described as having a mental disorder and those with other types of disabilities or problems, the mental disorder condition nearly always received the lowest-ranked attitudinal responses from participants.[18]

By the early 1980s, Link and Cullen were explicitly considering the possibility that expressed attitudes toward mental disorder could be misleading. They proposed that the typical response format of attitude measures prompted socially desirable answers that did not accurately reflect underlying attitudes. Utilizing an innovative methodology, they had participants respond to vignettes of disturbed behavior under three different instruction sets: (a) what *most people* would feel about the person in question; (b) what their *own feelings* were; and (c) how an *ideal* person (i.e., one with admirable qualities) would respond. The hypothesis was that responses in the "most people" category would better represent actual underlying attitudes than responses related to "own feelings" or those of the "ideal" person, with the latter condition expected to produce the highest levels of social desirability.[19]

Indeed, when vignettes were labeled with a mental hospitalization history, participants opted for social rejection more strongly in the "most people" condition—the one believed to indicate deeper levels of attitudes—than in the other response sets. Accordingly, most attitude research may have been conveying a falsely optimistic view of reductions in stigma. Moreover, additional investigations during the 1980s revealed that even with straightforward attitude surveys, more than half of the rural Americans serving as participants ascribed the symptoms of paranoid schizophrenia to moral weakness.[20] The upshot was that stigmatizing attitudes were still rampant.

Behavioral Research

Since the late 1960s, a different experimental tradition had been developing, featuring randomly assigned conditions (such as social interaction with a person labeled as mentally disordered versus someone not so labeled) as the independent variable and actual behavioral responses of the participants as the outcome variables. I begin with a key figure in the history of this work, Amerigo Farina. In his early studies, confederates presented themselves to research participants as either normal or having a history mental illness. Clear effects of the mental illness label were evident: Participants perceived inadequacies of the labeled individuals, avoided them, and even inflicted electrical shock as a punishment.[21] Such observable responses provided evidence that prejudice, discrimination, and stigmatization were at work.

In an intriguing examination of the effects of labels on stigmatized people themselves, Farina and colleagues next had individuals participate in dyadic interactions. In these exchanges, one member of a pair (person A) was randomly assigned to a condition in which that person was told that the interaction *partner* (person B) had information regarding person A's history of mental breakdowns and hospitalizations. In actuality, however, the interaction partner had no such information; the experimental variable was A's *belief* that B had knowledge of such a history. Although experimental participants performed *better* on a cooperative task than those in the control condition (perhaps to compensate for the effects of the label they believed their partners had received), they were more likely to be *ignored* by B, suggesting that their own fear of rejection initiated a self-fulfilling prophecy culminating in more negative interactions.[22]

In a replication study, participants who had actually been patients in mental hospitals were assigned to conditions in which they believed that interaction partners, who were to interview them, thought that they were (a) former psychiatric patients or (b) former medical patients. Again, however, the partners had received neither form of information. Participants in the psychiatric condition performed worse on objective tasks and were rated by the interviewer as more tense and poorly adjusted than those in the medical condition.[23] As before, the mere belief that a social partner knew of one's mental illness history launched a set of reactions that culminated in actual rejection. Note that such results may *underestimate* the power of stigmatization, given that these interactions were set up as one-shot patterns of interchange. In real life, negative expectations may be formed and consolidated over much longer time periods.

Other relevant research was also revealing. Rosenhan's famous investigation of "pseudopatients" (i.e., healthy volunteers who gained admission to mental hospitals and then languished at the hands of staff, who seldom reconsidered whether these individuals were actually patients) served as a warning that, even for staff members, self-fulfilling prophecies could powerfully influence interactions with mental patients. In addition, Sibicky and Dovidio performed an experimental investigation of college students interacting in dyads, in which one of the partners was led to believe that the other was either (a) in treatment at the college's therapy clinic or (b) simply a classmate. With this relatively benign manipulation, the partners rated the "therapy" individuals less positively, even before being formally introduced. They were also more evasive and less open during the interaction, with reciprocal effects on the targeted member of the pair, who had been unaware of the manipulation.[24]

In a simple yet compelling series of behavioral investigations spanning two decades, Page had his own staff members make telephone contact with landlords who had advertised rooms for rent. These staff were randomly assigned to one of two conditions: the caller either (a) inquired about the availability of the room or (b) made the inquiry with the additional sentence that the caller was receiving "some mental health treatment in a hospital" but would soon need a place to live outside the hospital. Results were clear across the 1970s, 1980s, and 1990s: Landlords receiving calls in the experimental condition were far less likely to indicate room availability than those in the control condition.[25] Indeed, only a small percentage of rooms were made available for viewing to callers identifying themselves as mental patients, providing clear evidence of the continuing discrimination toward those with mental disorders, particularly if hospital treatment were specified. As Page stated during the 1990s:

> It would appear that persons invoking even an ambiguous reference to mental illness still face many of the same rejecting situations they faced three decades ago, at least when such rejection is privately expressed, seemingly legitimate, and very likely perceived by its perpetrator as undetectable. . . . Unfortunately, much psychological research in this area has repeatedly relied on a naïve acceptance of interviews, surveys, or questionnaire-based data.[26]

In short, behavioral research was yielding a far different set of conclusions about the persistence of stigma and discrimination than were the more optimistic attitude studies.

Effects of Labeling—and Dangerousness— Reconsidered

Another debate was occurring with respect to the effects of the label of mental illness or "ex-mental patient." Do labels exert negative effects on perceivers' expectations or interactions, or are the tenets of labeling theory overstated?[27] To help resolve this controversy, Link and colleagues performed systematic research aimed at disentangling the effects of the label from those related to mentally disordered behavior per se.

Investigations had already begun to indicate that deviant behavior patterns were more likely to shape negative reactions than were labels themselves. That is, in head-to-head contrasts, the label of mental illness served as a less powerful predictor of social distancing and other indicators of stigma than did depictions of disturbed behavior.[28] Still, Link's research group aimed to clarify when and how labels of mental disorder could show their effects. The paradigm was to ask a representative sample of participants in a Midwestern city to make social distance ratings in one of six conditions, with the experimental factors constituting (a) the objectionable nature of the behavior (no disturbance, mild disturbance, severe disturbance), as crossed with (b) the label (ex-mental patient versus ex-general hospital patient). In keeping with prior research, participants expressed desire for greater social distance in the behavioral disturbance than in the no disturbance conditions, with minimal overall effects of the label of mental hospitalization.

The research team, however, had included additional questions that probed the respondents' perception of the *dangerousness* of mentally disordered individuals. Some respondents were quite likely to believe this stereotype, but others did not hold such a belief. Those respondents believing that mental illness was associated with a high degree of dangerousness were extremely influenced by the ex-mental patient label, in the direction of increased social distance. Yet for those who did not hold this general belief, the labeling effect was in the opposite direction, such that the ex-mental patient label actually *reduced* social distance.[29] In short, labeling *did* predict stigmatization but only when respondents believed that dangerousness or violence was linked with mental illness.

This finding raises an important question: What is the actual level of association between mental disturbance and violence? As Chapter 6 emphasizes, media portrayals are highly stereotypic in this regard, promoting the view that mental illness and violent behavior are inextricably intertwined. Are such media portrayals an accurate reflection of reality?

The fact is that serious mental illness does have a small, but discernible, connection to violent behavior; it is a mistake to say that there is no association. Yet several important qualifiers are essential to note. In the first place, the vast majority of those with mental disorder are not violent—in fact, only one variant of mental illness increases the risk appreciably (as discussed below)—and the contribution to overall levels of violence from mental illness is quite limited. In other words, societal violence has many roots, ranging from the personal to the institutional; the role of mental disorder is statistically significant but small in effect. Being male, for example, makes a greater contribution than does having a history of mental illness.

Second, the linkage that exists pertains only to those who are *currently* displaying mentally disordered symptomatology. The risk of violence for those who experienced psychiatric symptoms in the past but are currently in remission is not above chance levels. Active engagement in treatment is also likely to reduce the risk, given that noncompliance with treatment is a key predictor of increased tendencies toward violent behavior.

Third, the risk is strongly intensified when alcohol or substance abuse is added to the mix. In fact, the association between substance use and violence is far stronger than the mental disorder-violence connection. Given the substantial overlap between many forms of mental illness and the use and abuse of various substances, it is important to distinguish the role of mental disorder versus the role of co-occurring substance use in propelling aggressive or violent tendencies.

Fourth, the only type of psychiatric symptomatology clearly associated with violence involves a particular form of psychotic thought, involving delusions in which the individuals believe their thoughts are controlled by others who wish to do them harm.[30] Other forms of mental disorder, even those involving serious symptom levels, are not linked to increased rates of violence.

On the whole, although there is a small association between mental illness and risk for violence, this linkage pertains only to certain forms of psychotic behavior and is greatly exaggerated by newspaper and television accounts. At the same time, the media hardly ever mention the strong tendencies for people with serious mental illnesses to become victims of violent crime; rather, the stereotyped focus is on the perpetration of violence.[31] To the extent that such stereotypes are believed, the label of mental illness or ex-mental patient is likely to promote stigmatization.

Current Investigations

Large-scale investigations of public attitudes have reemerged in recent years, with provocative results. For example, in a Harris Poll inquiring about attitudes toward disabilities, Americans reported that they were more comfortable with deaf individuals, those in wheelchairs, or persons with facial disfigurements than they were with people with mental disorders. The overall conclusion was that, as was the case decades before, mental illness was the most disturbing type of disability-related condition for the general public.[32]

During the 1990s Link and colleagues updated the classic Star vignettes, devising a more modern set of descriptors of mental disturbance based on *DSM-IV* criteria. These vignettes were administered to more than 1,400 adults, representative of the U.S. population, through the General Social Survey. The vast majority (88%) stated that the schizophrenia vignette described a person with "mental illness," compared to 69% for major depression and 49% and 44%, respectively, for alcohol and cocaine dependence. The figures for schizophrenia and depression are much higher than comparable statistics during the 1950s, revealing gains in knowledge on the part of the American populace.[33] Crucially, however, the desire for social distance regarding schizophrenia and major depression was even *greater* than it had been during the initial era of the Star vignettes, nearly half a century before. With regard to depression, for example, almost half of the sample wished for considerable social distance. With regard to schizophrenia, the rates were higher still—exceeding those from nearly fifty years earlier. [34] What might have promoted this paradoxical increase in stigma regarding severe forms of mental illness, even as knowledge of mental illness was growing?

Phelan and colleagues explained this trend in terms of the finding that more than twice as many respondents (12%) were likely to associate mental illness with dangerousness than had been the case in the 1950s (5%). One reason for this association in the public's mind may have been changes in civil commitment laws: During the 1970s, most states had restricted involuntary institutionalization, with "danger to self" or "danger to others" constituting one of the few criteria for such restrictive placement.[35] Through exposure to such terms, the public may have come to associate serious mental illness with danger. In short, gains in knowledge over the last few decades appear to have been accompanied by *increases* rather than decreases in stigmatization, at least for severe forms of mental disorder.

In Canada, Thompson and colleagues reported a telephone survey of 1,200 adults from three sites in the province of Alberta. Responses revealed relatively impressive knowledge of schizophrenia, along with a belief in the potential efficacy of treatment and the professed willingness of many respondents to spend more tax dollars on intervention programs. On the other hand, perceptions of the dangerousness of persons with schizophrenia were strong, desired social distance was still considerable, and "loss of mind" was viewed by the respondents as the most handicapping condition that could befall an individual. Although some cause for optimism is evident, particularly regarding treatment, stigmatization is evident.[36]

In Britain, Crisp and colleagues sampled 1,737 representative adults during the 1990s, inquiring about a number of attitudes with respect to seven different mental disorders (severe depression, panic attacks, schizophrenia, dementia, eating disorder, alcohol addiction, and drug addiction). Responses varied widely with respect to the different disorders, highlighting that attitudes toward mental disorder should be examined specifically rather than as a whole. Receiving the most negative responses were schizophrenia and alcohol/drug addiction, both overwhelmingly perceived as dangerous and unpredictable. Reflecting greater public awareness of improvements in treatment methods, the vast majority of respondents perceived all of the disorders (except dementia) as likely to improve if treated. They also, however, appraised individuals with eating disorders and alcohol/drug addiction as "having oneself to blame" and as being "able to pull themselves together," indicating the belief that these conditions are controllable and blameworthy.[37] Nearly a quarter of the respondents viewed people with severe depression as dangerous.

Although not performed with a representative sample, a recent investigation by Ben-Porath examined the responses of 400 undergraduates to written vignettes that contrasted two factors: type of illness (depression versus back pain) and treatment seeking (receiving care versus not). The most negative ratings pertained to the vignette depicting both depression and treatment seeking. Receiving clinical intervention for mental disorder still receives stigmatization from educated young persons in our society.[38]

Regarding the international nature of stigmatizing attitudes, recent studies have revealed clear evidence for stigma in relation to mental disturbance in Norway, India, China, and Germany. Indeed, in the latter nation, social distancing of the general public in relation to mental disorder has not fundamentally changed in the past two decades. Stigma is global.[39]

Behavioral/experimental research has also continued to document stigmatization and discrimination. As discussed in Chapter 4, the work of Mehta and Farina has revealed that biogenetic attributions for mental disorder can induce punitive responses. Furthermore, in a groundbreaking investigation, Graves and colleagues recently demonstrated that, when presented with an experimentally manipulated label of schizophrenia (as compared to no diagnosis), participants not only expressed the desire for greater social distance but also revealed psychophysiological increases in brow muscle tension and heart rate deceleration—with the latter finding thought to be an indicator of preparation for action. Notably, these indicators of physiological reactivity predicted greater preferences for social distance. In this, the initial investigation of mental illness stigma to utilize automatic levels of response, findings revealed clear physiological effects in response to the label of a serious mental illness.[40]

Overall, recent surveys reveal that although public knowledge of mental disorder is more sophisticated than in past decades and although optimism regarding treatment is increasingly present, considerable distancing and stigmatization remain in place, particularly for the most severe forms of mental illness. These findings occur at the level of overtly expressed attitudes, which may underestimate true stigmatization because of the potential for socially desirable response tendencies. Furthermore, investigations featuring behavioral and psychophysiological response tendencies reveal that stimuli related to mental illness produce discrimination and punishment, as well as biological indicators of reactivity and stress. Conclusions that stigma had disappeared were clearly premature—and wrong.[41]

Stigma in Persons With Mental Disorder, Family Members, and Professionals

Individuals With Mental Illness

Initial research on this topic concluded that persons with mental disorder were likely to hold the same negative stereotypes regarding mental illness as did the general public. In fact, a clear majority of both inpatients and outpatients with mental disorder believed in generalized expectancies that people with mental illness would be rejected. Coping strategies of secrecy and social withdrawal were common, as would be expected for a stigmatized condition that is potentially concealable (i.e., a history of mental disorder or mental hospitalization). Not surprisingly, these strategies were associated, in turn, with a lack of social support. In short, persons with mental disorder tended to hold the same conceptions and stereotypes of mental illness as the general public, and these expectations of rejection and stigmatization promoted a vicious cycle of secrecy, withdrawal, and isolation, decreasing the chances for adaptive responding in society.[42]

However, research that deals with the effects of stigma on people with mental disorders must contend with a thorny problem: disentangling the effects of stigmatization from those related to the symptoms of mental conditions themselves. Without consideration of this potential confound, it could easily be the case that the effects of stigma are overinterpreted, particularly given that many forms of mental illness can breed hopelessness, despair, social and vocational limitations, and other adverse consequences.

In a longitudinal study intended to address this issue, Link and colleagues investigated men with both mental disorder and substance-abuse histories. Although twelve months of community treatment produced considerable improvement in symptoms, stigma-related expectations remained strongly present. In addition, both general expectation of stigma and individuals' direct experiences of social rejection continued to predict depressive symptoms following treatment. In fact, these factors were as predictive of posttreatment depression as were the patients' initial levels of depression. Stigma was as important, if not more so, than the effects of mental illness itself.[43]

In another longitudinal study, Wright and associates showed that social rejection fueled decreases in self-esteem among deinstitutionalized individuals. Furthermore, two types of perceptions—perceived devaluation and discrimination, and perceived rejection—were strong predictors of lowered self-esteem as much as two years later. In fact, those at the ninetieth percentile of such stigma perceptions had sevenfold lower levels of self-esteem at follow-up than did those low in stigma perceptions, even with statistical control of other relevant factors that might have predicted self-esteem.[44]

Ritsher and Phelan have found that among adults with serious mental illness, self-reports of internalized stigma—particularly related to a general sense of alienation from society as a function of having a mental illness—predicted increased depression and lowered self-esteem across a 4-month interval, even with initial levels of these outcomes statistically controlled. Importantly, it was not so much direct experiences of discrimination but rather the internalized sense of alienation (along with practices of social concealment) that predicted the strongest effects. Perlick and colleagues also found that perceived stigma predicted poor social adjustment over a 7-month period in a sample of adults with bipolar disorder, controlling for baseline social adjustment.[45] Although not every individual with a mental disorder experiences or processes stigmatizing messages in the same way, overall effects clearly suggest the negative consequences of stigma on optimism, morale, and life opportunities.

Additional investigations have demonstrated that both anticipated rejection and actual discriminatory experiences predict negative outcomes. For example, when older outpatients with unipolar depression expect stigmatization, they are likely to discontinue therapy prematurely. This finding is important, as it signals that stigma may directly hamper engagement with treatment. Also, in an investigation of outpatients with schizophrenia, all but one participant recalled stigma-related experiences, with avoidance of telling others about their disorder a common coping strategy. Furthermore, in a British survey of nearly 800 persons in advocacy groups for mental disorder, nearly half reported having been harassed in public, and more than a third had been terminated from jobs. Overall, whereas individuals with mental disorder may be particularly sensitive to social rejection because of the nature of their illnesses, stigmatization adds to their burden over time.[46]

Wahl performed a large-scale investigation in which 1,301 adults with mental disorders in the United States completed surveys, with a representative subsample of 100 selected for more intensive interviews.[47] The participants were found primarily through the rolls of the National Alliance on Mental Illness (NAMI); they were therefore likely to have been self-selected for some degree of activism and awareness of stigma. Bipolar disorder, schizophrenia, and unipolar depression were the most frequent diagnoses. Respondents averaged 42 years of age and were quite likely to have spent time in mental hospitals.

Nearly 80% reported having heard people make disparaging or offensive comments about mental disorder, with a similar percentage having experienced offensive media depictions, reflecting prevalent experiences of what is termed *indirect stigma* (i.e., stigmatizing messages given to others or conveyed globally throughout the culture). More direct experiences of stigma included shunning or avoidance by social contacts (e.g., coworkers and friends) and the experience of others' telling them to lower their own expectations. Not surprisingly, coping responses of secrecy and avoidance were prevalent.

In sum, people with mental disorders recognize the castigating attitudes and lowered expectations regarding mental disorder that are found in the general culture. Longitudinal investigations emphasize the lasting effects of stigma for the lives of those with mental disorders, even accounting for earlier levels of mental illness or adjustment. Stigma therefore produces a negative influence on the life course of individuals with mental disorders, over and above the impairments and problems associated with the conditions themselves. Some of the key strategies for coping with stigma, such as secrecy and withdrawal, promote further isolation and demoralization, suggesting that self-stigmatization is an insidious by-product of stigma. Yet self-stigma is not inevitable; there are large individual differences in coping styles that include, at least in some people, strength, resolve, and active efforts to fight discrimination.

Family Members

The potential for shunning and rejection of family members of individuals with mental disorder exemplifies Goffman's notion of "courtesy stigma," whereby those associated with a stigmatized individual are themselves devalued. Systematic research on the responses of families to mental disorder in their relatives began in the 1950s. Early studies dealt primarily with the responses of wives to their husbands' serious mental disorders. Stages of response were documented, with initial anxiety and denial giving way to adoption of a "sick" role and eventual acceptance of rehabilitation. In an illuminating study, Yarrow and colleagues discussed the data from intensive interviews with the wives of a sample of 33 men who had been hospitalized because of mental illness. The accounts of the fear of detection are graphic:

> I live in a horror—a perfect horror—that some people will make a crack to Jim [the son], and suppose that after George [the husband] gets out [of the hospital] everything is going well and somebody throws it in his face. That would ruin everything. I live in terror of that—a complete terror of that.[48]

The silence and denial of the time period in question are quite evident from these words. A third of the wives developed coping strategies termed "aggressive concealment," attempting to cover up their husbands' hospitalizations to nearly everyone in their social environments, and another third engaged in at least some degree of concealment and secrecy. In terms of relations with in-laws, many of the wives blamed the husband's family members for having caused or elicited the mentally disordered symptoms. Only one member of the sample had engaged in any meaningful conversation with her children about their father's mental disorder, revealing the silence within which most offspring were growing up regarding their father's hospitalization.[49]

Psychodynamic models were in ascendancy at this time, and family systems perspectives were gaining credence; both emphasized familial origins for all forms of mental disturbance. Little wonder, then, that guilt and shame were common, particularly for parents with respect to their offspring's mental disorders. Families of this era also sensed their own "marginality"—that is, the fact that they had few resources available to help their relative's plight, as well as their own.[50]

Changes occurred during the 1970s and 1980s with the advent of modern-day biological perspectives on mental disorder. Parents and relatives were now seen as reactors and responders to the relative's mental disorder rather than as causal agents—except, perhaps, for the genes they had transmitted to their offspring. Because institutionalization rates were plummeting, families were confronted with questions of how to support their offspring or other relatives in the community. E. Fuller Torrey describes the resultant scenario with respect to family strain:

> Imagine what it would be like to have a member of your family afflicted with a condition whose sufferers, whenever the condition is depicted on television, are portrayed as violent 73% of the time, and homicidal 23% of the time. Imagine what it would be like to have your neighbors afraid to come to your house, and your children ashamed to bring their closest friends home to visit. Imagine your relatives obliquely talking about your ill family member, unmistakably implying that your side of the family is guilty of something akin to original sin.[51]

Investigators were by this point documenting the kinds of problems family members experienced: first, *objective burden*, constituting caregiving tasks, financial costs, and barriers to obtaining resources; and second, *subjective burden,* involving the emotional distress that results from having a relative with a mental disorder. Despite the importance of objective burden, subjective burden emerged as even more problematic, in particular the embarrassment and shame associated with the relative's norm-violating behaviors.[52]

Lefley has been a key figure in the research effort to document family burden. In a summary of research through the early 1990s, she stated the following:

> In many cases mental illness in the family jeopardizes relationships with friends and neighbors; in extreme situations it may lead to an almost total social isolation of the family unit. . . . Emotional reactions to major mental illness in a family member frequently include bewilderment, fear, denial, self-blame, sorrow, grieving, and empathic suffering. . . . The added perception of stigma may elicit rage and resentment or intensify depression and social withdrawal. Normative ambivalence toward mentally ill loved ones—the typical swing between exasperation provoked by the patient's behavior, guilt at the reaction, and sorrow evoked by the patient's suffering—may be exacerbated by social stigmatization of families.[53]

Comprising a mixture of clinical impressions and systematic surveys, empirical data continued to document the isolation and confusion experienced by family members.

Wahl and Harman conducted a large-scale survey during the 1980s, sampling 487 family members who were chiefly mothers of young adults with serious mental illness, recruited through NAMI. The data revealed that the vast majority perceived stigma to have been a major issue for their relative, particularly in the domains of self-esteem, friendship, and employment success. The caregivers also believed that negative media characterizations of mental illness, as well as societal epithets and jokes, were major contributors to stigma. Among a list of eight potential coping resources for combating stigma, the respondents ranked the act of talking with mental health professionals as the least helpful alternative. Indeed, although mental health professionals were not universally viewed as harmful, they were "often perceived as adding to the stigma that troubles families."[54] Although the recruitment of the sample from an advocacy group probably involved self-selection for active relatives who were sensitive to stigmatization, the data lead to questions about the role of mental health professionals as sources of stigma (see below).

What is the magnitude of family burden? In a telling comparison, Struening and colleagues documented that the subjective burden of those caring for seriously mentally disordered relatives was equivalent to the burden of having a homeless relative and stronger than that associated with having a relative with multiple sclerosis. The burdens of caregivers may translate into marked stress, in addition to anxiety, depression, and shame. Siblings of adults who suffer from serious forms of mental disorder also carry a great deal of subjective burden, comparable to the levels that parents experience. Interestingly, greater levels of "felt stigma" have been reported by families with higher educational levels than by those from lower socioeconomic strata, perhaps reflecting such families' increased expectations for their offspring. The clear majority of caregivers believe that most people in society devalue persons with mental illness, and nearly all of them sense that society devalues family members as well.[55]

Stigmatization is not limited to family members of persons with the most severe forms of mental illness. A sample of parents of children with high-functioning autism (i.e., those with age-appropriate language and intellectual skills but clear social deficits) reported experiencing strong amounts of both (a) hostility and rejection from others and (b) embarrassment and fear in themselves. Even though the behavioral problems of their offspring youth were not, by definition, as severe as those of children with the usual forms of autistic disorder, these parents received clear disapproval from members of the community in relation to their children's lack of appropriate communication and occasionally erratic or aggressive behavior.[56] Much remains to be learned about the stigmatization experienced by parents of children with a broad range of mental and developmental disorders.

Family burden and perceived stigma are not restricted to the United States. In Sweden, a majority of relatives of persons with mental disorder perceived "stigma by association," with 18% admitting that they thought, at times, that the mentally disordered relative would be better off dead. In Chinese society a high degree of shame and embarrassment accompanies familial mental illness, and the burden of the illness tarnishes family honor and the ancestral lineage. In fact, siblings of an individual with a mental illness may be considered ineligible as marital partners. Also, 60% of Chinese family members of adults with schizophrenia stated that stigma had moderate-to-severe effects on the afflicted person's life. Such effects were stronger for patients with serious levels of pathology and in families with high levels of negative emotion regarding the relative with schizophrenia. They were also higher in families with more education, paralleling the situation in the United States. In recent investigations, stigma was also strongly perceived by caregivers in Ethiopia, Nigeria, and India.[57]

In the United States, Tessler and Gamache undertook two longitudinal investigations of working-class family members who frequently interacted with their seriously mentally disordered relatives, typically diagnosed with schizophrenia, depression, or bipolar disorder. This account documented that, although the objective burden associated with providing home care was difficult, the degree of subjective burden (e.g., coping with the disturbing and embarrassing behaviors of relatives in the community) was even stronger.[58] Moreover, family burden may include tangible costs for the relatives in question. In fact, Perlick and colleagues recently found that the burden experienced by families of individuals with bipolar disorder predicted worse outcomes in the offspring more than a year later; this effect of high family burden was carried, in part, by reduced medication adherence during treatment.[59] In their review of family stigma, Corrigan and Miller make the important point that, beyond the blame typically assigned to parents for having caused mental illness in their offspring, siblings and spouses may also receive blame for failing to ensure treatment compliance in their relatives or partners. Furthermore, the offspring of parents with mental disorders may become wary of their own risk for mental illness, a process referred to as fear of contamination.[60]

Mental Health Professionals

An initial issue is the status of mental health professionals among the general public. Such professionals are less highly valued and more negatively appraised by members of society than are other health-care personnel, as originally documented by Nunnally in the 1950s and 1960s. The situation does not appear to have appreciably improved in the last 50 years.[61] With such low status and with the often-difficult task of treating patients who display difficult emotional and behavioral patterns, considerable stress may attend to this role.

Still, on the face of it, this whole topic might seem unusual: Wouldn't mental health workers and professionals, who have selected careers to aid those with mental disorders, be expected to hold positive attitudes and hopeful expectations regarding those with whom they are working? The limited evidence available reveals, unfortunately, that such is not always the case. As found through the large survey of Wahl in the late 1990s, cited earlier in this chapter, families tend to perceive mental health professionals as adding to, rather than eliminating, stigmatizing attitudes and practices.

In the 1950s, Nunnally's groundbreaking research included a survey of several hundred general medical practitioners. Although these doctors had reasonably good knowledge of mental disorder, their attitudes were as negative toward mental illness as those of general community respondents. Indeed, on semantic differential measures, the medical professionals described the term "psychotic" as ineffective, twisted, dangerous, and dirty. Because the majority of professional contacts for those with mental disorder emanate from general practitioners rather than specialists (e.g., psychologists or psychiatrists), such stigmatization may be widely felt.

In work from the 1960s, the most ambitious period of empirical research on professional attitudes, the majority of investigations appraised the attitudes of different categories of mental health workers, typically those still employed in large treatment facilities and mental hospitals.[62] Overall trends indicated that employees in lower status positions (e.g., psychiatric aides or technicians) showed the most authoritarian and pessimistic attitudes, which may have reflected their lower socioeconomic status in general, whereas professional-level staff were generally more optimistic and humanitarian. Furthermore, such attitudes of authoritarianism or benevolence were associated with worse patient outcomes.[63]

As mental health care shifted from institutional to community care, empirical investigations of the attitudes of mental health staff personnel became less frequent. Still, a pattern of stereotypic beliefs and stigmatizing attitudes continued to be noted. For example, the staff of a Veterans Administration facility ascribed a host of negative traits, including apathy, hostility, immaturity, self-ishness, and aloofness, to persons branded as psychiatric patients as opposed to general medical patients. As recently as 2002, it was found in London that half of the medical students and physicians surveyed held beliefs in the dangerousness and unpredictability of people with schizophrenia and drug/alcohol problems. In Switzerland, a recent report indicates that psychiatrists are just as likely as the general population to desire social distance from persons with schizophrenia.[64] Although the actual prevalence of such attitudes and practices among practitioners is not known, even a small number of instances is too many.

Children and Stigma

Do children and adolescents with mental illness receive stigma? As social perceivers, when do children develop knowledge of mental illness, and how early might stigmatizing attitudes and practices emerge? What are the effects of family stigma on children whose parents have mental disorders? Although all too little is known about these important developmental topics, I briefly review the limited information that exists.

Labeling Effects

Several investigations have revealed negative effects of child and adolescent labels. For example, when adolescents are adjudicated and labeled as delinquent, a number of processes are set in motion (negative expectancies, court procedures) that accentuate, rather than relieve, deviance processes. This phenomenon exemplifies secondary labeling theory (see Chapter 2): The labels do not create the initial delinquency, but, once set in motion, labeling can propel a worse course. Being labeled as sexually abused may also have negative consequences for youth. Such effects of labels extend downward in age, as experimental research indicates that labeling of infants as "cocaine exposed" or "depressed" produces pejorative ratings of the babies by observers or even parents.[65]

On the other hand, appropriate diagnosis and labeling can produce positive effects. If diagnosis leads to responsive treatment, empowerment for youth and their families may result, through reduction of guilt and the provision of a hopeful intervention plan.[66] To the extent that society exhibits less stigmatization of mental illness in the future, accurate diagnosis may yield even greater benefits.

Regarding the responses of peers to labels, two key investigations are noteworthy. First, Gillmore and Farina performed an experimental study in which fifth- and eighth-grade boys individually interacted with a peer, who was actually a confederate of the experimenter. Prior to the interaction, the partner had been described as an ordinary child, an emotionally disturbed child, or a mentally retarded child. The research participants expressed desire for greater social distance from the labeled children, in contrast to the ordinary child. During the interaction, they also behaved in a less friendly and more negative fashion to the labeled boys.[67]

Second, Harris and colleagues performed a study in which elementary-school-aged children interacted with an age-mate. The manipulated variables were the *actual* diagnosis of the peer (ADHD versus non-ADHD) and the child's *expectation* for the partner's behavior (i.e., the framing of the partner as having a "behavior problem" or no label). Both variables negatively influenced the child's response to the peer, with the labeling effect suggesting strongly that stigma processes may be at work during middle childhood.[68] In all, messages about "emotional disturbance" and about conditions such as ADHD clearly filter down to children and adolescents; much more remains to be learned about their effects.

Children as Perceivers

In the small literature that has emerged on the development of children's views on mental illness, one finding is that children have more difficulty recognizing other youth as having mental disorders than they do in comprehending that adults can have such difficulties. There is also evidence for general age trends: Children's accurate knowledge of mental disturbance grows during the period from early childhood through adolescence. In addition, from ages 5 through 12, children are increasingly likely to claim that internal, psychological problems (and not just overt problem behaviors) are appropriate to treat. Still, negative attitudes are rampant. Even children aged 7–9 years attribute negative qualities to neutral behaviors that receive a label of mental illness.[69] Furthermore, in one of the few longitudinal studies in the field, it was found that desired social distance from a "crazy person" increased rather than decreased from childhood through adolescence. By the eighth grade, the crazy person label had replaced "convict" as the least acceptable category.[70] Although knowledge of mental disturbance increases throughout childhood, stigmatizing attitudes appear to intensify during this age span.

By adolescence, stigmatizing attitudes have solidified. The Annenberg Public Policy Center of the University of Pennsylvania performed a random telephone dialing procedure to sample 900 youths and young adults aged 14–22 years. Although the vast majority of participants showed good knowledge of the four conditions of depression, bipolar disorder, schizophrenia, and eating disorders, stereotypes were quite prevalent, such that propensities toward violence and low academic performance were ascribed to each condition (with the exception that eating disorders were not linked to violence). Stereotyped views did not differ appreciably as a function of male versus female status of respondents or their educational levels, although adolescents of color were somewhat *less* likely to engage in stereotypic thinking.[71] In short, adolescents hold the same stereotypes and prejudices regarding mental illness as do adults.

On the whole, the stigmatization of mental disorder appears to begin relatively early in development. Considerably more remains to be learned about the processes that fuel such negative attitudes and behaviors, including those that relate to cognitive development and those that emanate from socialization experiences (e.g., family communication or exposure to media).[72] All too little is known about the impact of stigma on children and adolescents who have themselves experienced it; a crucial research need is understanding how stigmatizing messages are interpreted and processed by the children who receive them.

Conclusions

What key issues emerge from this review? First, even though public knowledge of mental disturbance has increased over the last half of the twentieth century, attitudes and behavioral responses have not shown parallel improvement and may actually have deteriorated, particularly with respect to the most serious forms of mental disorder. Whereas relatively high proportions of the general public, across social classes, can today identify patterns of disturbed behavior as emanating from mental disorders, such increased recognition does not automatically translate into increased acceptance or reduction of social distance. The association of mental illness with violence and dangerousness plays a major role in this regard, signaling that media portrayals may be a particularly important target for reform. Overall, mental disorder is still ranked at or near the bottom of other conditions or disabilities with respect to public acceptance, and behavioral studies reveal strong tendencies to stigmatize and discriminate against people with mental disorders.

Second, which is more stigmatized: underlying behavior patterns or the label itself? Most of the relevant investigations reveal that, when behavior and labels are directly contrasted, the behavior patterns tend to receive greater stigmatization. Yet when behavior is normative or benign, the effects of labels are strong. Furthermore, when respondents associate labels with expectations of violence or dangerousness, stigmatization is high regardless of accompanying behavior patterns. In all, the labeling of mental disorder is an important aspect of stereotyping, prejudice, discrimination, and stigma. On the other hand, labels in the form of accurate diagnoses can be empowering, bespeaking the complexity of this entire issue.

Third, the relatively recent attempt to brand mental disorder in reductionistic fashion as the product of a genetically caused "brain disorder" may not promote the kinds of benign responses initially expected (see discussion in Chapter 4). Such ascriptions can fuel high degrees of punitiveness toward persons with mental illness. Although reducing moral blame and self-denigration for mental disturbance is a worthy goal, exclusively biomedical attributions may spur notions of chronicity, helplessness, and genetic difference or inferiority.

Fourth, stigma casts a considerable shadow. Negative social messages tend to be internalized by people with mental illness, and the negative effects of stigma appear even when the individual's preexisting symptoms or adjustment levels are taken into account. Family burden is often strong in the face of caring for relatives with mental disorders. Stigma's effects "ripple" not only to afflicted individuals and family members but also to mental health professionals (who are victims of courtesy stigma) and children, who learn to reject mental illness at early ages.

Fifth, several gaps are evident with respect to our understanding of stigma. For one thing, attitudes and behavioral responses toward mental disorder have been investigated almost exclusively for the most severe and psychotic forms of disturbance, such as schizophrenia, bipolar disorder, and major depression. Stigmatization of other types of mental disturbance, particularly those that are less severe in nature, is worth investigating with precision and rigor. Also, much of the current research on perceptions of racial and ethnic groups is based on implicit or covert forms of prejudice, but investigations of the stigmatization of mental disorder have focused almost entirely on overt attitudes. Investigation of deeper levels of stigma is therefore a priority. In short, the degree of hidden, unconscious, implicit biases on the part of the general public regarding mental disorder is almost entirely unknown.

Indeed, the stigmatization of mental disorder may be even more pervasive than portrayed by the results of formal research investigations. I next consider indicators of stigma from a range of everyday practices.

6

Indicators of Stigma From Everyday Life

A paradox emerges in the search for evidence of widely held and shared cultural beliefs and practices. That is, the very pervasiveness of such tendencies may mask attempts to find specific evidence for them. How can this be the case? An intriguing and troubling example is provided by Goldhagen, who wrote a compelling account of German society's intolerance of Jewish individuals before and during the Second World War. In this book *Hitler's Willing Executioners,* he has described just such a perplexing situation regarding the attempt to ascertain the presence of anti-Semitism at that time. Commenting explicitly on the difficulty of inferring prejudiced, even virulently hateful attitudes and beliefs in prewar Germany, Goldhagen states the following:

> A general problem in uncovering lost cultural axioms and cognitive representations of societies . . . is that they are often not articulated as clearly, frequently, or loudly as their importance might suggest. In the words of one student of German attitudes during the Nazi period, "to be an anti-Semite in Hitler's Germany was so commonplace as to go practically unnoticed." Notions fundamental to the dominant worldview and operation of a society, precisely because they are taken for granted, often are not expressed in a manner commensurate with their prominence and significance or when uttered, seen as worthy by others to be noted and recorded.[1]

In other words, pervasive and ingrained cultural beliefs and practices may escape notice precisely because they are so common. As a current example, Goldhagen suggests that pro-democracy attitudes among U.S. citizens would be difficult to document because of their thorough acceptance. It would take a larger-scale view of our society's policies and mores to find conclusive evidence:

> We could scour the utterances, both public and private, the letters, and the diaries of Americans, and . . . we would find comparatively few professions of their democratic temper. Why? Precisely because the views are uncontested, because they are part of the "common sense" of the society. Obviously, we would find that people participate in the institutions of democracy, just as Germans massively complied with and enthusiastically lent support in a variety of ways to the antisemitic institutions, legislation, and policies of their country.[2]

The lesson here is that those who are searching for indicators of prejudice and stigma must examine a culture's underlying messages, which have typically become embedded in everyday practices and which, as a result, may be relatively hidden to casual observation. To uncover their presence requires a fresh look at often-unnoticed indicators.

Language

The very language used in everyday conversations is quite revealing. During the course of an argument about even trivial matters, one participant may ask the other, with respect to statements that appear out of line with the flow or logic of the discussion, "Are you out of your mind?" If the logic is more convoluted, the person may state, "You're insane!" Unpopular ideas are commonly dismissed as "crazy" or "nuts," and outlandish plans are branded as "madness." When individuals say or do things that fail to show foresight or forethought, they are all too commonly called "idiots," "imbeciles," or "morons"—terms from the early part of the twentieth century used to denote various levels of mental retardation.[3]

Other examples abound: "What a deranged idea!" "Are you some kind of lunatic?" "She's more than a little strange—she's psycho." "Those people are really weird . . . mental cases." The ubiquity of such language use is telling: Its frequency of use signals a preoccupation with the rationality of social partners. When a hint of irrationality emerges, perceivers are quick to cast aspersions in the language of mental afflictions. It is tempting to infer a major concern, residing just beneath the surface, with the potential threat to the perceiver's own sense of order, mental stability, and normality. Particularly threatening is the perception that social partners may not be fully and coequally engaged, perhaps invoking the exclusionary module related to violations of social reciprocity or fairness (see Chapter 2) but also conveying a threat to one's own vulnerabilities about rationality and control.

Other linguistic practices are even more graphic. Murderers are "psycho killers," even in popular rock songs. Purveyors of strange ideas are "wacked," and facilities for those with mental illness are "loony bins" or "nut houses." Such language reveals fear, fascination, and ridicule: fear that the affliction could befall the perceiver; morbid fascination with the illicit, mysterious, and dangerous behavior patterns underlying the terms and labels; and ridicule through the baseness of the terms utilized.

Children begin to use variants of such terms at young ages, signaling the pervasiveness of the disparagement of persons with mental disorders. Indeed, pejorative labels of "retard" or "crazy" are among the first terms used by children, even before the start of formal schooling, to downgrade socially rejected peers. Such early learning and early put-downs reveal a concern with mentally disordered behavior even at the time of a child's initial forays into social groups.

Overall, language patterns signal a preoccupation with mental disorder across childhood, adolescence, and adulthood, with a host of terms related to mental illness used to scapegoat and demean those who violate social norms. The sheer number of terms in use, the high level of disparagement they convey, and their early onset during development are all signs of the pervasiveness and automatic nature of the stigmatization of mental illness, as well as the sense of deep threat conveyed by persons showing signs of irrationality or violations of social reciprocity. I am not contending that every utterance to the effect that one had a "crazy day" or that a line of reasoning is "nutty" signals deep stigma. Rather, the ubiquitous nature of language related to mental functioning reveals a preoccupation with mental stability and control, embedded in everyday words and phrases.

Public Media

Perhaps the strongest evidence in modern culture related to the stereotyping and stigmatization of mental disturbance is found in media portrayals of those with mental disorders. Although media depictions of mental disorder have recently begun to be less disparaging than has been the case for many decades, the pervasiveness of distorted media images is a major issue for anyone concerned with stigma.[4]

As he did with respect to public and professional attitudes (see Chapter 5), Nunnally began the trend of examining media accounts. In this work, conducted during the late 1950s and early 1960s, he had coders appraise various forms of media (television, radio, newspapers, magazines) for their portrayals of mental health and mental illness, focusing on the specific contents and the underlying attitudes toward mental disorder they conveyed. The key finding was that media coverage featured extremely stereotypic depictions:

> In particular, media presentations emphasize the bizarre symptoms of the mentally ill. . . . In television dramas, for example, the afflicted often enters the scene staring glassy-eyed, with his mouth widely agape, mumbling

incoherent phrases or laughing uncontrollably. Even in what would be considered the milder disorders . . . the afflicted person is presented as having bizarre facial expressions and actions.[5]

With respect to censorship and regulation of media messages at the time, there was already pressure for broadcast officials and film boards to censor words and terms that might be viewed as pejorative, including "nuts," "idiot," and the like. Although such recognition of the potential for stigma was progressive, people with mental disorders were often shown to be facially disfigured and behaviorally bizarre; the censoring of symbolic terms did not eliminate the inclusion of stereotyped images and themes.[6]

In addition, when coders applied semantic differentials to the content of media images, the negative pole of nearly every adjective pair was found to characterize media accounts of mental disorder. People with psychotic-level disorders, as well as milder disturbances, were portrayed as ignorant, dangerous, dirty, unkind, and unpredictable. Then, as now, film, television, and periodical writers attracted audiences by making characters easily identifiable and larger than life; exaggerating and caricaturing mental disorder were part of the process.[7]

What has been the pattern since that time? Across multiple forms of media, coverage of mental health and mental illness grew sharply in the latter decades of the twentieth century. On television, mental disorders were the most frequently portrayed form of disability during the 1960s and 1970s; during the following decade the inclusion of characters with mental illness on prime time television shows more than doubled. Yet the overwhelming majority of media portrayals continued to emphasize negative stereotypes, bizarre symptoms, and the propensity for violence. Data from the early 1980s essentially replicated Nunnally's findings from a quarter of a century earlier, revealing that depictions of persons with mental disorder were characterized by negative adjectives such as "confused," "unpredictable," and "dangerous." Fully 72% of prime-time portrayals of people with mental disorders featured violent tendencies; nearly one-fourth of adults with mental disorders were depicted as killers. Television also continued to show people with mental disorders as unemployed or as failures in their jobs.[8] By the late 1990s crime and, in particular, violent crime were still ten times more likely to be evidenced by characters with mental disorders than by other adult characters on prime-time programming.[9]

Several years ago Wilson and colleagues investigated the content of children's television programs and cartoons. Nearly half of the programs investigated contained references to mental illness; among major characters so depicted, none had even one admirable quality.[10] Hence, derogatory media-related portrayals of mental disorder begin quite early in children's lives.

Regarding print media, in Canada, newspaper accounts of persons with mental illness overwhelmingly featured coverage of schizophrenia: 77% of the newspaper descriptions over a 7-year period from 1977 through 1984 focused on this disorder, greatly outstripping its actual prevalence. Such accounts stereotypically emphasized the traits of unpredictability, dangerousness, unemployment, and unproductiveness. With respect to United Press International newspaper stories about former mental patients, it was found in the early 1990s that 86% of such features focused on commissions of violent crimes. In addition, stories on dangerous actions of mentally ill individuals were precisely those that tended to become front-page news.[11]

When all of the print media in New Zealand were examined over a prospective, 4-week period, nearly half of the articles referred to "mental illness" quite generally, with no further specification as to diagnostic category. Such global depiction can itself be construed as stereotyping, given that everyone with a mental disorder was lumped together. Over half of the pieces portrayed the mentally disturbed individuals in question as dangerous to others, with nearly that many referring to their criminality. On the other hand, a quarter of the articles had by this time included positive features, such as educational accomplishments, leadership, or human rights activities.[12] Although positive accounts are beginning to emerge in the United States as well, dangerousness and violence still pervade media coverage of persons with mental disorder, conveying the message that they are perpetrators rather than victims, although the latter is far more likely to be the case.[13]

Several issues are salient. First, do media portrayals really matter—that is, do they truly influence public opinions, attitudes, and behaviors? The general assumption would certainly be that exposure to media can sway public opinion; indeed, advertising would not be the multibillion dollar industry that it is unless there were strong belief that media exposure affects consumer attitudes and behavior. Yet relatively little research has tackled the specific question of whether negative portrayals of mental disorder predict stigma. A correlational study did reveal that, among college-age individuals who reported gaining their primary information about mental illness through television, there was a clear association between the number of hours of television watched each week and the extent of their intolerant and stigmatizing attitudes.[14] Although correlation does not imply causation, this linkage is provocative.

Experimental investigations have also revealed, at least in the short term, negative effects of stereotyped depictions. For instance, a television movie depicting homicidal violence on the part of a mental patient who had received a day pass from the hospital promoted negative audience attitudes on a well-validated scale; after seeing this film, viewers tended to reject community placements for persons with mental illness. Even when a narrated "trailer" accompanied the film, pointing out that violence is not characteristic of most persons with mental disorder, attitudes remained unchanged following the viewing.[15] Images matter, and they are unlikely to be outweighed by factual information.

Second, how graphic are messages conveyed by the media? The infamous *New York Post* has featured, within the past decade, a barrage of banner headlines related to stories of mentally ill people committing violent crimes in New

York (e.g., "GET THE VIOLENT CRAZIES OFF OUR STREETS," along with an accompanying two-page editorial titled "Hospitalize the Deranged"). Wahl's classic book, *Media Madness,* shows magazine advertisements as well. For example, John Deere showed "the world's first schizophrenic lawnmower"—that is, one with three different functions. Such a depiction is not only demeaning but also ignorant, betraying the common misconception that schizophrenia is equivalent to a "split" or multiple personality. In addition, news stories often present the most lurid of psychiatric symptoms as representative of all forms of mental disturbance, serving to brand the entire population of individuals with mental disorders in stereotypic fashion.[16]

The internet contains increasing numbers of references to and chat rooms about mental disorders, some of which are laden with valuable information laden but many of which contain pejorative, stereotypic information, including ridicule. For example, in recent years Netscape has featured on its homepage (or links emanating from the homepage, in the "Fun and Games" section) an "Insanity Calculator" to determine the answer to the question "How crazy are you?" If a respondent answers yes to questions such as "Have you ever played a record backward looking for hidden messages?" or "Do you ever talk in silly voices when alone?" instructions present a calculation as to the "percentage of your brain that's insane."

Relatively recently, media personalities have begun to reveal their own experiences with mental illness. For example, *Larry King Live* has featured disclosures by television personalities and entertainers including Mike Wallace, Ashley Judd, and Art Buchwald with regard to their mental disorders. Terry Bradshaw, the quarterback for the four-time Super Bowl champion Pittsburgh Steelers, has divulged his lifelong struggles with serious depression, both in print and on HBO's *Real Sports.* As noted in the introduction to this book, Jane Pauley and Brooke Shields have written autobiographical works pertaining to their own experiences with bipolar disorder and severe, postpartum depression, respectively.[17] Although various forms of mental illness still lack the kinds of "star power" that bring publicity and funding to other diseases and disorders (for example, Michael J. Fox and Muhammed Ali with respect to Parkinson's disease), public disclosures are beginning to emerge. These may serve both to normalize mental disorder and to raise its regard through linkages with celebrities and sports heroes. Still, the overall picture is discouraging, as public media continue to portray mental disorder in globalized, stereotypic, and negative fashion. Because little is known about the mechanisms by which media depictions foster stigmatization, this entire area is ripe for further analysis.[18]

Attitudes and Practices of Mental Health Professionals

Anecdotal, narrative, and survey evidence reveals that those entrusted with the care and treatment of mental illness can themselves display stigmatizing attitudes and practices. Although the extent of such practices is unknown, the topic is worth exploring.

To provide historical context, I note that large state mental hospitals dominated mental health care for more than a century, from the mid-1800s through the 1950s (see Chapter 4). Goffman's classic accounting of such "total institutions" emphasized their practices of systematically stripping the inmates of their personal identity from the moment of entering the facility (e.g., giving up personal clothing for institutional garb) to the mass schedules of eating, socializing, and sleeping.[19] Stigmatization was overt, in that the institution staff directly forced changes in the patient's appearance and behavior to promote anonymity and control, under the guise of benevolent protection.

Institutional care has been severely curtailed in recent years, and in its wake are a number of community-based alternatives. A few are exemplary facilities, yet others are venues in which neglect and even abuse are daily occurrences.[20] Mental health workers at the latter types of settings, who spend far more time with residents and patients than do professional staff, are typically employed in low-status, low-paying positions. In addition, all levels of mental health staff and professionals are victims of "courtesy stigma," receiving lower status from the general public (and their colleagues as well) than any other health care workers and professionals.[21]

An added indicator is that the health and mental health professions have been extremely slow to accept that mental disorders exist in their own membership. A recent survey reveals that among such professionals receiving any form of mental health treatment, the majority report that they do not disclose this fact to their peers, and many do not even discuss it with their spouses or partners. When such disclosures were in fact made, significant numbers noted ostracism and damage to their professional reputations.[22] The upshot is that stigma exists within the health and mental health fields.

The situation is therefore ripe—via low-prestige jobs, stressful work situations, and denial and shame regarding mental disorder within the field—for mental health staff and professionals to "externalize" and blame their clientele. Such tendencies have doubtless been compounded by prevailing scientific and clinical models, which link mental disorder to both inner weakness and faulty family socialization practices (see Chapter 4).

What are the specific messages to patients and clients? In the words of an individual with severe mental disorder, interviewed as part of the national survey by Wahl:

> What about statements that we got this way through cowardice, or that our illness is just a cover-up for ugly things inside of us or a result of our inability to love another human being? If this is stigma, then many of the things I learned from the mental health system as a child, teen, and young adult would have to be called examples of stigma.[23]

Other accounts from patients and consumers reveal that themes of infantilization, dehumanization, and lowered expectations have characterized the views of some professionals toward people with mental disorder.[24] Wahl asked the 100 participants in the interview subsample of his large survey of adults with serious mental illness to discuss their treatment experiences. A frequent comment pertained to hurtful jokes, as well as more frankly pejorative terms used by mental health workers and professionals with one another—often directly in front of recipients of services, as though the clients were not present— and with clients themselves. In the words of one respondent, a former medical student who described the practices of the teachers who trained the medical trainees:

> Once we were on the wards in the third year of medical school . . . the treatment of psych patients in all rotations was awful. They would laugh at them, poke fun at them on rounds, disbelieve any physical complaint they had. . . . The treatment of suicide attempts was the worst. They would tell them too bad they hadn't succeeded.

From another: "In med. classes, the professors often told jokes and put-downs. Acronyms, such as GOMER (Get Out of My Emergency Room) were taught. . . . My classmates would joke in front of me about antipsychotics, loony tunes, etc."[25] If those responsible for training other mental health professionals are themselves engaged in stigmatizing practices, there are bound to be lasting effects that spread to trainees and patients.

In pondering such practices, I find it tempting to speculate about the kinds of gallows humor employed by those working in pressured, stressful circumstances, who may let off steam and release tension by seeing the light side of their jobs. It is one thing, however, to utilize humor confidentially with a trusted colleague but quite another to provide explicitly derogatory messages to trainees, other professionals, and patients themselves. Even if the tone is less pejorative, mental health workers may still communicate low expectations for their clientele. When this is done, themes of hopelessness are picked up on by recipients of services, who comment frequently on the limits or caps on their potential communicated by professionals.[26] Views of the chronic, intractable nature of mental illness carry with them the sense that mental afflictions are permanent indicators of flawed status.

At the same time, mental health bureaucracy can be frustrating and dehumanizing. Paperwork is daunting, insurance documentation is time consuming and burdensome, and regimentation in the assignment of diagnoses and treatments may foster dehumanization. Even though the authors of *DSM-IV* caution mental health diagnosticians to label the mental disorder itself and not the entire person who suffers from the disorder, there is a tendency to view one's caseload as full of "schizophrenics," "bipolars," "psychotics," or "mental retardates." As I have emphasized repeatedly, if the essential humanity of the person with mental illness is lost, a host of stigmatizing and discriminatory practices will be close behind.

There are numerous clinicians and scientists who show the utmost respect for both the field of mental health and the clients who receive services.

Furthermore, doctors and other professionals have, at key points throughout history, been leaders of efforts to humanize care for those with mental afflictions and to destigmatize mental disorder. Both psychotherapeutic interventions and medication treatments are effective for large numbers of people with mental disturbance.[27] It is difficult to assert, with any accuracy, the frequency of pejorative and stigmatizing messages from mental health workers and professionals, as opposed to the presence of helpful, respectful attitudes and practices. Yet even a small percentage translates into many thousands of such communications per year, and evidence from existing reports and interviews reveals that such negative messages are, in fact, transmitted.

Policies and Laws

Practices of discrimination provide an essential window on the plight of stigmatized groups.[28] This section features information about discrimination in four crucial domains: housing, employment, insurance coverage for treatment, and legal rights.[29]

(1) *Housing* is a major issue for people with mental illness. Formerly housed (or, more accurately, warehoused) in large institutions, the vast majority of those with severe forms of mental disorder now live in the community. Large numbers undoubtedly reside with parents or other relatives, while others live in semi-independent apartments or halfway houses. Yet many such persons end up homeless. In fact, it is estimated that, overall, nearly a third of homeless individuals have a history of serious mental disorder. Other people with severe mental illnesses come to live in marginal, dangerous, inner-city neighborhoods.[30]

A major part of the problem has to do with the poverty-level existence experienced by many people with serious mental illness. Mental disorders deprive them of motivation and compromise their organizational abilities; they also serve as a tremendous drain on financial resources, given the problems of obtaining and funding treatments. To provide relief for individuals with disabilities, including specified mental disorders and developmental disorders, in the 1970s the federal government established a form of entitlement called Supplemental Security Income (SSI), which provides monthly stipends.

However, in 2002, the average price of a modest one-bedroom apartment in the United States exceeded the entire monthly stipend funded by SSI, which would be expected to cover not only housing but also other life expenses.[31] The cost of housing is therefore simply out of reach of many people with mental illness unless they can become employable and earn living wages.

Beyond economics, recall the experimental work of Page, who showed that if individuals disclose a history of mental disorder or mental hospitalization when seeking an apartment, they incur a great risk of being immediately shut out by the landlord. Securing housing plays a key role with respect to both survival and a sense of integration into the community;[32] yet a combination of discrimination by landlords, poverty, and high prices conspire to render afford-able shelter beyond the scope of many people with mental disorders.

(2) *Unemployment* and *discrimination at the workplace* are also key prob-lems. Rigorous economic analyses recently revealed that each year in the United States between 5 and 6 million individuals with mental disorders lose, fail to seek, or cannot find employment as a consequence of their mental ill-ness. Impoverishment is a common consequence. Although the behavioral and emotional problems and skill deficits of persons with chronic forms of mental disorder clearly contribute to problems with employability, discrimination re-garding employment opportunities is a reality as well. Indeed, a history of men-tal disturbance (and particularly mental hospitalization) makes employers not only reluctant to hire an individual but also prone to demote or dismiss a person if such a history is disclosed.[33] Compounding the problem is that if a recipient of SSI payments finds work beyond menial, low-paying jobs, benefits will be cut or lost. As a result, there is a strong disincentive for SSI recipients to seek employ-ment and clear motivation to fail to report employment opportunities if they be-come available.

The Americans with Disabilities Act (ADA) became federal law in 1990 and stipulated that employers make "reasonable accommodations" to employees with major disabilities, including mental disorders. Such accommodations in-clude instituting flexible or part-time schedules or restructuring job specifica-tions and altering work environments. Informal and formal evidence, however, suggests that such accommodations are frequently not offered or enforced with respect to mental illness. Furthermore, as just noted, disclosing a disability to an employer runs its own risks of incurring termination of employment, so that many choose not to disclose.[34]

Because employment status is linked not only with economic viability but also with self-esteem and perceived quality of life, unemployment and under-employment can fuel a vicious cycle of low standards of living, difficulties with obtaining housing, low self-perceptions, and hopelessness.[35] Additional consequences are important to note: A survey revealed that the majority of se-riously mentally ill individuals living in a city in the western part of the United States have, at most, one hour of daily structured activity. The predominant complaint from them was one of boredom and unemployment, outpacing psychotic symptoms per se as sources of trouble and despair.[36] This sense of idleness, meaninglessness, and lack of contact with the mainstream is often pres-ent for people with mental illness, bespeaking the importance of finding and keeping jobs.

(3) Major barriers exist for persons with mental disorders in the attempt to obtain *health insurance* or to get sufficient benefits if coverage is secured. For those lacking employment, benefits are limited to public assistance, which fea-tures substantial limits on coverage and low access to providers.[37] Such cover-age may reimburse only substandard forms of care—for example, psychothera-pies without an evidence base for efficacy or older formulations of medications that incur substantial side effects.

Even for employed individuals, exclusions often encompass preexisting conditions, which typically include many forms of mental illness. Additionally, mental disorders continue to receive lower rates of reimbursement than do physical illnesses, known as a lack of *parity* for funding of mental health services. This problem fuels the telling statistic that many people with mental illness either do not receive treatment or receive inferior intervention if services are actually secured. Indeed, current figures place estimates for the lack of access to services at up to 50% of those with mental illnesses in the United States.[38]

Although a majority of the states have enacted some type of mental health parity laws, some of these are limited to a small subset of diagnoses, thereby restricting access to treatment for many conditions. In 1996 the U.S. Congress passed the Mental Health Parity Act, but large loopholes exist. Although this legislation eliminated annual and lifetime dollar limits for mental health care in companies with more than 50 employees, many employers placed other restrictions on mental health benefits, such as limiting outpatient visits or the number of days for inpatient care. Furthermore, small to medium-sized businesses are exempt. As a result, needed treatments often do not get reimbursed.[39]

Large numbers of individuals with treatable mental disorders therefore cannot afford the interventions that are available. This problem reverberates throughout additional levels of analysis: Without effective treatment, one may not be able to secure employment; then, without a job, one cannot afford housing. Also, when treatment is lacking, the return of symptoms may fuel further stigmatization, compounded by hopelessness.

Parity is not the only relevant issue in this regard. In many cases individuals and families may be unaware that behavioral and emotional problems are related to a mental disorder. This sheer lack of knowledge contributes to underutilization, compounded by deeply held beliefs that (a) emotions and behaviors are entirely volitional, (b) mental afflictions are signs of weakness, and (c) seeking help is shameful. Alternatively, the realization that one (or one's family member) is suffering from a mental illness may confirm a set of "worst fears," given the pervasiveness of media images and societal views about the personal weakness and faulty parenting associated with mental disorder. This kind of self-stigma may prevent the display of hope and optimism needed to motivate treatment.

(4) The *legal rights* of those with mental disorders are often curtailed. Corrigan and colleagues present information on the civil rights (more particularly, the lack thereof) pertaining to persons with mental disorders. With respect to five crucial rights (voting, holding office, getting married, maintaining child custody, and serving on a jury), up to half of the states in the United States currently restrict one or more of these regarding persons with mental illnesses.[40] Disclosing a history of mental illness may therefore mean that one loses custody of one's children, cannot vote or run for office, or in some cases cannot get married. Overt discrimination with respect to mental illness is not an abstraction but rather a distinct reality.

Furthermore, many states prohibit persons with mental disorders from obtaining or renewing a driver's license. Elimination of driving privileges greatly restricts independence, and such discrimination may also have large effects on self-esteem, family burden, and even employability. Certainly, there are complex issues regarding rights and privileges in these domains. While actively symptomatic with psychosis, for example, some persons might not be able to drive safely. Yet does having a history of depression, bipolar disorder, or an eating disorder inevitably lead to unsafe driving—especially if treatments are in place? The issue here is one of restricting rights for identifiable disabilities rather than labels per se; in the case of mental illness, the label itself has far-reaching impact.

Overall, the assumption that all mental disorders are permanent and untreatable, precluding the possibility of marriage, voting, child custody, jury service, or safe driving, reveals clear stigmatization. It includes an a priori presumption of incompetence.

Additionally, for medical personnel, a history of mental illness can lead to restrictions on, or even denials of, professional licensure. It is once again the label rather than any specific evidence of disability that may cause this denial of professional privilege.[41] Even for highly trained health professionals, a history of mental disorder incurs the assumption that the individual's condition is untreatable, that professional judgment is grossly distorted, and that competent practice is no longer possible. This stance perpetuates silence and denial, as well as a lack of motivation to pursue needed treatment.

Finally, civil and criminal commitment to mental facilities is relevant. In terms of civil commitments, until the past few decades people with mental illness could be involuntarily hospitalized with frightening ease. Typically, a judge's order could be written, based on a single psychiatrist's recommendation, with little recourse for discharge once the individual was admitted. Changes in civil commitment statutes during the 1960s and 1970s have made it far more difficult to place people in a mental hospital against their will and have placed major limitations on the length of the involuntary stays that do occur.

Yet there is concern that the pendulum has swung too far in direction of protection of these rights, such that a number of severely mentally ill individuals, lacking insight into their behavior and often living in squalor, cannot get needed treatment.[42] The sheer numbers of people with mental disorders who are living on the streets, visible to most citizens as pariahs, promote stereotyping and stigma. Finding the optimal balance between unnecessary institutionalization and a lack of access to needed treatments will continue to be a contentious issue. Also, as noted earlier, prisons and jails have become the largest facilities for those with mental illness during recent years, with almost no adequate treatment provided.[43]

As for criminal commitment, individuals can be hospitalized involuntarily if they are deemed "insane" at the time of committing a crime. The nineteenth-century M'Naughten Rule, which still applies in many jurisdictions, holds that insanity is indicated only if the defendant did not know the difference between right and wrong at the time of the crime. This definition is quite restrictive, as even persons with severe psychoses can tell the difference between right and wrong at a cognitive level. Over the past decades, newer formulations have included less-restrictive definitions.[44]

Yet the "release" of individuals from guilt and punishment as a result of mental illness raises hackles in many citizens. The perception that mental disorders—highly stigmatized in the first place—can eliminate imprisonment fuels the perception that mental illness is an excuse or even a faked condition through which guilty individuals can escape responsibility for criminal actions. In some trials arguments occur between expert psychiatric witnesses for the defense versus those for the prosecution about whether the accused is mentally ill. Such legal battles call into question the viability of psychiatric diagnosis; they also raise the specter that mental disorder is being used to perform an end run around responsibility and punishment.

In actuality, the insanity defense is seldom invoked, and its success rate is extremely low.[45] As a result, when persons with legitimate, severe forms of mental disturbance commit crimes, the appropriate use of insanity pleas is not often attempted. The insanity defense serves as a symbol of the ambivalent nature of public opinion toward persons with mental disorder, and its success in several highly publicized cases has served to stigmatize mental illness even further.

Personal and Family Accounts

Realistic, compelling accounts of mental disorder emanate from personal stories of individuals and family members and constitute an important source of information about stigma. As powerful as such accounts can be, however, they have typically been discounted and ignored. From a scientific perspective, there are well-documented limitations to case studies, whether written by clinicians or persons directly affected. Is the subject of the case study truly representative of the population of interest? And what about the many variables that are not controlled? In addition, because persons with mental disorders have been highly devalued, with their very rationality questioned, why would anyone be tempted to believe their personal stories? Until relatively recently, there have been only sporadic examples of personal accounts and narratives that have captured the public imagination sufficiently to motivate change in the mental health system.[46]

Like others from a variety of disciplines, I believe that a key step toward a more complete understanding of human phenomena is active consideration of narrative portrayals. The construction of narrative—integrated stories with beginnings and endings that create meaning for tellers and listeners/readers alike—is a uniquely human activity, through which personal and cultural identities take form. Studying narratives gives a sense of the narrators' personal interpretations of key events, of the variables important to their self-definitions, and of the relation of their actions and perceptions to cultural and historical contexts.[47] In addition, vivid narratives may effectively humanize social issues. More than statistics and facts, life stories engage listeners and readers in a way that can promote empathy and identification. To the extent that personal and family stories can portray the real person behind symptoms and treatments—that is, the individual who struggles and copes, who encounters and fights discrimination, and who experiences both triumphs and setbacks—a different view of mental illness may well emerge.

But are personal constructions generally accurate and believable? Or is much of the motivation behind human behavior beyond conscious, accurate deliberation and recall?[48] And what of the real limitations on self-awareness that characterize many forms of mental illness? Although debate over these issues is contentious, personal accounts may well be optimal sources for information about stigma. In other words, despite the potential for questionable validity of reports from at least some persons with severely disordered thinking patterns (particularly during actively psychotic episodes), to dismiss out of hand the narratives of those with mental disorder is to engage in a priori stigmatization, as though the person is never believable. Narrative accounts clearly must be balanced against other sources of information in order to approach "the truth," but such portrayals can provide essential information with respect to comprehending and humanizing mental disorder and understanding the personal experience of stigma.[49]

In their incisive critique of the concept of stigma, Link and Phelan have decried the absence of the voices and personal experiences of stigmatized individuals in current academic formulations of the concept, prompting scholars to pay attention to the underlying messages from those who are most affected by stigma.[50] In fact, personal accounts have mushroomed in the past several decades.

During the 1960s, a milestone in narrative accounts was the publication of Kaplan's anthology, *The Inner World of Mental Illness,* which focused on the phenomenology of mental disturbance from the perspective of those who were so diagnosed.[51] Isolation, loneliness, and confusion were salient themes from many of these accounts, but separating the symptoms of mental disorder from stigmatization (and its internalization) is not always an easy task. In citing several more recent narratives, I focus on those that feature accounts of stigma.

Personal Accounts

Kathy Cronkite's *Out of the Darkness,* a narrative of overcoming serious depression, contains a specific chapter on stigma. *An Unquiet Mind,* by Kay Redfield Jamison, provides a moving description of her lifelong struggle with bipolar disorder, including years of failing to admit it or receive needed treatment, largely as a function of stigma. William Styron's *Darkness Visible,* which recounts the story of his suicidal depression that emerged at age 60, includes a segment in which his psychiatrist strongly encouraged him to avoid hospitalization because of the stigma involved. In fact, it was only Styron's subsequent decision to admit himself to a hospital that initiated the treatment needed to overcome his life-threatening episode. In the realm of substance abuse, Caroline Knapp's *Drinking: A Love Story* is powerful, elaborating the intricate web of personal myths and societal reactions that foster a lifetime of abusive drinking—and the role of stigma in promoting extensive, pervasive denial. A fine source of brief personal narratives is the regular feature of first-person accounts found in the journal *Schizophrenia Bulletin,* many of which feature vivid descriptions of the stigma associated with this diagnosis.[52]

Esso Leete wrote such a narrative, focusing on stigma. During her first semester in college, she began having perceptual distortions that progressed to hallucinations and severely disordered thinking. Hospitalized, she received a diagnosis of paranoid schizophrenia:

> I was treated with medications and released after a few months. I have since been hospitalized 15 times, the longest hospitalization lasting a year. I have had twice as many doctors. I have had 10 diagnoses (most of them variants of schizophrenia), been prescribed nearly 20 medications, and had almost every kind of therapy imaginable, including four-point restraint and seclusion "therapy," as well as insulin coma therapy concomitant with electroconvulsive therapy (ECT) . . .
>
> It has been my experience that there is nothing more devastating, discrediting, and disabling to an individual recovering from mental illness than stigma. . . . Such a tainted person is seen as unbelievable and therefore, untrustworthy. And persons who cannot be trusted must be feared. . . . You understand stigma firsthand when:

> - You are given insulin coma therapy and ECT without being consulted or informed because your psychiatrist and your family assume you are too ill to understand.
> - Your college refuses to admit you after discharge from the hospital because you now have a history of mental illness.
> - You are denied a driver's license because you are naïve enough to answer their questionnaire truthfully.
> - A general hospital emergency room doctor brusquely explains, after reading in your chart the diagnosis of "residual schizophrenia," that your fever, nausea, and vomiting are "all in your head."
> - Your friends decide they need to develop other relationships on learning of your past troubles and treatment.

Leete goes on to discuss additional experiences with stigma and discrimination, referring to individuals with mental disorder as "us":

Another problem for us is locating housing. Typically, when my halfway house in Denver attempted to build a new facility, neighbors came from far and wide to protest and humiliate us and were successful in opposing our application. In addition, our history of mental illness prevents us from fair hearings in divorce and child custody hearings. Security clearance is virtually impossible. In short, we are literally branded for life.

She is especially concerned with the low expectations voiced by mental health professionals:

I type medical records for a state hospital in Denver as my occupation. . . . It is quite common for psychosocial histories [in reports] to state flatly that "vocational assessment is not warranted now or in the future." How do mental health professionals know that? . . . Instead of working with us to build on our assets and to help us learn coping mechanisms, professionals many times see us as beyond repair and hopeless, not worth expending much time and energy on in terms of treatment.[53]

Overall, Leete's impassioned words make it clear that experiences of stigmatization are extremely salient to people with mental disorders. This account also provides evidence that such persons can present cogent accounts of societal reactions and personal responses.

The 100 individuals in the interview subsample from Wahl's national survey provide vivid accounts of stigmatization. Continuing with the earlier themes on the attitudes of mental health workers and professionals, one interviewee recounted that a counselor told her that her life was a "dirty, four letter word"; another counselor laughed at her when she disclosed her earlier suicidal tendencies. When a different interviewee asked her doctor about medication side effects, the doctor replied with a laugh, "If you go on a shooting spree, be sure you don't come to *this* office."[54] Such demeaning, "joking" responses clearly contribute to stigma; it is hard to imagine a professional responding to cancer or heart disease in similar fashion. These accounts also echo the contention that at least some mental health professionals hold extremely low expectations for persons with mental disorders.

With regard to family shame and rejection, an interviewee stated the following in relation to her initial experiences of mental disorder: "My husband's family completely dropped us. They stopped sending me Christmas cards, stopped sending me birthday cards, stopped coming here. They live an hour and a half away. They haven't been to visit for at least ten years."

Regarding job discrimination, a woman reported the following:

I showed my portfolio [to the president of the company]. I was applying for a design, desktop publishing type position, and they said, "You've got a lot of experience. . . . Why haven't you been hired?" And I said, "Well, because I have an anxiety disorder. . . . It doesn't affect my work. I just can't take the elevator above a certain floor or take public transportation." And there was that kind of visual change in the person. They were basically ready to give me an offer [and then it was] "Well, we'll get in touch with you." And I never heard back from that.[55]

In terms of child custody, a woman with a history of depression who went to court in order to gain custody of her children stated the following:

During that time, I remained stable, worked, and continued medication and therapy. . . . My doctor had testified on my behalf, stating that I should have the children and there was no reason why I shouldn't. As a parent, they had nothing on me except that my kids got too much fast food and soda pop when I was working and going to school at the same time. . . . [My ex-husband] had a history of two DUI's, was arrested for possession of amphetamines . . . and perjured himself twice on the stand. BUT, because I had a history of MENTAL ILLNESS and was treated in a psychiatric unit of a hospital, he was the better parent.[56]

With wide dissemination, such personal portrayals of discrimination may be likely to evoke public sympathy and even outrage. Current attempts to engage the public media in realistic depictions of life struggles could help to outweigh the sensationalistic and stereotyped coverage related to mental illness and violence that still permeate most accounts.

Stigma Related to Disclosure

When individuals make disclosures of their struggles with mental disorder, negative consequences may ensue. For example, following the publication of *An Unquiet Mind*, Kay Jamison remarked on the reactions she received:

As someone who has taught in academic psychiatry departments all of my professional life, and who has also suffered from manic depression since the age of 16, I have been acutely aware of the kinds of jabs and wounding stereotypes that mental illness seems to conjure. Yet it was only when I wrote a book about my illness that I became truly aware of the discrimination and antipathy people face. . . . I received an astonishing number of letters, many of them quite psychotic and frightening, from people who simply hated the mentally ill, or who raved on about the terrible manic depressives they had known. Others told me that I deserved my illness because I had not been a sufficiently devout Christian; yet others said that I had no business writing, teaching, or seeing patients, despite the fact that my illness was well controlled. Several colleagues made it abundantly clear that it would have been best to keep my illness private. Others were obviously embarrassed by my disclosure and appeared to have no idea of what they should say or do in my presence.[57]

The act of disclosing may incur stigma in other ways as well. When Fiona Shaw was publishing her book-length account of her severe, postpartum depression, titled *Out of Me,* her publisher sought legal opinions with regard to her recounting of certain professional interactions:

> I talk in the book of my time in psychiatric hospital, including encounters with psychiatrists. Before the typeset went to proof . . . counsel sent back a list with 25 areas of concern. So, one afternoon I sat round a table with my editor, the in-house lawyer, and others to hammer out changes. . . . I submitted to this with resignation, fighting to keep my argument and the tenor of my exchanges with my doctors, though as keen as my publishers to avoid litigation. Later, while I was putting together this altered version, I heard of someone else in a similar situation. This person had been a cancer patient and had written a book about his plight. He had changed his doctors' names, but there still was one scene his publishers were worried about and which he insisted must not be touched. In order to publish the book with this scene intact, an affidavit was written vouching that the book's descriptions were accurate and true. Had a doctor accused him of defamation, this affidavit, signed by his mother as a witness, could have been used in a court of law.
>
> . . . I phoned my publisher's lawyer. Couldn't we do something similar, I asked, with my husband as witness? Unlike the man's mother, my husband had been present at many of my meetings with my doctors, and could back my account. The answer was no. Why? Because I had been a psychiatric patient. Because in the book I acknowledge that I suffered memory loss, due mainly to electroconvulsive therapy, and also depression. . . . So that was that. Although my memories of events and people have been corroborated by my husband, by friends, even by my hospital notes, I am in a different position from somebody who has had a heart attack or cancer. I am forced to censor more. . . . There is still the feeling that it's somebody's fault if they suffer from mental illness, so they should stay quiet about it. . . . More than a suspicion remains that psychiatrists are able to speak and act with near impunity, while the people they treat find it harder than others to speak publicly about their treatment.[58]

In short, despite the greater awareness and greater openness in the current era, the believability of persons with mental disorder is still lacking.[59]

Stigma, Health Professions, and the Failure to Disclose

Particularly in the medical and mental health professions, there is great shame related to disclosing a history of mental disorder. Over and above the fear that one is succumbing to the disorders one is supposed to be treating—which may yield considerable threat to one's self-image as a healer—colleagues may call into question one's competence and ability to perform clinical work or to do unbiased research. The potential for shame may become paralyzing, with silence and isolation perceived as the only option.

A poignant disclosure in this regard comes from the husband of a neuropsychologist who had taken her own life after years of contending with bipolar disorder. In a letter to friends and colleagues following her death several years ago, he emphasized the severity of her illness and the shame surrounding it, which had led to silence and withdrawal from friends, support, and treatment. The following excerpt, shared with me for this book on the condition of anonymity, is lengthy, but its points deserve attention:

> When we first met and fell in love she was vibrant, creative, beautiful, and full of love and joy. Soon though, it became evident that her emotional lows were deeper and more easily triggered than could be easily understood as normal reactions to adversity. At other times she became impossibly irritable and irrationally angry. . . .
>
> Though over the past several years the manic episodes were successfully controlled, her depression grew much worse. She became unable to experience pleasure, getting through the day was a struggle, and she withdrew from her friends, children, and from me as well. . . . Despite the best efforts of her doctors, our children, and me there had become no way to reach her anymore. . . . Having lost control of her life, she enacted a carefully planned death.
>
> She had spoken of suicide, on and off, for several years but had pledged to not kill herself as recently as 5 days before her death. In her suicide notes to me and to our children she asked forgiveness for having broken her promise. We willingly grant her request because we know that she had been suffering and dying of her disease for the past 15 years.
>
> I trust this is all a surprise for most, if not all, of the recipients of this letter. In truth, she had made a conscious decision to keep her illness a secret. In large part this was due to her fear of being stigmatized and professionally marginalized if her disease was to become known. She was ashamed. As she grew sicker, she had an increasingly strong desire to not divulge the truth to outsiders. She never even discussed it frankly with our children, though they were the only others who weren't on the "outside." In service of the secret we had no social life, and she discouraged contact between me and our former mutual friends who had also been colleagues. By so doing, she lost all sources of support and became terribly isolated. . . .
>
> At the end she rejected ECT because she feared that her recuperative absence from work, and the temporary amnesia, would breach her secret. Pleading with her did no good. She would rather be dead than lose control of her professional identity.

So why should I now share so much of our personal tragedy? There are many reasons. First, I have long known that the secrecy and lies surrounding her illness represented a terrible mistake. I believe that if she had allowed her friends to know more about her and her life that she would have suffered less; and might not have felt impelled to kill herself. . . .

She was always terribly upset that people with neuropsychiatric disorders, like hers, were treated in a prejudicial manner in the health care arena. Now that modern clinical behavioral and neuroscience can actually offer a great deal of help and hope to the psychiatrically ill patient, it is agonizing to see the "ghettoization" of mental health care by the insurance industry. . . . Diagnosis and care of the sickest patients have been largely assigned to the least well trained and most underpaid segments of the health care community. Innumerable administrative and financial barriers to care frighten, dissuade, and discourage access. This happens because of the same shame that killed her. Mentally ill people are routinely derided and blamed for their conditions. . . . To date, there has been inadequate social pressure and political will to change this state of affairs. The mentally ill should have as much access to the finest doctors and technologies as those with cancer, cardiac disease, or epilepsy. She and I had money and expertise enough to obtain care. Most people are inadequately insured for mental health treatment or confined to bargain basement "carved-out," capitated clinics, which have a financial interest in denying care. Most senior psychiatric and psychological clinicians cannot afford to accept meager insurance payments, and clinically oriented psychiatry departments around the country have been decimated. You all know the story.

Although it is almost unthinkable that people in the psychological fields could accede to such silence and denial, the stigma attending to persons in this line of work can produce devastating consequences.

Family Narratives

A growing number of accounts of mental disturbance are appearing from relatives of those who have experienced mental illness. Jay Neugeboren has written poignantly about his experiences with his brother, who since adolescence has suffered from psychosis. Nathaniel Lachenmeyer eloquently describes his falling out with his increasingly paranoid father and his subsequent retracing of his father's last years, which were spent homeless and destitute, plagued by schizophrenia.[60] Both works vividly portray the increasing sense of despair and even hopelessness that characterize their reactions as sibling and son, respectively; they also document the increasing isolation of their brother and father as mental problems persisted and stigma intensified over the years. Other examples convey a wide range of experiences.[61]

Several years ago I undertook a family narrative by publishing *The Years of Silence Are Past: My Father's Life With Bipolar Disorder.*[62] My father, Virgil Hinshaw Jr., was a philosopher with lifelong bipolar disorder, misdiagnosed for 40 years as schizophrenia since his first psychotic episode at age 16. In order to illustrate several points regarding stigma, I present a brief synopsis.

Born in 1919 in LaGrange, Illinois, the fourth of four sons of a missionary mother and a Quaker, Prohibitionist father, Virgil experienced his first major loss at the age of 3, when his mother died suddenly following surgery for an ovarian tumor. After the family moved to the West Coast, settling in California, a second marriage produced two more boys. Strong value was placed on academics and on religious training in the family home, with foreign visitors interested in the Prohibition movement frequent guests. Virgil's stepmother (a former missionary herself) entered into a singular relationship with him, praising his academic and athletic success but also beginning a pattern of ritualized punishments, which entered the realm of abuse.

In 1936, at the age of 16, my father began ruminating about what European visitors had said about Hitler's rise to power and the Nazi domination that would ensue. Sleepless and increasingly irrational, he wandered the streets throughout the night, finally coming home one morning to climb to the roof of the family home and jump to the ground below, with the delusional belief that he could both fly and send a message to the world to stop Hitler. He was subsequently placed in a public mental institution, because the family did not have funds for any kind of private care. During his 6-month hospitalization, often tied to his bed, he heard celestial voices singing in his ears and came to believe that the food was poisoned. Indeed, he refused to eat and lost more than 50 pounds from his muscular frame; the superintendent called in my grandfather to prepare him for his son's likely death. Without any real treatment, Virgil finally remitted: His thinking cleared in the spring, and once released, he returned home and completed his eleventh-grade year in 3 months, earning a 4.0 grade average. Although one doctor noted that he had manic-depressive psychosis, his lasting diagnosis was schizophrenia.

He remained free of episodes throughout his junior college and university days, earning a BA at Stanford and a PhD in philosophy at Princeton, where he studied with Bertrand Russell and interviewed Albert Einstein. Yet, soon after completing his dissertation in 1945—with a deferment from World War II based on his Quaker background and history of mental hospitalization—he experienced a prolonged episode for which he was hospitalized at the infamous Philadelphia State Hospital at Byberry. As mentioned earlier, this institution housed up to 80 men per dorm room and was the model for the novel and film *The Snake Pit.* He received insulin shock therapy; he was also assaulted by fellow inmates. At several points he had the delusion that he was being housed in a concentration camp in Europe.[63] Upon his release half a year later, he applied for academic jobs, accepting a position at Ohio State, where he taught from 1946 until his death in 1995.

He was a brilliant assistant professor. He met his future wife, a graduate student in history, during the late 1940s but failed to tell her much about the more troubled aspects of his past. Indeed, stigmatization and silence were now ingrained in him; the last thing he wanted to disclose was a history of irrationality and mental hospitalization, which were the source of great shame. Following their marriage, my mother's pregnancies served as triggers for major episodes in my father. He received antipsychotic medications, newly available in the 1950s, as well as numerous ECTs, but additional, psychotic-level manias followed.

During the early weeks of an episode in the late 1950s, he became obsessed one evening with a female singer on a television variety show. Experiencing the symptom called "ideas of reference"—in which everyday events take on extremely personalized meanings—he believed that she was communicating messages specifically to him over the airwaves. Growing agitated and obsessed, even though my sister and I were asleep in our bedrooms nearby, he insisted that his wife accompany him to drive 100 miles to the station in Cincinnati so that he might find the singer and communicate more deeply.

My mother is terrified: To Cincinnati, in the car, at this time of night? She knows better than to try and talk him out of such a plan when he has reached this state, as his anger will escalate. So should she let him drive off—and perhaps learn of a fatal accident the next day, given his growing impatience and irrationality? Or should she accompany him to Cincinnati . . . but then what of the children? There is no reasoning with him; he must leave. Thinking fast, she decides to go along, fighting her terror that the children may awaken in the night with no one to look after them. . . . At speeds of over 90 miles per hour, they fly through the night.

Somehow they arrive in Cincinnati after 11:30 P.M., managing to find the TV station from which the show had originated, the huge broadcasting tower providing a beacon. Almost as if in a dream—but if this is a dream, it's fast becoming a nightmare—my father insists on leaving the car to enter the station and find the singer. . . . My mother struggles to maintain her composure, concentrating on reining him in. Will he try to jump the fence? She talks simply and rationally, convincing him that the singer has left and that there is no use in staying. His internal struggle is apparent, but finally he relents, suddenly eager to return home.[64]

Miraculously, they made the return trip without incident; my sister and I had remained asleep, oblivious to the disruption. But what of the uncertainty and the terror? And because of the silence and stigma of the time, nothing was said, even to close relatives, of such incidents. My mother had to fend for herself, revealing the uncertainty, fear, and despair that spouses, partners, and relatives experience when attempting to cope with serious mental disturbance in a family member. Indeed, the term "subjective burden" from the research literature hardly captures what must often be endured.

My father's doctors stated categorically that he must never tell my sister and me about mental illness because "children can't understand." Always compliant with professional orders, he said nothing. Somehow he and my mother hid the worst of his florid episodes from us. His longest hospitalization, which occurred when I was in the third grade, lasted nearly a full year, but nothing was said other than that daddy was resting in California. After his return home, he was a sensitive father, helping to calm me during nighttime awakenings that included fears of sickness and dying, telling me that the miracles of modern medicines would help me live to be 100 years old. Perhaps he was wondering whether any such miracles might ever help him escape his episodes.

Unbeknownst to me at the time, his intellectual prowess was beginning to fade; only the tenure he had received at the university kept him his job following bouts of manic, irrational behavior. Sometimes he suffered from flat depressions, but these never escalated into suicidality. It was only when I began college and returned home on vacations that my father called me into his study, daring to go against medical advice while beginning to disclose his life's story.

My father sits at his large wooden desk near his manual typewriter in this, his sanctuary. . . . He is serious. I can tell that he wants to talk, not just about my year in college but about something more substantial. . . . With rapt attention, I listen, still frightened but quite alert. He begins describing his nighttime journey in Pasadena, at age 16, framing it in terms of his fear of Nazi domination. . . . I am not used to this kind of disclosure from anyone in my family, particularly my father . . . and so it began. Several times each year, at nearly every school break or holiday that I returned home, my father and I would find one or two afternoons to return to the study, close the door, and resume our discussions. These talks signified my coming into adulthood and my awakening to the realities of my father, my family legacy, and my vision of who I was and who I might be in the world.[65]

Following college, I helped to get him accurately diagnosed with bipolar disorder and treated with lithium. Not surprisingly, my own interests had gravitated toward psychology. But the disclosures from my father, on top of years of silence, fueled my own conflict and anxiety, with particular worries about becoming crazy or psychotic. Control became a key theme for me, with any potential for loss of control linked in my mind with the possibility that I might emerge with mental illness. And what of having children—would they be tainted, too? It took a number of years of doubting before I realized that being a father was important to me. The stigma surrounding mental illness, along with realistic fears about one's own risk, can incur great doubts and fears in offspring.

Attending graduate school at UCLA and performing an internship rotation with Kay Redfield Jamison at the Affective Disorders Clinic there, I invited my father for a major conference on mood disorders. Although he enjoyed and learned from the conference, one evening back at home with me:

He describes his enjoyment of Southern California, where he grew up, and the colorful scene at Venice Beach. At one café, where he had eaten some lunch, he describes sitting near several "interesting characters" and tells me that he could immediately tell that some of them had been hospitalized in facilities for mental patients. "When you've been in mental hospitals as much as I have," he explains, "you can spot the psychotics like yourself right away."

I am stunned, not knowing how to respond. Have I heard him correctly? Has he not just attended the elite symposium at UCLA and learned that bipolar disorder is a highly heritable, biologically based condition? Hasn't he "owned" his rediagnosis as a person with this disorder? Apparently, his largely successful treatment with lithium and his book knowledge of manic-depressive illness have failed to put a dent in his underlying self-image: that of "a psychotic," an inmate of hospitals.[66]

This narrative reveals that mental disorder originating in childhood or adolescence may fuel a lifelong sense of unworthiness and self-blame, particularly in a culture that fosters stigmatization of aberrant behavior and promotes silence about a history of mental hospitalization. In fact, in personal journals that my father had written over many years, he revealed his conviction that he was somehow responsible for his episodes. That is, he had internalized the belief that his misbehavior as a child led to his stepmother's punishments, generalizing this view to self-blame for his adult episodes. Yet he also told me, during his latter years, that he would not have traded any of his life experiences, even the terrifying episodes of paranoia and psychosis that marked his episodes and hospitalizations. He remained philosophical to the end, despite a Parkinson-like illness that culminated in his death in 1995 at age 75.

This summary conveys several key points. First, mental disorder is both devastating in its consequences and human in its everyday manifestations. Personal and family accounts are a testament to such reality. The hope is that the humanization of mental disorder through narrative can be an antidote to ignorance and stigma. Second, accuracy in diagnosis and responsiveness of treatments are of paramount importance. Despite advances in so many other fields of medicine, progress in research and clinical endeavors related to mental illness has lagged, largely because of stigmatization of the entire topic. Third, despite stereotypes, even severe mental illness can be accompanied by strength, courage, kindness, and resilience. My father maintained his family and job; his sensitivity as a parent never wavered once he recovered from his episodes. Narrative accounts may convey this essential fact with particular vividness. Fourth, when mental disorder exists in a family, open communication to children in age-appropriate and comprehensible language should prove far superior to silence and denial.[67]

The more that personal and family accounts can bring the realities of mental disturbance to light, the greater the likelihood that mental illness will be humanized and that societal discussion will become part of daily conversation. Shame, silence, and distance promote ignorance and fear, which, in turn, induce even stronger tendencies toward distancing and closed attitudes. On the other hand, sensitive and accurate narratives provide a window on intimately human stories while providing an antidote to stigma. Promoting such narratives is a key objective for all who are interested in reducing the stigmatization of mental illness.

7

Stigma of Mental Illness

An Integration

This chapter synthesizes some of the key concepts presented in the preceding chapters, in an attempt to provide a working model of the stigmatization of mental illness. The main issues addressed are (a) the reasons mental illness is so likely to be stigmatized, even as knowledge and scientific progress accumulate rapidly in our current era, and (b) the kinds of responses that can be expected from those who receive stigmatization because of their mental disorders.

First, however, what is the viability of the stigma concept? Do scientists and policy makers believe that the stigma of mental disorder is real? Has this concept exerted influence over research, thought, and action in research and policy endeavors? To provide answers I present several accounts of the growing recognition of the impact of stigma in relation to mental disorder.

Stigma of Mental Illness: A Viable Concept?

During the past decade a consensus has formed among research and clinical experts, as well as policy and political leaders, that mental disorders are, in fact, highly stigmatized, with far-reaching consequences.[1] Both scientific investigators and social commentators have written about the topic with increasing directness.

Otto Wahl, an expert on media influences and a host of other stigma-related topics, puts it bluntly: "It is still socially acceptable for cartoonists, policymakers, health-care professionals, and the public-at-large to mock, stereotype, avoid, and otherwise denigrate people who experience a mental disorder."[2] That is, despite progress in the effort to eliminate overt bias and prejudice regarding other stigmatized groups, individuals with mental disorders receive regular castigation with impunity, as part of everyday encounters.

Patrick Corrigan and David Penn, influential investigators interested in both the origins of stigma and programs to eliminate it, state the case succinctly: "Stigma's impact on a person's life may be as harmful as the direct effects of the disease."[3] In other words, mental illness causes considerable impairment and suffering, but the stigmatization of people with such disorders brings with it a major set of additional problems and consequences at psychological and structural levels. The dual burden of mental illness and stigma is a formidable hurdle.

At an international conference on stigma and global health, Link and Phelan noted that stigma "plays a major role in shaping public health outcomes by exposing stigmatized persons to health-harmful circumstances, by increasing stress, decreasing coping resources, and by posing a significant health barrier to receiving optimal health care."[4] In short, stigma produces problems in multiple life domains, which combine to limit key life opportunities.[5]

Without my belaboring the point, many influential figures have come to the realization that stigma is a crucial issue for the entire endeavor of mental health care. The contentions of several decades ago—that the stigmatization of mental illness had essentially faded from view and that any pejorative views resulted solely from the severity of the symptoms, with no added or independent damage resulting from stigma processes—have simply not held up under the onslaught of evidence from systematic research and examination of everyday practices in the general culture.

A key indicator that the topic of stigma had "arrived" occurred in 1998, when the eminent medical journal *Lancet* sponsored a special section titled "Stigma of Mental Illness." The articles and commentaries dealt explicitly with the consequences of stigma in relation to mental disorder for individuals, families, and society at large. Publicizing this topic in as established an outlet as *Lancet* was a major sign of professional and scientific recognition of the importance of stigma.

As part of this series, psychiatrist Norman Sartorius made the following statement regarding schizophrenia in particular, which can generalize to all forms of mental illness:

Why then invest in programmes that might change attitudes and improve the acceptance of those with mental illness? Because stigma and discrimination are the most significant obstacles to the development of mental health care and to ensuring a life of quality to people suffering from mental illness. Because there is enough money around to help those with mental illness but it is not available because of the attitude of most decision makers and a large part of the general public toward mental illness and all that surrounds it. Because all other efforts that are undertaken to treat mental illness and rehabilitate people impaired by it are likely to be of little use if we do not make people think about schizophrenia differently, if we cannot ensure that patients and their families do not suffer from discrimination, exclusion and injustice because of their illness.[6]

From this perspective, all important issues pertinent to mental health emanate from the fundamental fact of its stigmatization.

Even the U.S. military is recognizing stigma. In a study published in the prestigious *New England Journal of Medicine,* Hoge and colleagues found that sizable percentages of the U.S. forces sent to the Afghanistan and Iraq conflicts over the past few years have developed mental disorders, in particular depression and posttraumatic stress disorder. Fewer than half, however, sought treatment for these conditions, with fear of stigmatization noted as a primary reason for failing to seek care.[7] This article received major play in the media, alerting the public to the importance of stigma in the armed forces.

International recognition of stigma has increased as well. The global nature of mental illness stigma is evidenced by book volumes and conferences emphasizing worldwide concern with stigma processes.[8] Furthermore, national and international efforts to counter stigma are mounting, revealing a growing consensus that something must be done about this long-standing problem. Given the increasing realization that mental illnesses are among the most debilitating and impairing of all health threats worldwide,[9] stigmatization is a topic for all cultures; no nation or society appears immune to its presence and effects.

Finally, as noted in the introduction to this book, former U.S. Surgeon General David Satcher issued his groundbreaking report on mental illness in 1999, voicing the clear conclusion that stigma was the main barrier to mental health funding and care across the nation. According to the report, the costs are enormous, as stigmatization

reduces patients' access to resources and opportunities (e.g., housing, jobs) and leads to low self-esteem, isolation, and hopelessness. It deters the public from seeking, and wanting to pay for, care. In its most overt and egregious form, stigma results in outright discrimination and abuse. More tragically, it deprives people of their dignity and interferes with their full participation in society.[10]

In combination with the White House Conference on Mental Health of the same year, this report ended a history of official silence about mental disorder and its stigma at the highest levels of government. Official recognition continued with the report of the President's New Freedom Commission on Mental Health in 2003, which decried the deplorable state of fragmented mental health services in the United States and called for fundamental reforms in mental health care.[11]

In short, it is difficult to escape the conclusion that the stigma related to mental disorder has risen to the fore of clinical, professional, scientific, and policy-related attention. Over and above the symptoms and impairments directly related to mental illness, stigma adds a unique and troubling layer of problems for individuals, families, communities, and societies. Key questions, however, are why it continues to be such a vexing aspect of personal and social responses to mental illness and how victims of stigmatization contend with its negative messages and imposed limitations.

Despite the potentially devastating effects of stigma, it would be a mistake to think that stigmatizing responses on the part of the public are incomprehensible. In fact, negative reactions to mental illness are in many respects quite understandable. The varied symptoms mental disorders—social isolation (and other deficits in social interactions), angry outbursts, self-preoccupation, despair, confusion, dysregulated emotions, and (in the case of psychosis) highly irrational behavior patterns—can be extremely off-putting. These behavioral and emotional patterns are difficult to understand and accept, making it unrealistic to contend that social responses to such displays should be uniformly warm and accepting. For family members and close friends, in fact, encountering such behaviors can cause considerable strain; for strangers, interchange may incur an almost automatic tendency to distance oneself. Some aspects of stigmatization may be understood as self-preservation on the part of perceivers.

To guide the ensuing discussion, I present two core principles. First, both the constituent behaviors of many forms of mental disorder and the label itself can signal threat to social observers. The nature of this threat is worth exploring in some depth, given the intensity of stigma phenomena and the pervasive consequences of stigmatization. Second, stigma is relational, formed through messages delivered by perceivers and the responses to those messages from its victims. To understand stigma requires analysis of both components, with the reactions and responses of those who are stigmatized mandating careful analysis.[12]

Mental Illness and Threat to Perceivers

Nature of the Threat

Clear evidence exists that the symptoms of psychosis and mood disturbances, as well as many anxiety disorders and childhood conditions, are present cross-culturally. These syndromes display at least moderately strong genetic risk, which interacts with multiple environmental triggers to induce dysfunction. Mental illness is real, incorporating symptoms, family patterns, correlates, and underlying predispositions that have been scientifically validated and that yield impairment that far transcends terms such as "problems in living" or other euphemisms used by those who deny its existence. These conditions are prevalent enough to affect society broadly. Indeed, the depth of their impact has been captured in investigations such as the Global Burden of Disease, which place mental disorders as the most impairing conditions on earth.[13]

Many of the relevant symptoms are replete with irrationality and unpredictability, particularly when psychosis is present. Psychotic behavior is, in fact, disorganized to an extreme degree; the delusional beliefs, aberrant perceptual experiences, and loss of contact with reality signal an utter loss of control to social perceivers. Other disturbed behaviors may defy decorum and threaten social codes—for example, the perennial checking of the person with obsessive-compulsive disorder, the intense self-absorption characteristic of some cases of depression, the near absence of social awareness among individuals with autism, the impulsivity and disorganization of ADHD, and the angry outbursts that can be associated with mania as well as conduct disorder or some personality disorders. Such behavior patterns disrupt social interactions and produce fear on the part of partners, prompting both curiosity and revulsion. There may also be an element of relief in some observers, who are thankful to have avoided the symptoms or conditions they are observing.

Some forms of threat emanating from mental illness may be overt, to the extent that out-of-control behavioral patterns violate personal space or physical integrity. Other features challenge the perceiver's sense of stability and disrupt perceptions of a predictable and orderly world. Regardless of the particular behaviors encountered, the very term "mental illness" connotes irrationality, chaos, and loss of volitional control, eliciting conditioned responses characterized by stereotypic thinking and fear.[14]

Although responses to symptoms of mental disorder can certainly differ across communities, cultures, and nations, the patterns of behavior characteristic of serious mental illness tend to evoke emotional and behavioral response patterns that are universal. Indeed, the evolutionary account of Kurzban and Leary (Chapter 2) postulates the existence of naturally selected exclusion modules, with (a) social reciprocity violations likely to trigger anger and punishment and (b) fear of contamination or parasitic infestation linked with disgust and banishment of the afflicted individuals. Many forms of mental illness are likely to invoke one or both of these modules, given their norm-breaking nature and, in the case of the most serious conditions, poor social skills, irrationality, and unkempt appearance. Furthermore, as discussed in Chapter 4, reductionistic ascriptions of mental disorder to biogenetic causes may well invoke tribal stigmas related to the victim's fundamentally flawed status and subhumanity, which can result in the harsh responses of exclusion or even extermination.

The key point is that people with mental disorder tend to produce both real threats to perceivers' health and well-being and symbolic threats to their sense of rationality and order. According to the dimensional analysis of Jones and colleagues, the *unpredictability, peril,* and *chronicity* of the disturbance are particularly likely to heighten such threat, over and above automatic reactions to the behavior patterns per se. Media depictions and cultural lore reinforce these images—and serve to provide them to members of society who have not yet encountered mental disturbance, including children.

The symbolic aspects of such threat are particularly important. Specifically, the out-of-control nature of the symptom patterns (or, alternatively, their passivity and despair) may well give rise to perceivers' fears regarding their own abilities to maintain behavioral and emotional control. In other words, seeing individuals who appear to "have lost their mind" via irrational, agitated, despairing, or extremely repetitive behavior may cause observers to question their own abilities to hold it together, diminishing their sense of stability. Such fears have deep roots.

Existential Fears

The provocative work related to terror management theory (TMT) is relevant here. As highlighted in Chapter 2, the basic tenet is that "a substantial proportion of human behavior is directed toward preserving faith in a cultural worldview and securing self-esteem in the service of death transcendence."[15] In other words, humans anticipate their own deaths, and this anticipation induces considerable anxiety and dread. When perceivers are primed with thoughts of mortality, their tendencies to stereotype and discriminate against those in outgroups rise precipitously, as a means of preserving self-esteem and stability and warding off the terror. Such preservation is likely to take place through a number of psychological mechanisms, each of which can uphold stability and permanency: identifying with ingroups, clinging to long-held cultural worldviews, showing stereotyped thinking (which occurs when observers are cognitively overloaded or stressed), and denigrating members of outgroups.

The kinds of stimuli most likely to invoke the reactions characteristic of TMT are those that produce unconscious, indirect threats to one's integrity.[16] In other words, situations or experiences subtly prompting mortality fears engender the strongest attempts to preserve stability—and to promote the harshest reactions against members of outgroups. Both the behaviors underlying mental disorder and the mental illness label are prime candidates for producing just this sort of indirect threat: Their upsetting, nontraditional, and sometimes antisocial and irrational features cause fear and threaten stability and integrity rather than directly broadcasting mortality. In other words, although some characteristics of serious mental disorder may cause a direct threat, it is the indirect and symbolic threat value of irrational, out-of-control, despairing, or otherwise disturbed behavior that may be particularly likely to tap existential fears and precipitate both generalized prejudice and the specific motivation to be rid of the source of the threat. Fear of the unknown can induce deep levels of response.[17]

Overall, the deep levels of symbolic threat posed by mental illness may help to explain the pervasiveness and severity of human responses to it. Mentally disordered behaviors are unsettling and serve as reminders to perceivers of their own tenuous sense of rationality and volition. The worst fear that many people have is of not having full control over mental and emotional faculties. The temptation to distance oneself from the source of such messages can be strong and swift, with tendencies toward punishment not far behind.

Stages of Response

Stangor and Crandall present a three-stage model of stigmatization. In the initial phase, following the types of real or symbolic threat engendered by members of a stigmatized group, perceivers engage in distortions that exaggerate differences between themselves and the stigmatized individuals in question.[18] Such distortions include stereotypes that progress to "us versus them" distinctions, through which group differences are further amplified and prejudice can emerge. In other words, to keep the threat at bay, motivation exists for creating further psychological barriers between the perceiver and the source of the irrational, unexpected behavior. This distancing magnifies the initial threat and promotes the fundamental tendencies for humans to consolidate their identities with ingroups and to differentiate themselves from outgroups.

Second, such deviance-amplifying strategies are likely to progress to the view that the deviant individuals in question are less than human—in other words, that they lack the fundamental qualities of the rest of humanity. Extreme reactions are now expectable, as a review of the human history of responses to racial and ethnic minority groups (as well as people with mental illness) quickly reveals. From such a view, full justification is in place to rid the community (or indeed the world) of the pernicious influence of such persons, for the good of one's ingroup and all of society.

Third, societal communication consolidates the stereotyped and now-feared images of the stigmatized group. Such transmission may occur in terms of general conversation and gossip; in more technologically sophisticated societies, the mass media play a key role in consolidating stereotypes. Threat value is further amplified and magnified through such broadcasting, typically developing into wide cultural consensus about the flaws and moral reprehensiveness of those in stigmatized groups.

In their own theory of stigma in relation to mental disorder, Link and colleagues posit the major phases of (1) labeling of individuals with mental disorder, (2) stereotyping related to the label, (3) separation into "us versus them" categories as a result of the stereotyping, (4) emotional responses on the part of perceivers (e.g., anger, fear, pity, anxiety) and complementary emotional reactions of those who are stigmatized (embarrassment, shame, fear, alienation), and (5) resultant status loss and discrimination.[19] Like that of Stangor and Crandall, this model progresses from the individual processes of labeling and differentiation to social and structural ramifications such as discriminatory policies.

Two key points are worth highlighting. First, the emotional responses of both social perceivers and their targets are core components of the model. In particular, the emotions of disgust, fear, and anger, which are linked closely to avoidance strategies, banishment, and punishment, respectively, are likely to characterize many facets of the public's responses to mental illness. Second, the discriminatory practices constituting the final step of this model will, by definition, promote social inequities, as well as a loss of rights and social standing for persons with mental illness. Yet such structural inequity is itself a trigger for processes related to system justification; it promotes further denigration of the individuals in question. In other words, to the extent that people with mental illness occupy the low rungs of social status and prestige, perceivers are likely to blame them for their own poor standing, keeping intact a sense of the fundamental fairness of society and reinforcing their own hard efforts to maintain rationality. A vicious cycle is now in place, with individual, social, and institutional levels of stigmatization mutually supporting one another.

Social Power

Link and colleagues also emphasize the important role of social power in stigmatization. That is, stigma occurs only when a dominant social group devalues the attributes of a less powerful group. Stereotyping or labeling performed by those low in power typically does not have significant ramifications for those near the top of the chain, psychologically or politically. As a result, stigmatization cannot be separated from the values of powerful constituencies in a given society, who set the tone for the kinds of behaviors and values that are accepted versus those that are threatening.

The positive side of this perspective is that, as ideologies change, traits or behaviors considered inappropriate and unacceptable may shift, with the potential for decreases in prejudice and discrimination. Despite the likely presence of naturally selected modules related to the exclusion of persons exhibiting certain classes of threatening behavior, such modules are particularly likely to be triggered by value judgments made in relation to a given culture's standards. In the future, the predominant view may emerge that certain forms of deviant behavior related to mental illness are not evil, that there are strong (but not exclusive) biological predispositions for their display, and that treatments can and do produce real benefits. Such a perspective has the potential to foster important changes in underlying attitudes. When standards change, stigma may well decrease.

Self-Stigma and Coping Responses

What are the effects of stigmatization on those who experience it? Current formulations emphasize that personal responses are part of a dynamic process of coping, differing across individuals and changing over time.[20]

First, unlike ethnic characteristics or physical disabilities, a history of mental disorder is usually concealable, meaning that the individual in question is likely to face the dilemma of whether to reveal such a history to social partners. Concealable stigmas invoke a great deal of anxiety. During social interactions, there is therefore high potential for preoccupation with potential "leakage" of one's history and possibly the fear that behavioral deviance may emerge. Goffman's original work explicitly discussed the adjustments made by people with concealable stigmas, and more recent formulations continue to point to the difficulties they experience—for example, wondering whether the stigmatized condition will emerge despite attempts to suppress it. In fact, compared to persons with overt stigmas, those with concealable stigmas typically show lower self-esteem, as well as more distress and negative emotion.[21]

Not surprisingly, secrecy and withdrawal are often selected as tactics for contending with concealable stigmas like mental illness, given the status loss, discrimination, and shame that can result from public knowledge of a history of mental disorder. Even though these strategies may preserve self-esteem in the short run, they further isolate the individual from social support. Furthermore, attempts to suppress symptoms and relevant history during a social encounter require great mental effort. People who are engaging in these efforts are likely to be peppered with intrusive thoughts about the concealed attribute in question and to experience high levels of cognitive and physiological activation. The act of suppression may well backfire, fueling discordant interchanges.[22] Even at a dyadic level, the stigmatization of mental disorder can produce intense consequences.

Second, current perspectives highlight the very different responses to shunning and devaluation displayed by people with mental illness. Although research has documented a number of general consequences of stigma—including social rejection, isolation and secrecy, the strong possibility of financial loss, lack of access to fully responsive treatment, and internalized shame[23]—these response tendencies are far from uniform. Models are emerging that analyze the reasons some stigmatized individuals respond with righteous anger, some ignore the prejudice and stigmatization and proceed with their lives, and still others show the classic pattern of internalization of negative messages with resultant damage to self-image. Amidst a host of reasons for such individual differences, Watson and River highlight two: (a) perceptions of the legitimacy of the discrimination received and (b) identification with a like group of stigmatized individuals.[24]

Legitimacy of Feedback and Attributional Ambiguity

Potential victims may hold to the belief that unequal treatment or negative feedback does not reflect their own flawed nature but rather that stigma results from prejudice on the part of perceivers. Because this belief may prevent internalization of negative messages, attributing stigma to the wrong-minded values of the majority would appear to be adaptive. Yet there is a potential cost, as such external attribution provides little motivation for change. That is, if stigma exists solely because of prejudice, why should one pay attention to any social feedback?

This phenomenon is particularly problematic for mental illness. Unlike many other stigmatized conditions, mental illness is a form of disability rather than a physical difference from others. In other words, mental disorders are dysfunctional conditions that merit treatment. If feedback about one's condition is attributed wholly to prejudice or stigma, there may be little motivation to consider intervention. Of course, the other extreme—that of internalizing all negative feedback as resulting from one's personal flaws—is likely to be debilitating, with the potential for the recipient of the message to close off any further communication.

A relevant concept here is *attributional ambiguity*, which refers to the difficulties of knowing how to ascribe negative feedback about a stigmatized condition. In other words, should recipients ascribe such feedback to prejudice in perceivers or to something about themselves?[25] An exclusive attribution to external causes may preserve one's self-image but at the expense of considering needed internal change. On the other hand, ascription solely to internal flaws may promote personal devastation. The ideal resolution, particularly in terms of mental disorder, would be to achieve a balanced perspective, which could include the view that stigma often emanates from prejudice but that at least some aspects of personal feedback may still be useful. Gaining enough perspective to understand how to apportion and balance such attributions is not a simple task.

Group Identification

If members of stigmatized groups become strongly identified with other victimized individuals and particularly if they become invested in working toward social change with the goal of countering stigma, empowerment may emerge. Such strategies have been embraced by racial, ethnic, and sexual minorities, with consequent building of group identity. Until quite recently, however, there has been very little opportunity for such identification with others suffering from mental disorders. People with mental illness have often been isolated, missing out on opportunities for social support because of both the social impairments related to many forms of mental disorder and the lack of solidarity or group identification among those with such conditions.

Self-help and advocacy movements are now part of the landscape for persons with mental illness and their families. One of the explicit purposes of these groups has been to foster social support and shared goals, which may go a long way toward reducing some of the effects of stigmatization. In Chapters 9 and 11 I elaborate on the potential of such involvement to help overcome stigma.

Stereotype Threat and Identity Threat

In the areas of racial and sexual prejudice, much current theorizing about the response of stigmatized individuals emanates from two perspectives in social psychology: stereotype threat and identity threat.[26] Stereotype threat is invoked when (a) a relevant stereotype exists (e.g., women are poor at math) and (b) a performance situation occurs in which the stigmatized person's abilities may be judged in relation to this attribute (e.g., a math test is branded as diagnostic of mental ability). Performance is lowered (controlling for initial test abilities) for stigmatized groups under conditions of such stereotype threat. Whereas relevant research has dealt largely with groups carrying overt stigmas, such as racial minorities and women, and usually in relation to cognitive performance, the applicability of stereotype threat to mental illness, which is largely concealable and invokes a wide range of stereotypes—for example, irrationality, lack of control, and social ineptness—is not known.

The implications are alarming, however. For example, consider the stereotype that mental disorders are inevitably associated with violence, an image highly promoted by the media. It is possible that this stereotype could be activated in situations of conflict, instigating a kind of self-fulfilling prophecy. In other words, in situations earmarked as frustrating, the individuals with mental illness might be so concerned with the violence stereotype that they adopt aggressive or acting-out tendencies out of frustration, thereby confirming it. Social perceivers may inadvertently fuel this tendency through their own expectations for discordant behavior and their own communications of fear or hostility. Although these possibilities are speculative, they constitute an important area for investigation.

Second, under identity threat models, a key assumption is that stigma places its victims at risk not only for poor performance in certain situational contexts but also for denigration of their whole social identities. Several factors are likely to be at work in this regard. For one thing, social representations of different stigmatized groups vary: Some are rather subtle (e.g., the stigma of left-handedness), whereas others are quite blatant (e.g., media depictions of Muslims or of mental illness). Key contextual factors are also relevant. For instance, being placed in a situation with a high percentage of "majority group" members can threaten identity for those in outgroups. In addition, personal characteristics such as stigma consciousness (i.e., the awareness of the stigma that exists in a given culture) and rejection sensitivity (e.g., the expectation of being shunned by others) may greatly fuel the experience of stigmatization.

In identity threat models, stigma victims are conceptualized as active appraisers of both their social worlds and their own capabilities for dealing with discrimination.[27] The ultimate responses of stigmatized individuals will be determined largely by cognitive appraisals, that is, how they construe both the situation and their coping responses. First, stigma may be perceived as either enormous (potentially overwhelming one's identity) or more circumscribed. Second, as for self-appraisals, some people may believe that they can handle a given stressor or threat, whereas others may perceive that they cannot cope at all. If stigma-related threat is believed to be of greater magnitude than one's coping responses, several types of voluntary and involuntary responses are likely to ensue, including lowered self-esteem, decreased achievement, and even compromised physical health. On the other hand, if the threat is viewed as manageable, the situation is likely to be viewed as challenging rather than overwhelming. Here, discrimination and stigma may come to be seen as forces that can and should be overcome, allowing active coping strategies to come to the fore. Yet almost no research has applied such models to mental illness.[28]

One of the most discouraging aspects of the stigmatization of mental illness is its tendency to induce shame, silence, and hopelessness in its victims. Yet self-stigmatization is not inevitable; a range of factors (structural, situational, personal appraisals) may produce the ability to ignore stigmatizing messages or to engage in active, problem-focused coping. Still, as discussed in Chapter 2, the very symptoms and impairments related to mental disorder, which often include low motivation, pessimism, and a lack of an integrated sense of self, mean that active coping will be a real challenge.

Greater or Lesser Stigmatization in the Current Society?

What can be made of findings that serious forms of mental disorder receive even greater stigma than they did a half century ago? If this is indeed the case—in other words, that stigmatization is increasing despite greater public knowledge related to mental illness—what could the relevant factors be?[29]

First, increased urbanization makes displays of deviance salient to greater proportions of the population. More and more of the world is marked by modernization and crowded urban settings; at the same time, policies in many nations have forced the closing of mental hospitals and institutions. Greater proportions of the pubic are therefore exposed to larger numbers of individuals with serious mental illness than ever before. In short, Westernization and urbanization could be associated with decreased tolerance and enhanced stigma simply because of increased exposure to mental disorder.

Second, greater educational levels in many societies, along with the increased skills required by technologically sophisticated jobs, make the educational failure and unemployment often associated with mental disorder more noticeable and more costly than they would be in rural, nontechnical cultures. In other words, factors that thwart upward mobility, such as mental illness, may receive more rather than less stigmatization because of the increasing importance attached to academic and vocational skills in modern societies.

Third, the extensive growth of a middle class may cause a tendency toward standardization of behavior. Middle-class values often emphasize conformity and decorum in behavioral displays; as such, nonconforming behavior may be experienced as particularly deviant and disturbing in technological cultures.

Fourth, mass media reach increasing numbers of people in the current times, particularly in industrialized nations, with rampant promotion of widely stereotyped views of those with mental illness. In cultures with electronic media as a pervasive cultural influence, there are multiple channels through which stereotyped images of mental illness can be spread. These images appear to play a major role with respect to stigma.

Overall, industrialized societies place a premium on technological sophistication, as well as conforming, uniform behavior; they also rely on mass media to portray predominant worldviews and stereotypes. All of these factors may be related to increases rather than decreases in stigmatization. In addition, the exaggerated association between serious mental illness and violence—widely disseminated not only by the media but also by civil commitment statutes in which a key criterion for involuntary hospitalization is "dangerousness"—fuels high levels of stigma. There is no doubt that fighting stigmatization is a particularly daunting challenge in an increasingly Westernized, education-conscious, and technologically sophisticated world.[30]

Indeed, a paradoxical situation now exists. On the one hand, recent scientific and clinical advances, centered mainly in Western nations, have witnessed an unprecedented degree of hope for the provision of effective and responsive treatments for many forms of mental illness. On the other hand, data exist to the effect that the cultures most likely to produce positive outcomes for serious mental disorders such as schizophrenia are certain non-Western, nonindustrialized societies in Africa and Asia. That is, although schizophrenia has a nearly uniform prevalence around the world, some traditional cultures without urbanization appear to produce better long-term outcomes. The societies in question are characterized by an allowance for a period of time in which an individual can display seriously irrational behavior without subsequent penalty and by the existence of vocational and residential opportunities when more normalized behavior patterns reappear.[31]

It is therefore likely that rehabilitating mental illness and fighting stigma will require more than providing modern-day treatments. Also necessary is a fundamental reexamination of the place for behavioral deviance in modern society, as well as practices that can promote a good fit between individuals with disturbed behavior and existing societal institutions.

Attributions of Control Revisited

In terms of the acceptance or rejection of those with mental illness, what is the role of perceivers' beliefs regarding control of and responsibility for deviant behaviors? Because of the importance of this topic, I amplify the discussion of several points made in Chapter 4.

First, much social psychological research suggests that when negative or socially deviant behaviors are thought to be controllable—that is, under the personal responsibility of the person in question—harsh responses are the norm, whereas attributions to noncontrollable and nonresponsible causes produce more benign reactions.[32] Beginning with Hippocrates, many reform efforts have been explicitly based on the contention that mental disorder is a noncontrollable condition of biomedical origin, "a disease like any other." Recent efforts to brand mental illness as brain disease are predicated on just such an attributional shift.

Second, however, it is apparent that harsh stigmatization can apply to attributes that are completely outside of one's personal control. The clearest example pertains to ethnicity and skin color, uncontrollable traits that have nonetheless evoked extremely harsh prejudice and stigma throughout history. It is naïve to think that uncontrollable "problems" or stigmas are automatically or routinely viewed in benign terms.

Third, when disturbed behavior is the topic, the nearly reflexive distancing on the part of perceivers may precede and override attributional accounts. Some types of threatening behavior patterns may incur automatic revulsion, and many emotional responses do not require cognitive explanations or inferences to be triggered.[33] Attributional models of stigmatization may be of secondary importance regarding mental illness, in that many responses emerge before attributions are even invoked.

Fourth, throughout history explanations for mental disturbance have contained complex blends of causal factors. For example, in demonologic accounts the individual's possession was held responsible for the behavioral aberration, but it was also believed that personal weakness or lack of faith led to the risk for such possession. People with disturbed behavior often find themselves in "double jeopardy" from an attributional perspective, with external, noncontrollable causes for deviant actions believed to emanate from internal, controllable flaws or weaknesses. Even naturalistic accounts, through which mental disorder is held to result from disease processes, can become tinged with controllable ascriptions when the symptoms are mysterious or threatening: "Unstable" or "weak" character traits may be perceived as underlying the development of symptoms.[34]

Fifth, we are now in a period of renewed interest in biomedical, brain-disease, and genetic models of mental illness, which promote the ascription of behavioral deviance largely or entirely to noncontrollable causes. These models are not always an easy sell, given the pervasive view that behavior and affect are a function of volition and personal control. But when perceivers *do* come to believe in biomedical/genetic ascriptions, accepting the proposition that abnormal behavior is a manifestation of faulty genes and/or neurochemical abnormalities, this shift in perspective may promote the belief that there is little, if anything, the individual can do to alter these behavioral and emotional problems, now presumed to be immutable and lifelong. Such an essentialist belief is likely to incur pessimism and even despair, linked to perceptions of chronicity and fundamental difference.

This perspective may also promote the conviction that the person in question is genetically inferior and flawed. To the extent that the condition is believed to reflect the exclusive product of aberrant genes, the perception may emerge that the sufferer is qualitatively distinct from the rest of humanity, akin to belonging to a foreign, subhuman tribe or nationality. As a result, the extremely harsh and even exploitative responses associated with tribal stigmas may come to the fore. In fact, experimental evidence suggests that when deviant behavior is ascribed to genetic/biomedical abnormalities, as opposed to psychosocial influences, punishment increases.[35]

The actual state of affairs is neither black nor white. As I noted earlier, some evidence exists that attributing mental illness to biomedical causes can reduce blame and decrease social distance, at least with respect to overtly expressed attitudes. But other research on this topic points to the conclusion that these attributions are no panacea for stigma reduction, given that exclusively biomedical causal models can potentially foster a view of the individual as tainted and flawed. On a mass scale, negative eugenics models, which emphasize the genetic inferiority of certain classes of people (such as those with mental illness), can lead to policies of forced sterilization, which occurred widely in the United States during the early decades of the twentieth century, or genocide, as they did in Nazi Germany.

Recent survey data reveal that the general public holds multidimensional views of the causation of mental illness, blending life stresses and biological factors as risk factors.[36] It may be the case that *exclusively* biogenetic attributions underlie punitive social responses to mental illness. In other words, if mental disorders are the sole product of defective genes, there is little humanity left. A parallel exists with respect to former views positing that mental illness was solely the result of faulty parenting, which prompted the extreme stigmatization of family members. The moral is this: Reductionistic views that isolate, stereotype, blame, and dehumanize persons with mental disorders or their relatives are inherently stigmatizing.

Two sets of beliefs appear crucial for positive responses. One is the concept that mental disorder comprises underlying psychobiological risk that is fueled by responses to difficult life events and shaped (but not directly caused) by families and environments. In other words, mental illness has biological roots, but personal and social factors are still important in forming the symptom picture. The second is the view that despite the biological and even genetic risk for serious mental illness, efforts from the individual and family are still crucial in shaping ultimate outcome—and in effecting meaningful change. That is, personal and family *blame* for the origins of mental illness should be minimized, but at the same time personal and family *responsibility* for obtaining treatment is critically important. This message can be difficult to convey in an era that calls for single, simple sound bites as answers to complex questions.[37]

Less Severe Forms of Mental Disorder?

Many forms of mental disturbance are not as disruptive, threatening, and irrational as schizophrenia, serious depression and bipolar disorder, agoraphobia, obsessive-compulsive disorder, autism, and severe eating disorders, to name several of the most striking examples. The question is whether the arguments raised in these pages are relevant for mild or moderate forms of mental disorder, such as learning disorders, phobias, and relatively mild attention problems.[38]

For one thing, current diagnostic systems have come to encompass many different types of mental disturbance that were formerly viewed as part of human variability or as problems in living. The terms "mental disorder" and "mental illness" now apply to such behavioral and emotional concerns. Because these labels are associated with stereotypes, deviant behavior may be stigmatized whenever the mental illness label is invoked, regardless of the specific form of the underlying behavior. Recall from Chapter 5 that the effects of "mental illness" labels are strongest when they are associated with *normal-level* behavior patterns or with *mild* disturbance. Furthermore, labeling is particularly likely to trigger extremes of distancing and castigation when the perceiver believes that mental disorder connotes violence and danger.[39] If members of society have internalized the view that people with mental illness are inevitably violent or morally deficient, the label is likely to trigger a chain of stereotypes, even if the behavior patterns in question are not at the extremes of severity.

There are other consequences of the widening scope of mental disorder. For example, it goes against the grain to think that a quarter or more of the current population now suffers from a mental disorder—or that the lifetime risk is nearly half.[40] A growing view, in fact, is that the pharmaceutical industry is pushing an agenda to lower the thresholds for diagnosis and treatment of a large number of physical and mental disorders in order to maximize profits. The resulting tendency, serving as a kind of backlash, may be for the public to disbelieve in the reality of *any* forms of mental illness.[41] The sheer amount of problem behavior that now falls under the rubric of "mentally disturbed" challenges the validity even well-established forms of disturbance.

On the one hand, the increased numbers of persons diagnosable with a mental illness could reduce stigma, as more and more individuals self-identify as having a range of conditions falling under this rubric—and as psychotherapy and medication treatments become more widespread. Indeed, the potential for stigma reduction as a function of increasing acceptance of beneficial treatments should not be overlooked. On the other hand, there is potential for the trivialization of mental illness if the boundaries are stretched too far, prompting doubt as to the viability of any form of mental disorder. In terms of stigma, the gap appears to be growing between those less severely afflicted people who voluntarily select treatment for self-enhancement versus those more severely affected persons with behavior patterns marked by serious irrationality and the need for restrictive or coercive treatments. The most severe forms of mental illness, already the subject of major stigma, may be at further risk when biogenetic ascriptions are emphasized to the exclusion of other contributory factors.

Still, less severe variants of mental disorder may incur substantial stigma precisely because they are not as clearly noticeable or irrational as other forms of disturbance. In other words, if certain people look, act, and seem "normal" much of the time but show problems in particular situations (e.g., specific objects or settings for those with phobias; social encounters for those with high-functioning autism), the attribution may emerge that they are willfully acting out during those times and that they—or their parents, in the case of children or adolescents—are exerting insufficient control and restraint. The sporadic, situational presentation of the symptoms and the lack of immediate recognition that the individual is pervasively disturbed could engender higher expectations and a consequent increase in stigma when deviance does emerge. All too little is known about this set of issues.

Closing Points

First, schema formation and at least some degree of stereotyping are bound to occur in any social groups, given the ubiquity of social cognitive processes (including categorization and stereotyping) and the pervasive nature of ingroup identification. At the same time, it is not inevitable that such automatic responses will be translated into deep prejudice, extreme discrimination, or views of the subhuman status of those with mental illness. In other words, it is a mistake to conflate normal social cognitive processes of categorization and stereotype formation with the belief that mental illness is unchangeable and inevitably flawed. Chapters 9, 10, and 11 directly tackle the issue of how to combat the stigmatization of mental illness, under the explicit assumption that humans can become aware of and modify their tendencies to show bias and prejudice.

Second, because mental illness stigma is not likely to vanish overnight, perspectives on self-stigmatization are essential to keep in mind. Specifically, when conditions and traits linked to mental illness receive social disapproval and structural discrimination, consequences such as shame, humiliation, and decreased self-worth on the part of recipients are likely—but not universal or impossible to overcome. Much remains to be learned about the processes that fuel positive coping rather than despair on the part of those with mental illness.

Models of the stigmatization of mental illness should grow in sophistication in the years ahead. The brief synthesis in this chapter may provide starting points for such future formulations.

8

Research Directions and Priorities

In many of the previous chapters I have indicated gaps in knowledge about the stigmatization of mental disorder. My aim here is to suggest directions for future research, which may be of use to the next generation of investigators.

Measurement and Appraisal of Stigma

This large topic deals with issues such as basic definitions of stigma in relation to mental disorder, knowledge-attitude-behavior distinctions regarding measurement, and explicit versus implicit forms of stigma. At the outset, I highlight the scholarly review of Link and colleagues on the topic of measurement of stigma related to mental illness.[1] I cannot hope to recapitulate the many points made in this authoritative article; rather, my objective is to note several key considerations in framing accurate evaluation of stigma and stigma processes.

Distinguishing Stereotyping, Prejudice, Discrimination, and Stigmatization

Investigators often do not operationalize stigma stringently enough or measure it carefully enough. For example, many studies of the "stigmatization" of mental disorder utilize surveys of cognitions or attitudes as the chief or only measurement tool. Others infer the presence of stigma from a single behavioral indicator. Ideally, measures of stigmatization should incorporate more than a lack of knowledge about mental illness, the invocation of stereotypes, the harboring of narrowly defined negative attitudes, or an act of behavioral exclusion. The process of stigmatization draws upon stereotyping, prejudice, and discrimination but also goes further, invoking the notion of a fundamental mark or stain related to membership in a devalued group. When individuals are stigmatized, social interactions may be strained as a result of the "marked" attribute or the fear of its emergence (as is often the case for concealable stigmas). Stigma also has major impact on the self-perceptions and coping styles of those who are its recipients, reverberating throughout families and communities.

It would be too much to ask of any given investigation to incorporate all such aspects of stigma. After all, few studies can span multiple social networks across lengthy time periods and include data on both perceivers and those who experience stigma. The point, however, is that investigators must seriously examine what they intend to capture in their studies of stigma processes and select, when possible, several channels to aid in understanding the relevant variables. They should also attempt to discern underlying mechanisms of stigma, including dimensions of concealability, course/chronicity, disruptiveness, aesthetics, peril/danger, and origin, as well as the interpersonal dynamics surrounding stigma. Optimal research should examine the impact of devaluation on victims. In order to elucidate the cyclic nature of stigmatization, its effects across time, and its differentiation from the ramifications of mental illness per se, understanding reciprocal processes of influence is a priority.

In all, if the research base in the field is characterized by a thin set of attitude items or isolated behavioral indicators, the contention that mental disorders receive stigma could be viewed as a trivial assertion, with the potential for a reemergence of the view that mental illness is not truly stigmatized. The burden is on the next generation of investigators to ensure that documentation of stigma is as complete as possible—and that the measured attributes of stigma are aligned with key conceptual models. Investigators would be wise to (a) specify when they are measuring knowledge, when they are tapping attitudes, and/or when the indicator is behavioral discrimination; and (b) discuss the implications of their results for the complex nature of stigma-related processes, including limitations of the measurement approach they have chosen.

Linking Knowledge, Attitudes, and Behaviors and Using Sound Research Principles

In building models of stigma, investigators should make no automatic assumption that knowledge about mental disorder is directly associated with attitudes toward people with mental illness or that either of these is a perfect predictor of behavioral responses per se.[2] In other words, having knowledge about a topic does not translate into a certain attitudinal stance toward that issue, and behavioral tendencies do not necessarily follow directly from attitudes and preferences.

Several more general research principles are worth noting. First, when possible, researchers would do well to utilize the types of large and representative samples evident in many early studies in the field.[3] Convenience samples of undergraduates may provide important information but are far from representative of the age, education, and social class of the population.

Second, to make an obvious point but one that is underappreciated in practice, expressed attitudes may be subject to social desirability. Participants may convey benevolent attitudes toward those with mental disorder on questionnaire responses chiefly because they do not want to appear callous or prejudiced and because social norms have tended, over time, to proscribe derogation of disadvantaged individuals (although this may be less true for mental illness than racial minority status). The work of Link and Cullen was instrumental in showing that respondents displayed social desirability in terms of attitudes toward mental hospitalization.[4] Investigators should consider the response formats advocated by these researchers ("most people," "own response," "ideal person") in order to obtain a less biased picture of respondents' beliefs. Furthermore, research teams should consider going beyond explicit attitude measures to include implicit tasks, as well as behavioral indicators.

Third, and more specifically, the following point about the ways of asking questions is provocative. Specifically, measures of racial attitudes that request evaluations on bipolar, semantic-differential scales often reveal no evidence of differences in evaluation of Blacks versus Whites. For example, respondents tend to rate these two groups at the same point on the "lazy-ambitious" continuum. Yet when positive adjectives are separated from negative ones, an interesting pattern emerges: Respondents tend to rate Blacks and Whites equally negatively (e.g., equally "lazy") but to rate Whites more positively (e.g., more "ambitious").[5] Without such separation, evidence for prejudice or stigma could be missed.

Fourth, regarding mental disorder, Brockman and colleagues found that questionnaires with fixed, objective response formats yielded weaker evidence for stigmatization than those requesting open-ended responses, with the latter presumably allowing for freer answers that were not suggested by multiple-choice items or other preselected formats. Only a minority of research in this area has utilized such narrative response formats. Although scoring of responses is time consuming, such methods are worth considering.[6]

Fifth, a key problem in reviewing research on public conceptions of mental disorder is that attitude measures across different investigations and across time are difficult to compare. In other words, what levels of reduction in social distance or what types of changes in the adjectives endorsed in semantic-differential scales would constitute evidence for "improved" attitudes? Helpful in this regard are studies in which respondents directly compare people with mental disorder to those with other forms of disability. In fact, such forced contrasts reveal that, along with substance abuse and homelessness, mental disorder continues to be the least preferred type of disability or deviance (see Chapter 5). Absolute change in attitudes may be difficult to determine, but the relative ranking of mental disorder can provide an anchor.

Sixth, a basic disconnect still exists between investigations of attitudes and those focused on behavioral indicators. It is nearly impossible, for example, to come up with a study in which respondents in behavioral, interactional research—that is, those interacting directly (or expecting to interact) with a person labeled as mentally disordered—have also been asked to provide general attitudes about mental disorder. Admittedly, giving attitude or social distance measures to respondents who will soon interact with persons suspected of having mental disorders could color the experimental manipulations, if done without planning and thought. Yet it would be a significant advance in knowledge to see just what behavioral tendencies and responses emerge from those participants whose responses on attitude measures are also recorded. A clear research priority is to integrate attitude and behavioral measures in the same investigation, with appraisals of stereotyping and knowledge welcome additions as well.

Implicit Versus Explicit Expression of Prejudice and Stigma

Many who study ethnic and racial prejudice have come to the conclusion that overt measures of attitude and acceptance fail to tap underlying attitudes and biases—those that are the most likely to be exhibited in current times, when it is no longer socially acceptable to express overt prejudice. In other words, whereas respondents may have learned to present more desirable or accepting attitudes through traditional, explicit measures, they may still hold deeply seated, unconscious proclivities and response tendencies. Concepts like symbolic racism have come to the fore, signifying belief systems that not expressed overtly but that are instead revealed through substitute means such as strongly favoring the Protestant work ethic or believing in meritocracy.

A major advance in research on prejudice and bias has been the development of instruments designed to tap covert or implicit attitudes, which are defined as those that exist without the respondent's conscious knowledge. A key example is the Implicit Association Test (IAT).[7] Here, the outcome measure is response latency, or reaction time, as participants associate pairs of concepts with the stimulus of interest. To illustrate the operation of this measure, I use the example of implicit attitudes toward young versus old people. Respondents initially see (on a computer screen) a picture of an old or a young face. From a pair of adjectives (e.g., "old" versus "young"; "good" versus "bad"), they are asked to select the one that best describes the picture. Eventually two sets of adjective pairs are presented, which cross-list the positive and negative terms with the "old" versus the "young" words.

Implicit bias toward elderly faces would be revealed by a quicker latency to the pair "old or bad" than to "old or good." Similarly, bias in favor of younger faces would be signaled by faster response times to "young or good" than to "young or bad." In fact, many individuals who profess no age-related bias on explicit attitude measures show just such implicit biases. Again, because respondents are asked to respond quickly and because the variable of interest is reaction time, the assumption is that unconscious attitudes are being appraised. Measuring implicit attitudes provides a window on the types of response biases that exist below individuals' usual levels of awareness. Importantly, such unconscious biases show predictive validity for specific indicators of prejudice, often with a different (and stronger) pattern of correlations to criterion measures than those obtained from explicit scales.[8]

A key question is whether such a paradigm can be applied to the area of mental disorder. Initial forays are occurring. For example, the careful work of Teachman and colleagues reveals that antifat bias exists at implicit but not explicit levels and, recently, that implicit bias against mental illness exists in both normative samples and persons with mental illness.[9] The overall objective of such research is to circumvent the common problems related to explicit means of appraising prejudice—namely, social desirability and a lack of self-awareness of deeply conditioned, underlying response proclivities.

Further demonstration of implicit prejudice of persons with mental disorder would be troubling, if not unexpected, providing evidence that many respondents are not even aware of their biases toward people with mental disorder. Yet such findings should not promote undue pessimism among those who attempt to combat stigma. Indeed, in the field of racial and ethnic prejudice, it has been shown that individuals who evidence unconscious, implicit antipathy can still make strides to overcome such biases via intentional, planned means. In addition, implicit biases can be conditioned away by repeated exposure to counterstereotypic images, such as presentation of stigmatized group members in conjunction with positive attributes.[10]

Appraising the Independent Variable
of Mental Disorder

What is actually stigmatized in the realm of mental disorder: the symptoms themselves, particular diagnostic entities, or general labels of "mental illness" or "ex-mental patient"? Evidence exists that each of these may be the focus of stereotypes, prejudice, discrimination, and stigma; the independent variable must therefore be specified with precision.

Many early investigations of stigma related to mental disorder dealt with the presentation of vignettes that presented symptoms of various forms of mental disturbance in order to determine whether such descriptions would be recognized as forms of mental illness and to ascertain how much social distance would be desired from an individual displaying such symptoms (see Chapter 5). Although evidence exists that greater segments of the general public recognize such portrayals as falling under the rubric of mental disorder than was the case decades ago, such "accuracy" in recognition is not necessarily associated with more favorable attitudes, as I have repeatedly discussed.

A central issue is that a great diversity of mental aberrations exists, belying the conception of an overall, uniform construct or label of "mental illness" or "mental disorder." Indeed, considering mental disorder to be undifferentiated is not only ill informed but also potentially stereotypic, given its implicit assumption that people with mental illnesses are "all the same." Recognition of the key differences across diagnostic categories has led investigators of recent large-scale surveys of public attitudes, in both the United States and abroad, to present distinct vignettes of separate conditions. Different forms of mental illness are, in fact, associated with unique profiles of misinformation and stigmatization, even though all of the types continue to receive at least some degree of negative response.[11] In most research, it therefore makes sense to study stigma in relation to the independent variable of different forms of mental illness— unless, of course, the generic label of mental disorder or mental illness is the conceptual focus. In fact, research on secondary labeling theory emphasizes that the general label of mental illness or ex-mental patient can produce considerable stigma.

Several related issues emerge from this general point. First, given that the chronicity or permanence of a stigmatizing condition is highly likely to be related to negative attitudes, it would be helpful to include items tapping respondents' beliefs about the long-term course of various conditions. The public's attitudes may well reflect strong beliefs in the inevitably permanent nature of most mental disorders.[12] Such perceptions of chronicity may well be related to the metaphoric linkage of conditions like schizophrenia with despair, hopelessness, and devaluation.[13] Focusing on depictions of distinct forms of mental illness and understanding the public's association of these discrete forms with features such as chronicity or controllability can help to make attitude research more precise and conceptually rigorous.

Second, viewing mental disorder in its specific, variegated forms rather than as a global, amorphous entity prompts consideration of the crucial point that many forms of mental disturbance are less severe and less inherently threatening at a behavioral level than schizophrenia and other psychotic-level disorders. As Chapter 7 highlights, far too little is known about the responses of the general public, family members, mental health professionals, and patients themselves to these forms of mental disturbance. A key objective is to extend work on prejudice, discrimination, and stigmatization to the full range of mental disorders.

Third, mental disorders are almost always depicted in the form of written vignettes that describe various symptom patterns. Alternatively, the manipulation may relate to the presence or absence of the label of mental illness or ex-mental patient. Yet direct confrontation of the behavioral and emotional patterns associated with mental disorder would constitute a far more powerful stimulus than written accounts or verbal labels. It would be worthwhile for investigators to consider paradigms in which symptoms of mental disorder are presented in videotaped formats—or even virtual reality simulations.[14] Such portrayals are more likely to incur real, rather than artificial, encounters with the manifestations of mental disorder, opening the door for research that is more accurate. Indeed, virtual reality simulations could provide the additional benefit of enhancing empathy for those experiencing mental disorder, if the simulations were presented with appropriate framing and contextualization.

Overall, researchers must complement their work on carefully selecting their *dependent* variables related to stereotyping, prejudice, discrimination, and stigma (see the section Measurement and Appraisal of Stigma at the beginning of this chapter) by specifying their conceptions and measurements of the *independent* variable of mental disorder.

Attributional Analysis of Stigmatizing Responses to Mental Disorder

A key theme of this book pertains to a fundamental tenet of attribution theory—namely, that attributing negative behavior to controllable causal factors should increase stigma, whereas ascription to noncontrollable factors (such as naturalistic, disease models) should reduce stigma. In several instances I have noted that this view is significantly challenged with respect to mental disorder. In fact, the tendency for biogenetic attributions to fuel punitive responses is both troublesome and fascinating (see Chapters 4 and 7).

Future investigators will need to take social psychological and attributional accounts of mental disorder to more sophisticated levels. That is, we still do not fully know *how* persons in current society view mental disorder, particularly in terms of its biomedical attributions.

It may be the case, for example, that when respondents receive biological or genetic attributions for mental disorder as part of experimentally assigned research conditions, they continue to believe that the individuals in question actually could have controlled their behavior—and that the biomedical ascription is a kind of modern-day excuse for aberrant behavior. Such respondents may take a perspective that is parallel to demonological accounts of mental disorder in former eras, in which a supposedly uncontrollable causal factor—namely, possession by evil spirits or the devil—was linked to the belief that the afflicted person was still responsible for vulnerability to the possession, perhaps through a moral weakness or lack of faith. In other words, an alleged "biogenetic" causal condition may actually constitute a blend of controllable and noncontrollable features.

Other respondents may undergo a radical attributional shift, dropping volitional ascriptions altogether and coming to the belief that the behaviors in question are the result of a deep, underlying, and permanent inborn flaw. If these possibilities (and others) are counted in the same experimentally assigned condition, there is bound to be confusion in interpreting findings.

Furthermore, in the coming years, when genetic aspects of one's offspring are likely to become far more intentionally directed than has been the case throughout human history (i.e., through gene selection), carrying "deviant genes" may be viewed as an entirely *controllable* facet of one's makeup (at least, controllable by one's parents). It will be quite important to know how respondents view individuals who show the behavioral manifestations of a presumed genetic inferiority, particularly one that could have potentially been controlled or prevented through prenatal selection or genetic manipulation.[15]

More open-ended, narrative responses than those encountered in traditional multiple-choice attributional scales may be necessary to understand how members of society actually process and comprehend various explanations of mental illness. It is also likely that some aspects of respondents' schemas may not be fully amenable to conscious introspection. Exploration of intensive personal narratives, content analyses of advertisements and media portrayals, probing of implicit attitudes, and examination of cultural practices and language structures (e.g., jokes, common stories told in various cultures) are all required to uncover the nature of personal representations of and attributions for mental disorder.

Responses of Individuals With Mental Disorder to Stigma

Although systematic research on the attitudes and behavioral responses of the general public to mental disorder has been proceeding for 60 years, less is known about how people with mental disorder comprehend, internalize, and/or cope with the devaluation and stigmatization they experience. It was originally assumed that victims of stigmatization would inevitably respond by internalizing the aspersion foisted upon them, but as emphasized throughout these pages, current perspectives posit that lowered self-esteem and shame are not universal.[16] Indeed, many individuals in minority groups display levels of self-esteem fully as positive as those in the majority group, utilizing a variety of coping tactics in response to identity threat.

Still, individuals with mental disorders may be particularly likely to evidence shame and reduced self-esteem. Part of the reason for this response pertains to the very symptoms of many forms of mental illness, which include difficulties in interpersonal relationships, sad or dysphoric mood, isolation, and a loss of the sense of an integrated self. In addition, persons with mental disorder are not as unified or as self-identified as a "group" as many ethnic and racial minorities. Political solidarity—which would tend to foster group identification, as well as recognition of the arbitrariness and inhumanity of discrimination and stigmatization—has been a relatively recent occurrence with respect to mental disorder. For such reasons, internalization of blame would be expectable.

Basic questions remain unaddressed. What, for example, are the relative proportions of persons with mental disorder who display the three types of coping outlined by Watson and colleagues—yielding to stigma, ignoring it, or actively combating it? Are these, in fact, the only three types that exist? What are the relevant cognitive and emotional strategies utilized by individuals in such categories? Along these lines, it is essential for researchers to allow those with mental disorders to be heard. In other words, studying narratives has a clear role in the initial phases of research programs aimed toward understanding personal experience.[17]

Other questions are important. What are the most adaptive and maladaptive coping responses to stigma? Are different strategies optimal for different diagnostic categories, different personality types, or different points in the "careers" of persons with mental disorder? How can self-stigmatization be prevented or remediated once it has occurred? And what determines appraisals of the threats to identity posed by stigma and discrimination for persons with mental disorders? These questions are essentially unexplored at this time.

Two additional themes are salient. First, research in the past decade has revealed that some persons in the general population are particularly sensitive to interpersonal rejection and that such *rejection sensitivity* incurs negative consequences for subsequent relationships and for the individual's sense of self-worth.[18] It is quite likely that that individual differences in coping with social rejection may predict adaptive versus maladaptive responses to stigmatization in people with mental disorders. Indeed, a degree of imperviousness to rejection could fuel persistence and patience on the part of individuals as they struggle to complete education, find jobs and housing, and establish meaningful relationships in a stigmatizing and discriminatory society.

Second, at least a subgroup of people with mental illness has probably gained the sense that societal rejection is arbitrary and wrong minded and that it does not relate to their own shortcomings or weaknesses. For them, rejection may be viewed as a political rather than personal issue, predicting preservation of self-esteem.[19] However, such a cognitive stance may prevent the individual in question from obtaining needed feedback from social partners—or even from seeking treatment. Again, the relevance and applicability of these concepts and processes for mental illness stigma are almost completely unexplored.

Overall, investigators will need (a) additional instruments that effectively tap self-blame, shame, and internalization of castigating messages, including open-ended strategies, and (b) research paradigms that can separate features of self-stigmatization from the symptoms of mental disorder. Also crucial is measurement of a wide range of coping responses on the part of individuals with mental disorder and appraisal of the linkages between their coping styles and personal adjustment. Developing a thorough taxonomy of coping options would be an important step. Regarding stereotype threat, relevant stereotypes related to mental disorder and pertinent tasks that tap these stereotypes need to be identified. Finally, regarding identity threat, little is known about the cognitive appraisals of persons with mental illness regarding social messages that could erode social identity—or similar appraisals of their own coping mechanisms.

Current Social Issues in Relation to Stigma and Mental Disorder

A number of political and social events and issues in recent years have important implications for the stigmatization of mental disorder. I note several of these briefly in the hope of stimulating relevant inquiries.

Funding Cutbacks in the First Decade of the Twenty-First Century

Many if not most state budgets across the United States have become awash in red ink during the early years of the current century. Education, welfare, and mental health are often the first victims of the fiscal slashing in an attempt to balance budgets. Will stigmatization of persons with mental disorder increase in such times of economic downturn? Or will other social and political currents outweigh these economic trends? Furthermore, as budgets tend to improve (a trend that appears to be occurring as of 2006), will mental health expenditures show an increase—and will levels of stigmatization decrease?[20] Linking public attitudes with economic and political trends is not a simple task, requiring longitudinal data, as well as a large number of control variables. Still, investigations of this topic could shed light on important macrolevel processes that relate to stigmatization, with the eventual goal of forecasting linkages between economic and political factors and stigma processes.

Prejudice and Stigma in the Post-9/11 World

Since the terrorist attacks on the United States in September 2001, a surge of ethnic and cultural hatred, often directed against persons of Middle Eastern descent or those of Islamic faith, has surfaced. It is unknown whether such intolerance has spread (or will spread) to persons with mental disorder. Two reasons make such an occurrence likely, however. First, the huge, media-driven stereotype that persons with mental illness are prone to violence would be likely to fuel such beliefs. That is, fears of violence have increased in the wake of the terrorist attacks, and those whose behavior patterns are stereotypically linked with danger and aggression—namely, individuals with mental disorders—would be expected to increase in visibility during such fearful times.

Second, recall the principles related to terror management theory, which posit a linkage between fears of mortality and intolerance of those who are deviant.[21] Current levels of general fear in society make it likely that the blaming of scapegoated individuals, such as those with mental illness, would increase. Research on such possibilities could help to reveal systems-level processes (and their interaction with individual-level, existential perspectives) related to prejudice and stigma.

Documentation of Structural Discrimination

Link and colleagues make the key point that indicators of structural discrimination against persons with mental disorders—for example, lack of adequate insurance coverage or nonenforcement of equal housing acts—are almost entirely neglected in the research literature. Both qualitative, ethnographic investigations and quantitative studies are important priorities in this regard. Topics for future research could include the following:

The spatial location of board-and-care homes for people with schizo-phrenia, pay scale differentials for professionals whose work involves the chronic mental illnesses as opposed to much milder conditions treated in private practice settings, historical differences in research funding . . . and the social isolation of treatment facilities for people with severe mental illnesses. These institutional arrangements need to be understood from a stigma perspective both as consequences of stigma and as factors that create and reinforce stigma on the individual level.[22]

I concur and strongly suggest that the next generation of investigators pay as much attention to discrimination and policy as to individual and social factors related to stigma.

Families and Stigma

Family members and caregivers must contend with both objective burden—such as financial costs, finding housing, and providing care—and subjective burden, a term that entails embarrassment, shame, and a host of additional neg-ative emotions related to the difficulties of caring for their afflicted relatives.[23] Subjective burden often leads to a primary coping mechanism of concealing the relative's mental illness from all but essential contacts. Documentation of such burden and of resultant tendencies toward secrecy and concealment is plentiful, extending well beyond the United States (see Chapter 5).

Beyond description, however, the next phase of research will need to ad-dress more specific questions, as well as issues related to underlying mecha-nisms. For example, which forms of mental disorder are particularly linked with subjective burden in families? It is a reasonable assumption that the most severe forms are the top candidates in view of the fact that these would appear to incur the greatest costs, the greatest investments of time and energy, and the least hope. It may also be the case, however, that in an increasingly meritocratic society valuing educational and financial success, conditions affecting atten-tion, learning, and motivation (e.g., childhood ADHD and learning disorders) may be particularly painful and stigmatizing for many families—particularly as rates of diagnosis for these conditions continue to rise.

Furthermore, which types of family coping responses are associated with relief from subjective burden, and what kinds of contextual factors (friends, community supports, religious institutions) promote such relief and optimal coping? It would be tempting to assume that disclosure and active coping are always superior to concealment, but it is highly likely that some families cope best in quieter ways. Probing for specific kinds of familial response and for the processes that predict healthy or maladaptive family outcomes is a priority.

Now that causal models of mental disorder have largely shifted from direct blaming of families and caregivers, an explicit objective of many family self-help and advocacy movements has been to promote a biological, medical model of mental disorder. It is simply not known, however, whether such frameworks have led to reductions in familial burden. Given the many issues related to the consequences of biomedical attributions for mental illness, understanding their application to family stigma is essential. Does a biogenetic set of attributions decrease families' sense of self-blame? Alternatively, does it foster a search for "which side of the family" may have been responsible for the genes in question, thereby fueling guilt? At the same time, do such attributions tend to engender support from other families of individuals experiencing mental illness, or do they tend to isolate the family as deviant and genetically distinct?

Finally, to what extent does the presence of a relative with mental illness foster empathy, concern, sensitivity, and strength on the part of family members? As noted below with respect to resilience, mental illness is not invariably associated with despair and disability. Similarly, for some family members, the amounts of objective and subjective burden experienced may be outweighed by a host of learning experiences that result from living with and caring for a relative with a mental disorder. In some cases, unprecedented courage and compassion may emerge. Empirical literature on this topic is nearly nonexistent.

Mental Health Professionals and Stigma

Evidence presented in earlier chapters documented the tendencies of at least some members of the mental health professions to display stigmatizing attitudes toward clients and to hold low expectations for change. Yet extant information is limited primarily to anecdotal accounts or broad surveys; far more remains to be learned about how those entrusted with the care of people with mental disorders perceive and treat their clients and the relatives of these clients.

First, what are the actual rates of stigmatizing practices? It could well be that the majority (even the vast majority) of both newly trained and more seasoned mental health professionals hold positive, nonstigmatizing attitudes toward persons with mental disorder. Yet it might also be the case that tendencies to see clients as "them" versus "us" are salient. Second, does stigma exist in staff and professionals at implicit, as well as explicit, levels? And, if so, which is more predictive of caring versus demeaning behavioral responses?

Obtaining relevant information will not be simple. One avenue is to systematically determine the perceptions of recipients of mental health services. Large-scale mental health care organizations might include, beyond client satisfaction indicators per se, questions about the kinds of attitudes and behavioral practices exhibited by their providers. Note that the difficulties brought on by mental illness and the problems that are often inherent in therapeutic relationships could negatively bias such reports. Even so, this information would be important to have.

Once such responses are better known, it would be productive to probe underlying assumptions. Is it always the case, for example, that maximum warmth and empathy on the part of professionals produces the best outcomes? Do people in some categories of psychopathology fare best with greater structure, even at the expense of some degree of perceived flexibility? How can professional and staff attitudes and practices convey respect while simultaneously promoting adherence to the types of treatment strategies that have been shown to work? A whole set of provocative questions is relevant to this area of study.

Recent research reveals tendencies toward concealment among mental health professionals with respect to their own psychological and psychiatric treatment.[24] To the extent that such findings are generalizable, how might professionals' reluctance to disclose their own status as consumers of psychotherapy or psychopharmacology shape openness toward and acceptance of their clientele? It will be important to probe deeper into the experiences of mental health personnel regarding their own sense of being stigmatized and to relate these self-perceptions to their attitudes toward and practices with clients.

Children, Development, and Stigma

Only a small amount of research has focused on children's knowledge of and attitudes toward mental disorders, and almost no work has centered on the experiences of children with mental illness who themselves confront stigma. These are major issues that could themselves merit chapter-length coverage.

Children as Perceivers

First, a number of fundamental questions are unanswered. What do youth know about mental illness (and related terms, such as being "crazy"), and when do they know it? Are there regular developmental progressions regarding such knowledge—and related attitudes? Can children recognize mental disorder in other children, or is their knowledge largely restricted to adult manifestations of abnormal behavior? Beyond cross-sectional research on children or adolescents of different ages, it will take prospective, longitudinal research to address these questions, in order to understand the development of such knowledge and attitudes across time. The development of attitudes toward racial minority groups has been an important research focus; parallel work on mental disorders is sorely needed.

Second, what is the relationship between knowledge and attitudes in youth? Wahl's review reveals that increments in knowledge across childhood appear to be accompanied by *increases* rather than decreases in negative attitudes.[25] Given the pervasiveness of negative media images of mental disorder, such findings may not be surprising, but the next step is to better understand the mechanisms underlying associations between knowledge and attitudes. Is mental illness portrayed in sufficiently frightening terms that more knowledge automatically predicts greater desire for social distance? Are there ways in which children can be taught about mental illness to enhance empathy rather than increase distancing? Although difficult to address, these questions are of great theoretical and clinical importance.

Third, how are children's attitudes related to family socialization practices? In other words, what language and attitudes do parents and families convey about mental illness, and how do children internalize and comprehend such language and understanding? Alternatively, are media messages or peer influences sufficiently pervasive that family socialization is of relatively little importance? Does the age of the child matter here? Answers to these questions are virtually unknown.

Children With Mental Illness

Little is known about how children and adolescents with mental disorders perceive stigmatization.[26] Work on perceptions of stigma in children who are members of various racial groups has yielded important findings, revealing that those who are members of underrepresented minorities appear to develop awareness of cultural stereotypes and show stigma consciousness earlier in development than do nonminority children.[27] Do children with mental disorders display similar "precocity"? How do they process and understand the social rejection and blaming that may accompany their diagnostic labels? Alternatively, do their diagnoses afford access to treatments that outweigh the potential stigmatization they receive, with the potential for such intervention to diminish self-blame and enhance positive coping? Creative research along these lines is a priority.

Developmental Effects of Stigma

Across the developmental span, it might be expected that mental disorders in children's earliest years (infancy, toddlerhood, preschool) would not constitute a major issue, given the child's immaturity and lack of self-reflection. However, for parents of children with early-onset conditions (e.g., autism), stigma may be considerable, in that families are extremely likely to receive blame for such disorders. Alternatively, the origin of such conditions during the early stages of life may be ascribed to aberrant genes, which, as I have indicated, can induce punitive social responses. The family's ability to receive early intervention is of paramount importance for conditions that begin during the first years of life, meaning that stigma and resultant concealment have the potential to thwart needed preventive work.

In middle childhood, conditions that emerge or receive initial diagnosis (e.g., ADHD, learning disorders, some types of anxiety disorders) may be particularly confusing for children, who are likely to be uncertain about the meaning of these labels—and the resultant stigma that may emerge from them. The extent and quality of family support around diagnosis and labeling are therefore crucial topics.

Conditions likely to arise in adolescence (e.g., bipolar disorder, major depression, schizophrenia) would be expected to interfere with the youth's developing identity. Peers at this age are exquisitely sensitive to conformity and difference; behavioral extremes that remove an adolescent from the mainstream can be damaging to self-image and social status. In particular, the experience of hospitalization or residential treatment for adolescent conditions may initiate a lifetime of negative self-image if providers are not sensitive to the implications of a potentially permanent label of "mental patient" for adolescents.[28] Mental illness in adolescence may predict a fundamentally altered identity, particularly if providers and family members are insensitive to the disruptions incurred by symptoms and invasive treatments. In short, far more remains to be learned about the firsthand experiences of adolescents who experience stigma.

Children of Parents Experiencing Mental Illness

When children grow up in families in which a parent displays mental illness, several important processes create enhanced risk for their own development of psychopathology. For example, shared genes may mediate such risk: Mental illness may run in families because both parents and children have similar genetic propensities. In addition, problems in parenting may accompany the adult's mental disorder, with negative implications for the child's development. Also, the child may witness emotionally dysregulated behavior on the part of the parent and experience marital discord and a lack of parental consistency and coordination. As children mature they may also sense that they are members of a "contaminated" family system, in which they are fated to experience the same problems as those of their mother or father—or in which they are expected to contain the family secret. In all, there are potentially numerous factors that may help to explain the increased risk for distress and mental illness in children of parents who themselves have a mental disorder.[29]

Another relevant process pertains to the stigma received by the parents in such instances. Because of the shame associated with mental illness, parents may understandably be reluctant to discuss their condition with their offspring (if, in fact, they are even aware of a mental disorder). In other words, if families practice strategies of concealment, this stance is likely to include failing to tell the offspring as well. Yet when children experience silence about behavioral aberrations, parental arguments, or ruptures in caregiving, all of which may accompany a parent's mental illness, their natural tendencies will be toward internalization, blaming themselves for the disruptions they are witnessing.[30] The point here is not to promote wanton disclosures of concepts that will bewilder or frighten children—or expose children to irrational behavior patterns— but rather to consider investigation of the kinds of messages that facilitate greater comprehension and reduced self-blame on the part of the offspring of parents experiencing mental illness. Knowledge of such processes could help to inform the further development of family interventions (see Chapter 11).

Resilience, Mental Illness, and Stigma

Can individuals experiencing a mental disorder, with accompanying stigma, show strength and competence? What processes predict positive outcomes as opposed to despair and hopelessness? Can knowledge of healthy functioning in people with mental disorders help to change pervasive cultural stereotypes about mental illness, thereby serving to reduce stigma? These are key research questions related to resilience and mental illness.

It must first be emphasized that mental illness produces negative impact on many aspects of life functioning. Painting a rose-colored picture of mental disorder is not advisable. At the same time, stereotypic views of mental disorder as inevitably predicting lifelong despair and disability are incorrect: The attainment of positive outcomes is a documented phenomenon that mandates formal recognition and intensive investigation. A focus on strength and adaptation may, in fact, help shift the view of both professionals and the general public to one filled with far more optimism than is typically the case.

Defining Resilience

Resilience has been conceptualized as an individual's capacity to adapt successfully and to function competently despite experiencing stress, adversity, or trauma.[31] In other words, resilience reflects unexpectedly good outcome in the face of conditions that would normally predict problematic consequences. Early work related to this concept focused on traitlike characteristics that produce "invulnerability" or "resiliency" in the face of significant trauma or stress.[32] More recently, experts have converged on the view that resilient functioning is not a static condition that exists wholly within the individual but rather reflects a transactional, dynamic set of processes inside and outside the person.

Although modern research on resilience dates to the 1970s, the occurrence of positive outcomes in the midst of risk has captured the interest of scholars and writers over the ages. From the view that good outcomes in the face of stress were rare, chance-driven occurrences, the focus has shifted to identifying subgroups of high-risk individuals who show better-than-expected outcome in predictable ways. Work in this domain has been wide ranging, with target populations including those with schizophrenia, persons exposed to poverty, children who endured the Great Depression, adults reared in foster homes and institutions as children, and delinquent youth with criminal fathers. Response to trauma has also been salient, with studies involving people exposed to the extreme violence of Northern Ireland, children of the Holocaust followed into adulthood, and individuals exposed to natural disasters.[33]

At least three levels of variables promote resilient functioning: those within the individual (e.g., positive self-esteem, easy temperament, high intelligence, a sense of humor), factors pertaining to family and relationship processes (e.g., certain child-rearing styles, positive relations and identifications with an adult outside the home), and characteristics of broader social environments (e.g., school settings, certain types of neighborhoods). Moreover, efforts have shifted from the mere description of characteristics associated with positive outcomes (so-called protective factors) to the attempt to understand *how* certain factors contribute to positive outcomes despite the presence of adversity.[34] For example, Kim-Cohen and colleagues, who examined antisocial behavior and intelligence in the face of economic deprivation during childhood, found that identical twins were more similar in their patterns of resilience than were fraternal twins. These findings strongly suggest that genetic factors can substantially contribute to resilient functioning with respect to cognitive skills and the absence of aggressive tendencies.[35] Yet parenting practices also lowered the odds of aggression and antisocial behavior, even after genetic influences were controlled. Social factors are important as well.

Critiques of the Concept

Difficult questions surround the concept of resilience. For example, do protective factors work only in conditions of high risk, or can a person be resilient even under normative circumstances? Should positive outcomes be measured in one key domain, or would truly resilient functioning require healthy adaptation across several life areas? In addition, because protective factors may actually constitute the reverse ends of risk factors for negative outcomes (e.g., strong versus weak family support), are there actually any special factors that enable a mysterious process termed resilience? Despite these contentions, understanding of processes predictive of healthy functioning in conditions of high risk can provide a needed counterpoint to the nearly exclusive focus on pathology and maladaptation across the mental health fields.[36]

Mental Disorder and Recovery

A key perspective on mental illness is the belief that psychopathology is static and unchanging (e.g., once someone is mentally ill, that person is always mentally ill). In actuality, individuals with mental illness commonly shift between phases of more versus less pathological functioning.[37] People with mental disorders who are in remission or who have been treated successfully may not differ significantly from nondisordered individuals at such times. Even though mood disorders are highly recurrent phenomena and many other mental disorders often have lingering effects and impairments, most forms of mental disorder are not unrelenting. Views that deny the possibility of recovery can also lead to substandard care.[38]

Even for schizophrenia, long characterized as an unrelenting and chronic condition, some forms of rehabilitation are possible, particularly when the disorder is treated soon after its emergence and when comprehensive and coordinated services are provided.[39] In fact, the concept of *recovery* from serious mental illness has been championed by those who have themselves shown sufficient improvement to be able to write about their experiences.[40] The term suggests that even in the face of serious mental illness, progress can occur and individuals can develop a sense of meaning and purpose. Key research goals are to discover the range of long-term outcomes of individuals with mental illness—and the types of factors and processes that can facilitate optimal adjustment. Coping with stigma is bound to be a key issue in such formulations.

Positive Features of Mental Disorder

Can persons with mental disorders excel in certain domains despite their illness? Furthermore, can a history of mental illness facilitate strength, compassion, and courage, which might not otherwise have surfaced? Anecdotal evidence suggests that such is indeed the case. My father, a philosopher with a 40-year history of misdiagnosed and maltreated bipolar disorder, provides a clear example (see Chapter 6). Despite the adversity associated with his mental illness, along with the shame he endured because of the almost universal silence about mental disorder during much of the last century, he clearly stated to me that he would never have traded any of his life experiences. This perspective, one that is held by many people who have struggled with mental illness, suggests that the personal experience of mental illness can enrich and broaden one's life.[41] A key to understanding resilience in the face of mental illness lies within the subgroup of individuals who, despite adversities related to mental illness and its frequently accompanying stigmatization, have succeeded in professional, personal, and family domains and grown in wisdom and compassion.

What of the linkage between mental disorder and creativity and productivity? Many contend that mental illness can confer a special status among humans. Neurologist Oliver Sacks has discussed conditions such as Tourette's disorder and autism as potentially reflective of special abilities rather than uniform deficiencies.[42] Storr comments on the potential for mental disorder to be linked to political and artistic success.[43] On the one hand, when mental illness is equated with uniqueness, difference, or a sense of being special, the potential for stigmatization may be reduced. On the other hand, it is important not to romanticize the experience of mental illness or to assume that everyone who displays aberrant behavior is somehow uniquely creative or gifted. Bipolar disorder is the condition with the strongest evidence for linkage with creativity and productivity, but manic and depressed states are far more linked to disorganization and despair than to any kind of sustained output. In fact, a depiction of inevitable associations between mental disorder and creative genius may actually serve to promote stigmatization, given its inaccuracy, its fostering of false hope, and its potential to undermine motivation for treatment if people cling to the belief that symptom remission is equated with the waning of creativity.[44]

Few people with mental illness are demons or geniuses. Portrayals that emphasize humanity, normality, and everyday coping, as well as resilient functioning, may go far in reducing the stereotype that mental illness is equated with extremes. Research on the ability of such accurate depictions to enhance empathy and decrease stigma is sorely needed.

Ethnic, Cultural, and Cross-National Perspectives

Although stigmatization of mental illness transcends national and cultural boundaries, the vast majority of relevant research focuses on Western societies. Indeed, many of the measures used to appraise stigma processes in international research are Western in origin.[45] Furthermore, in United States-based research, ethnic and racial diversity of stigma recipients is not always achieved. In order to avoid portraying stigma as an exclusively white, middle-class phenomenon (which is clearly not the case), it will be vital to include variables of race, culture, and social class into research.

As indicated in the supplement to the Surgeon General's report on race, ethnicity, and culture in connection with mental health in the United States, problems of both mental illness and stigma are compounded for individuals of color, particularly when poverty is involved.[46] Being a member of a minority group and simultaneously having a mental illness constitutes a kind of double stigma. Prejudice against each of these attributes may interact, and the lack of resources that accompanies minority status and/or poverty may render access to treatment even more difficult. More research is needed to document the kinds of experiences of individuals with doubly stigmatized attributes.

In addition, given the worldwide nature of the stigmatization of mental illness, investigations detailing cultural similarities and differences in the experiences and ramifications of stigma could facilitate an understanding of what is universal and what is culturally specific with respect to stigma.

9

Overcoming Stigma I

Legislation, Policy, and Community Efforts

It should be clear by now that stigma is exhibited and experienced by individuals, families, social groups, communities, and societies. It is also conveyed via stereotyped media images, as well as the attitudes and practices of at least some personnel providing services in the mental health arena. Each of these systems and levels is a potential target for intervention. But where should those interested in reducing or eliminating stigma begin?

This is a difficult question. The long-standing nature of stigmatization and the multiple levels at which stigma occurs mean that efforts targeting any particular level may be insufficient. For instance, changing employers' attitudes toward mental illness may not contend with broader structural issues of discrimination or the lack of funding for appropriate accommodations in the workplace. Encouraging treatment for persons with mental illness—a crucial aspect of stigma reduction—cannot in and of itself address those forms of prejudice that are deeply embedded within the culture's practices and laws. Altered social policies may have difficulty in filtering down to meaningful change inside the minds (and hearts) of members of society. And when perceivers make a genuine attempt to overcome stereotypes and prejudices, there is the possibility that the images intended to be banished are instead locked in place via "rebound" mechanisms.[1]

The implication is clear: Underlying mechanisms related to stigma must be addressed, and change efforts must occur in multiple settings and at multiple levels. In the words of Link and Phelan:

> [An] approach to change must ultimately address the fundamental cause of stigma—it must either change the deeply held attitudes and beliefs of powerful groups that lead to labeling, stereotyping, setting apart, devaluing,

and discriminating, or it must change circumstances so as to limit the power of such groups to make their cognitions the dominant ones. In the absence of fundamental changes, interventions targeted at only one mechanism at a time will ultimately fail, because their effectiveness will be undermined by contextual factors that are left untouched by such a narrowly conceived intervention.[2]

From this sobering perspective, single-strategy programs could lead to false hopes and subsequent demoralization, as other sources of stigma may well remain unaltered or become even more entrenched. In other words, it is possible that only the most coordinated, multifaceted interventions may be able to reduce stigmatization in meaningful ways.

However, given that intensive, multilevel programs may be quite expensive to mount, where can efforts begin? Should change emerge in bottom-up fashion, such that individual consciousness raising must take place before larger systemic reform can occur? Or are top-down strategies optimal, whereby new laws or policies promote the kinds of structural change that, in turn, produce alterations in individual citizens' behavior and attitude?

Meaningful change will certainly require both processes. Yet if a choice is necessary, I would argue that the priority is instituting reform through the passage of legislation and the formulation of social policies that can guarantee fundamental rights for those with mental disorders. Without such a top-down approach, individual efforts may take too long to build and fail to address the essential point that stigmatization comprises a fundamental social injustice that needs to be redressed at the level of coordinated policy efforts.[3]

A parallel can be drawn with the civil rights movement of the 1950s and 1960s, when racial bias in the United States finally began to be addressed through laws and judicial decisions banning discrimination. Although many individuals had been opposed to racial prejudice throughout our history, it took top-down legislative and policy changes to motivate large-scale reform. Readers of a certain age may recall that opponents of such action often voiced the point that "legislating morality" was impossible. Although it may be true at a certain level that laws alone do not alter individual morals and values, structural changes in society are often essential for breaking down barriers and ensuring rights, which may lead to changes in individual attitudes once freer contact emerges.

Reform was not simple for civil rights advocates. For example, the 1954 Supreme Court ruling of *Brown v. the Board of Education,* which outlawed school segregation, encountered massive resistance in a number of states. It took federal involvement to enforce the ruling, even to the point of sending the National Guard to certain schools.[4] Still, half a century later, racial prejudice and discrimination are far from being solved. Indeed, legal and judicial reforms cannot overcome automatic, unconscious forms of bias, of which perceivers are typically unaware.[5] Nonetheless, top-down approaches may well be the optimal places to begin.

In this chapter I therefore address legislation, social policy, and community-level efforts. Chapter 10 considers public media and mental health professionals, and Chapter 11 takes on family and individual strategies to combat stigma, emphasizing support and advocacy groups for families, access to responsive treatment, and promotion of active coping mechanisms to combat self-stigma. The core point is that coordination across all of these levels is greatly needed.[6]

Legislation and Policy

The current era has witnessed activism regarding mental health legislation and judicial rulings. The report of the President's New Freedom Commission on Mental Health, issued in 2003, recommended a system of coordinated care, responsiveness to family and consumer needs, greater integration of information about causes and treatments, and early detection of mental disorders.[7] In response to this mandate, a coalition of the nation's largest mental health advocacy groups, including the National Alliance on Mental Illness (NAMI), the National Mental Health Association (NMHA), and the Bazelon Center for Mental Health Law, joined forces to create the Campaign for Mental Health Reform, with many other advocacy groups quickly signing on (by the summer of 2006, 16 organizations had joined the campaign). Its stated goal is to call attention to two core issues: (i) Mental health is crucial for overall well-being, and (ii) mental disorders must be investigated and treated with the same urgency as physical illnesses.[8] Although the campaign is pursuing a number of legislative and judicial initiatives, perhaps the most crucial pertains to parity, the policy of placing insurance coverage of mental disorders on the same level as coverage for physical illnesses.

Parity

The issue here is that mental health services are not reimbursed at the same rates that hold for other conditions and diseases. It is hard to think of a more concrete example of stigma: Physical illnesses receive one level of compensation, whereas mental illnesses receive another, lower level. As a result, even if people recognize and seek treatment for their mental disorders, which itself constitutes a major step, a lack of parity means that they typically cannot afford such treatments or can afford only substandard care.

In a recent national survey conducted in the United States, it was found that the time span from the onset of most forms of mental illnesses to the individual's seeking of treatment is measurable in years, even decades.[9] Although there are many reasons for such delays in seeking treatment, including lack of awareness of mental illness, denial, and the threat of social disapproval—all of which reflect the pernicious effects of stigma—inadequate funding for services is high on the list.

The federal Mental Health Parity Act of 1996 began the process of providing access to insurance coverage for mental illnesses that is equivalent to the coverage for other diseases. As Chapter 6 points out, however, there are major loopholes in this legislation. For instance, it is still legal for employers of small firms to deny or restrict mental health coverage. Even for larger companies, there are ways of circumventing the full, equitable funding of mental health services. The total number of days of inpatient care, for example, is often severely capped across an individual's lifetime.[10]

A more stringent bill to guarantee parity, known as the Senator Paul Wellstone Mental Health Equitable Treatment Act, is being debated in Congress. This legislation is named for Paul Wellstone, Democratic senator from Minnesota, a reformer for health and mental health care who was killed during a campaign airline crash in 2002. One Senate sponsor is Edward Kennedy, a liberal Democrat from Massachusetts and a longtime advocate of mental health reform. Recall that his brother John Kennedy, as president, enacted the Community Mental Health Centers Construction Act in 1963 (see Chapter 4).[11] The second sponsor is Senator Pete Domenici, a conservative Republican from New Mexico. His advocacy stems directly from family experiences, as one of his daughters has been diagnosed with schizophrenia for many years. It took this personal experience with the consequences of serious mental illness to convince Senator Domenici that discrimination is a central problem and that parity is a priority.[12] Personal contact and family experience can be real motivators for change.

Given the lack of true parity at present, the message to people who suffer from debilitating depressions, impairing anxieties, severe disturbances of thinking, or other mental disorders is that mental health problems are of secondary importance, unworthy of being considered or treated in the same ways as "regular" medical conditions. A cascade of negative consequences is likely to follow, including worsening of symptoms, lack of employability, difficulties securing housing, and hopelessness. As a result, public stigma is bound to intensify, completing the vicious cycle.

What would the financial consequences of parity be? It has been estimated that health insurance premiums would rise approximately 1% with the passage of more complete parity legislation. Although this is certainly an expenditure that must be borne, estimated costs to U.S. government and businesses from untreated mental disorder are over $100 billion annually in terms of lost productivity and unemployment.[13] Given these astronomical figures, parity would appear to be cost effective. Time will tell whether Congress and the executive branch will invest strongly enough in parity to effect meaningful change.

Yet parity is not a complete solution. The increasingly large number of citizens who lack health insurance will be unaffected by parity legislation, which deals only with persons who have insurance coverage. For the noninsured, more basic health care reform is the real issue, so long as treatments for mental illnesses are included. In fact, being uninsured means that mental health care is almost unattainable except through poorly funded entitlement programs such as Medicaid and Medicare.[14]

Even when treatment is available, poor people who are confronted with mental illness often receive inferior treatments. Continuity of treatment providers is rare, as interns and residents rotate through low-income clinics in teaching hospitals, and patients are often shuffled from one provider to the next. When medication is prescribed, it is too often done quickly and without sufficient rationale or education. Clear information on possible side effects and follow-up appointments to monitor patient response are often absent. The experience of Betty, a mid-30s single mother of a 6-year-old boy, illustrates the issues faced by recipients of public assistance:

Betty has struggled with chronic depression since adolescence. Sometimes she has episodes of depression that are quite severe, rendering her hopeless and even suicidal. Yet even when these episodes recede, her mood and energy are low nearly all of the time. It has been this way for more than 20 years, and she has come to believe that her mood will never really change.

Despite the presence of this mental illness, which began when she was 14, she managed to attain a high-school equivalency diploma. She got pregnant in her late 20s and had a son, but the boy's father was never present. Her depression has continued to exert a negative impact on her functioning, particularly because she is so isolated socially. She and her son live in a small, crowded apartment, and she has no social contacts or friends. She works part time, takes classes at a community college, and receives SSI benefits related to her depression.

Through a public clinic, Betty began to receive a form of treatment called interpersonal therapy a year ago. This is an evidence-based type of psychotherapy that emphasizes both insight into long-term patterns of functioning and the importance of relationships with others. A key goal was to expand supports in her social network. However, her hopelessness and low energy continued to limit her efforts to develop meaningful relationships; an underlying pessimism seemed to thwart her reaching out. Her therapist, a psychologist, suggested that she obtain consultation with a medical doctor about adding antidepressant medication to her treatment regimen.

Betty was extremely resistant to considering medication for her depression, as she believed that she should be able to cope without "chemicals." In fact, she thought that it would be a sign of weakness to rely on pills for her own personal issues. However, having developed trust in her therapist, she agreed to visit the medical clinic where she received her care to get information about antidepressant medication. She had an appointment with a physician's assistant, who reviewed her records and spoke with her for a few minutes about her mood and functioning. An antidepressant was prescribed, but the overworked assistant did not provide any detailed information about how to take it or what it might do. Fearing side effects and lacking any understanding of how the medication might work, Betty decided not to begin.

Her therapist became aware of the situation and began to talk with Betty about issues such as exactly when to take the medication and what to be aware of when she took it. Only then did Betty feel safe enough to begin taking the medicine. Yet she had not been prescribed its more recent extended-release form. Given her hectic schedule of work, school, and parenting her son, who had been recently diagnosed with learning problems and was often quite demanding, she often forgot to take the second pill of the day.

Her therapist intervened with the medical clinic, and the staff finally wrote a new prescription for a longer-acting form of the medication, which provided all-day coverage. Gradually the medicine and therapy have combined to take away some of the hard, sad edge of her depression. She has begun to feel some hope.

It will take both parity legislation and general health-care reform to provide access to sound care for persons with mental illness. At the same time, this vignette makes clear that mental health professionals need to provide clear, supportive guidance in order for treatments to be accepted. In addition, anticipating the section below on mental health research, it will take a continued commitment to funding the highest-quality research on causation, diagnosis, and treatment of mental illness—as well as basic psychological and social processes that may be relevant to mental disorder—to guarantee that effective interventions continue to be developed and promoted. Efforts at multiple levels are clearly needed.

Additional Laws and Policies

A key issue related to legal initiatives for persons with mental illness is that, in democratic societies, rights for certain individuals should be restricted only for due cause, related to demonstrable limitations or disabilities that would imperil the freedom, safety, or rights of others. Restrictions of rights for extremely global reasons—for instance, the label of mental illness or a history of the same—are inherently discriminatory.[15] Yet as Chapter 6 emphasizes, many states currently prohibit people with mental disorders from having custody of their children, as well as from voting, marrying, serving on juries, or holding public office. Examining and changing state laws with respect to such restrictions is a priority.

Would Abraham Lincoln ever have been able to vote under such statutes, much less become a member of Congress or president, given his history of mood disorders? Could Winston Churchill ever have been elected prime minister of England with his clear propensity for alcohol use and his legendary mood swings? Again, denial of rights may be appropriate for just cause—but not for a history of mental illness that is stereotypically believed to create a permanent affliction that dominates an individual's entire character and rationality. The range of rights that are denied individuals with mental illness requires serious reform efforts at local and state levels.

Beyond laws related to civil and human rights, I address the policy-related areas of employment, housing, research funding, and criminalization of mental illness.

Jobs   Rates of unemployment and underemployment among those with mental disorders and the resultant poverty and alienation that emanate from them are strikingly high.[16] Without meaningful work, a pattern of dependency, boredom, alienation, and lack of fulfillment is likely to develop. Societal stigma is also prone to increase, as a function of perceivers' observations that persons with mental disorders are not able to support themselves and therefore require welfare funds.

Ending job discrimination is crucial. Although it is illegal to prohibit persons with disabilities from being employed (under, for example, the Americans with Disabilities Act, or ADA), such discrimination is often hard to prove in the case of mental illness. Indeed, potential employees with a mental disorder are likely to be caught in a bind. They can either (a) fail to tell the prospective employer about their history and hope that perseverance and determination can lead to job success—but without support or accommodations; or (b) disclose such history but then run the risk of failing to be hired or having to fight to obtain workplace accommodations if a position is secured. Means beyond legislation alone will be necessary to convince employers that individuals with mental disorders are worth hiring. Attitude change could emanate from education about employee success, from assurance that accommodations can be funded, and from firsthand experience with employees who have worked out well.

In terms of the workplace, ADA bans discrimination in public facilities, as well as places of employment, for individuals with physical and emotional disabilities. Yet most of its provisions have been utilized for persons requiring accommodations for physical conditions; less clear are the sorts of procedures that are required for those with identified mental disorders in either public facilities or work settings.[17] In an important survey, MacDonald-Wilson and colleagues found that individuals with serious mental disorders—for whom job tenure was noted to be quite short overall—often needed accommodations related to acquiring social skills, learning work tasks, maintaining stamina, and tolerating stress, differing from the mobility or physical access accommodations often needed for physical disabilities. Indeed, this study identified job coaching and flexibility of scheduling by supervisors as key contributors to success for people with mental disorders. Other accommodations could include job restructuring, workplace modifications (e.g., a more secluded workplace for individuals with marked social anxieties), or short bouts of sick leave hours to accommodate needed psychological or psychiatric services.[18] Providing specific training in job-related skills to overcome skill deficits, low levels of education, or low motivation may also be quite significant. Funding for such endeavors is essential, requiring policy-level change that transcends legal mandates per se.[19]

Housing Housing is a clear prerequisite for independent functioning, safety and integrity, and many other aspects of well-being. The Fair Housing Act of 1988, along with various amendments, outlaws housing discrimination against individuals with physical and mental disabilities. Unfortunately, enforcement of fair housing statutes is not ensured, particularly because discrimination against people with mental disorders may be difficult to document. In addition, the empirical research of Page reveals that landlords are extremely unwilling to show apartments to prospective tenants with histories of mental disorder.[20] Overall, major problems regarding housing access for persons with mental illness exist.

Even if housing is made available and provided without discrimination, a large number of persons with mental disorders cannot afford a place to live. Recall from Chapter 6 that the cost of basic apartments in many states outpaces the entire monthly allocation received from SSI benefits. As a result, inadequate housing or facilities obtainable only in high-risk, dangerous neighborhoods may be the only options. Living in such neighborhoods doubtless contributes to the huge risk for people with mental illnesses to be become victimized by violent crime.[21] It is hard to imagine a more important priority area for stigma reduction.

Lobbying and advocacy are crucial to the extent that additional legislation can help to ensure greater rights in this domain. At a policy level, provision of community residences and group homes is extremely important for many with serious mental disorders—those who need more social and therapeutic support than is typically available in independent apartments. Because of stigmatization, however, neighborhood resistance is often strong with respect to locating such facilities in desirable venues. Advocates may need to testify at town meetings or in front of zoning boards. For independent housing, subsidies must be increased if any sort of decent living quarters can be obtained. Of course, viable employment is a crucial step toward affording housing; integrated strategies are needed across housing and employment policies.

In sum, housing options for persons with mental illness may be limited to living with relatives, often under stressful circumstances; obtaining substandard housing in marginal neighborhoods; competing for a few slots in supported living facilities or community residences; or, in the worst case scenario, not having any viable housing at all, leading potentially to homelessness. A combination of enforcement of antidiscrimination laws, enhanced subsidies for housing, improved employment opportunities, greater support for community residences and halfway houses, and nondiscrimination on the part of landlords are all needed to address this crucial problem.

Funding for Research Research on mental health includes two broad categories of investigations: (a) studies of basic social, emotional, cognitive, developmental, and neurobiological processes, which provide the "raw materials" for under-standing problems in mental and behavioral functioning; and (b) investigations into the causes of and effective treatments for mental illness. Both types are essential for ensuring progress. In fact, basic research and clinical investigations must work in tandem to make inroads regarding mental disorder and its amelioration. Given how much remains to be learned about mental illness, if adequate funds for continued research are not forthcoming, persons with mental disorders would have good reason to lack hope.

Although research and services for mental health have received funding at increased levels in recent years, the amounts still lag behind rates of funding for physical illnesses.[22] This is an untenable situation, especially given the in-creasing recognition that mental disorders are among the most impairing ill-nesses worldwide.[23] Permitting basic and applied research on mental illness to fall behind comparable investigations of other diseases and conditions is itself strong evidence for stigma.

How can such funding be prioritized? In a participatory democracy like that of the United States, advocacy and lobbying are necessary. But building a constituency behind mental health efforts has historically been difficult, given the invisibility and lack of organized efforts of persons with mental illness. Advocacy groups such as NAMI and the Campaign for Mental Health Reform are lobbying intensively for continued funding increases with respect to the National Institute of Mental Health (NIMH), the federal agency supporting re-search on mental disorders, and the Substance Abuse and Mental Health Services Administration (SAMSHA), which explicitly funds service-related ef-forts. These efforts are crucial to reducing stigma: Indeed, after years of record increases in federal funding for the National Institutes of Health (including NIMH) in the late 1990s, funding is now nearly stagnant.[24]

The fight to conquer mental disorder will not be a quick one, despite the progress that has been witnessed over the past decades. Although increasingly viewed as treatable conditions, mental disorders have been part of the human condition for millennia, and their consequences and impairments are often ex-tremely severe. As I have noted throughout these pages, they result from multi-ple genes and multiple environmental risk factors, which interact to tip the balance toward pathology rather than positive adaptation in ways that are still being discovered.[25] Given the complexity of the development of mental disor-ders, long-term investments in concerted research are a national priority.

Criminalization   Mental health issues have become increasingly folded into the criminal justice system in recent years.[26] Several trends have converged: (a) deinstitutionalization of mental facilities, which too often leaves individu-als with severe mental disorders in inner-city settings without adequate sup-port; (b) criminalization of status offenses, particularly those related to sub-stance use and abuse; (c) tightening of civil commitment statutes, which makes it extremely difficult to get individuals with serious mental illness into mental facilities against their will; and (d) a general trend toward "law and order" (e.g., three-strikes laws). As a result of such occurrences, jails and prisons are witnessing large increases in inmates with mental disorders. Furthermore, the lack of preparation in such facilities for mental health problems—and the dearth of relevant services—are alarming.[27]

Several issues are relevant. First, it is not at all clear that the criminalization of deviance related to mental disorder (e.g., substance abuse, disruptive public behavior) does anything to help the underlying mental conditions. It is highly arguable, in fact, that jail and prison facilities will only exacerbate underlying instability. Second, if persons with mental illnesses are indeed imprisoned, it is essential that treatment be made available, but this is rarely the case. Third, the low status of prisoners in current society, along with the increased stigmatization of mental illness in recent years, constitutes a double stigma for incarcerated individuals with mental disorders, particularly given the general cultural and media-promoted view of mental illness as inevitably linked with violence. Reform inside prisons, including diagnosis of underlying mental disorders and provision of responsive treatment, will need to dovetail with advocacy for the decriminalization of certain forms of deviance. Other needed reforms involve the training of police (as well as other legal personnel) to be sensitive to mental illness in persons they are likely to apprehend and improving media portrayals that inextricably link mental illness to incompetence and violence (see Chapter 10).[28] In short, the reinstitutionalization of individuals with mental illness into prisons and jails provides few solutions and is instead a trigger for recidivism, stigmatization, and hopelessness.

Children and Adolescents With Mental Disorders

Several policy-related issues are important for reducing the stigmatization of children and adolescents with mental disorders. I highlight three: special education laws and funding, medical checkups that could be expanded to include the monitoring of behavioral and emotional health, and existing policies that seriously threaten family unity.

Special Education   The Individuals with Disabilities Education Act (IDEA) was first passed into law in 1975, as the Education for All Handicapped Children Act, and then reauthorized in 1991 and again in 2004. Over the years, it has stipulated that youngsters with suspected special needs receive a school-based assessment. If this evaluation reveals the existence of a learning disability, emotional disorder, or other health-related condition that compromises school performance, an Individual Education Plan (IEP) is developed and implemented, with the goal of providing reasonable educational objectives, accommodations to meet these goals, and a systematic means of monitoring progress.

The accommodations written into the IEP exist along a continuum. Children with milder disabilities may receive resource room assistance, through which they go to a smaller class with trained teachers several hours per week. Another option could be to obtain the assistance of an aide in the regular classroom setting. At a more restrictive level, special day classes may be mandated, where the child attends a substantially separate classroom on an all-day basis, perhaps with limited mainstreaming for lunch or physical education. In the most severe cases, entirely separate school facilities may be required, constituting either day programs or residential care. The principle guiding such accommodations is that of the *least restrictive alternative,* meaning that the child should be placed in the setting that provides needed learning supports with as much mainstreaming in regular educational settings as possible. The intent is to avoid unnecessary exclusion or stigmatization.[29]

Several points are important to consider. First, the potential benefits of obtaining a diagnosis in order to justify services must be weighed against the potential for stigmatization that could attend to the label. Recall the behavioral study of Gillmore and Farina, where fifth- and eighth-graders responded to classmates labeled as mentally retarded or emotionally disturbed with a desire for greater social distance and with less friendly and more negative social interactions.[30] Stigmatizing attitudes are apparent in children and adolescents, and it may take intervention beyond mainstreaming alone—at the level of educating all children about behavioral and emotional distances—to promote optimal chances for youth with mental disorders in the classroom.

Second, federal funds are not specifically earmarked to help districts implement these procedures. In other words, IDEA is the law, mandating IEPs and appropriate accommodations, but federal monies have not been set aside to fund its full provisions. Increasingly strapped for funds, school districts are struggling to maintain mandated special education services for all who need them. As a result, parental requests for an IEP and appropriate accommodations may be denied. In many such cases, parents become adversaries of school districts, insisting on further evaluations (or provisions of specific diagnoses) to justify needed services. In short, access to appropriate and responsive special education services for youth whose mental disturbances preclude adequate academic achievement should enhance learning and ultimately reduce stigma; nevertheless, in this era of limited funding for adequate public education across much of the United States, extra funds for children with special needs related to mental illnesses are at a premium.

Viable educational and therapeutic programming for children with mental disorders will take investments of funds to be implemented with quality. Such investment should pay dividends if all youths can receive a quality education, enabling them to lead productive lives. In particular, when separate programs are truly warranted, they must have the kinds of trained personnel in place to ensure that learning goals are met while maladaptive behavior is not being modeled as a function of exposure to other children or adolescents with deviant behavior. Far greater support is needed for regular classroom teachers as well, in order to accommodate youths with special needs in their classrooms.

Third, the kinds of problems for which school systems are willing to provide accommodations typically include cognitive or language problems or attention deficits that directly interfere with classroom learning. Depression, social skills deficits, or problems at home are typically ignored or denied services. As a brief example, take the case of a 6-year-old boy with a history of severe physical abuse. The boy was quite intelligent and therefore able to keep up academically with his first-grade classmates, although his performance could have been even better. And, because he was depressed, he rarely interacted with anyone and had no friends. He would respond if called on in class but did not initiate interactions with teachers or peers.

It was argued to his home school district that, despite his superior intellect, his depression was interfering with his academic and social learning. Yet the chairperson of the district's special education committee stated bluntly that the district was not concerned about problems at home or social functioning. The verbatim response was as follows: "A child can burn down his house, but if he doesn't set a fire at school, it isn't our problem." At best, this attitude conveys an unhealthy distinction between school and home domains of functioning; at worst, it exemplifies clear stigmatization. School is the main arena where mental health problems can be identified and addressed for children and adolescents, given that they are in school settings many hours per day. The separation of academic learning from social and self-regulatory skills is counterproductive.

Fourth, services for children are often fragmented—divided across educational needs (school systems), emotional and behavioral needs (mental health systems), physical needs (medical systems), and home-related needs (welfare systems). Unfortunately, few systems of care look at the whole child to coordinate efforts. Integration and coordination of systems of care for children and adolescents are an essential component of stigma reduction.

In all, provision of support and treatment for mental disorders in the context of school-based services is a major educational, policy-oriented, and stigma-related issue for children and adolescents. Problems with respect to funding, inclusion versus exclusion, and fragmentation of services make the current system difficult for many school-aged youths with mental disorders. Better means of evaluating the effects of accommodations are also needed to ensure that provisions of special education statutes are being implemented with due diligence in ways that truly benefit the child and reduce stigma in the long run by promoting educational and mental health–related gains.

Preventive Behavioral Orientation for Health Checkups   In current medical practice, well-child visits are implemented throughout development to ensure that vaccinations have been given, developmental milestones are surpassed, and illnesses are reviewed. Although these do not occur with sufficient regularity for children in disenfranchised, uninsured families, the ideal is a preventive orientation to health care. Yet emotional and behavioral indicators play almost no role in such assessments, which are largely restricted to physical markers and milestones. Along with many allied professionals, I suggest that the pediatric (and general medical) profession incorporate evaluation of behavioral and emotional problems and strengths during routine care.[31]

Such assessment might include rating scales for parents and teachers (or, for younger children, child care workers) prior to the scheduled checkup, so that the professional has access to normed information about the child's behavior and performance. More detailed probing could be requested if there are potential issues requiring follow-up. As children develop, they could themselves complete brief screening questionnaires about crucial domains of functioning (such as depression or substance use in adolescence). Aimed at catching potential problems early, this approach is likely to be far more cost effective than waiting until behavioral and emotional problems are fully in place—and which may even then never come to the health-care professional's attention.

Such an orientation would signal an important shift toward recognition of the importance of mental illness and the promotion of positive social and emotional functioning. Attaining competence during early periods of life is bound to exert a positive influence on all facets of later development. Although additional training and funding will be required to implement such a focus on prevention, the potential benefits could be considerable.

In the past several years, much controversy has attended to the New Freedom Commission's advocacy for screening related to mental and emotional problems. Scientologists and others who deny the existence of mental illness contend that such an enterprise is actually a means of finding new cases of nonexistent conditions, which would be subjected to social control in the form of unneeded medication and other treatments. Both extremely conservative and extremely liberal political constituencies have espoused these beliefs, showing a convergence of different ideologies around the contention that early identification is actually a ploy by pharmaceutical firms and zealous mental health advocates to create new markets for psychotropic medication use in vulnerable young children.[32]

Although extreme caution needs to be exerted with respect to the process of labeling young children as "at risk" for mental disorder, it is simply wrong to deny that mental disorders often begin early in development and that they require preventive intervention before becoming entrenched.[33] The point is *not* to routinely and unthinkingly mandate labeling or early medication treatments for young, vulnerable children. Rather, it is to recognize the reality of mental disturbance and to include prudent assessment as part of examining the health of the whole child throughout development. The current system of waiting until problem behavior, a learning issue, or emotional disturbance becomes clearly established is simply not viable: It wastes needed time, it is ultimately quite costly, and it only enhances stigma.

This practice should not be limited to children and adolescents. Because the majority of adults with mental illness fail to receive treatment, mental health assessments can and should be incorporated into routine medical care for them as well. A good example is screening for signs of depression during yearly checkups.

Such practices could serve to normalize discussion of mental disorders and increase access to needed services. That is, doctors would routinely engage their adult patients in discussion of psychological symptoms, life stressors, and coping styles. Doctors commonly ask about family histories of heart disease or stroke during routine care but usually fail to inquire about mental disorders; such avoidant strategies keep mental disorders shrouded in secrecy and maintain the belief that exposure to or discussion of mental disorder, even in a doctor's office, is shameful. Moreover, when a mental disorder is detected in an adult who has children, preventive services could be considered for the family and offspring (see Chapter 11). This orientation would require training for the personnel involved, including safeguards to avoid overprediction of mental illness. The point would not be a rush to diagnosis but rather to embrace a stance that is preventive and encourages people to seek help when it is called for.

Family Unity In a number of instances, parents of youths with serious emotional and behavioral disturbances have had to relinquish custody of their children in order to obtain any meaningful services for them. It is only by this extreme step that public facilities or other therapeutic environments can sometimes become available. In fact, it is estimated that this scenario transpired for more than 25,000 families in the United States between mid-2003 and mid-2005. Such cases typically involve youngsters with high levels of emotional disturbance and acting-out behavior. Because of the shortage of residential mental health centers for such children and adolescents, along with the exorbitant costs of these facilities, parents may be able to obtain placements only if the court or the state takes over custody, so that public funds can be utilized.[34]

Consider this scenario: You have a 14-year-old boy who is exhibiting a severe mood condition, with a recent diagnosis of bipolar disorder. Episodes of mania (with uncontrolled rage, fueled by paranoia) and depression (with suicidal thoughts and behaviors) recur. He has punched out walls in the family home, the school has expelled him, and he refuses to be seen by a psychologist or psychiatrist. Your other children are terrified. Desperate for care, you consult a social worker at the county mental health center, who explains that no affordable residential care facilities are located in your region. Contending that the violent behavior is not grounds for accommodations related to learning and achievement, the school district has refused to grant an IEP.

One of the few remaining options is to declare yourself "incompetent" to parent this adolescent and then relinquish custody to the state so that he may be placed in a public facility. This is a sacrifice that too many families have had to make in order to keep themselves and their offspring safe. The federal "Keeping Families Together Act" intends to outlaw such practices. In addition, the "Family Opportunity Act"—which allows Medicaid benefits for families with children who have serious disabilities even though the family is somewhat above the federal poverty-level guides—is also under debate; it also has the objective of family preservation. Both of these bills could aid families in receiving services for their offspring without having to become impoverished or lose custody of their children altogether.[35]

Paradoxical Effects of Legislative Reform?

Are there potential problems with legislation designed to promote equality and parity for individuals with mental illness? It is hard to imagine, at first glance, that negative consequences could occur, other than increased costs in the short run to fund relevant initiatives. Yet laws designed to provide special benefits and rights for persons with mental disorders could well backfire by serving to further isolate this category.[36] In other words, specialized mental health laws may be inherently stigmatizing because they call attention to the underprivileged status of persons with mental disorder in a way that emphasizes their need for special protection. Stigma could actually increase if the public comes to view persons with mental illness in "benevolent" terms—that is, as victims who need pity rather than independent status and full rights.[37]

One potential solution would be to enact legislation applicable to *anyone* who lacks certain competencies, rather than singling out those with mental illness as a special category deserving of particular protections. Indeed, in the current political climate there is real risk involved in creating protected status for specific subgroups. Consider affirmative action laws and guidelines, against which a backlash has emerged, in the form of opposition to any kind of favored status for individuals of color regarding education or employment. A key tension therefore exists between singling out certain groups for special privileges and applying color-blind or other equity-based policies.

Parity legislation should not present a problem in this regard. If parity laws are framed as opening access to treatments for valid psychiatric conditions, rather than giving preferential status to a specific and favored subgroup, opposition should be minimal on this ground. In other words, parity regarding insurance coverage for mental health care must be considered as a necessary step toward ending discrimination, so long as such persons are not branded as a special interest group requiring privileged status or special treatment. Other laws discussed earlier, such as ADA, IDEA, and the Fair Housing Act, apply to individuals with physical as well as mental disabilities.

On the other hand, there is need for vigilance regarding statutes that mandate special status for mental disorders (for example, a piece of legislation that would create extra funds for this class of people). Once again, equality and parity rather than special, protected status must be emphasized. In short, those advocating for legislative reform should attempt to minimize unintended consequences of change efforts.

Summary

Increased advocacy for legislation related to the rights of people with mental illness is a priority. Because of the importance of ensuring that mental disorders receive the best available treatments, parity in insurance coverage for mental health treatments is crucial. At the same time, it is essential to provide access to health insurance (and mental health care) for the millions who are uninsured. Other policy-related strategies include providing needed job access and training for those with mental disorders, ensuring that accommodations in the workplace are upheld, enforcing fair housing practices (and implementing new policies to improve access to housing), and working to counteract the de facto reinstitutionalization of people with mental disorders in inadequate jail and prison facilities. Lobbying for increased funding for basic and applied research on mental illness and its treatment is also essential for stigma reduction: Without gains in knowledge regarding the causes of and effective interventions for mental illness, no progress can be made. Finally, legislation that limits rights regarding child custody, voting, jury service, marrying, holding public office, or driving on the basis of a diagnosis of mental disorder or disability (rather than on the basis of specific competencies or disabilities) should be challenged.

For children and adolescents, access to special services at school under IDEA requires sound financial backing, as well as considerable family education about legal rights, to prevent a situation in which the wealthiest or most legally savvy families are the only ones who can obtain accommodations. Also, a new orientation to medical care could incorporate the assessment of emotional and mental health problems of youth—and adults—during routine checkups. This could be of great value in preventing mental disorder and reducing stigma, so long as overzealous and premature diagnosis is avoided. Family preservation should be a core goal for parents of children with mental disorders to the greatest extent possible, and fragmentation of services for youth must be replaced by integrated models of care so that families do not have to engage with educational, mental health, welfare, and other systems separately and counterproductively. As a cautionary note, however, people with mental illness should not be further stigmatized by statutes that single them out as helpless, special recipients of extra rewards or accommodations. Equal access, not special protection or status, must be the priority.

Community-Level Interventions for Members of Society

What can communities and concerned citizens do to reduce the stigmatization of mental illness? Corrigan and Penn have divided empirically supported means of countering stigma into three main categories: (a) promoting personal contact between the general public and individuals with mental disorders; (b) providing education about mental illness to members of the community; and (c) mounting protest efforts against discrimination and stereotyped media portrayals of mental disorder.[38] Because the latter strategy (protest) has focused largely on countering the noxious effects of media depictions, I save relevant discussion of that approach until Chapter 10. Although personal contact and educational campaigns are ultimately intended to alter attitudes and behavioral practices of individual citizens, I present them as community interventions because they are ripe for adoption by large social groups. Other means by which citizens can alter attitudes and behaviors, such as changing patterns of stereotyped thinking and directly promoting the enhancement of empathy and compassion, follow this discussion.

Personal Contact

Pioneers in the fight against racial prejudice strongly believed that attitudinal and behavioral change requires face-to-face contact with members of stigmatized groups. The premise is that hearing about the plight of devalued individuals or attempting to alter prejudiced attitudes through mental processes alone cannot produce the same types of effects as directly interacting with outgroup members. The *contact hypothesis* has been a guiding force behind antidiscrimination laws and judicial rulings, as well as specific programs designed to reduce prejudice and bias.[39]

Is there supporting evidence along these lines—in other words, does contact change attitudes and behaviors? Regarding the area of racial prejudice, a number of investigations support the contention that when contact occurs, bias tends to diminish. Indeed, a systematic meta-analysis by Pettigrew and Tropp found support for the contact hypothesis.[40] In addition, a review from the 1990s showed that contact between students or mental health workers, on the one hand, and psychiatric patients, on the other, was associated with reductions in negative attitudes regarding mental disorder. Overall, corroborating evidence exists to the effect that contact with persons with mental illness is associated with reduced prejudice and stigma, although numerous qualifiers preclude the proclaiming of large effects in all cases.[41]

Indeed, the *kind* of contact or interaction is crucial. For example, if "contact" involves the public's making tours of mental hospitals or encountering disheveled homeless persons with severe mental illnesses on urban streets, fear, exclusion, and stigma are likely to increase rather than diminish. For children, if contact involves interacting with a disruptive, untreated peer with a mental disorder, it is likely that distancing and scapegoating will result, along with the belief that children with mental disorders are dangerous and untreatable. Simply knowing someone with mental illness or having a disordered relative is typically insufficient to reduce stigma (see Chapter 5). A critical issue, then, is related to the *conditions* of contact that can diminish prejudice and stigma.[42]

Equal Status   When majority group members and stigmatized individuals have relatively equal power and status, contact is far more likely to promote positive attitudes than when there is a marked power imbalance. Contact with stereotypic representatives of people with mental illness (e.g., through encountering homeless persons with mental illness on city streets) is likely to reinforce the belief such persons are deviant, powerless, potentially freakish, and extremely difficult to deal with. When a stigmatized group has low social power and when contact is not equitable, social interactions tend to promote the status quo precisely because they serve to reinforce prevailing notions and stereotypes.

The key question, then, is how to foster equal status. Structural and policy changes—access to housing, employment, and funding for adequate treatment, as discussed in the first section of this chapter—are a crucial step. At a less formal level, community settings that promote commerce, shopping, conversation, and interchange among equals can provide the kinds of contact that are likely to break down social barriers. To the extent that persons with mental disorder can be embedded in the social life of a community, chances for stigma reduction will be improved, so long as behavior patterns are not disruptive—meaning that treatment is an important ingredient. Employment and housing, as well as assurance of adequate treatment, are therefore crucial.

Closeness, Informality, and Regularity   When contact is informal and casual rather than formally arranged and when opportunities exist for shared mainstream experiences rather than artificial interchanges, perceptions of stigmatized group members are most likely to improve. Interactions should be regular events in the lives of citizens rather than sporadic, arranged contacts. In addition, when there are emotions to be shared (particularly positive emotions but also, potentially, shared sadness or righteous anger), the psychological closeness of the relevant interactions is likely to foster appreciation and acceptance. When humans can form bonds marked by social exchange, mutual valuation, and close acquaintanceships, boundaries tend to dissolve.

Institutional and Societal Support   If attempts at making contact encounter obstacles or ridicule, the disruption is likely to thwart meaningful change. For example, if school systems and teachers are opposed to mainstreaming, students will undoubtedly pick up on the resistance, and attitudes toward classmates with mental and emotional disorders are not likely to improve. The same would be true if employers are reluctant to promote meaningful contact between newly hired employees with mental disorders and the rest of the workforce. On the other hand, when interaction is bolstered by support from work settings, school administrators, or communities at large, reductions in stigma are likely. At the ultimate level, contact is likely to "stick" when it has the backing of the law of the land and is bolstered by governing bodies. Appropriate and sensitively enacted accommodations for individuals with disabilities, either physical or mental, may give the signal that exchange is valued and supported. In short, contact requires nurturance and support from social structures and institutional authorities.

Cooperative Tasks and Collaboration   If ingroup and outgroup members have shared goals and work toward common ends, attitude change is likely to be positive and contact is likely to continue. This cooperative framework is important for several reasons. For example, the mutuality of goals can reduce the perception of threat from an outgroup member. Such mutuality can also help to facilitate a more human, universal standard of comparison between ingroup members and those in outgroups. This perceived commonality will be fostered only when supports are in place for meaningful interaction—and when there are real, rather than contrived, problems to be worked on. In short, the more that people with mental disorders are able to be next to other members of society in school settings, jobs, and community organizations, working together on important issues, the more that true cooperation can emerge.

What are some practical means of ensuring these conditions of equitable contact? Providing treatment for persons with mental illness is essential so that contacts are not marked by huge disparities in behavior (see Chapter 11). Location of housing in neighborhood settings rather than isolated tracts or distant institutions is also essential to promote the kinds of informal, regular contact that can reduce prejudice and stigma. Facilitating employment opportunities that can afford regular, close contact at the workplace is a key step as well. For children and adolescents, contact should be facilitated by mainstreaming procedures, through which youth with mental disturbances are placed in regular classroom settings to the greatest extent possible, in accordance with the least restrictive alternative noted earlier. Yet simply placing children with physical or mental disorders in such venues is not enough. Without adequate preparation, education, and guidance from teachers, fellow students may reject their behaviorally deviant peers. Supports directed to students with special needs are also required in the form of interventions to help with academic and social skills.[43] On the whole, fostering optimal contact requires planning, enlightened social policy, and support from key citizens.

Education

Common community-level efforts to destigmatize mental illness involve education of the public about mental disorder. The assumption is that if citizens are better informed about the realities of mental illness, they will relinquish their tendencies to engage in stereotypic thinking and thereby reduce their prejudiced attitudes. If lack of awareness and understanding can be replaced by knowledge, such that the frightening, unknown aura and threat surrounding mental disorder dissipates, acceptance should emerge. From this perspective, ignorance is the key enemy.

There is a long history of public efforts to provide such education. Indeed, during the 1950s and 1960s, local, state, and federal programs were enacted in the attempt to convince the public that mental disorders were illnesses like all others. Results, however, were mixed, with initial optimism giving way to harsher appraisals of the actual attitudinal and behavioral changes that were produced.[44] Currently, governmental and private agencies are continuing to provide information about mental illness with the objective of destigmatizing it. Educational methods include workshops and seminars for employees, as well as films and videos. Also, a number of demonstration programs have been attempted, in which various audiences (e.g., police officers, mental health trainees, high school students) are exposed to workshops, films, and lectures.

Results from such programs are typically small but demonstrable.[45] In other words, various forms of education can produce benefits, but they are not universally found and are not likely, in and of themselves, to produce long-lasting effects. Still, public education has become mainstream. For example, during the 1990s Rotary International began an "erase the stigma" campaign in order to educate business professionals about the negative images of persons with mental disorder. A major federal agency responsible for mental health promotion and services, SAMSHA, has implemented an "Elimination of Barriers" initiative, providing funds in eight states for a variety of initiatives to educate the public and thereby reduce stigma.[46] The objective is to develop longer-term strategies that could make an important difference in the future.

Educational programs often include brochures—or today, website postings—that attempt to portray mental illness realistically and in common, human terms. Lectures and formal courses are sometimes offered. Some strategies are more creative, borrowing from efforts to raise the public's awareness of and compassion for physical disabilities. For the latter, simulations have tried to reveal to participants what it would be like to be blind or physically impaired. Extending this concept, some recent simulations have involved the experiencing of hallucinations, with the objective of promoting empathy for the confusion and even terror of hearing voices (and, as well, of revealing the reality of the symptoms of mental illness).[47]

In terms of benefits from these efforts, the research evidence is mixed.[48] From short-term educational programs there have been both successes and failures. For one thing, information alone may not change prejudicial attitudes, as emphasized in Chapter 5. Indeed, data that emphasize the chronic symptoms of mental illnesses may actually perpetuate stereotypes. More helpful is information about the adaptive potential for people with mental disorders. Longer-lasting educational interventions can produce substantial changes in attitudes, especially if they emphasize give-and-take exchange rather than strict lecture format. In other words, education should not be didactic and closed but rather open and interactive, to the greatest extent possible.[49] Also recommended are messages about competencies of those with mental illness—for example, information about their potential to live and work in the community rather than a listing of chronic social deficits. It would be quite interesting to see the potential benefits of early education about mental illness, initiated before prejudicial attitudes become entrenched. School-based educational programs, including those in the elementary grades, are an important area to be developed.

Recent research on adolescents indicates that interventions combining education (particularly about the effectiveness of mental health treatments) and contact (through hearing about mental illness directly from those who have experienced it) can produce demonstrable improvements in attitudes, which persist for many months.[50] It may therefore take a synthesis of education plus contact to product lasting benefits.

Community Action: A Vignette

What can community organizations do? Estroff and colleagues performed a national-level survey to review community-based programs with the express goal of reducing stigma related to mental illness.[51] Many of these are nontraditional and include theater and improvisational groups, peer-support training, education on mental illness for bus drivers and other transit workers, weekly radio programs on mental health involving high school students, and web-based and regional conference facilitation. The qualities of such programs, most of which have not received formal evaluation as of yet, include empowerment of individuals and families dealing with mental health issues, respectful language, creation of resources for jobs and housing, promotion of involvement and contact, connection with existing community agencies and supports (e.g., schools, political leaders, media outlets), and expression through humor (particularly in drama and theater). Combining education and contact is a common thread.

An organization in the San Francisco Bay Area, known as Stamp out Stigma (SOS), is in the vanguard of community advocacy groups pursuing the explicit goal of eliminating the stigmatization of mental illness. According to an informative article in PatientView, SOS was founded by Carmen Lee, a woman who had spent many of her adult years in and out of psychiatric facilities, related largely to her ongoing battles with severe, suicidal depression.[52] After starting an advocacy group in the 1980s, and along with serving as a county commissioner on disabilities, with the express goal of placing mental illness on a par with physical disabilities in terms of recognition and funding, Lee founded SOS to fund speaker bureaus.

The speakers are typically former or present consumers of mental health services, having been patients in outpatient or inpatient facilities. Serving on panels, they provide 70 or more presentations a year to businesses, community groups, and citizens' meetings. Their focus is on topics such as how to treat people with mental disorders as equals or how to manage, in the workplace, an individual with mental disorder who becomes symptomatic or even potentially violent. In addition, SOS consults with police officers regarding how to provide more humane care for apprehended individuals with mental disorders, dentists who may need to deal with symptoms in the office, local suicide prevention centers, and even the FBI regarding optimal attitudes and practices when questioning a person with mental disorder. As another means of transmitting information, the organization also facilitates website links.

Through its speaker bureaus, SOS first promotes *contact,* in that the agencies, businesses, and organizations contracting with SOS receive hours of direct interaction with the speakers. The sessions typically comprise give-and-take discussions rather than didactic lectures. Such contact is also on relatively equal grounds, in that the agency or organization in question has requested the service of the expert consumers of the speakers' bureau.

Next, many of the messages given by SOS are direct instances of *protest,* albeit of a gentle rather than a confrontational variety. The very nature of SOS is one of a protest organization, yet one that is willing to work with mainstream groups (e.g., police force, FBI).

The format of the interactive sessions clearly facilitates *education.* Information is transmitted about helpful attitudes for employers and agency staff, procedures for dealing with crisis situations, and legally and ethically sound options for handling disruptive behavior. Again, this education is transmitted interactively rather than didactically or pedantically.

Beyond these three core tenets of stigma reduction, the fact that SOS is an independent organization, staffed by persons with mental disorder and providing a needed service, attests to the kinds of endeavors that individuals with mental disorder can take on. It models independence, initiative, and resolve; this implicit message may be one of the most important pieces of information that recipients learn.

Like many other nonprofit organizations, SOS has been experiencing a financial crisis. Outreach efforts to secure foundation grants, federal funds, and contracts are ongoing. It is telling that an organization with the values and practices of SOS is struggling to receive adequate support: There is not a large funding base for disenfranchised persons (such as those with mental disorder) to sustain important advocacy and educational efforts. Overall, SOS serves as a model of the kinds of direct outreach to society—emphasizing a combination of personal contact, protest efforts, and an extremely interactive educational format—that can help to diminish stigma. Formal evaluation is a crucial need.

Further Strategies to Combat Stigma

Beyond contact, education, and protest, what steps can members of communities take to reduce their own tendencies to stigmatize? This is a fast-growing area of research in relation to ethnic and racial prejudice and discrimination; applications to mental disorder are speculative but potentially important.

At the outset, it is important to note that attitudes toward stigmatized groups are often resistant to change.[53] First, providing educational information about exemplary members of an outgroup may fuel the belief that such information pertains only to the special case under consideration—the "exception that proves the rule"—rather than to the group as a whole. The strength of the overall stereotype may well be enhanced. In other words, if information is presented about a person with mental illness who shows sensitivity and humanity, perceivers may quickly come to believe that this particular person is unique, leaving untouched (or even more entrenched) the general belief that most individuals with mental disorder are frightening, irrational, and untrustworthy.[54]

Second, newly formed, positive attitudes toward stigmatized persons may place perceivers in the uncomfortable position of feeling that they must expend energy to change the discriminatory circumstances that led to the devalued status of the outgroup. Consciousness raising may therefore unleash uncomfortable emotions, challenging the perceiver to reconsider the inequities in the world. Defensiveness and inertia may result.

Third, when perceivers are confronted with the discrimination received by a stigmatized group, such awareness may raise doubts about how fair and just the world really is. As Chapters 2 and 7 pointed out, however, such beliefs tend to promote system-justifying strategies of blaming victims for bringing on their own plight. In other words, confrontation with alarming realities may motivate the belief that it is the fault of the outgroup member for having failed.

Overall, attempts to increase sympathy for the plight of stigmatized individuals, such as those with mental illness, often motivate forces that counteract compassion. Furthermore, simply suppressing stereotyped images has a mixed record in short-term research.[55] More active approaches of fostering empathy and contact may be necessary.

One of the initial pioneers in the field of changing racial bias and prejudice was Rokeach. Several decades ago he enacted procedures of confronting majority-group individuals with their own prejudiced values and attitudes, prompting them to challenge their own beliefs. When this type of confrontation succeeded in inducing strong personal dissatisfaction in the participant, marked improvements in attitudes toward racial minorities were likely to ensue. Such attitude and behavior change (e.g., joining the NAACP) were found to persist for more than a year.[56] As powerful as such strategies may be, however, many potential recipients might strongly resist active confrontation of their own biases and prejudices. That is, this approach does not appear feasible for those who would not consent to participate in the first place.

Newer research suggests additional means of overcoming stigma: (a) presentation of counterstereotypic images, (b) reconstruing ingroup versus outgroup identification, and (c) enhancement of empathy.

Counterstereotypic Imagery   In fascinating experimental work, Bodenhausen and colleagues presented brief counterstereotypic images of ethnic minority individuals to white perceivers. These were in the form of portrayals of well-liked African Americans who were financially successful. Whereas it might be thought that reading such depictions would promote the belief that African American individuals could "make it if they only tried," these portrayals actually increased the perceivers' likelihood of identifying discrimination as a major problem for African Americans. Viewing stigmatized individuals via counterstereotypic information—that is, images emphasizing positive rather than negative attributes—appears to promote identification with and empathy for the kinds of discrimination received by the minority group as a whole. Could positive portrayals of mental illness also lead to increased understanding and sympathy?[57]

Additionally, the use of mental imagery, through which participants vividly imagine examples of counterstereotypes (e.g., women who are strong and assertive), can reduce both explicit prejudice and implicit, unconscious biases toward the stigmatized group in question. Moreover, educational programs that promote positive emotions related to attitude change, such as those fostering strong interpersonal bonds among the participants, are particularly effective in combating implicit racial biases.[58] Community interventions of the future may benefit from the use of counterstereotypes, mental imagery, and positive emotion to reduce stigma.

Reconstruing Ingroups and Outgroups   A major problem with many attempts to reduce prejudice, bias, and stigma is the pervasive tendency for humans to be suspicious and distrustful of outgroup members. Educational interventions with the goal of increasing sympathy for a member of an outgroup may be working against a fundamental social, even evolutionarily motivated tendency to devalue those who are not in one's primary group. One way around this dilemma is to expand perceivers' boundaries of what constitutes the ingroup.

Along this line, Gaertner and Dovidio have promoted the *common ingroup identity model,* which features explicit means of encouraging a wider conception of who belongs to the ingroup, under the hypothesis that doing so will offer the benefits of ingroup membership to previously stigmatized individuals. This strategy circumvents the problems inherent in trying directly to extend empathy and compassion for outgroup members, a process that may backfire.[59]

One important strategy is to provide collaborative goals for groups who are in conflict. This process is exemplified in the classic work of Sherif and Sherif, who intensively studied preadolescent boys attending a residential camp during the 1950s. To bring these issues to life, I provide a brief description of this research.[60]

The boys in this camp were first divided into subgroups with different names (Eagles versus Rattlers). After a week's encouragement to develop their separate group identities, the groups showed, as expected, both strong ingroup identification and considerable outgroup hostility, which included name calling and even physical attacks. Ingroup-outgroup distinctions formed quickly and were marked by considerable antagonism.

During the second week, the groups were placed together for various activities. Such proximity, however, did not change the antipathy that had developed; contact alone was not sufficient to overcome prejudice. It was only during the third week that the camp directors had the groups work together toward common goals. For example, both groups were first told that a water leak in the camp threatened all of the campers, forcing them to collaborate. In a second instance, the boys were informed that there was not enough extra money for renting a movie, ensuring that the two groups pooled their resources to have enough for the rental. Finally, staff members intentionally drove the camp truck off the road to become stuck in a rut, though the campers did not know of this manipulation. The only solution was for the Eagles and Rattlers to work together to pull the tow rope, in order to have enough pooled strength to lift out the truck. In all three instances, a shared vision of goals emerged from the very nature of the tasks, which ensured that positive outcomes could be obtained only through collaborative efforts.

Only after the groups collaborated on such superordinate goals, suspending their group allegiances and coming together, did real harmony develop. Even then, this process did not come about quickly. It took initial successes in the cooperative efforts before the boys began to call the entire group *we* rather than the usual *us* versus *them*. By the time of the last common challenge, the truck pull, a new ingroup identity had clearly formed that included both former groups. It was not interpersonal contact per se but rather the formation of a new identity that made the difference, through collaborative goals and efforts.

If entrenched groups can form mutual goals requiring cooperation, longstanding antagonism and prejudice may erode. The crucial question is how to foster such mutual, superordinate goals for groups that have traditionally not interacted or have done so with hostility. One example occurs when persons with mental disorder and other members of society work together in self-help and advocacy organizations toward legislative and policy change (see Chapter 11). More broadly, when depictions of mental illness emphasize positive features and attributes, many members of society may become motivated to collaborate on common aims. The hope is that such decategorization processes can lead to reductions in stigma regarding mental disorder.

Enhancing Empathy   Because it will not always be possible to expand the boundaries of the ingroup, it is still important to find ways of fostering empathy and compassion for members of oppressed or stigmatized groups. Empathy, according Batson and colleagues, is

> an other-oriented emotional response congruent with another's perceived welfare; if the other is oppressed or in need, empathic feelings include sympathy, compassion, tenderness. . . . Research indicates that empathic feelings often result when one takes the perspective of a person in need, imagining how that person is affected by his or her plight. [61]

The concept includes *cognitive empathy*, understanding what another person is feeling, and *affective empathy*, the actual matching of feelings with those of another. Empathy may exert its ultimate effects through the perception of a common humanity and destiny across individuals. When empathy is invoked, positive attitudes and helping behaviors typically follow.

But it is not always this simple. Sympathy for a victim's plight may initially increase the perceivers' own sense of threat, prompting fear that the problems could beset them as well. As a result, perceivers may paradoxically devalue the victim in order to distance themselves and reduce their own sense of danger (a process termed "defensive avoidance"). Empathy may also foster condescending attitudes—for example, "look at those poor, pitiful victims"—unless respect for the castigated group is also promoted.

Research has concluded that empathy enhancement should focus on personally relevant information, include examples of the group's oppression or discrimination in the present day (and not just in the past), and promote respect, as well as sympathy, for the group.[62] Relationships, particularly those that are prolonged and meaningful, are particularly likely to enhance empathic responding. People have the capacity to empathize with their fellow human beings, but fostering empathy requires attention to the kinds of procedures most likely to generate respect and compassion.

The positive news is that there are many productive avenues for community change. Evaluating programs to document whether stigma reduction works and how it does so is of great importance for future endeavors.[63] It is only through such evaluative efforts that stigma reduction programs can be self-corrective and gain from experience.

10

Overcoming Stigma II

Media and Mental Health Professionals

Media

The stereotyped and negative portrayals of mental illness in various forms of public media remain as a core issue for those interested in stigma reduction. Although movement toward more accurate coverage in major media outlets is occurring, depictions still convey biased images of mental disorder as linked to violence, incompetence, and irrationality. In this chapter I emphasize two sets of strategies geared toward altering such portrayals: organized protest and intentional media depictions that can convey a different set of images. The hope is that each approach can produce accounts emphasizing realistic portrayals of mental illness, featuring stories and disclosures that are inspiring and humanizing.

Protest

Protest movements can raise the consciousness of members of society with regard to the prejudice, discrimination, and stigma that exist for many devalued groups. Actions include letters to editors of periodicals, confrontation of producers and sponsors of biased programming, boycotts of groups that promote insensitive and demeaning portrayals, picketing of films, and other procedures intended to both raise public consciousness and put a stop to biased coverage. To build general consensus, advocacy groups have promoted "watches," in which consumers are directed to scrutinize media for stereotyped portrayals. These are directed largely toward television and film with respect to insensitive and prejudiced depictions of persons with mental disorders. Print media and advertisements can also be targeted.

For example, groups such as the National Stigma Clearinghouse aggressively communicate with the public and media outlets to confront negative images of mental illness in the media. Beginning in the 1980s, NAMI began to hand out "media watch kits" so that local chapters could monitor newspapers, television, and film for stereotypic, degrading images.[1] Protest efforts emanating from such scrutiny can serve to alert media outlets and their sponsors that demeaning depictions of mental disorder are no longer acceptable and that executives, managers, and publicists need to uphold a higher standard. In addition, boycotts can provide a powerful economic incentive to alter advertisements and images, particularly if they are widely publicized and supported.

Take, for example, the case of a 1990 motion picture titled *Crazy People*, a comedy starring Dudley Moore and Darryl Hannah. A large protest accompanied the initial advertising for the movie:

> The original newspaper and poster ads for this comedy . . . showed a cracked egg with hand and arms making a silly gesture and declared, somewhat ominously, "*Warning:* Crazy People Are Coming." Representatives from a variety of mental health advocacy groups wrote to executives at Paramount, the film's producer, about what they perceived as a totally unnecessary suggestion (and one inconsistent with the content of the film) of menace from "crazy people." As a result, advertising for the film was changed, with new ads saying simply "You wanna laugh tonight?" and showing a picture of the stars.

The film was to have a major opening in Philadelphia:

> A newspaper . . . ran a promotion offering free tickets to a screening of the movie for anyone who could prove that he or she was "crazy." Representatives from [several organizations] wrote letters, marched in the street outside the paper's offices, and arranged for a meeting with the paper's editor and publisher in order to convey how troubling it was to have the paper treat "being crazy" as a joke. The paper responded favorably and published an apology for the ad, saying "this was . . . mean-spirited and wrong." The paper also reportedly decided not to run any further ads for the movie . . . and to attempt to run more stories that presented other views of mental illness.[2]

Protest efforts like this can place considerable pressure on film producers and newspapers to correct images that are needlessly devaluing, with the hope that a key source of stereotyping and stigmatization can be stopped in its tracks. At the same time, protest efforts are energizing for those who initiate them, promoting identity and solidarity with respect to a group that deserves and demands justice.

As another example, a decade ago the editors of Superman comics planned the death of this beloved character to be shown in print. Advance publicity had revealed that his killing would be perpetrated by Doomsday, an evildoer from an interplanetary insane asylum, whose apparel featured a straightjacket. The National Stigma Clearinghouse learned of this content and contacted the publisher, D.C. Comics (and its parent company, Time Warner), to protest such a portrayal of the murderer of a much-admired superhero. When the issue was published (which quickly sold out), no reference to the mental status of Doomsday existed, and pictures of him did not include a straightjacket. In fact, D.C. Comics issued a statement in which it avowed sensitivity to nonprejudicial depictions in its comics.[3] As these examples show, protest efforts can raise consciousness, provide accountability to purveyors of media, and reduce grossly stereotypic and inflammatory messages.

More recent campaigns have produced results as well. NAMI Stigmabusters represents an e-mail alert network that provides notices about particularly stigmatizing contents of media portrayals. In 2000 this group helped to play a role in the cancellation of the ABC prime-time series *Wonderland*, which depicted a mental facility and its patients in graphic, violent terms. For example, in an initial episode a patient, after gunning down several other individuals, stabbed a pregnant physician in the abdomen with a hypodermic needle. One means of protest was conducted through direct communication with the program's major corporate sponsors. Much publicity ensued, and the program was cancelled after a few episodes.[4]

Are there potential downsides to protest efforts? For one thing, it is often a matter of judgment as to what is merely lighthearted and what is truly degrading. Some advocates with mental disorders have, in fact, contended that protest efforts can be overly serious in their goal of eliminating any and all humorous references to mental disorder. In fact, the ability to see humor in difficult situations can be an excellent source of coping—so long as the comic relief is not one sided, patronizing, or potentially humiliating. The point is not to remove appropriate humor from difficult life situations but rather to counter images that are patently unfair and stigmatizing, such as those that ridicule mental illness or feature incompetence or violence as the chief attributes of persons with mental disorders.

Another potential problem has already been mentioned: that of "rebound" when persons are asked to suppress established images. It is as though the efforts to push away the image trigger a set of mental mechanisms that actually reinforce the image.[5] The fear is that protest efforts may lead to an entrenchment of the very depictions that are intended to be banished.

Rebound phenomena appear to invoke complex cognitive processes. One mechanism is that the active mental energy needed to keep the image at bay may prevent other kinds of mental processing from occurring. In other words, if a person is fighting to keep an image of "dangerous mental patients" out of her mind as a result of protest efforts, she may not notice that an interaction partner with mental illness is actually cooperative.[6] The danger exists that when the public is forced to recognize biased accounts of stigmatized groups and asked to replace these images with more benign ones, the unwanted images may become more accessible and entrenched. Certain forms of protest in the name of destigmatization could therefore backfire.

Although this possibility is sobering, it is based largely on short-term social psychology experiments that reveal acute, paradoxical effects of mental suppression. Longer-term efforts to protest media portrayals may be far more successful. That is, when the replacement of images is gradual and when there is no call to suppress prior images, there may be little "bounce" in any rebound. Furthermore, to the extent that protests force media depictions to become more accurate and compassionate over the long run, future generations will experience a far different view of people with mental disorders than is provided by the current images. These long-term benefits are likely to considerably outweigh any short-term consequences related to suppression.

Finally, how can the effects of protest be evaluated? It is one thing to note that a particular protest effort has stopped a biased program or altered a stereotyped advertisement, but it is quite another to know whether such actions have fundamentally changed the attitudes and behavioral practices of the general public. Given the major role of mass media in people's lives, it is difficult to imagine a randomized experiment (outside of an extremely short-term laboratory study) that could adequately test the effects of concerted protest efforts directed against stereotyped media images. How, for example, could a control group be formed that lacks access to the relevant media or views alternative images? It will be a major challenge for future investigators to design appropriately controlled trials. Still, given the massive sums of money linked to newspaper, television, and radio programming and advertisements, many powerful individuals and corporations have faith in the persuasive power of media messages. Change in this domain is essential.

Overall, despite potential dangers of stereotype suppression, which could result in the unintended intensification of stereotyped images, alterations in the content of inaccurate and demeaning portrayals of mental illness, promoted through active protest, are a crucial part of destigmatization efforts. Concerns regarding potential rebound from protest efforts appear overstated, given that the ultimate benefits can fundamentally change media images for years to come, outlasting any short-lived negative effects.[7] Protest efforts also provide a means of empowerment for organizations and groups that band together to raise consciousness.

In 2005, as a positive means of promoting alternate media images, the federal Substance Abuse and Mental Health Service Administration (SAMSHA) sponsored the Voice Awards, presented to film, television, and radio writers, producers, and actors who portrayed realistic and sensitive characterizations of mental illness in 2003 and 2004. Among many contenders, "The Aviator," "ER," and "Monk" won in the film and television categories. The clear intention is to reward those who produce programs with accurate depictions of the realities of mental illness.

Marketing Strategies

In a breathtaking chapter, Sullivan and colleagues, who are professional marketers rather than mental health professionals or consumer advocates, place the issue of mental health stigma in the arena of marketing communications programs. Their analysis provides an intriguing window on the intentional fashion in which media experts create images through a host of strategies and public relations initiatives regarding various products, groups, and causes. I focus on their analysis of several types of procedures, with specific regard to mental health.[8] Because space limitations preclude full development of these ideas, this overview is intended to generate thought about procedures that could influence the public's view of individuals with mental illness.

One example is *cause marketing*. Here, a given product or service is linked explicitly with a cause, with proceeds from the product or service going to aid the cause. The expectation is that consumers will link the benevolence of the cause with the product or service in question, fostering loyalty to the product. At the same time, the cause is furthered via financial support and increased public awareness. An example is that of a lipstick product: Proceeds go directly to AIDS prevention research, with popular media celebrities headlining advertisements that make this explicit association.[9] AIDS prevention efforts receive direct benefit, at the same time that consumers feel altruistic and potentially link these positive feelings with the product line. A pertinent question is whether a company might risk a particular commodity for cause marketing related to research or treatment for a major mental illness.

Alternatively, the more traditional practice of *social marketing* is not tied to any product or service per se. Rather, it pertains to attitude change through building perceptions of a desired social good or social improvement. Public service advertisements, websites, ads in public transportation, and the like may serve the end of social marketing, which is intended to raise consciousness about important societal concerns. Causes related to environmental, health-related (e.g., teen pregnancy prevention; antismoking), and antiracial discrimination concerns have all received extensive social marketing. Mental illness lags behind in these efforts.

Sullivan and colleagues suggest that one way of approaching social marketing for this topic would be to accentuate the missed opportunities for all of society if the potential of persons with mental illness fails to be realized. Along these lines, the message could presumably target fundamental similarities across all types of people and highlight the past contributions of prominent individuals with mental disorders.

In practice, social marketing typically targets specific audiences predicted to be amenable to attitude change. What are the key subgroups that might be targeted with respect to reducing the stigmatization of mental disorder? In other words, should the entire populace constitute the target group, or are there particular niches or subpopulations to which the campaigns should be geared? Clearly, additional research is needed on the particular kinds of persons most (or least) likely to benefit from social marketing campaigns related to mental illness stigma. Because adolescence is a time of increased risk for the emergence of a large number of mental disorders and because peer relations in adolescence are especially crucial, social marketing is being increasingly directed to this age group. In addition, the World Psychiatric Association's programs to eliminate the stigma related to schizophrenia utilize social marketing strategies that are targeted toward students, employers, and criminal justice workers. Along these lines, speaker bureaus and media-watch organizations have been implemented in more than 20 nations, targeting these specific components of the population.[10]

The relatively new practice of *buzz marketing* involves the soliciting and compensation of "plants" to promote a particular product or service. For example, mothers of Little League teams or parents in parent-teacher associations might talk up a particular household product with other families in an attempt to generate "buzz" about that product line. Alternatively, attractive individuals may go to bars and clubs, promoting a certain brand of alcohol. The intention is to generate interest that is not tied to overt advertisement. Sullivan and colleagues ask whether mental health professionals would be willing to discuss, at community talks, positive images of mental illness, perhaps in return for incentives from local mental health associations. The relevant point is that the professionals would not be believed to be selling anything—rather, they would be perceived as delivering truthful messages in a realistic fashion. Indeed, the professionals in question may well be extremely truthful in such ventures. It is the incentives for providing such talks that characterize buzz marketing, the goal of which is to promote enthusiasm and commitment via word of mouth.[11]

More controversial are *stealth marketing* tactics. The example given by Sullivan and colleagues is that of a beverage company filling recycling bins in high-income, desirable neighborhoods with empty bottles of a particular product. Here, the objective is to link the product with the particular neighborhood in order to produce positive associations for the product, with the added benefit that typical advertising procedures (commercials, print ads) are completely bypassed. A core premise of both buzz and stealth marketing is to circumvent the usual modes of oral, print, or televised ads or "spots": The goal is for the public to believe that the promotion of the product or service in question is entirely natural. A possible mental health example of stealth marketing (quite related to buzz marketing as well) might include the preplanned discussing of positive experiences in therapy by movie or television stars on talk shows or in interviews.

Another procedure (or, rather, set of procedures) is termed *cultural seeding,* whereby the public is inundated with multiple images of a given brand across different forms of media but without knowing that there is a concerted effort to foster explicit linkages. This is not a new concept: For many decades children's products have appeared simultaneously on cereal boxes, television programs, and everyday items such as lunchboxes. Through more current efforts, products or brands are made mutually interdependent (e.g., via television commercials, CDs, websites, and clothing lines), presenting the consumer with multiple, linked references to their presence in everyday culture. The point is to have a multitude of images that do not always appear through direct advertising, toward the end of a "contagious" spread of the product or cause.

Along the line of several of these procedures, Sullivan and colleagues provocatively ask the following: "What if National Public Radio sponsored a reading series by authors who have a mental illness? Perhaps the subject areas in their writing could sensitize the public to stories of recovery and the complexities of living with mental illness."[12] The point here would be to link radio promotions, books, and television talk shows (or other means of communication) with the objective of providing mutual reinforcement of core messages. At least some media outlets are now promoting discussion of mental illness with compassion and reality. It will take concentrated efforts for advocates to position the right speakers and readers in the right media outlets, so that messages of disclosure become part of the general cultural dialogue.

For decades advertisers have promoted "integrated marketing communication," through which messages are repeated and echoed across multiple forms of media. In recent years, the venues of such coordinated messages have expanded into the internet and through means such as sponsorships (e.g., corporate naming of sports stadiums or college football bowl games). Saturating markets with brands and images therefore has an expanded base of operations, some of which intentionally attempt to move away from direct advertisement strategies.

The potential for communication about mental disorder to utilize varied sources and outlets is already occurring. For example, in a subtle yet powerful series of spots that aired on MTV and other youth-oriented outlets several years ago, the National Mental Health Awareness Campaign promoted depictions of eating disorders, as well as depression and suicidality, aimed at increasing recognition and discussion of these mental disorders among adolescents and young adults. These public service announcements were sufficiently youth oriented and subtle to escape detection as traditional, pedantic messages; they ended with the posting of websites that featured information about mental disorders and related services for adolescents. These sites yielded millions of hits.[13] This media project also exemplified the notion of targeting communication to a particular demographic niche—in this case, teenagers and early adults.

I add a final concept to this discussion, that of *framing,* which has recently emerged as a central theme of major political parties in the United States.[14] Based on George Lakoff's cognitive linguistic analysis, framing is the intentional attempt to use simple, direct, repeated messages about a political concept or cause, whereby the frame links to a deeper theme in the consumer's psyche.[15] For instance, the concept of "tax relief," emphasized by Republican administrations, has at its very core the frame that taxation has overly and unfairly burdened the populace. This frame is embodied in the term *relief,* which invokes images of the release of a long-standing, unfair imposition on fundamental rights. Hence, tax relief is a metaphor that taps into a deep human value, contextualizing lowered taxes as an act of freedom and a casting off of oppression.

Debates about the ultimate value of framing are now part of the political landscape. For example, many contend that a frame cannot fundamentally reshape attitudes in the absence of sound, underlying concepts and principles related to the social or political issues in question. Still, framing plays a large role in major party politics in the current era.[16] For mental health advocates, it would be an important exercise to come up with relevant frames regarding messages to the general public about mental illness and the rights and dignity of individuals who have such conditions. One such frame, promoted in recent years, is that mental illness is entirely neurobiological, constituting a disease like any other. As I have discussed repeatedly, however, this frame may promote images of mental disorder as immutable and indicative of a fundamental lack of humanity, despite the supposition that it will lead to blame reduction.

Alternate frames could emphasize notions of civil rights, which have a deep tradition in our society and are linked to core values that most members of the citizenry strongly hold. They could also link mental disorder to intensifications of problems that everyone encounters—facilitating a broadening of the boundaries of one's ingroup. Another provocative frame is that of "neurodiversity," a celebration of key differences in individuals' neurological and psychiatric status, which may link with the notion of individuality (a strongly valued theme in many Western societies).[17] Coming up with a viable message will not be an easy task, however, given the lack of consensus as to the underlying nature of mental disorder (see Chapter 1). Those interested in addressing media-related stigmatization would do well to rigorously explore the kinds of meaningful frames that could impart deeply held values and images while at the same time generating respect and compassion for people with mental disorders. Focus groups, public opinion polls, and astute political and psychological analysis could all play a role in such development.

On the whole, means exist beyond traditional public service announcements, with their penchant for dry facts and sober educational messages, to produce renewed media images of mental disorder and related personal and family struggles.[18] Such procedures have the potential to alter, in fundamental ways, perceptions of the general public. A key challenge for the years ahead will be to configure ways of intentionally utilizing the types of public relations strategies described herein to reshape public attitudes. Although some may find it distasteful or even potentially manipulative to enact some of these tactics, particularly buzz or stealth marketing, it is worth noting that at present a multitude of images are intentionally displayed to the public about a variety of characteristics and traits, often in ways that reinforce highly negative stereotypes about mental illness. From this perspective, if the ends are worthy and the means are not unethical, it may be worthwhile to implement a range of strategies for altering public perceptions, so long as (a) appropriate targets are considered, such as adolescents, [19] and (b) careful evaluation is performed in order to understand the impact of these strategies. Given the huge importance of media influences, discussion of this entire topic is sure to grow in the coming years.

Disclosure and Humanization

Beyond the tactics and strategies of protest that may alter media images and beyond the frames that may be invoked to contextualize mental disorder, what are the particular messages that should be included in media portrayals? A basic contention is that the more that mental illness can be humanized by its disclosure and "telling" in everyday narratives, the more that members of the populace can come to understand the underlying humanity of people and families who cope with its challenges. Realistic portrayals in books, stories, features, interviews, and commentaries, involving narratives of pain, strength, and coping, are the kinds of images that should promote interest, empathy, and compassion. Mental illness is certainly associated with despair, impairment, and threat, and these aspects should not be denied. Yet subtleties, competencies, and struggles are too often lost in the stereotyping (or occasionally the glorifying) of mental illness. Realistic, humanizing portrayals cannot substitute for face-to-face contact, but they may set the stage for such contact by enhancing interest and motivation.

What if stories of mental illness were prime-time, mainstream material? Despite its inaccuracies, the film *A Beautiful Mind* gave a humane depiction of schizophrenia that presented the counterstereotypic image of its association with extreme talent. As another example, on the HBO series *America Undercover,* the anxieties and panic disorder of actress Kim Basinger and former football star Earl Campbell have been vividly yet sensitively portrayed.[20] Mental illness is now out of the closet in many facets of everyday media, although it is too often accompanied by sensationalism and depictions of violence.

Star power, which has been an effective lobbying and consciousness-raising strategy for a number of physical illnesses, is relatively underutilized in the case of mental illness, revealing the stigma associated with it. The more that the public can link mental illness with highly valued people, the more that positive associations can form.

Still, case reports, personal narratives, and television portrayals should include not only noteworthy, exceptional individuals with mental illness but also average people who are neither stars nor outcasts. The idea that people with mental illness are either exceptionally talented or globally flawed belies the fact that that mental disorder is part of everyday life. Models need not be heroic to convey a humanizing image. Depictions of resilience can promote the association of mental illness with strength, courage, and resolve—and with the view that change is entirely possible. Not everyone with mental disorder overcomes adversity, and it would be a mistake to force rose-colored glasses on the eyes of readers or viewers. Yet overcoming the stereotype that mental illness is inevitably linked with despair, tragedy, and progressive decline is essential.

Harrington discusses an important trend over the past few decades in case studies of those with neurological and psychiatric conditions, which have moved away from dry, objective reports of symptoms and syndromes toward more vivid and personalized depictions of the unique human being who presents with the symptoms and syndromes in question.[21] For example, Oliver Sacks has published revealing portrayals of individuals with autism, Tourette's disorder, and many other conditions.[22] Along with first-person and family narratives about mental illness, these carry enormous potential for fostering increased humanization of neurological and mental disorders.

Disclosures are also important for the individuals who provide the narratives. The process of writing about difficult emotional events can promote psychological and even physical health.[23] Narrative can therefore promote a "virtuous cycle" of personal freedom, public gains in knowledge, and increased contact. At a fundamental level, it takes mental illness out of the realm of the mysterious and unknowable and into the arena of openness, familiarity, and empathy.

Mental Health Professionals

The actual extent of stigmatizing attitudes and practices on the part of mental health workers and professionals toward their clientele is unknown. But even a small amount translates into many, many thousands of negative social interactions in any given year—with the potential for long-term damage to morale and the promotion of stigma by the very personnel entrusted with helping those with mental illness. Indeed, if the social workers, educators, counselors, psychologists, medical practitioners, and psychiatrists who constitute the "front lines" of mental health service delivery convey stigma and disparagement, those with mental disorders have real reason for pessimism.

Whatever their actual frequency, such practices should be placed in context. Recall that the mental health professions have low status; the entire enterprise appears to have received a pervasive "courtesy stigma" through its association with a clientele that is viewed as weak, unproductive, and blameworthy. Not only do the mental health professions suffer in terms of prestige, but pay scales for many mental health workers are on the low end of ranges for other professionals, revealing decreased status associated with this line of work. Those in the mental health fields must also contend with potent and frequently derogatory media images of helping professionals. For example, Gabbard and Gabbard provide insightful commentary on the checkered history of depictions of psychotherapists and psychiatrists in film, most of which convey unscrupulous, exploitative, comical, or odd images but rarely realistic or optimistic ones.[24] Furthermore, work in the mental health fields can be quite stressful, given the problems related to mental illness itself and the lack of resources that often exist in current service delivery systems.

Mental disorder appears to be particularly stigmatized in the field of medicine itself. Michael Myers, a psychiatrist who specializes in physician health, contends the following about mental illness in general and the problem of suicide in particular:

> The stigma attached to mental illness is greater in the house of medicine than in the general public. Stigma, a pernicious force, reinforces denial in physicians that they might fall ill, contributes to their delay in getting medical care, compounds suffering, confuses and frustrates doctors' families, drives self medicating, and dangerously heightens the risk of death by suicide. And when physicians do kill themselves, the conspiracy of silence surrounding their deaths may aggravate feelings of isolation and shame in their survivors—and thwart our public health efforts at prevention.[25]

These pointed words speak to a fear of mental disorder among health professionals—an attitude that is likely to be communicated to patients and the public at large, whether explicitly or implicitly. That the medical profession does not tend to confront problems of depression and other mental disorders in its own ranks bespeaks the long-standing stigmatization of mental illness in a core profession intended to deal with such problems.[26]

As emphasized repeatedly throughout this book, the conceptual bases of mental health practice during much of the twentieth century involved a direct blaming of individuals and families for the mental health conditions they and their relatives suffered. Stigmatization of the very people being served was built into the theoretical foundations of the mental health profession almost from the time of its formal establishment.

All of these issues can set the stage for workers and professionals to "blame victims"—that is, to disparage the individuals who are intended to be helped by mental health services. Narrative evidence along these lines is disheartening.[27] However, it is not just overt stigma and criticism that are potentially problematic; views of mental illness that emphasize pity and hopelessness are also communicated directly to patients and relatives. Furthermore, the health care system is permeated by a hierarchical model of expert-sufferer, doctor-patient relationships.

What can be done? I reiterate that a great many mental health workers are dedicated, respectful, and tireless in their efforts; blanket aspersions should not be cast on the field. Relatedly, the huge advances in mental health must be recognized, and these could not have been possible without strong professional and scientific commitment and dedication. In the spirit of encouraging set-breaking strategies for promoting healthier and more productive attitudes and practices on the part of mental health workers and professionals, I list potential strategies and solutions in headline form.

Increased Status for Mental Health–Related Work   To the extent that the general public views mental disorders as important, impairing, serious, yet treatable conditions, rather than ones that are malingered or imagined, the status of those professionals entrusted with their investigation and care should increase. Although there is no way to legislate or impose such views unilaterally, the suggestions made in Chapter 9 regarding education, contact, and empathy enhancement, plus those from earlier in this chapter on media-related tactics, all have the potential to lift the general status of mental illness to new levels of respect and social concern. Such increased status could, in turn, promote a higher level of professional prestige for those who work in the field.

More direct means of enhancing the public's views of mental health professionals are possible as well. From their marketing perspective, Sullivan and colleagues call for intentional efforts to "brand" psychology and psychiatry in positive, humanitarian, and scientific terms via public relations campaigns. Some of the relevant terms and images could include the portrayal of those in the mental health field as a benevolent set of professionals and/or as humanistic healers. Catch phrases might include the perspective that therapy works, that it is continuously evolving, and that it causes more powerful benefits than one might think.[28] Other themes could include the view that it is a sign of strength, rather than weakness, to receive help from individuals who are trained in giving it. There are bound to be other ideas. In short, it will require the careful analysis of target audiences, the implementation of focus groups, and the hiring of creative directors and other marketing personnel (working in tandem with professional leaders) to uncover compelling images and themes.

Still, images devoid of substance will not make a real difference. That is, the mental health professions must continue to strive for scientific rigor and professional competence, so that campaigns have real meaning. If those working in the field show stigmatizing practices and convey low expectations and hopelessness to clients and caregivers, no amount of public relations work can be expected to succeed. Overall, promoting the many positive attributes of the related mental health professions is worth pursuing.

Enhanced Training Methods and Procedures   Mental health professionals need to be educated in the types of treatment that have been documented to work. With literally hundreds of schools of psychotherapy in existence, an ever-widening arsenal of psychotropic medications, and a huge (and growing) list of alternative treatments, consumers face a bewildering assortment of intervention options. It is often quite difficult for those seeking treatment to know with any certainty which interventions have shown effectiveness for particular conditions.[29] At the same time, many training programs promote treatment strategies that have little or no scientific support. "Empirically supported" and "evidence based" are the terms now used to signify those types of intervention that have undergone sufficient, well-controlled research to lead to firm conclusions as to their viability.[30] To the extent that professionals know of and are skilled in the practice of these kinds of treatment, they will be greatly increasing the odds of successfully treating their clientele. This stance should produce a host of positive effects, including consumer satisfaction, positive regard for professionals, and a reduction of the stigma that can emerge when symptomatology goes untreated.

There are admittedly problems inherent in mere adherence to lists of evidence-based treatments. For one thing, certain types of treatment for a number of disorders have not received sufficient study. Providers therefore need training in how to devise and evaluate newly created or newly synthesized forms of intervention for unique cases, understudied conditions, or ethnic minority or impoverished subpopulations (see below). Relatedly, the results of short-term, tightly controlled experimental studies of therapy outcome may not generalize to the kinds of real-world, seriously impaired, multiply diagnosed, and diverse clientele that exist in the community. In other words, treatments shown to demonstrate "efficacy" in highly controlled studies may not reveal much in the way of "effectiveness" in the real world.[31] Moreover, knowing that a treatment works does not tell us how or why it works; a huge need exists to discover the underlying mechanisms of change.[32]

Still, to the extent that the therapeutic field becomes more rigorous and evidence based, further improvements should appear in terms of client outcomes, enhanced status of professionals, and reduced stigmatization of mental illness. Such work cannot proceed without a renewed commitment to the funding of basic and applied research efforts in psychology and psychiatry.

At the same time, those involved in the selection and training of personnel in the mental health professions must consider the factors of responsiveness, respect, and empathy. Providers with the highest levels of technical skill cannot produce real benefit without the ability to enlist, connect with, and maintain contact with their patients and clients. Training efforts must emphasize the dual objectives of competence in empirically supported interventions and sensitivity to clientele, as well as their relatives and supports. To the extent that professionals and mental health workers can understand both the science behind treatments that work and the experiences of clients and family members, mutual respect and trust should build.

Cultural Competency   Staff members and professionals must also be aware of the increasingly multicultural nature of American society—indeed, of world society—and of the need for ensuring that clinical services are delivered with sensitivity to families and individuals of nontraditional backgrounds. In other words, training in *culturally competent* mental health practice is now being discussed and performed in training institutions.[33] The intention is not to teach stereotypes about individuals from various ethnic, cultural, or socioeconomic groups, which would clearly be a step backward. Rather, it is to raise awareness of the belief systems, cultural practices, modes of communication, and response tendencies that may characterize various ethnic and cultural subgroups in order to foster more accurate diagnosis and more responsive communication regarding treatment.

In the middle of the last century, an acronym was coined regarding the types of clientele most likely to respond to psychotherapy. Known as "YAVIS" (young, attractive, verbal, intelligent, and successful), the term connoted the unfortunate facts that (a) those individuals prone to do well in verbal therapies were those, in many respects, least in need of effective intervention and that (b) psychotherapies were not typically adapted to patients of color or those of lower class status.[34] Since this time, investigations of many forms of treatment (both psychological and pharmacologic) have indicated that clients with low resources, those who are single parents, and those of minority ethnic and racial status show greater likelihood of premature termination from intervention and a weaker chance of obtaining meaningful gains.[35] It will take concerted efforts to dispense treatments that can benefit all members of society. Doing so could also help to reduce the sense that mental health professionals are insensitive to a non-middle-class clientele. To the extent that providers come to understand different means of expressing stress or pain among diverse members of the public, their tolerance and respect for clients of different backgrounds should rise—and their status in the eyes of society should reciprocally increase.

Different Models of Treatment   Some have contended, in fact, that the very na-ture of traditional mental health services can be limiting or even stigmatizing for many clients, particularly those with severe forms of mental illness. For in-stance, doctor-patient relationships emphasize the expertise of the provider and the weakness (and need for acquiescence) on the part of the recipient of care. A more coequal set of therapeutic relationships, in which clients gain em-powerment, has been advocated. Corrigan and Lundin promote such alternate forms of care, marked by consumer-practitioner collaborations and, in some in-stances, the use of mental health consumers as direct providers of advocacy and self-help services to others in need.[36]

It is an open question as to whether all of the problems related to mental ill-ness will be solved through such modes and models. More traditional means of providing pharmacotherapy and psychotherapy may well be of enormous benefit, so long as they are provided with sensitivity and rigor. Certainly, how-ever, if providers can consider a more collaborative approach that includes the perspective of the sufferer, incorporates the understanding of the stigmatiza-tion that many individuals with mental illness experience, and offers a less au-thoritarian stance, enhanced care may result.

Support—and Therapy—for Professionals   Given the stresses inherent in mental health work, it would be advantageous for professional groups to provide sys-tematic means of providing relief and support for their members. Collabora-tions with other professionals, including consultation and mutual support, constitute one avenue. Keeping up with current research on mechanisms of psychopathology and advances in empirically supported treatments is another. Doing so can reduce a sense of isolation and keep clinicians in touch with the wider community of scientists and therapists. Individual or group therapy for providers can also provide a safety valve for pressures and stresses in order to

11

Overcoming Stigma III

Families and Individuals

Families

Family members of people with mental disorders often find themselves in extremely difficult situations, serving as caregivers, financial supporters, treatment seekers, and advocates while carrying a burden of shame and societal shunning. What can they do to combat stigma?

Family Education About Mental Disorder

One of the greatest enemies may be ignorance. If families get consultation from professionals who hold the view that child-rearing practices are the primary causes of schizophrenia, depression, bipolar disorder, ADHD, autism, and other mental disorders, it would be expected that such families would emerge with a deep sense of shame. Furthermore, if they accept media-promoted stereotypes about mental disorder—that it is hopeless and strongly linked to incompetence and violence—their pain and subjective burden will only increase. Receiving accurate information about mental disturbance is a high priority, and this information should include facts about not only the moderate to strong genetic propensities for many forms of mental disorder but also the role of life stressors and social supports as related to outcome, the importance of family advocacy in obtaining responsive treatments, and the need for family members to take care of themselves, as well as their relative with mental illness.

In the rush to debunk the myth that parenting practices cause the major forms of mental illness, the idea became widespread that these disorders are entirely products of genes, with social context and family interaction playing little or no role in the course of such disorders. This information is inaccurate.

Even though there are clear genetic predispositions for many forms of mental disorder, family context is still of major importance for the person's ultimate course.[1] Improvement often depends highly on environmental factors, including in many cases the family's pushing through to ensure that appropriate intervention is secured. At the same time, optimal family coping may serve to reduce guilt and improve life quality for all of the members.

Where can families obtain accurate information? In the current era, the internet can be an excellent source, yet one that must be used with caution because of the huge numbers of unsubstantiated claims and the great amount of misguided information often posted there. Self-help and advocacy groups strive to maintain quality control over their websites, with links to informative readings, workshops, question-and-answer pages, and other information-rich sources. In addition, television and radio broadcasts, as well as newspaper articles, can be good sources of information if the producers and writers have access to up-to-date, accurate data. Still, considerable misinformation abounds.

Antipsychiatry campaigns are clearly in place, promoting the concept that mental illness is a mythical set of medical labels for what are really just problems in adjustment.[2] On the opposite end of the spectrum, some officially sanctioned professional information promotes the notion that mental illness is a brain disease caused exclusively by genes, and direct-to-consumer advertisements from pharmaceutical firms run the risk of overmedicalizing many life problems. Amidst the information explosion that currently exists, balanced and informed coverage is at a premium.

Once again, the core messages should be that despite the biological underpinnings of many forms of mental illness, social support and provision of treatment are crucial—and personal and family efforts can go far in changing the course of mental disorders and providing a healthy climate for every family member. A critical point to communicate is that over and above the very real impairments that frequently accompany mental illness, rehabilitation is a distinct possibility, and treatments can and do provide benefit.

Family Involvement in Treatment and Family Therapy

Engaging family members in treatment plans is crucial. Even if the focus of the intervention is the individual with mental illness, other family members also need education and involvement in order to be appropriately supportive and to promote adherence to treatment regimens. An active stance is particularly critical when the family member receiving treatment is a child or an adolescent, but even if the "identified patient" is an adult, relatives must understand how best to support ongoing treatment.

In some models of intervention, family members are not just informants and supporters of the individual's treatment plan but also serve as direct participants in family-oriented therapies. It is now well known, for example, that a family's communication style about an offspring's schizophrenia or bipolar disorder plays a large role in the individual's chances for recovery—even though family communications had little to do with the condition's onset. Hostile and critical communication is, in fact, predictive of relapse and rehospitalization.[3] Modulating discordant family interaction is an important treatment goal, as is ensuring that the family maintains healthy boundaries in relation to their adolescent or young adult with mental illness. Doing so often requires support and reinforcement from professionals and other providers, particularly given the intense pain that can accompany a relative's mental illness. For conditions such as eating disorders (e.g., anorexia nervosa), direct engagement of the family in treatment is often essential for relieving symptoms and maintaining normal weight. With respect to many child disorders (e.g., ADHD, conduct problems, autistic disorder), there are major limitations regarding what can be achieved from individual work with the child alone. Family-based, behaviorally oriented strategies that feature training in the dispensing of regular rewards for adaptive skills and consistent consequences for problem behavior are the psychosocial treatments of choice for such conditions.[4] Overall, family involvement in therapy constitutes an essential component of the treatment plan in a great many cases.

Consider the family of 8-year-old Karina, who has been diagnosed with ADHD.

Following a pattern of inattentive behavior, below-average school grades, an impulsive behavioral style, and poor peer relationships, Karina's first- and second-grade teachers gave feedback to her parents at parent-teacher conferences. Her mother and father were increasingly upset with battles over homework and Karina's generally negative attitude. Finally, they sought an evaluation from a local psychologist who had received specialty training in learning and attention problems. After examining a series of parent and teacher rating scales, conducting interviews with the family, performing a school observation, and testing Karina in the clinic, the psychologist made a preliminary diagnosis of ADHD. She requested that the family begin parent training—that is, participating in a group with other families of school-aged children with similar problems, to learn a set of more consistent behavior management skills.

As they received more education and did some reading about ADHD, the parents realized that there may be a substantial genetic contribution to the condition. Upon reflection, they noted some of their own personal and family histories of learning and attention problems. Did this mean that their daughter was destined genetically? Fortunately, both the psychologist and the pediatrician reinforced the point that conditions like ADHD, although biologically based, show substantial benefits with tight, consistent expectations and regular schedules of rewards and punishments coordinated at home and school. The doctor also let the parents know that, despite controversy and depictions in the media of rampant use of medication for children, medication treatments for ADHD have a record of success for youth with this condition if they are carefully monitored. Still, the family was not in favor of a medication trial.

The parent training group, which included Karina's parents and five other sets of caregivers, was quite active. The leaders provided education about ADHD, instructions in using a structured reward program, role plays and rehearsals of the kinds of situations that "push the buttons" of the parents, and guided practice in de-escalating angry, emotionally explosive discipline procedures and using time-out and other consequences instead. Through the group, Karina's parents realized that they were not alone in their situation. They also came to learn that, although they could take the blame off themselves for having caused their daughter's ADHD, they were still clearly responsible for helping Karina to her realize her potential. Through engagement in treatment, they received social support, practical strategies for home management and school consultation, and a sense that openly discussing their daughter's condition with professionals and other families—and with Karina herself—was far preferable to silence and denial.

Some of the work was quite frustrating. Karina responded to initial limit setting with anger and defiance. At other times, she was tearful, wondering why she was so different from other girls and why other kids in her class teased her for being behind in her schoolwork. If it weren't for the support of the group, her parents may well have wanted to quit.

Essential to the process was learning how to work with the school system more productively. The family obtained an Individual Education Plan and are currently working out accommodations such as modifications of homework and some small-group supplements for Karina's reading skills.

At this point, the parents have noticed some improvements in Karina's behavior and feel encouraged that they have managed her problems (and their own frustration) more consistently at home. They are still wary of setbacks, however, as well as their own tendencies to stop the rewards when Karina shows some improvement. They still want to try to manage without any medication for their daughter, even though other families have related to them that it has been useful in their situations. What may be the most gratifying thing of all is that the family members feel as though they are working together toward a common goal and that the levels of intense negativity they experienced each night have been considerably reduced.

Indeed, ADHD is a condition particularly likely to be stigmatized. Its increasing rates of diagnosis, combined with the rising incidence of medication prescriptions and the pervasive cultural view that it is simply a product of lenient parenting, can be difficult for many families to reconcile. Reports of the strong genetic underpinnings of ADHD must be combined with clear messages regarding the importance of consistent family and school contexts for improving symptoms and impairments.[5] Treatments that emphasize active engagement in skill building and behavior problem management have the best empirical support among psychosocial options.

For a different kind of family involvement, consider the therapy designed by William Beardslee, which targets families in which a parent suffers from mood disorder—usually depression but also including bipolar disorder. Within such families, it is now well known that the offspring suffer a substantial risk of developing mood disorders (and other psychiatric problems) themselves.[6] One core premise is that if children or adolescents are met with silence about their parent's condition, they will be prone to blame themselves for the family disruptions that often occur, the erratic discipline that may exist in the home, and the suffering their parent experiences. This self-blame can dovetail with other risk factors to increase the odds that the children will develop adjustment problems or mood disturbances themselves.

In this therapy, a key objective is for the parents to work with the therapist to form a plan for a series of family meetings, where a key goal is to engage the child directly in discussions of the parent's depression. In other words, the parents create a narrative—a life story in language that the child can understand—that promotes effective coping with the parent's mood disorder and its consequences. Considerable support and guidance from the therapist are needed to help the family provide such communication in a direct yet sensitive way.

Results of this treatment program are encouraging. Not only does such family therapy, contrasted with control treatments, produce better coping and adjustment on the part of children and adolescents immediately after intervention, but it also may help to prevent their onset of subsequent depression.[7] In other words, family treatments that encourage openness rather than silence may have far-reaching effects on the next generation's risk for mental disorder, even for conditions with undoubted psychobiological aspects, such as depression. These effects appear to be tied to combating the silence and stigma that typically surround mental illness.

Beardslee recounts work with Fran and John and their 12-year-old son Frank:

> Families need to take time, proceed at their own pace, and feel safe in opening up. Information comes alive only when families deal with their underlying fears, and talking about depression is not simple. For many, it involves rethinking the depression they have experienced, the families that they grew up with, the events that led to depression—and the veil of silence that has surrounded these events . . .
>
> It became clear that the tradition in both their families had been to deal with adversities by not talking about them. In Fran's family, there was a deep-seated fear that talking about negative things might make them worse . . .
>
> Both parents were worried that they would somehow irrevocably alter their relationship with Frank if they labeled Fran's illness as depression. As she said, "I don't want him to think that I'm crazy." John had a different issue. "I've always felt he was too young to hear about it," he said. "I don't want him to think that Fran is impaired. . . ." With our help,

Fran and John planned their family meeting very carefully. . . . As they began, they talked specifically about what they'd been through together, and because they had taken the time to plan, it went well. They emphasized that Frank was not to blame. They outlined the actions they would take to protect him. . . . They described the depression, her irritability, and her upset, in terms that he could understand. Frank was mostly quiet but listened intently. At the most poignant moment of the meeting, Frank said, "I don't think you like me when you're depressed." Fran answered, "It's not that I don't like you. I love you, I will always love you."[8]

Regarding these types of family meetings, Beardslee notes six core principles: (1) Make sure that the timing is right, (2) gain commitment from the whole family, (3) start by addressing major concerns, (4) tie together the family history, (5) plan to have multiple discussions, and (6) use all of the available resources to cope with depressions (e.g., relatives, neighbors, additional treatments). In short, overcoming silence and stigma cannot take place overnight in the context of family treatment, but the effort toward greater contact can pay substantial dividends. Increased family communication may be an essential aspect of intervention and bring about lasting benefits.

Self-Help and Advocacy Groups

The last several decades have witnessed incredible growth of self-help and advocacy groups related to mental health awareness and mental health policy. This movement has marked a sea change in the status of people with mental disorders, and particularly their families, from passive, blameworthy, and largely invisible victims to advocates for personal and family well-being, as well as social change. Wahl's national survey from the late 1990s indicated that participants viewed such self-help, advocacy-related groups as an important source of support and coping.[9]

What can participation do for the family? First, it involves public recognition of the status of having a mental illness, directly countering the tendencies toward shame, silence, and concealment that have frequently been part of the family legacy of responding to mental disorder.[10] Second, it can provide a source of social support, particularly if group meetings and interpersonal encounters are part of the activities. When other individuals share resources and coping strategies, they provide models of active responding, removing some of the isolation that all too often accompanies mental disorder. Third, there is typically an educational component to such groups (e.g., guest speakers, books, websites), which can foster greater awareness and knowledge of mental disorder. Fourth, to the extent that outreach and advocacy are involved, active work toward social change is now an attainable goal. That is, the family is now part of an effort geared toward eliminating prejudice and discrimination, advocating for relevant legislation, or perhaps becoming involved in efforts to ease zoning restrictions on community residences for persons with mental illness.

Are there any downsides to such participation? One potential issue is the tendency for some advocacy groups to promote a view of mental illness in reductionistic, brain-disease terms. Such a stance is in many ways understandable, given the legacy of professional claims that parenting practices (as well as personal defenses or weaknesses) are the key contributors to mental disorder and the recent surge of interest in brain imaging, genetics, and medication treatments. As readers will clearly surmise from earlier sections of this book, however, a portrayal of mental disorder as related exclusively to flawed biology or deviant genes is not only inaccurate but also likely to promote pessimism, pity, and punitive tendencies, as well as stigma directed toward relatives. In addition, although recognizing the psychobiological reality of mental illness may provide a welcome antidote to the personal and family blaming that have dominated the landscape for far too long, a sole focus on biological causes and treatments may undermine motivation for understanding the importance of psychosocial aspects of treatment.

The following vignette gives a sense of the support that can emanate from these types of groups:

Recall Carl at the beginning of Chapter 1, the young man experiencing an increasingly severe episode of schizophrenia, whose close-knit family has become worried and even panicked about his condition since the deterioration that followed his high school graduation. Isolating himself in his bedroom, he often places his hands over his ears to shut out the voices he hears, with a growing sense that the house is bugged and that his thoughts can be heard by the FBI. For months now, his parents have refused to bring other people into the family home, fearing friends' and neighbors' responses to his increasingly disheveled appearance and irrational behavior. They also do not leave him alone, despite his 19 years, because they are unable to communicate with him effectively about his incessant cigarette smoking, even in bed, and his paranoid belief systems. Their own social lives have suffered as a result. The pain is sometimes unbearable—will their son ever get back to his normal self? Will he always mumble incoherently and verbally threaten others who dare to confront him about his ideas? Can their lives ever get out of this pattern?

An acquaintance has wondered where Carl's parents have been during their several-month hiatus from church attendance. One Sunday afternoon she stops by their home. At first, the couple is too ashamed to discuss Carl and his behavior, but even the friend can hear the increasingly loud and incoherent ramblings, as well as the blaring television volume that come from Carl's bedroom. Softly, the mother begins to explain her son's condition, tears welling in her eyes as she does so. Her husband is at first upset that his wife would talk in this way, but soon he also feels some relief just to be able to let someone outside the family know of their suffering, confusion, and pain.

The friend calls back the next day, first expressing sympathy and then providing information about a support group for families at the community center. The parents are noncommittal, afraid at first to discuss their situation openly with anyone but her. When she offers to accompany them, however, there is still the problem of leaving Carl alone. The father volunteers to stay at home so that his wife can attend.

The self-help meeting the following week is a revelation. Other families—some of whom the mother knows casually—begin to discuss hidden secrets of mental illness in their families. How could she not have known about their pain related to an aunt, an aging parent, or an adolescent son or daughter? She herself has little to say, feeling both awkward and shy, but she soon knows that she will return. A few meetings later, she hears a presentation about schizophrenia, and many of the symptoms in the talk match Carl's condition. She even stands up during the question-and-answer period to describe the situation with her son at home. Many people speak to her afterward, voicing empathy and asking about Carl's treatment. Embarrassed to admit he is getting none, she soon obtains the name of a psychiatrist, her voice trembling during the initial phone call to set up an appointment. She and her husband are able to go to the session, as one of Carl's sisters volunteers to cover at home.

Much planning ensues. Does Carl need to be hospitalized? Convincing him to see a doctor isn't possible, as his paranoia has become severe. While his parents strategize about how to effect hospitalization, they are grateful for the pamphlets and websites from the support group, which further explain schizophrenia. They consult a family therapist, who helps formulate a plan for a brief hospital stay. With great effort, they are able to implement the hospitalization, even though it takes some real doing, finally dragging Carl to the car to come with them.

During Carl's two weeks at the hospital, his parents call a meeting with several of their neighbors in order to openly discuss Carl's problems and struggles and to put an end to the silence they believe will increasingly isolate them in the neighborhood. Some of the neighbors are sympathetic; others remain silent. At least, however, the family need no longer deny or pretend.

Although the pain has never really left them, the family is actively coping, increasingly hopeful that Carl will recover much of his former level of functioning. They even watch television and read the newspaper differently these days, aware of the distorted stories of violence, incompetence, and hopelessness usually linked with schizophrenia. As worried as they still are about their son, they are beginning to channel some of that concern into anger over the stereotyped images of mental illness that they

continue to witness in the media and during everyday conversations in
the community.

Peer Support and Stigma Reduction

Beyond self-help and advocacy groups, explicit programs to increase family support and family coping are beginning to appear. For example, NAMI has developed the Family-to-Family Educational Program, a 12-week set of sessions in which caregivers meet with a trained family member who is a veteran of the issues involved in providing care for a relative with serious mental illness. This program is educational in nature, with information regarding mental illness and its treatment a core aspect of the curriculum. Training in coping skills, self-care, and advocacy is included. This program also explicitly features contact, in that the group facilitator is a peer who has undergone similar experiences. Initial evaluations are promising, particularly with respect to increases in the participants' sense of empowerment.[11] Additional appraisals with better control conditions and longer-term follow-up will be essential to document the long-range nature of the benefits of this and related programs.

Summary

The struggles, shame, and even outright humiliation that all too many family members experience as a result of stigma cannot be overstated. These forces predict coping responses of silence and secrecy, threatening the well-being and health of the relatives in question and preventing the procurement of needed services for the family member with mental illness. Obtaining up-to-date education about mental disorders, joining in collaborative treatment efforts, and participating in advocacy groups can provide levels of support and encouragement that were not possible a generation or two ago. Programs aimed explicitly at promotion of family coping are being evaluated as well. Still, far too many families do not avail themselves of these advances. In order for family support and engagement to become a reality, change is required at many levels: enhanced quality of media messages and portrayals, lobbying efforts for policy change, increased funding for and access to treatment, and the promotion of social support and empowerment. At the same time, advocacy and self-help groups need to provide balanced messages that remove blame for serious mental illness while emphasizing the need for both family responsibility and increased community supports to ensure the best outcomes possible.

Individuals With Mental Disorder

What realistic strategies exist to combat stigmatization at the level of individuals with mental illness themselves? Although much of the focus below is on adults, many of the suggestions may apply to parents of children with mental illness, particularly in terms of engaging with treatment.

Effective and Responsive Treatment

Background Issues   The core question is whether stigma-reduction efforts should include intentional efforts to change behavior or symptoms through engagement of individuals with mental disorders in treatment. My answer is a clear "yes," but an important question must first be raised: Could this stance be akin to the proposition that, to avoid stigmatization, persons in racial minority groups should change their skin color to match that of the majority—or that gay men or lesbian women must receive intervention to become straight? These sobering analogies reveal the dangers inherent in suggesting that stigmatized individuals must either alter themselves or become more like the ingroup to prevent castigation and prejudice. There is potential for "blaming the victim" in advocating for individual treatment as a means of fighting stigma if the underlying message is that nonconformity must be rooted out before any stigma reduction can take place.

But this argument is not valid. The situation with regard to treatment for mental disorder is clear: If properly diagnosed, mental illnesses are dysfunctional constellations of symptoms that cause substantial impairment and suffering. Treatment is essential not to eliminate "differences" or deviancy but rather to relieve pain and promote optimal functioning. An important effect of such treatment is the reduction of threatening, often noxious behavior patterns that produce stigmatizing responses on the part of social perceivers; promoting behavioral conformity is not the paramount goal. Rather, the legitimate therapeutic benefits of intervention are complemented by the potential for stigma reduction.

Racial status is a fixed characteristic that yields a difference of appearance and requires fundamental acceptance on the part of any society that claims to be tolerant and pluralistic. Similarly, being gay or lesbian does not signify mental illness—even though it was officially considered as such in the recent past[12]—and is therefore not a characteristic to be "treated away." Mental illnesses are different: They constitute a set of highly dysfunctional behavior patterns that require intervention. Advocating treatment does not therefore translate into a reactionary stance of demanding conformity. In fact, responsive intervention may serve the purposes of relieving individual suffering related to an underlying mental disorder, decreasing societal fears and distancing that emanate from its most extreme and debilitating symptoms, and enhancing the perception that mental illness is changeable.

It is naïve to think that if everyone with mental illnesses could simply receive intervention, stigma would disappear. Even successful intervention often leaves intact emotional displays and behavior patterns that are non-normative. In other words, acceptance of some degree of behavioral difference is required, so long as the behavior patterns in question do not harm others. At the same time, there are doubtless adaptive aspects to mental disorder, both in individuals and their biological relatives; otherwise, given natural selection, how could such conditions have persisted in humans until the current era? Advocates of neurodiversity, in fact, claim that fundamental acceptance of difference is of crucial importance (see Chapter 12). Yet to the extent that effective treatment can relieve suffering, combat dysfunction, and enhance growth, it may unleash important human potential and simultaneously serve to lessen stigma.[13]

The Value of Treatment   Evidence-based treatment strategies now exist for many mental disorders. Both psychotropic medications and various forms of psychotherapy are effective, to varying degrees, for a variety of mental conditions. Presenting the details of these treatments is well beyond the scope of this book, given the vastness of the topic and the growing research evidence for both child and adult intervention strategies. The bottom line, however, is that mental disorders can often be treated—and treated effectively.[14]

For example, antipsychotic medications can help persons with even severe, chronic forms of schizophrenia to function in society. Mood-stabilizing medicines allow individuals with bipolar disorder to overcome impulsive, suicidal behavior and lead productive lives. As controversial as medication treatments for ADHD have become, their careful use, with diligent oversight, can provide real benefit. For all such conditions, side effects must be appraised and the potential for adverse reactions carefully monitored, but medication treatment can be lifesaving.

Various psychotherapies can be as helpful as medications for unipolar depression and constitute the treatments of choice for a range of anxiety disorders, as well as conduct problems in youth. Combining medication and therapy often produces superior outcomes to either treatment modality alone: This clearly is the case for depression and sometimes for ADHD. Although severe autism defies effective treatment for the most part, intensive behavioral treatments in the early phases of autistic disorder have shown promise in altering its course and promoting greater communication and social responsiveness.[15]

The situation is far from perfect. Mental illnesses often co-occur in the same individual, and such patterns of comorbidity predict lowered response rates to treatment.[16] In addition, some people with mental disorders come to identify themselves in terms of their mental affliction, harboring the fear that, by treating the illness, they may lose part of their core identity. In such cases, advocates for treatment face an uphill battle, particularly with respect to those persons who may need intervention the most.[17] Treatments can also incur side effects, some of which may be direct—for example, physical symptoms can emerge from certain psychotropic medications, which themselves generate stigma. Other effects may be less direct, in that receiving medication or psychological therapy is still highly devalued in certain regions and subcultures, resulting in shame and humiliation. And response to treatment is far from universal. Response rates are well below 100%, and it is rare even for "responders" to obtain full normalization of functioning.[18]

In addition, gaining access to treatment requires acknowledgement on the part of individuals (and caregivers, in the case of children) that a psychological or psychiatric problem exists. Such acknowledgement requires understanding that the problems and impairments are related to a mental disorder, emotional acceptance of this fact, and the motivation to seek treatment. Each of these is a major step.[19] Furthermore, treatment cannot occur unless funding for mental health care exists. Once again demonstrating the multiple levels at which stigma reduction must occur, it will take a combination of societal tolerance, treatment access, personal knowledge and acceptance, and parity of healthcare coverage to promote the kinds of treatment seeking that are necessary for both personal benefit and stigma reduction.

Despite these issues, implications of the growing successes of various intervention strategies are considerable. It is now the case that if mental disorders are recognized, diagnosed, and treated, many of their debilitating symptoms and life impairments can be ameliorated, often substantially. The situation is highly likely to improve in the future, as clinical psychology, psychiatry, and the related mental health fields continue to mature. Success rates for mental health treatments already rival those for heart disease and cancer in physical medicine, meaning that there is reason for considerable optimism.[20] Views of mental disorder that emphasize its hopelessness and immutability may eventually become relics of past ignorance.

Implications for Stigma   Beyond the benefits of effective treatment for persons afflicted with mental disorders, as well as their families and caregivers, what are the specific implications for stigma reduction? First, if some of the more threatening symptoms of mental illness can be controlled and reduced through active intervention, then a key source of stigmatization—namely, its sense of peril or threat to observers—may diminish. Second, successful treatment is likely to increase a sense of personal agency and effectiveness on the part of the treated individual. Such autonomy and self-valuation may then fuel a more positive set of interactions with social partners, including employers, workmates, and community members at large, which can serve to promote reductions in stigmatization. This process can occur for children and adolescents, as well as adults.

To the extent that responsive and effective treatment strategies are put into place, the individual in question may be relieved of considerable personal suffering and propelled into a more active means of coping with life stressors and social and occupational challenges. For children, academic and social successes may be more attainable; for adults, economic hardship may also be reduced, given that treatment benefits may extend to increased employability. As members of society, in turn, encounter fewer symptoms that signal threat, hopelessness, and despair, they may be able to appreciate the person's positive traits, so long as equitable contact can occur. Perceivers who see the benefits of successful treatment may, in fact, realize that change is possible and that individuals with difficult mental and behavioral problems can, in a deep and human way, overcome adversity. Successful individual-level treatment may therefore set in motion a "virtuous cycle" of improved academic and social functioning, enhanced economic independence, and genuine acceptance.

There is a gap between this positive scenario and the current reality. Delays in seeking treatment are still quite long for persons who emerge with the symptoms of mental illness, even in this country.[21] Fewer than half of those with mental disorders in the United States and other developed nations receive any form of systematic care or treatment, with rates far lower in Third World nations.[22] Moreover, to reiterate a crucial assertion made earlier, because effective treatments are unlikely to eliminate evidence of mental disorder altogether, there must be societal acceptance of the reality of mental disturbance even if effective treatments are in place.

Still, the core point is that responsive and effective treatment can play a vital role in stigma reduction. The view that mental illnesses are hopeless and untreatable is simply false, even though in some cases the road to rehabilitation will be long and arduous. Along with systems-level changes in eliminating discrimination, fostering basic human rights, and promoting societal tolerance and acceptance, receipt of treatment can be a viable stigma-reduction strategy, and it must be a cornerstone of all future efforts.

Coping With Discrimination and Stigma

In this section the theme is not the improvement of psychological and psychiatric status through treatment procedures but rather the potential for people with mental illness to utilize various coping strategies to deal with the realities of societal prejudice and stigmatization. My implication is not that the primary means of stigma reduction should consist of teaching the victims of stigmatization to bear up more stoically to oppression and scorn. Such a stance would signal tacit acceptance of societal tendencies to stigmatize individuals with mental illness. Stigma exists, however, and enhancing the coping styles of people with mental disorder is an important part of decreasing the burden of mental illness.

In fact, even under the most optimistic of scenarios, the stigmatization of mental disorder will not soon recede. It is extremely likely that people with mental illness will encounter at least some degree of stereotyping, prejudice, discrimination, and stigma in the foreseeable future, even if all of the changes advocated in this book occur. Coping responses are a needed component of stigma-reduction tools, complementing both treatment-related benefits and change strategies at the level of media, professionals, and social systems.

What are the most effective coping strategies? It is a mistake to think that any one tactic is inherently the best means of dealing with stigma. Some persons undoubtedly do best through quieter and more reflective means; others may require action and the sense of working for social change. Investigators are just beginning to understand the different ways of responding to stigma among those with mental disorders.[23]

Stress and coping research has determined that some forms of coping are directed primarily toward the source of conflict or stress; these involve planning, as well as gathering instrumental and emotional support. Such *problem-focused* coping can be distinguished from *emotion-focused* coping, which features mental and behavioral disengagement from the stress and can also include denial.[24] In terms of mental illness stigma as a stressor, problem-focused strategies could involve the joining of self-help or advocacy movements that actively fight discrimination. Such tactics might also entail the securing of job training or obtaining additional information about accommodations for mental disorder. With the growth of self-help and advocacy movements for individuals and families encountering mental disorder, problem-focused coping is more of an option than ever.

Emotion-focused coping can sometimes yield benefits but is more consistently associated with distress and negative outcomes. Indeed, because such coping strategies do not actively deal with the source of the problem, they may promote rumination or preoccupation with the experience of prejudice and may cause difficulties in detaching oneself from hurt and pain. In some cases active, outward coping is simply not possible, so that emotion regulation strategies are needed.[25] The ability to understand that prejudice and stigma do not emerge from one's personal flaws—and the direct encountering of bias in everyday life—constitute a blend of emotional reframing and problem-focused strategizing that is likely to be helpful.

Active coping usually requires the ability and willingness to identify oneself as an individual who is experiencing mental illness. This kind of admission is not easy. Not only may people with serious mental disorder lack insight, but coming to terms with such a stigmatized attribute is difficult even if realization exists. In addition, disclosure is not always strategic in terms of personal advancement, given the stigma that still occurs throughout society, particularly at the workplace. Corrigan thoughtfully discusses the pitfalls and potential gains related to self-disclosure and makes an analogy to the process of coming out in gay and lesbian individuals. Goldberg and colleagues also argue that disclosure of mental disorders to an employer must be done with caution and appropriate timing.[26] Overall, to the extent that a strong sense of solidarity and community exists among members of a stigmatized group and to the extent that structural discrimination is decreased, personal disclosure will be facilitated.

In fact, disclosure of one's status as having a mental illness does not have to be "all or none." There may be some situations in which thoughtful disclosure may aid in coping and others in which it might generate responses on the part of perceivers that can trigger discrimination in relation to social or occupational goals. Because a history of mental illness is usually a concealable form of stigma, decisions about when and how to disclose productively constitute an important topic but one that has been seldom investigated.

It is also possible to envision some forms of psychotherapy as directly targeting one's ability to cope with stigmatization. Cognitive therapy, for example, may aid people with mental illness in dealing with self-statements and cognitive distortions. To the extent that stigmatizing messages from society become internalized, therapy that directly challenges such perspectives and enables the individual to try out alternative constructions, including those that can facilitate ascribing many aspects of stigma to external factors (such as prejudice) may be particularly valuable.[27] Overall, coping with stigma and its consequences cannot be neglected.

12

Concluding Issues

To close this book I present several issues and controversies that may be of interest to the next generation of individuals and groups interested in stigma. These include the conceptual models used to understand mental illness, the role of mental health screening in preventive efforts, basic versus applied research priorities, problems inherent in mounting stigma reduction, and the movement advocating neurodiversity. My final comments include a hopeful yet realistic appraisal of the chances for success in reducing stigma in the years ahead.

Conceptions of Mental Disorder

Widening Boundaries

An expanding number of conditions are now counted as forms of mental illness. This trend, exemplifying the increasing tendency to adopt biomedical models (see Chapter 4), produces several consequences. For one thing, negative connotations of the terms "mental illness" and "mental disorder," previously reserved for conditions such as schizophrenia, bipolar disorder, and autism, may now be invoked for a wide range of behavior patterns. Secondary labeling theory posits that stigmatization will be directed to behavioral displays formerly viewed as part of the general human condition but now believed to represent a feared and threatening category.

As an example, alcohol and substance use disorders now fall under the umbrella of mental illness, leading to a clash between the moral terms often used to understand such conditions and the biological connotations of medical-model perspectives. Are alcohol abuse, heroin use, or crack or methamphetamine usage truly disease states, or is this branding just one more attempt by secular scientists to take away personal blame and responsibility for most forms of human deviance? Furthermore, will there be a paradoxical weakening of personal resolve to fight such problems when they are construed as forms of mental illness—that is, uncontrollable outcomes of a disease? Modern social critics and antipsychiatrists have lambasted the tendency to place ever-widening forms of behavioral deviance under the rubric of mental illness, whereas those defending this model point to genetic predispositions, clear psychobiological risk factors, and sophisticated brain-imaging studies of neural correlates.[1]

This entire issue is complicated by the increasing realization that most mental disorders appear to differ quantitatively, but not qualitatively, from normal-range behavior.[2] In other words, most conditions appear to be "spectrum" in nature. Parallel to medical entities such as hypertension, when diagnoses are applied to continuous distributions of underlying processes, the question of where to draw the line between normality and pathology is not clear cut. Even though scientific efforts can help in this regard, when the underlying process is dimensional there is no indisputable criterion above which a disorder is present or below which it is clearly absent.

A major issue for future generations of both scientists and clinicians will be where to place these thresholds of deviance and dysfunction. Wider boundaries could, once again, stigmatize greater amounts of behavior. On the other hand, they could allow for the realization that normal and abnormal behavior are separated only by degree, with the potential for greater identification and empathy on the part of society and with the hope that help can become available to larger numbers of people. The underlying value judgments placed on conformity and deviance will serve as crucial determinants of ultimate acceptance.

Future Views of Mental Illness

Indeed, what will views on mental illness come to be a century from now and beyond? It is imaginable that advances in genetics, developmental psychopathology, and cultural psychology will be of such magnitude that current conceptions of what is disordered and what is normal will seem as primitive as the views of a century ago appear to us today. For example, considerably more focus may be placed on the potentially adaptive value of many forms of behavior today termed deviant or pathological. The benefits to human societies of having partial risk for mental disorder may be fully appreciated in terms of the diversity that can accrue to our societies and our species. Even now, for example, we know that biological relatives of individuals with bipolar disorder are particularly likely to achieve artistic, scientific, or financial success.[3] In addition, as the study of resilience continues to mature, it may become possible to identify those who are at risk for mental illness and provide them with the kinds of protective experiences that could significantly turn around the potential for negative outcomes without necessarily altering their underlying natures or their potential for unique contributions.

Yet this is undoubtedly an optimistic view. A more likely occurrence is that the increasing power of molecular genetic techniques will allow future neonatologists and clinicians to specify, within bands of probability, the extent of risk that a fetus or infant may carry for developing various forms of mental illness. Such designation may well promote tendencies to stereotype and pathologize, given the pervasive assumption that mental disorder should be avoided at all costs. There may be a rush to early intervention of the kind that involves abortion of the fetus or involuntary medication treatment for the child. Considerable blame may attend to those who could be accused of knowing about their (or their child's) genetic risk for mental illness but did not take steps to prevent it.

A strong form of genetic determinism and elitism could come to dominate societal views, with harsh discrimination against those of lower "castes" who carry what are deemed to be genetic taints. The "elite" without mental illness may view themselves as defenders of an increasingly restricted concept of normality, needing to use eugenic means to prevent despoiling the gene pool. After all, if unfavored genes can be selected out, great blame may accrue to families who opt not to enact such procedures. A new eugenics may emerge in the attempt to purify and improve the human species, with intensified stigma emerging with respect to "failures" in this effort.[4]

The ultimate question is likely to be how future scientists, clinicians, policy makers, and citizens will come to view the human potential of persons with mental illness. Will the perspective be one of enacting all means possible to prevent such conditions from ever emerging? Or will it instead be one of early identification, toward the end of enacting preventive care—but with the assumption that there may still be valuable contributions from those with mental disturbances and that unduly narrowing the gene pool may weaken diversity across our species? It is hard to imagine a more important set of ethical, clinical, and scientific questions.

Reactions Against Mental Disorder Designations

As ever-increasing domains of behavior continue to be annexed under the domain of mental illness, there are bound to be counterresponses. An example involves the pro-anorexia ("pro-ana") movement. Relevant websites glorify the extreme restrictions of caloric intake characteristic of anorexia nervosa, portraying them as lifestyle choices rather than symptoms. These views strongly deny that any biomedical causal factors could account for such behavior patterns; promoted instead is the perspective that the restriction of eating constitutes an individual, even politically motivated, lifestyle choice.[5] A clear message is that eating-related problems should not be stigmatized, as they are not a form of mental illness at all.

When eating problems are portrayed in this way, the young women receiving such messages would be expected to have little or no motivation to alter their eating patterns—which are in fact lionized by the pro-ana perspective.[6] In other words, the reductions in stigma that apply to an entirely volitional account like pro-ana may greatly reinforce and intensify eating pathology. As a wide variety of lifestyles proliferates in pluralistic societies, clashes between those who view certain forms of deviance as symptoms of an underlying illness and others who emphasize the voluntary, chosen, and rational bases of such behaviors are likely. There is potential for a paradoxical intensification of disturbed behavior patterns when stigma reduction is attempted by circumventing the biomedical perspective altogether.

Mental Health Screening

I advocated earlier for the inclusion of mental health and behavioral indicators into general health care screenings, certainly for children but also for adults. When screening recommendations were made by the President's New Freedom Commission in 2003, however, considerable backlash emerged.[7] I pause to analyze some of the issues involved and what they may tell us about the stigmatization of mental illness.

Clearly, there are very real scientific and clinical issues that surround the early prediction of mental disorders.[8] Detecting any relatively rare event in the general population is bound to be accompanied by a number of "false positive" appraisals (overpredictions), in which the assessment is made that the individual in question will contract the condition of interest when that person is not truly at risk. In fact, if the attempt is made to predict extremely rare events (for example, schizophrenia, with an overall prevalence of less than 1% of the population), overall accuracy would be maximized by predicting that such an outcome would *never* occur. In this instance, the prediction will be correct more than 99% of the time—at the expense, of course, of missing all of the actual cases. The real question pertains to the relative costs of overprediction of relatively rare events versus the failure to accurately detect true cases.

For nearly all physical illnesses, "false negatives" (underpredictions) are the crucial error to be avoided. A false negative appraisal could potentially be fatal, whereas a false positive may alarm the screened individual but, at worst, motivate further diagnostic tests. However, the strong stigma that attends to labels of mental illness (or to designations of high risk status for mental disorders) means that false positive errors are highly undesirable in this domain. Furthermore, until relatively recently, the virtual absence of effective treatments has meant that there was no particular advantage for the early screening and prediction of mental illness. This situation is clearly changing, however, given the increasing promise related to prevention and intervention strategies.

The relevant question remains as follows: in order to avoid underprediction with respect to mental disorder, how many false positive cases are we willing tolerate? The answer will hinge largely on the continuing presence of stigmatization with respect to mental illness, as well as the continued funding for prevention and treatment studies that can provide meaningful data on the personal and societal benefits from early intervention.

Strongly political arguments are being raised about the value and meaning of early detection. In particular, claims abound that mandatory screening of mental health–related problems will usher in an era of unprecedented use of psychotropic medications for at-risk children.[9] In such views, early screening efforts would not only incur potential stigmatization but also trigger the inappropriate and unethical prescription of medications. Increases in the use of psychoactive medications for children and adolescents in recent years make it clearer why such fears would develop.[10]

The goal of screening, however, is not to promote automatic prescription of medication at the first sign of future risk for mental illness via mandatory procedures. Rather, a preventive approach to mental health issues should be embedded in the kinds of medical checkups now in place—so long as there is full realization that better access to medical care is a key priority—in order that trained health professionals can help to gauge potential high-risk situations for mental disorder. If positive screenings occur, the first step would be to perform additional evaluation not only of the child but also of caregivers, as well as school or neighborhood settings. In many cases, the information could suggest the provision of psychosocial interventions or accommodations. As medication treatments become validated for certain conditions in young children, these may be recommended in such cases, but only with better data as to their safety and efficacy and not as the primary option.[11]

In all, a "positive" screening should not automatically place the source of the problem in the children themselves and should not mandate forced treatment. The objective is to find problems in their incipient stages and in their full contexts rather than to wait until they have become fully entrenched. It is just as stigmatizing to deny the potential value of early screening and detection— under the misguided assumption that mental illnesses are imaginary constructs invented by pernicious agents of social control—as it is to promote universal and mandatory screening without parental consent and with an inevitable push toward involuntary treatment.

Research Priorities

In recent years there has been an explicit policy shift at the National Institute of Mental Health (NIMH) toward prioritization of the types of research that can fundamentally ease the burden of mental illness in society. In other words, an increased emphasis has been placed on research efforts that directly target understanding the causal factors for mental illness, their epidemiology (i.e., distribution throughout society), the optimal assessment and treatment strategies for such conditions, and the viability of current service delivery systems intended to guarantee their care. De-emphasized are investigations of basic processes related to cognition, attention, emotion, social processes, development, and neurobiology, unless these studies have direct application to mental disorder. The belief is that NIMH should be geared toward clinical application.[12] This shift has been prompted by analyses, conducted by both scientists and advocates, which highlight the acute lack of funding for serious mental illnesses (e.g., schizophrenia, bipolar disorder, severe forms of depression, autism, panic disorder, and obsessive compulsive disorder) in relation to the societal costs of such debilitating conditions.[13]

There is no doubt that funding for research on and treatment of serious mental illnesses must become a priority. Indeed, these are the most stigmatized variants of mental disorder, and they have received a disproportionately low level of funding in relation to their long-term human and economic costs. It is worth considering, however, the costs incurred in the other direction—namely, those related to an intentional neglect of basic psychological, biological, and social research.

This stance is reminiscent of the attempt 35 years ago by the Nixon administration to lead a "war on cancer" by earmarking federal funds for research and clinical efforts with direct relevance to combating this vicious disease (or, rather, set of diseases).[14] Given the state of the art of molecular biology, virology, and other basic sciences at that time, the rush to end cancer without funding basic research efforts was fundamentally misguided. In other words, in the absence of considerably more knowledge about how and why cells proliferate as they do, a budgetary focus devoted exclusively to application was premature.

Parallel arguments apply to the current situation in mental health. Despite clear advances, the entire field is still in a period of ignorance about a great many fundamental processes related to both normal and atypical functioning. Genetic propensities, neural pruning in early brain development, prenatal environments, temperament, emotion and emotion regulation processes, developmental changes linked to puberty, attention, memory, family socialization, wider environmental influences (e.g., schools and peer groups), and cultural factors are just a few examples of such processes. Without better understanding of these and other systems, how can we be sure that intervention efforts are being directed toward the right targets?

Furthermore, it is not even known whether the current means of classifying mental illness is correct. There may well be underlying dimensions of dysfunction at neurobiological, psychological, and social levels that cut across existing psychiatric classifications. Basic knowledge of genes, brains, and environments (and their nearly infinitely complex interchanges) is surely required before mental health and mental illness can be understood with sufficient clarity to devote complete resources to applied endeavors.

Admittedly, there are hard choices to make, given the enormity of the problem and the relatively limited resources available (in comparison, for example, with the vast sums of money used to promote current defense and war efforts). Although important work on prevention, treatment development, clinical trials, evaluation of long-term outcome, and dissemination must be promoted, careful thought needs to be given to the appropriate weighting of research on basic processes versus more applied endeavors. Scientists, policy makers, and the general public need to be engaged in continuing self-education and debate about these priorities before we realize, some years down the road, that funds were squandered on attempts to cure mental illness that were implemented too quickly and without full knowledge of the underlying causes and mechanisms.

The call for clinical relevance applies to research on stigma as well. Investigations of basic psychological, evolutionary, and social processes that may be of major pertinence to stigmatization are now viewed as less crucial than work with direct implications for reducing stigma. Again, it is wonderful that NIMH has finally recognized the clear importance of stigma for all aspects of mental health and mental illness, but the balance of basic versus applied investigations needs serious thought.[15] At this time, do we really know all of the most promising targets for viable antistigma efforts? How do basic social psychological and evolutionary psychological mechanisms link with structural factors in relation to stigmatization? Which targeted areas are likely to have the best chance producing change? Debate about these vital issues is required.

Stigma Reduction: Trends and Challenges

Following the coverage of strategies to overcome stigma in Chapters 9, 10, and 11, I note several issues of direct relevance to future efforts.

First, in any educational campaigns regarding mental disorder, two important talking points should be strongly considered: Mental disorder is more common than often thought, and stigma harms all of society. In other words, the message needs to be circulated widely that it is *your* parent, *your* offspring, *your* uncle or aunt, *your* boss, *your* employee, *your* student, or *your* teacher who may be dealing with a mental disorder, often in silence. Another component of the message is that without giving these members of our families and our social networks a chance to receive treatment and be part of the mainstream of society, we all lose.

Even considering the most serious mental disorders, a prevalence of 6% means that, on average, at least one child in every classroom, one close or extended relative, or one workmate is contending with mental illness. When moderately severe forms are included, the presence of an additional 20% or more of the population makes mental illness far from a rare occurrence. Rather, it is a part of everyday life for each citizen and every family.

Mental illness has been so often hidden from public view and so frequently relegated to the back burner of public concern that many individuals are surprised at just how frequently it can and does occur, even in its most serious forms. The wasted potential within families, communities, businesses, and the nation as a whole is both tragic and unnecessary. Finding ways to deliver such messages should be an essential part of future campaigns, along with portrayals that emphasize the underlying humanity of persons and families who contend with mental illness.

Second, recall the provocative point from Chapter 6 that some individuals and groups interested in eradicating stigma may be overly serious and overly sensitive. Is this in fact true? Should those engaging in antistigma efforts lighten up in crucial respects? Is political correctness receiving greater priority than meaningful change? For example, attempting to erase our language of all offhanded references to mental illness or other stigmatized conditions makes little sense. Should we actually attempt to ban the use of phrases such as "what a crazy idea"? These kinds of provisions would be impossible to implement and serve no real purpose. As a parallel, for instance, should we stop using the phrase "left-handed compliment" to reduce the stigma of non-right-handed individuals?

There is a major caveat here, however: A great deal of the stigmatization of mental illness, parallel to a large amount of racial and ethnic bias and prejudice, is not performed at the level of mild teasing or poking fun but instead consists of grossly mean-spirited and degrading language and images that dehumanize those with mental disorders. This is a difficult legacy to overcome, and individuals and family members who have contended with mental illness stigma are justifiably sensitive to slurs and ridicule.

Some gay and lesbian individuals now use the word "queer" to refer to themselves, and some African American persons may playfully refer to one another as "niggah." Yet it is still extremely derogatory for persons outside of these minorities to utilize such language. Because of the history of massive stereotyping, prejudice, discrimination, and stigma of sexual minorities, racial groups, and those with mental illness, those in the majority should be sensitive to the roots of the hurt and shame felt by those who have been stigmatized. They should also be aware of the one-sidedness of the legacy of stigmatization. Still, we are all human, and to the extent that the climate changes, some lightness of tone and message may be welcome and may signal interpersonal closeness between people with mental disorder and the rest of the population.

Third, should antistigma campaigns be directed at the populace at large or instead targeted to specific groups? Marketing strategists often deploy targeted initiatives under the assumptions that certain segments of the population will be more responsive than others to input and persuasion regarding specific programs. But who are the relevant groups or subgroups for receipt of antistigma messages? As we come to know more about children's development of attitudes toward mental illness, targeted programs in grade schools or middle schools may be productively developed. Furthermore, adolescence is an extremely important age of risk for the development of mental illness, as well as for peer relations and the consolidation of prejudicial attitudes. Media campaigns have already been developed for adolescents and young adults who are viewers of MTV and other youth-oriented outlets. Regarding adults, it is difficult to conceptualize particular subgroups who might be particularly amenable to antistigma efforts or who may be considered the most likely purveyors of stigma. This remains an important research direction.[16]

Fourth, related to the essential area of changing media portrayals of persons with mental illness, presentations of truly human stories of mental disorder could go far in changing public opinion. In addition, the intentional use of newer (and in some cases more controversial) marketing tactics should be actively considered by those interested in fighting the stigma of mental illness. Although buzz marketing and stealth marketing are controversial, it is worth considering all of the alternatives to spread messages about mental illness that can overcome stigma. Indeed, powerful political and commercial interests commonly use a wide range of intentional media strategies related to a host of products, services, and topics. Furthermore, there is nothing unethical about intentionally framing important messages about mental illness—for example, that it is not inevitably chronic and tragic, that resilience is a possibility, and that human potential is wasted if we let people with mental disorders languish. It may take novel means of communicating such messages to the public at large; media watch groups, advocacy organizations, and clinical entities interested in overcoming stigma should weigh them carefully.

Fifth, the mental health professions need to confront their own views toward mental illness and promote change, where indicated, with respect to their attitudes and practices (see Chapter 10). Even if displayed by only a small minority of professionals and staff members, the stigma revealed by those working in the mental health fields is unacceptable. Raising the status of mental health professions, countering the stress that attends to mental health work, and removing the shame that attends the admission of any sign of personal weakness are potential components. Additional solutions include increased scrutiny in the selection of students, trainees, and personnel for the professions of interest; self-examination of stigmatizing attitudes and practices, including probing of their roots in outmoded conceptual models; admission of mental health workers' need for support and access to therapy without shame; and a revamping of training models and methods to include a less authoritarian view, replaced by one incorporating respect, flexibility, and rigor regarding best practices.

Finally, more careful attention should be paid to other cultures' means of dealing with and caring for persons with mental illness, with special focus on non-Western societies. Industrialized nations do not necessarily provide the best outcomes for individuals with serious mental disorders.[17] Effective care requires more than the provision of optimal individual and family treatments; it must also include the availability of social and vocational roles for individuals whose experiences of mental disorder have temporarily prompted removal from the mainstream. Although some forms of mental illness may never become completely nonthreatening to social observers, systems that can promote societal and familial reentry following episodes are crucial for positive prognosis.

Neurodiversity and the Acceptance of Difference

Even if treatments do a better and better job of alleviating core symptoms and fostering adaptive functioning for persons with mental disorders, no intervention will be able to remove a history of mental illness or the difficult life experiences and self-perceptions often left in its wake. Particularly for severe forms of mental illness, the most effective intervention strategies cannot, as of yet, promote complete normalization of functioning. Residual symptoms, recurrences, lingering impairments, and permanent alterations of self-image are often likely to survive effective treatment. It is mistaken to think that, if treatment were universally available, all of the problems related to mental illness, including its rampant stigmatization, would suddenly disappear.

The concept of neurodiversity has become a potent topic in recent years.[18] Its premises are that (a) many important and gifted individuals throughout history have had various forms of mental or neurological disorders and that (b) appreciating the contributions from people with this kind of diversity is essential. Given the pervasively negative images promulgated about mental illness through general language and the media, it is indeed crucial that narratives of strength as well as weakness, normality as well as deviance, and diversity as well as conformity filter to the public's consciousness if inroads are to be made against stigma.

The potential danger here is that overemphasis on neurodiversity could end up romanticizing or glorifying mental illness, which is clearly not a worthy goal. The impairments accruing from many forms of mental disorder are real and often devastating. Still, to the extent that normality and pathology exist on a continuum—and to the extent that it is difficult to say with certainty which traits and propensities will have the greatest chances of being adaptive as societies and cultures continue to evolve—the neurodiversity construct is provocative.

Along these lines, Corrigan emphasizes that, in the final analysis, stigma is an issue of social injustice. In other words, civil and human rights cannot be denied on the sole basis of a mental disorder label, and antistigma campaigns centering solely on access to treatment may ignore systemic and structural roots of bias.[19] Although mental illness is indeed dysfunctional and requires excellent treatment, reduction of stigma requires joint emphasis on individual and family treatment, encouragement of a better fit between individuals and social institutions, enforcement of basic rights, and appreciation of human diversity. These objectives are not mutually exclusive but instead complementary.

Overall Perspective

If I had to state in one phrase my view of the likelihood of successfully combating stigma in the years to come, I would term it "extremely cautious optimism." In other words, I am well aware of the historical, cross-cultural, and in all probability hard-wired nature of human tendencies to be exquisitely sensitive to interpersonal dysfunction and to stigmatize outgroups. It is also clear that mental disturbance poses both real and symbolic threats to social perceivers. The battle before us is indeed uphill, particularly given our increasingly education-dominated, technologically sophisticated, and conformity-conscious world.

At the same time, I am swayed by those eras in history when bravery trumped ignorance and compassionate views of mental illness emerged. I am cognizant, too, of the great progress in science and clinical practice of recent decades and the potential for humans to overcome their proclivities to categorize and stereotype, by empathizing and providing justice. Still, wide-eyed visions related to quick attainment of destigmatization are not productive. Despite clear progress toward eliminating racial bias over the last 50 years, the United States is facing harsh evidence of the pervasive, lingering effects of its own racism, as evidenced by the hugely inadequate efforts to rescue the largely poor, minority, displaced victims of Hurricane Katrina in New Orleans in 2005. Implicit bias, as well as explicit policies of racism, institutionalized poverty, and bureaucratic inertia, remain in place.

Indeed, it will take a long, dedicated, and patient fight to grant fundamental rights, change media images, ensure adequate treatment, and foster real compassion with respect to mental illness. The length of the struggle is important to keep in mind, as overzealous promises of quick reform invariably lead to resentment and subsequent retrenchment.[20]

Several concluding points are in order. First, the most severe forms of mental illness receive major stigma, yet those experiencing and dealing with other types also confront rejection. For instance, caregivers of children with ADHD, high-functioning autism, and learning disorders are constantly reminded of the shortcomings of their offspring—and, tacitly, of their own parenting—at school, in social groups, and in public venues, often receiving considerable blame. In societies concerned with achievement and, to a large extent, conformity, many forms of mental illness may be prone to receive stigmatization because of the widespread belief that exerting volitional control and providing stricter child rearing are all that is required to eliminate the problems. In nearly all instances mental disorder exists on a continuum, so that stigma does not pertain solely to the most virulent forms of disturbance.

Second, it will take creative efforts to emphasize the fundamental humanity of people who contend with mental illness, particularly those with the most severe forms. Exposure to personal and family narratives that document everyday realities is critical, as I have repeatedly emphasized. Mental disorder retains an aura of mystery, confusion, and threat; we simply cannot afford the repeated promotion of stereotypes of violence, constant and utter irrationality, and hopelessness that surround mental illness. Narratives of strength, courage, and resilience matter, and showcasing them is essential. Stories on treatment-related successes do not make for sensational headlines, yet they should receive far more media attention than tales of horror, crime, or despair.

Third, mental illness touches far more individuals and families than many people would ever suspect. Exposing to public consciousness the facts and realities that nearly all families know at a private level, but rarely voice in public, would go far in eliminating the denial that still constitutes a major barrier to effective change. We cannot afford to bury the realities of mental illness any longer.

Fourth, *realistic* strategies for change must be emphasized. By this I mean that promises of eliminating mental illness through modern psychopharmacology or universal means of primary prevention—or comparable promises of eradicating stigma solely through public education—are simply not attainable in the foreseeable future, if ever. To the extent that such quixotic objectives are promoted, there is bound to be discouragement and demoralization in the aftermath. A likely consequence is that the problems related to mental illness will be perceived as all the more intractable, with subsequent increases in the blaming of persons with mental disorders or their families. In implementing meaningful, multilevel approaches to combat stigma, it will be important not to overpromise. At the same time, momentum toward change must be sustained.

Finally, the ultimate question regarding stigma may well be whether we as a society and a species are content to keep in place attitudes and policies that allow such a shocking waste of human talent and potential. The ultimate irony of stigmatization and discrimination is that all of society and all of humanity lose when these practices are perpetuated. I have the hope that too many concerned people are now dealing with mental illness on a daily basis—suffering from the degrading and wasteful consequences of stigma—to allow mental illness to stay hidden and to allow practices of neglect, punishment, and banishment to remain in place. Change must emanate from altered policies and laws, but the motivation for reform must emerge from a multitude of impassioned, informed pleas from individuals and families and from a continued insistence on promoting and funding effective treatments. The challenge is real, but we all stand to gain from joining the fight.

Notes

Introduction

1. Dukakis and Tye (2006); Pauley (2005); Shields (2005); Styron (1990). See http://www.nydailynews.com for a May 25, 2005, story on Alex Rodríguez's enthusiastic disclosure of his involvement in psychotherapy (Rodríguez also donated $200,000 for children's mental health services in New York City).

2. Rabasca (1999).

3. U.S. Department of Health and Human Services (1999, p. 3). See also U.S. Department of Health and Human Services (2001), which is the supplement to the Surgeon General's report dealing with the particular challenges of providing mental health services to ethnic minority populations, who often receive double stigmatization. Of many recent works elaborating on the importance of stigma in relation to mental illness, see Corrigan (2005c), as well as Otey and Fenton (2004), which introduces a special section of key articles on the stigmatization of mental illness. See also Hinshaw (2005, 2006).

4. New Freedom Commission on Mental Health (2003). Note that the commission did not advocate for increased government expenditures related to mental health care.

5. These include, first, the United Kingdom's 5-year program, from 1998 to 2003, titled "Changing Minds: Every Family in the Land." Second, in 2001, the World Health Organization began the Mental Health Global Action Program to tackle the huge problem of upgrading services and access to care around the world. Third, the World Psychiatric Association (WPA) has also embarked upon an international antistigma program. See Crisp (2000); PatientView (2004a); Thompson, Stuart, Bland, Arbodele-Florez, Warner, and Dickson (2002); for a summary of the effects of the WPA's global program, see Sartorius and Schulze (2005).

6. Teplin, McClelland, Abram, and Weiner (2005).

7. For wrenching accounts of the degraded state of community residences in New York City within the past several years, see the Pulitzer Prize–winning series of Levy (2002a, 2002b, 2002c). These articles open with the story of a man with schizophrenia, in his early 50s, in a "home" in Brooklyn (housing more than 300 people), who was often unattended during his major seizures and who was found by an aide after he had been dead for 12 hours (he was so stiff from rigor mortis that he could be fit into a body bag only after his back was broken). Staff neglect, suicides of residents, and a pervasive lack of any records or accountability are the legacies of such current models of "care." Regarding conditions at public hospitals, see J. Doyle (2005), who reported on recently uncovered conditions at Napa State Hospital in northern California, described briefly in the text. For a grim account of mental health care in developing nations, see Miller (2006), who notes that a third of the world's countries have no mental health budgets.

8. Wang, Berglund, Olfson, Pincus, Wells, and Kessler (2005).

9. As noted throughout the book, personal accounts of people with mental disorders are growing and constitute a powerful means of portraying the full humanity of individuals with mental illness. For a review of the insights yielded by these kinds of disclosures, see Angell, Cooke, and Kovac (2005).

10. Zilboorg (1941, p. 313).

11. Torrey (1997).

12. Lamb and Weinberger (1998).

13. French (2002); C. S. Smith (2005); Tsang, Tam, Chan, and Cheung (2003); World Health Organization (2001). Although the long-term prognosis for persons with schizophrenia may actually be better in underdeveloped nations than in the United States and other Western nations, as discussed later in the book, the harsh stigmatization of mental illness transcends national and cultural boundaries; see Miller (2006).

14. Phelan, Link, Stueve, and Pescosolido (2000).

15. Kessler, Chiu, Demler, and Walters (2005).

16. I am indebted to Kay Redfield Jamison for making this astute point.

17. In Hinshaw (2002b), a book that is currently being rewritten, I wrote about the life of my father, a philosopher who had his first, life-threatening episode when he was 16, followed by 40 years of diagnosis with schizophrenia. Along with a narrative of his fascinating yet harrowing life, the book contains information about his many strengths, the shame and silence that permeated society's reactions to mental illness during the last century, and his opening up to me about his life's experiences once I attained late adolescence—which triggered my own deepening interest in psychology and mental health. See Chapter 6 for an account.

Chapter 1

1. For information on prevalence, see Kessler, Chiu, Demler, and Walters (2005), who reveal, first, that about 26% of the U.S. population is likely to have experienced a mental disorder within the past 12 months. The majority of these disorders are mild or moderate in severity, but 5.7% of the population can be classified as having a serious disorder, which by definition involves suicide

attempts, job loss, psychotic features, or substance abuse leading to impairment. Furthermore, fully 46% of Americans have a lifetime experience of mental disorder—again, the clear majority of these are mild to moderate—with a high proportion beginning in childhood or adolescence; see Kessler, Berglund, Demler, Jin, and Walters (2005). Early recognition is therefore a high priority. Figures on suicide are available in the fact sheet from the Campaign for Mental Health Reform, posted July 15, 2005, at http://www.mhreform.org/news/715-05-roadmapfactsheet.htm.

2. Kutchins and Kirk (1997). For an initial and influential denial of the existence of mental disorder, see Szasz (1961).

3. As discussed in greater detail in Chapter 2, attribution theory originated in social psychology and pertained to the pervasive tendency of humans to seek causal explanations for unusual, atypical, or threatening events; for a review, see Weiner (1985).

4. Wakefield (1992).

5. Wekerle and Wolfe (2003).

6. D. Myers (1996).

7. Polubinskaya (2001); Spitzer (1981).

8. Hinshaw (1999).

9. The official classification system in the United States is the American Psychiatric Association's *Diagnostic and Statistical Manual of Mental Disorders,* now in its revised fourth edition (see American Psychiatric Association, 2000). Although it is termed a handbook of "disorders," nearly all of the conditions it lists are actually syndromes—that is, collections of associated symptoms—given that underlying, unified causes for these conditions have, with rare exceptions, not yet been found. Haslam (2000) contends that a medical or disease model contains four key elements: (a) Causes are disturbances in biological structures, functions, or processes; (b) each condition has a distinct etiology; (c) disorders are discrete categories, and afflicted individuals are qualitatively distinct from the nonafflicted; and (d) the disorders are universal across all humans rather than culturally bound. Such conditions are rarely met in medicine, much less psychology or psychiatry.

10. This example highlights the fact that an individually-based medical model of mental illness may so completely overlook the reality of the social norms that define the deviant behavior in question as to be oppressive, ludicrous, or both.

11. Fannon, Chitnis, Daku, and Tennakoon (2000).

12. In the words of Steven Hyman, former director of the National Institute of Mental Health, "Thus, even if one day we find ourselves with our genomes on a chip in our wallets, our genotypes will provide only probabilistic information about our behavior." See Hyman (2004, p. 12).

13. Wakefield (1992, 1999).

14. Lilienfeld and Marino (1999). For example, consider the well-known example of black versus white moths in England: As the environment changed in the nineteenth century as a result of industrialization, tree barks became dark because of the soot produced, making the genes for white moths (formerly protective against white tree bark) clearly "dysfunctional" in the new context. See also Wakefield's counterreplies (1999).

15. Cicchetti and Cohen (2006); Rutter and Sroufe (2000).

16. Walker and Diforio (1997).

17. Cicchetti and Rogosch (1996); Sroufe (1989).

18. For discussion of plasticity in brain development, see M. Johnson (1999). Also, readers may wonder whether the models in this chapter, proposed largely by scientists and clinicians, are consonant with most people's general perceptions of psychopathology. In a pathbreaking synthesis, Haslam (2005) has probed the ways in which people generally perceive deviant behavior, comprising what he terms a "folk psychiatry." He terms the four dimensions in his analysis as *pathologizing, moralizing, psychologizing,* and *medicalizing,* corresponding roughly but not completely to the social norms/social deviance, moral, personal impairment, and medical models, respectively, of the analysis here. It is worth noting, however, that lay conceptions do not, as of yet, appear to fully incorporate the complex notions of reciprocal causation and transactional influence found in developmental psychopathology models nor the notions of fit in the ecological model.

19. Alloy, Acocella, and Bootzin (1996); Davison, Neale, and Kring (2004); Oltmanns and Emery (1998).

20. American Psychiatric Association (2000, p. xxxi).

21. See Cicchetti and Rogosch (1996).

22. For reviews of dimensional versus categorical perspectives, see Beauchaine (2003) and Pickles and Angold (2003). With respect to setting a cutoff on an underlying dimension, in medicine blood pressure clearly forms a continuous, normal distribution, but it is still clinically important to assign a cutoff value for the diagnosis of high blood pressure (i.e., hypertension). In fact, the official criteria for hypertension have been lowered in recent years in order to apply treatments before more serious problems develop. This process reflects the lack of a "gold standard" for assigning a diagnosis, even in many aspects of medicine.

23. Haslam and Ernst (2002) provide extended discussion of the important distinction between categories that are utilized for practical purposes (e.g., recommending treatment) versus categories that they term *natural,* which reflect "essentialist" categories with causal factors that are completely distinct from other designations.

24. To give a sense of the scope of the *DSM-IV,* the major categories of adult conditions include delirium, dementia, and other cognitive disorders; substance-related disorders; schizophrenia and other psychotic disorders; mood disorders (e.g., depression, bipolar disorder); anxiety disorders (e.g., recurrent panic attacks, phobias, posttraumatic stress disorder); somatoform disorders (i.e., those with physical symptoms not explainable by a medical condition); factitious disorders (the intentional taking on of symptoms); dissociative disorders (amnesia, fugue, and dissociative identity disorder—the new name for multiple personality disorder); sexual and gender identity disorders; eating disorders (including anorexia nervosa and bulimia); sleep disorders; impulse control disorders; adjustment disorders (those triggered by identifiable stressors); personality disorders (representing long-standing, maladaptive clusters of traits); and a range of other conditions. There is also a large section of disorders usually first evident during childhood (e.g., ADHD, oppositional defiant disorder, learning disorders, conduct disorder). To enhance precision, definitions of specific disorders typically include the following: (a) an operational list of constituent symptoms; (b) a criterion involving the duration of the symptoms (e.g.,

two weeks for major depressive disorder; six months for schizophrenia); (c) exclusionary criteria—that is, symptoms or features that rule out a given diagnosis; and (d) explicit statements about the types of impairment that must be yielded by the symptoms in question.

25. See, for example, Moynihan and Cassels (2005). For a view of pharmaceutical firms' creation of markets for all kinds of prescription medications in the United States, see Critser (2005).

26. Regarding ADHD, despite stereotypes that it is a label applied to mildly bothersome children, it is actually an impairing condition that shows strong heritability, clear evidence for neurobiological substrates, and existence in multiple cultures; see Barkley (2003) and Hinshaw (1999). The issue of substance abuse is a thorny one. The *DSM-IV* lists three types of alcohol and substance disorders (substance use disorders, substance abuse disorders, and substance dependence disorders); such conditions often coexist with other mental disorders. The stigma associated with alcohol and substance problems is extremely high, related to the assumption of personal culpability in the individual who "succumbs" to the influence of drugs. Although substance use and abuse receive some coverage herein, their manifestations and stigmatization fall largely outside the scope of this book.

27. The field's understanding of mental disorder is changing rapidly at present, with the result that current conceptions of mental illness may seem as misguided and outdated to future generations as those of past centuries appear to us today. Because the status of current models is uncertain, keeping a broad perspective on what is considered mental illness may be wise for a work on stigma.

28. Murray and López, eds. (1996, p. 3).

29. As discussed in footnote 1 to this chapter, Kessler, Chiu, Demler, and Walters (2005) recently provided evidence that 5.7% of the U.S. population have experienced, within the past year, a mental disorder causing severe impairment such as psychotic thinking, loss of employment, suicidal behavior, or serious substance use.

30. D. Myers (1996); Biernat and Dovidio (2000).

31. Allport (1958); Oskamp (2000).

32. For a classic work on attitude-behavior linkages, see Ajzen and Fishbein (1980), and Fishbein and Ajzen (1975). For more current discussion of the fluid boundaries between cognitive, affective, and behavioral components of stigmatization, see Dovidio, Major, and Crocker (2000).

33. Research reveals that stereotypes are linked only weakly with actual discrimination. Prejudice has a clearer association with discriminatory practices, but even here, the prediction is far from perfect. See Struch and Schwartz (1989), who found that measures of aggressive attitudes were nearly uncorrelated with behavioral aggression. For a meta-analytic review of attitude-behavior relations, see Krauss (1995).

34. Erlich, Flexner, Carruth, and Hawkins (1980); Stein and Flexner (2001).

35. Goffman (1963, p. 1).

36. Ibid. (pp. 5–6).

37. See ibid. regarding individual and social processes; Jussim, Palumbo, Chatman, Madon, and Smith (2000) for fascinating information on self-fulfilling

prophecies; and Major and O'Brien (2005), for a comprehensive synthesis of identity threat theory.

38. The PsycInfo database, comprising social science articles from psychology and related fields, lists over 4,100 citations under the keyword of "stigma," the vast majority of which emanate from the past 15 years or so.

39. Link and Phelan (2001a).

40. Goffman (1963, p. 7).

41. See Scambler and Hopkins (1990) for information about the concepts of enacted stigma (implying prejudice and discrimination from perceivers) versus felt stigma (related to the self-perceptions of those who are stigmatized).

42. For the earlier view, see Allport (1958); for later perspectives, see Cioffi (2000); Crocker and Quinn (2000); Miller and Major (2000).

43. Jones, Farina, Hastorf, Markus, Miller, and Scott (1984).

44. If judgments of deviance are at least somewhat relative, then there may be no absolute attribute that induces stigma; a person is stigmatized because of "having a devalued social identity in a particular social context" (Crocker, Quinn, and Steele, 1998, p. 506).

45. See Sternberg (2003) for an elaborated theory of hatred, one aspect of which is the negation of intimacy with the blamed individual or group, leading to the perception of subhumanity. Another aspect is the use of mass communication via propaganda to justify the hatred.

46. See, for example, Corrigan and Watson (2002) and Watson and River (2005). Yet, as discussed in subsequent chapters, there is also potential for members of stigmatized groups to show different kinds of coping responses, including empowerment (see also Major and O'Brien, 2005).

Chapter 2

1. See Crocker, Quinn, and Steele (1998); Fishbein (2002); Fiske (1998); Jones, Farina, Hastorf, Markus, Miller, and Scott (1984); Katz (1981).

2. For key readings on the social psychological approach to stigma and discrimination, see the review chapters of Crocker et al. (1998), Dovidio, Major, and Crocker (2000), and Major and O'Brien (2005); the book-length accounts of Goffman (1963), Jones et al. (1984), Katz (1981), and S. Sontag (1978/1989); and the edited volume of Heatherton, Kleck, Hebl, and Hull (2000). Ottati, Bodenhausen, and Newman (2005) provide a recent review of social psychological accounts; this chapter has a different organization from the present one yet provides a view that is roughly parallel. Sociological views are provided by Scheff (1974, 1984), Link, Cullen, Frank, and Wozniak (1987), Markowitz (2005), and Wright, Gronfein, and Owens (2000). The integrative accounts of Corrigan and Kleinlen (2005) and Link and Phelan (2001a) are of crucial importance, as is the seminal work on stereotype threat by Steele and Aronson (1995). Identity threat theory, the complex and fascinating perspective regarding stigmatization that involves appraisals of threats versus coping responses, is reviewed in Major and O'Brien (2005).

3. Goffman (1963, p. 4).

4. Jones et al. (1984).

5. Goffman (1963); see also, more recently, Quinn, Kahng, and Crocker (2004) regarding the pros and cons of strategies of concealment for persons with mental illness.

6. Jones et al. (1984); Langlois, Kalakonis, Rubenstein, Larson, Hallam, and Smart (2000).

7. Gupta, Mosnik, Black, Berry, and Masand (1999).

8. Weiner (1985); for a more recent elaboration with respect to mental disorder, see Corrigan (2000).

9. Weiner, Perry, and Magnusson (1988). See also Farina, Holland, and Ring (1966), in which experimental participants gave higher levels of electric shock to confederates alleged to have mental disorders when the participants believed that the afflictions were more personally controllable than when they were not.

10. I take up this issue directly in Chapter 4 when I address the effects of the current zeitgeist toward biomedical/genetic views on mental disorder. The question of the potential benefits and potential liabilities of exclusively genetic and biological ascriptions for mental disorder is addressed by Corrigan and Watson (2004) and Hinshaw (2005, 2006).

11. Lerner (1980).

12. Jones et al. (1984, p. 59).

13. Allport (1958); D. Myers (1996).

14. Crocker et al. (1998); Devine (1989). Whether those in the outgroup believe the stereotypes is a crucial factor in their response to stigmatizing messages (see Major and O'Brien, 2005).

15. Fiske (1998). It is also the case that conscious efforts to suppress the automatic stereotypes in question may backfire when the perceiver has limited or overtaxed cognitive resources, fueling a paradoxical overaccessibility of the negative stereotype, as shown by Wegner (1997). Similar mechanisms appear to be at play for those with a concealable stigma who attempt to suppress or cover up their condition, as articulated by Smart and Wegner (2000).

16. Regarding implicit attitudes, see, for example, Dasgupta and Greenwald (2001) and Greenwald, Nosek, and Banaji (2003). As described in subsequent chapters, some of these tests involve measures of reaction time to various stimuli, with the idea that quickness of response is not susceptible to conscious control. For the first study of implicit attitudes in relation to mental illness, see Teachman, Wilson, and Komarovskaya (2006).

17. See Katz (1981) and Katz, Wackenhut, and Hass (1986) for extensive accounts of ambivalence.

18. Experimental research confirms that responses to stigmatized persons are fluctuating and volatile, reflecting ambivalence. See Hebl, Tickle, and Heatherton (2000) for detailed examples of the ambivalence that often attends to interactions between perceivers and members of stigmatized groups.

19. A related point pertains to the strong likelihood of discrepancies between attitudes and behavior on the part of social perceivers. That is, because of the conflicts raised by contact with a member of a devalued outgroup, there may be key differences between *attitudes* (e.g., in surveys, the respondent may profess openness toward those with mental disorders) and *behavioral responses* (e.g., the same respondent would not give a job or rent an apartment to an ex-mental patient). Discrepancies can also go in the other direction, such

that prejudicial attitudes are counteracted by benign behavioral responses. These points reflect a major issue in social psychology—the differences between expressed attitudes and actual behavioral response (see Krauss, 1995).

20. See McConahay (1986). Gaertner and Dovidio (2000) describe a variant termed aversive prejudice or racism, in which an individual consciously committed to nonstigmatizing views still holds overlearned, unconscious, negative attitudes that may "leak" when there are no cues related to egalitarian expression—and that may be self-justified on the basis of factors other than race. Even those who deeply believe in equality are prone to express prejudice and discrimination.

21. Crocker et al. (1998); Hebl et al. (2000).

22. Macrae, Bodenhausen, Milne, and Jetten (1994); Wegner (1997). Yet, as summarized in Major and O'Brien (2005), stereotype suppression does not uniformly result in rebound and may in fact be a helpful means of counteracting stigma. This area of research is complex.

23. See the synthesis of findings in Major and O'Brien (2005).

24. Regarding rejection sensitivity, see Downey and Feldman (1996); for stigma consciousness, see Pinel (2002) and Brown and Pinel (2003). Stigma consciousness may develop in any member of society, although it is likely to develop earlier and be more intense for members of stigmatized groups—see McKown and Weinstein (2003).

25. For the use of these terms, see Scambler and Hopkins (1990).

26. Erlich, Flexner, Carruth, and Hawkins (1980, p. 835).

27. Crocker and Major (1989); Crocker et al. (1998); Dovidio et al. (2000); Major, Kaiser, and McCoy (2003); Twenge and Crocker (2002). See, for example, Crocker, Cornwell, and Major (1993), who showed that overweight women who received negative feedback tended to attribute such criticism to their weight and not to characteristics of the evaluator, with consequent negative mood. The ability to externalize these types of feedback may protect self-esteem.

28. For overviews, see Crocker et al. (1998); Fiske (1998).

29. See Tajfel and Turner (1979). Note that, outside of experimental research studies, individuals often perceive themselves to belong to multiple ingroups, ranging from small and exclusive entities (e.g., one's family) to neighborhoods, racial groups, cities, states, and nations. It may be more difficult, however, to consider all of humanity as part of one's ingroup.

30. The discussion in this section draws on Allport (1958); Brewer (1999); Crocker et al. (1998); Dovidio et al. (2000); Gaertner and Dovidio (2000); Hewstone, Rubin, and Willis (2002); Jones et al. (1984); Jost and Banaji (1994).

31. Alllport (1958, p. 51).

32. Pettigrew and Meertens (1995). An extreme form is found in Hitler's explicit blaming of Jews, gypsies, and people with mental illness and mental retardation as threats to Germany's economic well-being and national security, a practice that clearly fostered prejudice and hatred.

33. A related principle pertains to self-affirmation theories, whereby threats to self-image are met by attempts to maintain or bolster self-concept. See Wills (1981); see also Crocker et al. (1998) for a review.

34. Fein and Spencer (1997).

35. Hewstone et al. (2002) comment on additional theories of mechanisms underlying what they term intergroup bias—that is, the tendency to promote one's

ingroup and devalue the outgroup. One is *optimal distinctiveness theory*, which deals with humans' need to balance assimilation with others and differentiation from others; it posits that a fundamental motivation for ingroup bias is the psychological need to feel differentiated from other groups. Another is *subjective uncertainty reduction theory*, namely, the motivation to hold on to clear, sure beliefs in the world, which could be facilitated by the castigation of outgroups.

36. For example, Pratto, Sidanius, Stalworth, and Malle (1994).

37. For example, see Solomon, Greenberg, and Pyszczynski (1991). For a more recent review, see Solomon, Greenberg, and Pyszczynski (2000). Also, Biernat and Dovidio (2000) contend that mortality fears are particularly likely to be raised by Goffman's category of "abominations of the body" (i.e., physical signs that may signal fears of illness, contagion, and vulnerability in the perceiver).

38. Becker (1963); Scheff (1974, 1984). For an excellent synthesis, see Markowitz (2005).

39. Scheff (1984). The negative implications of labeling theory for mental illness were extended by the often-cited investigation of Rosenhan (1973), in which "pseudopatients" (individuals posing as patients in mental hospitals) were subject to strong expectations of deviance on the part of the hospital staff, who in some instances kept them on the units for lengthy periods of time and subjected them to dehumanizing care.

40. See, for example, Gove (1982); Weinstein (1983).

41. Markowitz (2005, p. 137).

42. Link et al. (1987); Markowitz (1998); Wright et al. (2000); see the review in Markowitz (2005). In Chapter 5 I review empirical evidence on the actual effects of labels.

43. Such a multilevel conception has been applied to many phenomena in the social sciences. For example, in the ecological/transactional models of Bronfenbrenner (1979), Lynch and Cicchetti (1998), and Sameroff and Chandler (1975), there are four nested levels of influence: (a) the microsystem, involving the immediate social and physical environment (family, neighborhood, and school settings); (b) the mesosystem, involving the interactions that occur between various microsystems (e.g., family and school); (c) the exosystem, involving those influences in which the individual is not directly involved (e.g., for children, parental work environments, which may affect parenting but are not directly experienced by the child); and (d) the macrosystem, including societal influences such as government, the media, and economic conditions.

44. Macrae, Milne, and Bodenhausen (1994).

45. Stoessner and Mackie (1993); see the discussion in Haghighat (2001).

46. Gaertner and Dovidio (2000).

47. Devine (1989, p. 16).

48. The classic work on this topic is found in Adorno, Frankel-Brunswik, Levinson, and Sanford (1950). From a psychological perspective, the authoritarian personality was thought to emerge from harsh child-rearing practices and other psychosocial processes.

49. See Corrigan, Edwards, Green, Diwan, and Penn (2001) for relevant evidence. Another personality characteristic, termed benevolence—which indicates a belief in the childlike quality of those with mental disorder—yields a parental kind of concern over the lack of responsibility of those with mental disturbance and fuels tendencies toward distancing and even punishment.

50. Sidanius and Pratto (1999); Hewstone et al. (2002). Crandall (2000) presents an interesting analysis linking SDO with earlier notions of social Darwinism and other system-justifying belief systems.

51. Merton (1948) provided the initial conceptualization of the self-fulfilling prophecy. Jussim, Palumbo, Chatman, Madon, and Smith (2000) cogently discuss the role of self-fulfilling prophecies related to stigma. Intriguingly, although evidence shows real yet small effects related to self-fulfilling prophecies at the dyadic level, far stronger effects appear to exist at the level of social institutions. In fact, Jussim and colleagues argue that social-level self-fulfilling prophecies for those in stigmatized groups, such as tracking in school districts or the presence of job ceilings for those with serious mental disorders, may be particularly pernicious.

52. Steele and Aronson (1995); Steele (1997).

53. Quinn et al. (2004) showed that revealing a history of mental illness led to declines in test performance; such disclosure may well invoke stereotype threat.

54. For an integrative summary of relevant theorizing, see Stangor and Crandall (2000) and Stephan and Stephan (2000). For an interesting perspective on the mutual threats that occur when stigmatized and nonstigmatized individuals interact, see Blasovich, Mendes, Hunter, and Lickel (2000).

55. Major and O'Brien (2005).

56. See Link and Phelan (2001a) for emphasis on the role of social power in stigmatization.

57. Clark and Clark (1950).

58. Belluck (2005).

59. Kitayama (2002); Mendoza-Denton and Mischel (in press).

60. Jones et al. (1984, p. 100).

61. Hovland and Sears (1940). Reanalyzing the same data with more sophisticated statistical techniques, Hepworth and West (1988) upheld the original findings, though the reanalyses attenuated the strength of the effects. On the other hand, Green, Glaser, and Rich (1998) performed further reanalyses and claimed that the relationship was tenuous. It appears, then, that more sophisticated analyses provide a cautionary note on the strength of this putative association.

62. Wilson (1975); see also Williams (1966) and Tooby and Cosmides (1992). For lucid writing on the promise and pitfalls of evolutionary approaches, see deWaal (2002).

63. Cosmides and Tooby (1994); Kurzban and Leary (2001); see also Neuberg, Smith, and Asher (2000).

64. Neuberg et al. (2000, pp. 35–36).

65. Kurzban and Leary (2001); Neuberg et al. (2000). Others are beginning to incorporate both social psychological and evolutionary psychological perspectives into integrated theories of stigmatization of mental disorder. See, for example, Haghighat (2001), who posits six levels of stigma: cognitive, affective, behavioral/discriminatory, denial, economic, and evolutionary.

66. Neuberg et al. (2000, p. 34).

67. Kurzban and Leary (2001, p. 192).

68. Coryell, Scheftner, Keller, Endicott, Maser, and Klerman (1993); Neale and Oltmanns (1980).

69. Goffman (1963).

70. Kurzban and Leary (2001, pp. 197–198).

71. Grammer and Thornhill (1994).

72. Kurzban and Leary (2001, p. 199) address this point: "We wish to stress that the evolutionary view should not be construed to suggest that stigmatization is genetically determined or inevitable." Neuberg et al. (2000, p. 35) contend that "just because some stigmas were (or even are) adaptive or 'natural,' this does not make them 'good,' 'right,' 'morally justifiable,' or anything of the sort; the morality of any stigma is independent of its existence." Fiske (1998, p. 357) states that "Stereotyping, prejudice, and discrimination are partly automatic and socially pragmatic, yet at the same time individually controllable and responsive to social structure."

73. Oskamp (2000).

74. Kurzban and Leary (2001).

Chapter 3

1. For detailed accounts of relevant history, see Alexander and Selesnick (1966); Cockeram (1981); Deutsch (1948); Foucault (1965); Mora (1992); Torrey and Miller (2001); and Zilboorg (1941). The coverage in this chapter borrows heavily from these sources. Particularly with regard to ancient eras and medieval periods, the classic work of Zilboorg is a key source.

2. As Zilboorg stated (1941, p. 267), "No new step is ever made and no new discovery is ever brought forth without the shadows of the past hovering over it."

3. B. Smith (2003).

4. Maher and Maher (1985) contend that the intent behind trephining was more medical than psychiatric, to aid in the freeing of splinters or clots.

5. Alloy, Acocella, and Bootzin (1996); Zilboorg (1941).

6. Although there is indeed a link between at least some forms of mental disorder and creativity (see Jamison, 1993), the tendency to romanticize serious mental illness can be pernicious. For example, Kramer (2005) discusses the myth that depression is linked to rebellion and creativity and concludes that historical figures who suffered from depression made contributions in spite of (rather than because of) their mood disorders.

7. Henry (1941).

8. Mora (1992).

9. In Zilboorg's words, "If Hippocrates strove toward the liberation of psychiatry from mystical prejudice and toward a unified, biological point of view on mental diseases, he did so without many established scientific facts at his disposal" (1941, p. 50).

10. Ibid.

11. Ibid. (p. 92).

12. Alloy et al. (1996).

13. Davison, Neale, and Kring (2004).

14. By legend, in the seventh century A.D. several lunatics witnessed the beheading of an eloped daughter of an Irish king, Dympna, who had renounced Christianity and fled to Belgium. They were so moved by this sight that they became cured, and this miracle became widely known. Pilgrimages to the

religious shrine at Gheel thus occurred, in the hope of similar cures by the intercession of Dympna, soon considered the patron saint of "mad" individuals (see Henry, 1941).

15. Allderidge (1985). She also claims that close examination of the historical record reveals some degree of enlightenment in many of the policies of Bethlehem, contradicting the uniformly negative legacy typically associated with this institution.

16. Henry (1941).

17. In fact, Neugebauer (1979) points out that sweeping historical accounts that utilize secondary sources can lead to stereotyped notions of the practices and beliefs of a given era, whereas the historical pursuit of original documents from given time periods leads to more accurate depictions of societal attitudes.

18. Zilboorg (1941, p. 141).

19. Davison, Neale, and Kring, (2004).

20. Comer (1999).

21. Mora (1992).

22. Foucault (1965).

23. Henry (1941, p. 569).

24. Dain (1964).

25. Rosenhan and Seligman (1994).

26. Zilboorg (1941, p. 313).

27. Torrey and Miller (2001).

28. Cited in Zilboorg (1941, p. 323). Pinel's actions came at a particularly dangerous point in the French Revolution, so that he was roundly criticized for harboring potential enemies of the revolution among the insane he was intending to liberate. When an angry mob of Parisians seized him on the streets of Paris, he was saved from probable death by one of the former patients of the hospital, Chevigne, who, as Pinel's bodyguard, turned the crowd away.

29. Cited in Henry (1941, p. 572).

30. Cited in Davison and Neale (1989, p. 38).

31. Henry (1941, p. 581). For a complete accounting of moral treatment, see Bockoven (1963) and Brizendene (1992).

32. Grob (1994).

33. Cited in Shannonhouse (2000, pp. 8–11; italics in original).

34. Alloy et al. (1996, p. 18).

35. Griesinger (1867); cited in Achenbach (1974).

36. See Aries (1962) and deMause (1974/1988) for extensive coverage of various historical conceptions of childhood.

37. Donohue, Hersen, and Ammerman (1995).

38. Ibid.

39. Phares (2003).

40. Achenbach (1974).

41. Donohue et al. (1995); Phares (2003). Note that subsequent, comparable laws have been on the books until quite recently in states such as Massachusetts, allowing families to place "stubborn children" in outside placements with few legal obstacles.

42. Rhodes (1999).

43. Dain (1964); Foucault (1965); Grob (1994); Zilboorg (1941).

Chapter 4

1. Haslam (2005); Herman (1995).

2. Link and Phelan (2001a).

3. Beers (1908/1945).

4. For a revealing history of this movement, see the authoritative text of Kevles (1985). See also Black (2003), who presents a graphically detailed history of the eugenics movement in the United States, including depictions of sweeps of impoverished Appalachian areas for poorly educated families, California's leading role in negative eugenics, and strong institutional support through major laboratories such as Cold Spring Harbor, IBM, and several major foundations.

5. Kevles (1985) noted that more than 20 states still had such statues on the books in the 1980s, but federal regulations had nearly eliminated the practice; see also Black (2003).

6. See Alliance for Human Research Protection, listserve posting, October 17, 2003, which cited the release, from the former German Democratic Republic, of documents revealing 200,000 euthanasia crimes against physically and mentally disordered individuals in Germany from 1939 to 1944 (see http://www.ahrp.org). Another estimate is that an additional 25,000 psychiatric patients died from systematic starvation in the period immediately following World War II, from 1945 to 1948. Black (2003) documents that U.S. policies inspired the lethal German eugenics provisions.

7. See Eidelson and Eidelson (2003) for discussion of "superiority" as a key worldview that promotes intergroup conflict. In fact, a primary element of hatred is the gap between the ingroup's perceptions of its own superiority and the outgroup's inferiority and subhumanity; Sternberg (2003).

8. Goffman (1961); Grob (1994).

9. Grob (1994).

10. Gessel, cited in ibid. (p. 171).

11. It is important to note that modern ECT is an effective treatment for severe forms of depression that have not responded to medications or psychotherapy; see Sackeim, Devanand, and Nobler (1995); Dukakis and Tye (2006). For an indication of the fervor surrounding biological interventions like psychosurgery (including prefrontal lobotomies), heavily promoted by advocates such as Walter Freeman, as well as the enthusiasm for interventions related to autointoxication (i.e., germs in the gut and colon that could allegedly leach out and infest the brain), espoused by Henry Cotton—both of which ended up with disastrous results—see Nuland (2005).

12. Deutsch (1948); Ward (1946).

13. Joint Commission on Mental Illness and Health (1961).

14. See Frost and Bonnie (2001) for thorough coverage.

15. For example, in California the Lanterman-Petris-Short Act restricted the criteria for involuntary civil commitment to three features: (a) dangerousness to self, (b) dangerousness to others, or (c) grave disability, with the latter implying the inability to perform basic self-care functions. An underlying premise was that, when governments acted as "therapeutic states," promoting easy means to institutionalization, basic rights were seriously truncated in many instances.

16. Breakey, Fischer, Nestadt, and Romanoski (1992).

17. Levy (2002a, 2002b, 2002c).

18. For a thorough and alarming overview of the rates of persons with severe mental illnesses in jails and prisons, see Lamb and Weinberger (1998), who contend that deinstitutionalization, an utter lack of community-based care, and the lack of training of police officers are key reasons for this increase. See also the PBS Special titled *The New Asylums* (2005; http://www.pbs.org) and the fact sheet from the Campaign for Mental Health Reform (2006; http://www.mhreform.org).

19. For a report on the hearings held by a public commission on the devastating effects of the all-too-common practice of prison rape for both male and female inmates, see Marshall (2005).

20. Grob (1994, p. 311).

21. For additional historical perspective, Burt (2001) posits three major "revolutions" in attitudes toward mental health in U.S. history: the moral treatment/institutional care movement of the early 1800s, the Progressive reform era of the early 1900s, and the community mental health/mental health law "revolution" of the 1960s and 1970s. According to Burt, each of these three movements led in cyclic fashion to major setbacks and eras of retrenchment.

22. Beers (1908/1945).

23. Much of this historical material is found in Achenbach (1974) and Donohue, Hersen, and Ammerman (1995).

24. See, for example, Bettelheim (1967).

25. American Psychiatric Association (1952, 1994, 2000).

26. Hibbs and Jensen (2005) and Kazdin and Weisz (2003) provide in-depth guides to empirically supported treatments for child and adolescent mental disorders.

27. Helfer and Kempe (1968).

28. Szasz (1961); Laing (1965); Foucault (1965). For a cogent review of the antipsychiatry movement, see Rissmiller and Rissmiller (2006).

29. The major shift occurred with the publication of *DSM-III*, see American Psychiatric Association (1980). Blashfield (1984) reviews the poor reliability of psychiatric diagnosis under *DSM-I* and *DSM-II* and the subsequent resurgence of interest in the Kraepelinian model to validate mental disorders.

30. Antipsychiatrists are still active, fueled by sources such as the Church of Scientology. Considerable media attention has been devoted to ardent advocates like Tom Cruise, who has used his star power to denounce psychiatry and psychotropic medications on national television. At another level, there is still active scientific debate about the extent to which current classifications accurately capture the actual, more dimensional nature of psychopathology (see Beauchaine, 2003). Still, the reality of mental illness is clear (Hyman, 2002).

31. See Bloom and Kupfer (1995) for a compendium of advances in psychopharmacology. Controversy over the proliferation of medication treatments has not abated, based on incomplete response rates, the potential for side effects, and more recently the direct-to-consumer advertising of such medications by pharmaceutical firms, which has led to a renewed set of campaigns from antipsychiatry groups.

32. See Barondes (1998); McGuffin, Riley, and Plomin (2001); and Rutter and Silberg (2002).

33. See, for example, Hyman (2002).

34. Murray and López (1996).

35. For a fascinating perspective on the history of genetic views of mental disorder, ranging from initial, reductionistic accounts to the multifaceted, polygenic theories that are currently in ascendancy, see Schulze, Fangerow, and Propping (2004).

36. D. Johnson (1989). Note that this is not a new plea; as Chapter 3 points out, it recapitulates the work of Griesinger and other German nosologists from the middle of the nineteenth century. Despite its title ("Schizophrenia as a Brain Disease"), Johnson's article contains a reasonably well-balanced set of arguments related to interactive influences on schizophrenic symptoms. Still, there is considerable impetus for making reductionistic ascriptions to exclusively medical model perspectives in relation to mental disorder, fueled by reactions against the moralistic and family-blame models that predominated in earlier eras.

37. More technically, such genes are "polymorphic," meaning that they are not rare mutations but rather those with multiple alleles, some of which are distributed in the population with high frequency. Despite their having been naturally selected, however, certain alleles may be less adaptive under current cultural conditions, particularly if paired with either other alleles that confer risk, environments that potentiate risk, or both. In other words, it is a mistake to assume that moderate-to-strong heritability for mental disorder implies the work of a "defective gene."

Along this line, I highlight a crucial point that is often overlooked in current conceptions of the biogenetic basis for mental disorder: Even for conditions with substantial heritability, environmental input (including family socialization, school climate, or social supports) may have important influences on a person's outcome. In other words, heritability reflects the proportion of individual differences in a trait or condition attributable to genes. But even for highly heritable conditions (a) environmental factors may well influence the overall levels of the behavior or trait in question across the population (e.g., height is extremely heritable, yet the entire population is taller than several generations ago, largely because of dietary influences); and (b) key environmental factors in one's life can strongly influence the subsequent course of the disorder—see Hinshaw (1999), Hinshaw, Owens, Wells, Kraemer, Abikoff, Arnold, et al. (2000), and Rutter and Silberg (2002). It is therefore a mistake to believe that heritability automatically implies genetic destiny.

38. For important research on this issue, see Martin, Pescosolido, and Tuch (2000). The latter used a representative sample of the United States population from the General Social Survey, with excellent methodology. As described further in Chapter 5, "social distance" measures are those that ask respondents to indicate their desired levels of social closeness to or separation from people in different groups (e.g., willingness to be a neighbor versus having one's offspring marry such an individual). A thoughtful, balanced review of this entire topic can be found in Corrigan and Watson (2004), who highlight the pros as well as the cons of biogenetic attributions.

39. Mehta and Farina (1997). Note that as in the classic Milgram experiments (see Milgram, 1974), there were no shocks actually administered, but the participants believed that they were, in fact, punishing the partners with shock.

40. Phelan, Cruz-Rojas, and Reiff (2002); Phelan (2005). Recent work has be-

gun to examine the influence of genetic attributions on unconscious, implicit forms of bias and stigma. For example, Teachman et al. (2003) found that genetic ascriptions for obesity did not reduce implicit bias toward obese individuals. This is a major area for research development related to mental disorders.

41. Read and Law (1999); Read and Harre (2001); Walker and Read (2002). See also the earlier work of Morrison (1980), and consider the findings of Dietrich, Beck, Bujantugs, Kenzine, Matschinger, and Angermeyer (2004). Read and his colleagues also found that (a) psychosocial causal attributions were associated with more positive attitudes and that (b) contact with persons with mental disorders also predicted positive attitudes. I return to the "contact hypothesis," which promotes actual behavioral contact with members of stigmatized groups as a means of countering stigma, in Chapter 9.

42. See Watson and Corrigan (2005).

43. Read and Harre (2001). Indeed, there may well be a backlash in current society against the "excuses" for personal responsibility perceived to emanate from those who claim that biology, psychological trauma, and the like serve as mitigating factors for deviant or unlawful behavior. Overmedicalized views may be perceived by some as inappropriate cop-outs for behavior rather than as viable explanations.

44. See the discussion in Hinshaw (2002b); see also Phelan et al. (2002).

45. Haslam (2000, pp. 1049–1050).

46. S. Sontag (1978/1989). See also Finzen and Hoffman-Richter (1999), who comment on Sontag's powerful illness metaphors in relation to schizophrenia.

47. See Read and Harre (2001); Watson and Corrigan (2005).

48. Engel (1977); see also Bronfenbrenner (1979), who emphasized the need for ecological perspectives and the importance of context.

49. In fact, at a cross-cultural level, evidence exists that societies that emphasize harmony and those with clear social and vocational roles for deviant individuals are linked with a more benign course for serious psychopathology than those with a more competitive, individualistic bent. See Grob (1994); Lin and Kleinman (1988); and Warner (1999).

50. This is an issue of fundamental importance, with debates ranging far beyond the scope of this work. For a lucid review, see Pickles and Angold (2003).

Chapter 5

1. See Nunnally (1961). See also the seminal work on semantic differential scales by Osgood, Suci, and Tannenbaum (1957). For a current review of methodologies regarding the assessment of stigma, see Link, Yang, Phelan, and Collins (2004).

2. Rabkin (1972, p. 154). For a searing portrayal of conditions inside an infamous leper colony on the Hawaiian island of Molokai, see Tayman (2006).

3. Allen (1943); Nunnally (1961); Ramsey and Seipp (1948a, 1948b).

4. Whatley (1958); see also Bogardus (1925, 1933) for early use of social distance scales to measure attitudes toward ethnic and racial minority groups.

5. Cumming and Cumming (1957).

6. Rootman and Lafave (1969).

7. Ibid., p. 265.

8. Gussow and Tracy (1968).

9. See reviews in Rabkin (1972, 1974). See also Crocetti, Spiro, and Siassi (1971) for a review of "optimistic" conclusions.

10. Crocetti et al. (1971, p. 1126).

11. Lamy (1966).

12. Tringo (1970).

13. Phillips (1963).

14. Phillips (1966).

15. Crocetti, Spiro, and Siassi (1974).

16. Gove (1982); Gove and Fain (1973); Lehman, Joy, Kreisman, and Simmons (1976).

17. Rabkin (1984), cited in Link, Cullen, Frank, and Wozniak (1987).

18. Olmstead and Durham (1976); Albrecht, Walker, and Levy (1982).

19. Link and Cullen (1983).

20. Neff and Husaini (1985); for a review, see Wahl (1999b, Chapter 2).

21. Farina, Holland, and Ring (1966); Farina and Ring (1965).

22. Farina, Allen, and Saul (1968).

23. Farina, Gliha, Boudreau, Allen, and Sherman (1971).

24. Rosenhan (1973); Sibicky and Dovidio (1986); Piner and Kahle (1984). For commentary, see Biernat and Dovidio (2000).

25. See the review in Page (1995).

26. Page (1995, p. 67).

27. Gove (1980, 1982).

28. See the review of pertinent investigations in Link et al. (1987); see also Segal (1978), Cockeram (1981), and the longitudinal investigation of Huffine and Clausen (1979).

29. Link et al. (1987). They described this latter finding as an "extra break" phenomenon, also termed an "affirmative action" effect by Monahan (1992). The implication is that the label can actually fuel benevolence if the respondent does not associate this ascription with dangerousness.

30. See Corrigan and Cooper (2005); Monahan (1992); Steadman, Mulvey, Monahan, Robbins, Appelbaum, Grisso, et al. (1998); see also Hiday (1995). The particular delusional type linked to violence is termed "threat control-override symptoms," as discussed in Link, Monahan, Stueve, and Cullen (1999). See also Phelan and Link (1998) for discussion of the tendency for modern respondents to associate mental illness with dangerousness because of changes in civil commitment laws. Corrigan and Cooper (2005) present an extremely well-balanced perspective, acknowledging the association between violence and mental illness but emphasizing (a) that most forms of mental disorder have no linkage with violence and (b) that the association is grossly exaggerated in media accounts. See Carey (2006) for a poignant story about the dilemmas posed when serious mental illness does lead to violence.

31. Teplin, McClelland, Abram, and Weiner (2005).

32. Cited in Wahl (1999b). In this and other recent investigations, overt attitudes are typically measured with "traditional" scales that ask for the respondent's own views, meaning that the cautions of Link and colleagues—that such self-report measures underestimate actual stigma—should be taken into account. That stigma is found to be strong in current times even with use of such measures is revealing.

33. Link, Phelan, Bresnahan, Stueve, and Pescosolido (1999).

34. Link, Phelan, Bresnahan, Stueve, and Pescosolido (1999); Phelan, Link, Stueve, and Pescosolido (2000). Note that the greatest levels of social distance were desired for the cocaine- and alcohol-dependence vignettes, revealing that substance abuse received more stigma than mental illness per se in this survey; see Pescosolido, Monahan, Link, Stueve, and Kikuzawa (1999).

35. See Phelan, Link, Stueve, and Pescosolido (2000), and Phelan and Link (1998). Regarding perceptions of violence, I note parenthetically the findings of Schnittker (2000), who showed that the respondents in the General Social Survey desired somewhat less social distance when presented with vignettes of women, as opposed to men, with mental illness; they also perceived such female characters as less dangerous.

36. Thompson, Stuart, Bland, Arbodele-Florez, Warner, and Dickson (2002). The survey was performed in preparation for the World Psychiatric Association's worldwide antistigma campaign, which was taking place in several nations.

37. Crisp, Gelder, Rix, Meltzer, and Rowlands (2000). This survey was done to prepare the Royal College of Psychiatrists for its 5-year (1998–2003) antistigma campaign in the United Kingdom, titled "Changing Minds: Every Family in the Land." See also Crisp (2005) for additional information on the stigmatization of eating disorders.

38. Ben-Porath (2002).

39. See Angermeyer and Matschinger (1997, 2004); Hamre, Dahl, and Malt (1994); Hillert, Sandman, Ehmig, Weisbecker, Kepplinger, and Benkert (1999); Lee, Lee, Ching, and Kleinman (2005); and Raguram, Raghu, Vounatsou, and Weiss (2004).

40. See Graves, Cassisi, and Penn (2005). As Chapter 8 notes, the first investigation of implicit attitudes regarding mental illness was performed by Teachman, Wilson, and Komarovskaya (2006).

41. A core reason for increases in stigma may relate to greater urbanization in recent years, a point developed in Chapter 7 (see Sartorius, 1999).

42. For examples of research on the effects of stigma on individuals with mental illness themselves, see Markowitz (1998), Read and Baker (1996), and Rosenfeld (1997). Incisive reviews are found in Fife and Wright (2000), Major and O'Brien (2005), and Watson and River (2005). Such theorists and investigators view the effects of the personal experience of stigma in terms of social rejection, subsequent isolation, financial loss, and a tendency (though not an inevitable one) toward internalization of shame.

43. Link, Struening, Rahav, Phelan, and Nuttbrock (1997).

44. Wright, Gronfein, and Owens (2000).

45. Ritsher and Phelan (2004); Perlick, Rosenheck, Clarkin, Sirey, Salahi, Struening, et al. (2001).

46. See Dickerson, Sommerville, Origoni, Ringel, and Parente (2002); Sirey, Bruce, Alexopoulos, Perlick, Raue, Friedman, et al. (2001); PatientView (2004a). In one survey of patients and consumers in the United Kingdom, the results of which were published in a report titled "Just One Percent," it was found that only 1% of mental health consumers rated themselves as happy with the quality of their lives, more than one-fourth reported being shunned when they did seek help, and more than a third had not received any written information or descriptions about services or treatment options (see PatientView, 2004a).

47. Wahl (1999a, 1999b). Wahl intentionally utilized the term "consumers" in describing persons with mental disorders to avoid any pejorative connotations of the words "patient," "mental patient," "ex-mental patient," and the like. For an excellent discussion of the issue of what term should be used to describe such individuals, see Penn and Nowlin-Drummond (2001). In their investigation, undergraduates and community members were randomly assigned to viewing four different labels: *consumer of mental health services, person with schizophrenia, person with a severe mental illness,* and *schizophrenic* before providing social distance and attitude responses. Whereas the "consumer" label was associated with lower levels of perceived dangerousness and lowered social distance on the part of respondents, as well as greater ratings of the condition's ability to change with time, it was also linked with higher attributions of responsibility to the target individuals for their condition, and it did not predict any greater intentions for behavioral contact. Designating persons with serious mental disorders as "consumers" may produce a mixture of positive and negative consequences. Furthermore, politically correct designations may not necessarily be those that would be selected by persons with mental disorders themselves; such terms may, over time, come to be just as stigmatized as the traditional labels.

In Japan, the official term for schizophrenia since the 1930s has been "seishin bunretsu byou," which translates to "split mind." Sugiura, Sakamoto, Tanaka, Tomada, and Kitamura (2001) found that this term, when paired with vignette descriptions of psychotic behavior, fostered stigmatizing responses. Japan therefore enacted a formal change of the term to "loss of coordination disorder," expressly to reduce stigmatization, as reported by Desapriya and Nobutada (2002). Clearly, at the level of national policy and terminology, the assumption is that terminology does matter.

48. Yarrow, Clausen, and Robbins (1955, p. 34). See Clausen and Yarrow (1955).

49. For more recent discussion of family silence, see Beardslee (2002); Hinshaw (2004).

50. Kreisman and Joy (1974).

51. Torrey (1988), cited in Lefley (1992, p. 128); see also Tessler and Gamache (2000).

52. See Hoening and Hamilton (1966) for use of these terms. Relatedly, Hatfield (1978) noted the "psychological costs" to relatives of those with schizophrenia, including stress, anxiety, depression, and anger. See also Thompson and Doll (1982).

53. Lefley (1992, pp. 128–129). See also Lefley (1989).

54. Wahl and Harman (1989, p. 136).

55. Citations for this paragraph include Struening, Stueve, Vine, Kreisman, Link, and Herman (1995); Struening, Perlick, Link, Hellman, Herman, and Sirey (2001); Greenberg, Kim, and Greenley (1997); Muhlbauer (2002); Szmulker, Burgess, Herrman, Benson, Colusa, and Bloch (1996); and Phelan, Bromet, and Link (1998).

56. Gray (2002). The levels of perceived stigmatization in families of children with the more usual forms of autism, which involve clear delays in language and cognitive functioning, are undoubtedly quite strong, as well, if not stronger.

57. See, for example, Ohaeri and Addullahi (2001); Oestman and Kjellin (2002); Shibre, Negash, Kullgren, Kebede, Alem, Fekadu, et al. (2001); Thara and Srinivasan (2000). For an overview of mental illness and its stigmatization in Islamic countries, see Al-Issa (2000).

58. Tessler and Gamache (2000).

59. Perlick, Rosenheck, Clarkin, Maciejewski, Sirey, Struening, et al. (2004).

60. Corrigan and Miller (2004).

61. Nunnally (1961); see also Dichter (1992). This process exemplifies, once again, a "courtesy stigma" attending to persons associated with those suffering from mental disorders, even those entrusted with their care.

62. See the review in Rabkin (1974).

63. Cohen and Streuning (1962).

64. Fryer and Cohen (1988); Keane (1990) (1991); Lauber, Anthony, Ajdacic-Gross, and Rossler (2004); Mirabi, Weinman, Magnetti, and Keppler (1985); Mukherjee, Fialho, Wijetunge, Checinski, and Surgenor (2002); Scott and Philip (1985).

65. Regarding delinquency, see Farrington (1977), as well as Adams, Robertson, Gray-Ray, and Ray (2003) and Ray and Downs (1986). Regarding sexual abuse, see Holguin and Hansen (2003); cocaine exposure, Woods, Eyler, Conlon, Behnke, and Webie (1998); and infant depression, see Hart, Field, Stern, and Jones (1997).

66. Klasen (2000). See also MacDonald and McIntyre (1999) for information that does not support negative effects of labels on children with developmental disorders.

67. Gillmore and Farina (1989). The desired social distance and behavioral negativity were similar for the disturbed versus retarded peer; effects were also parallel for the 5th- versus the 8th-grade boys.

68. Harris, Milich, Corbitt, Hoover, and Brady (1992).

69. Spitzer and Cameron (1995); see the review in Wahl (2002).

70. Weiss (1994).

71. This research is discussed in Penn, Judge, Jamieson, Garczynski, Hennessy, and Romer (2005).

72. For excellent work on the development of racial prejudice, see Doyle and Aboud (1995).

Chapter 6

1. Goldhagen (1996, p. 32).

2. Ibid. (p. 33).

3. The adjectives *mild, moderate,* and *severe* are now applied to the varying degrees of mental retardation.

4. Coverdale, Nairn, and Claasen (2002); Diefenbach (1997); Wahl, Ward, and Richards (2002); see the extensive review in Stout, Villegas, and Jennings (2004). Recall that in the 1972 campaign for the U.S presidency, the Democratic nominee for vice president, Sen. Thomas Eagleton, was dropped from the ticket when media stories emerged that he had a history of depression and treatment with electroconvulsive therapy (ECT). Stigma plays a role also at the highest levels of government.

5. Nunnally (1961, p. 74).

6. A parallel can be made with regard to the elimination of pejorative racial terms from broadcasts dealing with African Americans. Despite such censorship, it was still commonplace to depict this ethnic group as able to perform only menial work. Today, given the broadening standards of what is considered acceptable language on the air, the censorship of words like "nuts" in the 1950s seems incredibly naïve. Far stronger language is heard every night during prime time.

Nunnally also found that mental disorders were typically portrayed as originating from former injuries (e.g., war wounds, childhood head injuries) or from traumatic environmental events, such as the loss of relatives or a house being burned down. In the latter scenarios, there was often a sudden cure when the environment changed for the better. A lack of accuracy was therefore quite salient. As is the case today, the brief nature of most newspaper articles, as well as the "23-minute" format of most half-hour television dramas (i.e., 30 minutes minus commercial time) usually precludes subtlety, complexity, or realism regarding the interplay of causal factors for mental illness.

7. Snow (1983); Wahl (1995, 1999b). An intriguing sidelight is found in Nunnally's early work (see Nunnally, 1961, Chapter 7). Here, he posited that newspaper and magazine features on mental disorder peaked during economically good times but did not appear as frequently during times of war or economic recession. His conclusion was that news about mental disorder was essentially a "luxury item," presented only when more pressing accounts of serious problems did not predominate. Although coverage of mental disorder is far more extensive today, it would be instructive to see whether this trend is still evident.

8. Wahl and Roth (1982); Gerbner, unpublished data, cited in Link and Cullen (1983); Wahl (1992).

9. Diefenbach (1997).

10. Wilson, Nairn, Coverdale, and Panapa (2000); see the review in Wahl (2003).

11. Key information in this paragraph emanates from Byrd, McDaniel, and Rhoden (1980); Cassata, Skill, and Boadu (1979); Day and Page (1986); Matas, el-Guebaly, Harper, Green, and Peterkin (1986); and Shain and Phillips (1991).

12. Coverdale et al. (2002).

13. For evidence of at least some positive portrayals, see Wahl et al. (2002). Note that few pieces, however, include any kind of personal perspective from the points of view of individuals with mental disorder themselves, a crucial omission given the importance of first-person accounts (see later section in this chapter; see also Chapter 10). For data on the tendencies for people with severe mental illness to be victims of violent crimes, see Teplin, McClelland, Abram, and Weiner (2005).

14. See Wahl (1992) and Angermeyer and Schulze (2001) for discussion. For the correlational study, see Granello and Pauley (2000).

15. Wahl and Lefkowitz (1989).

16. Wahl (1995); see also www.CineMania.com.

17. Pauley (2004); Shields (2005). See also Wertheim (2003) for an article in *Sports Illustrated,* in which major athletes on professional sports teams disclose their experiences with depression and in which the responses of the

teams and the leagues in which they play are documented. The byline of the article is as follows: "Mental illness still carries a powerful stigma in pro sports, but there are signs that teams are finally facing the problem and trying to help troubled athletes."

18. In other words, conceptual models are lacking to provide guidelines for understanding media influences. For elaboration, see Stout et al. (2004), who make the important points that (a) only a handful of experimentally controlled studies of media influences currently exist, so that few causal inferences can be made about such influences; and (b) underlying models of media influence are generally restricted to social learning accounts (e.g., observational learning occurs from exposure to media images) and cultivation theory (i.e., increased viewing time of television cultivates a worldview consistent with media images). Gerbner, Gross, Morgan, Signorelli, and Shanahan (2002) provide further discussion of the need for conceptual models of media influence.

19. Goffman (1961).

20. Levy (2002a, 2002b, 2002c).

21. Dubin and Fink (1992). Along these lines, psychiatry is low on the status hierarchy of medical professions, and clinical psychology is often viewed as the weakest subfield among psychology's disciplines.

22. Goode (2003); Gottfredson (2004).

23. Cited in Wahl (1999b, p. 56).

24. See Angell, Cooke, and Kovac (2005); Deegan (1997); Penn, Judge, Jamieson, Garczynski, Hennessy, and Romer (2005). Again, Wahl's survey included people with serious forms of mental illness, who were members of an advocacy organization; it would be surprising if they were not particularly sensitive to their interactions with professionals. But the repeated anecdotal evidence regarding staff and professional attitudes and practices cannot be ignored.

25. Wahl (1999b, p. 111).

26. Angell et al. (2005); Wahl (1999b). Deegan (1997) also discusses the tendency of some practitioners to become hardened with respect to the suffering of their clientele, failing to realize that the low expectations they convey may well lead to apathy—instead interpreting such reactions as a symptom of the underlying mental disorder.

27. Bloom and Kupfer (1995); Nathan and Gorman (2002).

28. Corrigan and Kleinlen (2005); see also Lamb and Weinberger (1998). Discrimination may be direct (e.g., a landlord may deny rental to a person with a history of mental disorder). It may also be structural, entailing the general curtailing of rights of those with mental illness based on broad social policies (e.g., lack of adequate health insurance coverage for mental as opposed to physical disorders). Discrimination can also emanate from self-stigmatization, a subtle but pernicious process through which individuals' internalized stigma prevents their fully utilizing life opportunities.

29. Corrigan and colleagues make an important point about discriminatory practices: Restrictions of an individual's rights may be justified on the basis of actual levels of disability or incompetence, but only if these disabilities are assessed accurately and specifically. As an example, persons with visual impairments should not be allowed to drive if they possess a disability that is uncorrectable. Fundamentally unjust, however, is discrimination made on the basis of a general label (including that of mental illness). Yet much in the way

of mental illness discrimination is made on just such a global basis, with no documentation of underlying disabilities (see, for example, laws restricting voting rights or child custody, discussed subsequently in this chapter). Furthermore, unless appropriate accommodations are made for persons with disabilities—including those with mental disorders—the underlying problems and their associated impairments are likely to persist, leading to higher levels of subsequent discrimination. For discussion, see Corrigan and Kleinlen (2005). Additional commentary on discrimination as an indicator of stigma is provided by Corrigan, Markowitz, and Watson(2004).

30. Corrigan and Kleinlen (2005). Such living situations doubtless fuel the strong tendency for people with serious mental illness to become victims of violence; see Teplin et al. (2005), with commentary by Eisenberg (2005).

31. For example, see Breakey et al. (1992).

32. First, Cooper and O'Hara (2003) discuss the gap between housing prices and SSI benefits, noting that even though some states supplement the federal SSI standard, many apartments are still well beyond reach financially. Second, see Page (1995) for an example of research on discrimination by landlords. Third, for evidence of the difficulties incurred in seeking housing for persons with mental illnesses, see Wahl (1999b). Fourth, Carling (1990) discusses the importance of housing for empowering individuals with mental disorders and fostering their community integration.

33. It is for this reason, among many others, that secrecy and concealment of a history of emotional or mental problems are key coping strategies for many individuals with mental disorders.

34. Wahl (1999b). It is also the case that ongoing court cases have debated whether ADA should apply to only the most severe physical and psychiatric disorders (those, for example, that would be limiting of the individual in almost any circumstance) or those that may yield impairment only in certain restricted situations.

35. Vanden Boom and Lustig (1997). See also Goldberg, Killeen, and O'Day (2005) regarding the pros and cons of disclosing a mental disorder to an employer.

36. Warner, Taylor, Wright, Sloat, Springett, Arnold, et al. (1994); see also Fromkin, cited in Warner (1999). Indeed, Warner contends that "The mentally ill may be the most alienated people in our society" (p. 118).

37. For poor individuals with mental illness, recent shifts in Medicaid and Medicare policies have made it exceedingly difficult to get refills of needed prescriptions, so that symptoms and impairments are highly likely to return. See Pear (2006).

38. See Wang, Berglund, Olfson, Pincus, Wells, and Kessler (2005). This problem appears to be even more striking for members of ethnic minority groups; see U.S. Department of Health and Human Services (2001).

39. See Feldman, Bachman, and Bayer (2002); Pear (2000). Furthermore, at a different level of medical discrimination, Druss, Bradford, Rosenheck, Radford, and Krumholtz (2000) found that with respect to angioplasty following heart attacks (i.e., myocardial infarctions), persons with mental disorders were less likely to receive this technique (see discussion in Corrigan and Kleinlen, 2005). Discrimination may exist even with respect to general medical procedures.

Another perspective on parity, pointed out by an anonymous reviewer of a draft of this book, is that because mental health treatments are less well established than medical treatments, it is more difficult for insurers to know the risk incurred by funding them, therefore justifying a lack of parity. I am not at all convinced that this is the case. For instance, many surgical procedures have never undergone clinical trials, and a large number of psychological and psychiatric treatments are now as validated empirically as key medical treatments.

40. Corrigan, Markowitz, and Watson (2004). See also Corrigan and Kleinlen (2005); Hemmens, Miller, Burton, and Milner (2002). Corrigan, Watson, Heyrman, Warpinski, Gracia, Slopen, et al. (2005) provide information on recent bills in state legislatures that may be able to redress some of the current restrictions on rights, most of which have not undergone major improvements over the past decade.

41. Hansen, Goetz, Bloom, and Fenn (1997).

42. Torrey (1997).

43. A related issue is that police officers may well show stigmatization in their interactions with members of the public suspected of breaking the law who may simultaneously exhibit signs of mental disorder. For coverage of issues related to police contacts with persons with mental illness, see Watson, Ottati, Lurigio, & Heyrman (2005). See also Lamb and Weinberger (1998) for additional information on the plight of persons with mental illness in prisons.

44. Whereas many past notions of mental disorder have emphasized personal control and responsibility for such behavior patterns, the explicit assumption underlying insanity pleas is that the person's serious mental disturbance has relinquished that individual from such control.

45. Davison, Neale, and Kring (2004).

46. For example, in the 1860s, Packard's account of her husband's involuntary commitment of herself stirred up great sentiment against forced hospitalization, particularly of women; see Packard (1873) in Shannonhouse (2000). In the early 1900s, Clifford Beers's *A Mind That Found Itself* was highly influential in igniting public opinion in the direction of reform; see Beers (1908/1945).

47. See Josselson, Lieblich, and McAdams (2003); see also Bruner (1986, 1990); Ochs and Capps (2001).

48. See, for example, Nisbett and Wilson (1977).

49. Davidson et al. (1998) and Strauss (1989) integrate subjective/phenomenological accounts of serious mental disorder into accounts of pathology and resilience. Understanding such perspectives may facilitate the formation of truly collaborative research efforts between scientific investigators and participants, fostering empowerment in those who have traditionally been considered solely as subjects of research. For elaboration on the confluence of narrative and empowerment, see Mankowski and Rappaport (1995) and Rappaport (2000). See also Angell et al. (2005) for a review of the ways in which first-person accounts of stigma can inform the public and clarify crucial themes related to the stigmatization of mental illness.

50. Link and Phelan (2001a); see also Angell et al. (2005). For a listing of personal accounts of mental disorder through the late 1990s, see Sommer, Clifford, and Norcross (1998).

51. Kaplan (1964).

52. Cronkite (1994); Jamison (1995); Styron (1990); Knapp (1997); see also the many issues of the *Schizophrenia Bulletin* over the last several decades.

53. Leete (1992, pp. 18, 19, 20, 22).

54. Wahl (1999b, pp. 56–57).

55. Ibid. (pp. 51, 83).

56. Ibid. (p. 99); capitals in original.

57. Jamison (1998, p. 1053).

58. Shaw (1998, pp. 1050–1051).

59. Quinn, Kahng, and Crocker (2004) present experimental data on the effects of disclosing mental illness, demonstrating that when college students with a history of mental illness reveal such history, their scores on a test of reasoning decline, compared with their baseline academic performance. Disclosure of highly stigmatized conditions like mental illness may therefore incur costs, at least until mental disorders receive less societal stigma.

60. Neugeboren (1998); Lachenmeyer (2000).

61. For a review, see Angell et al. (2005). See, for example, Moorman (2002), who writes poignantly about her sibling's mental illness. See also Beard and Gillespie (2004) for a collection of family narratives.

62. Hinshaw (2002b).

63. Although this may appear to be a completely irrational delusion, photographs of the dorms at Byberry reveal an uncanny resemblance to the quarters in German and Polish camps during World War II; see Grob (1994).

64. Hinshaw (2002b, pp. 10–12).

65. Ibid. (pp. 106–107).

66. Ibid. (pp. 127–128).

67. Beardslee (2002).

Chapter 7

1. Byrne (1997); Corrigan (2005c); Crisp (1999); Haghighat (2001); Jorm, Korten, Jacomb, Christensen, and Henderson (1999); Link and Phelan (2001a).

2. Wahl (1999b, p. ix).

3. Corrigan and Penn (1999, p. 765).

4. Link and Phelan (2001b). For an overview of the entire conference (Stigma and Global Health: Developing a Research Agenda), see the special section in *Lancet, 367* (2006), introduced by Keusch, Wilentz, and Kleinman.

5. See additional evidence for such consensus in Corrigan (2005c) and Hinshaw and Cicchetti (2000).

6. Sartorius (1998, p. 1058).

7. Hoge, Castro, Messer, McGurk, Cotting, and Koffman (2004).

8. See Guimon, Fischer, and Sartorius (1999).

9. Murray and López (1996).

10. U.S. Department of Health and Human Services (1999, p. 8).

11. New Freedom Commission on Mental Health (2003).

12. Key references for this chapter include the seminal contribution of Goffman (1963); the work of Stangor and Crandall (2000) on the threat incurred by mental illness; the evolutionary theorizing of Kurzban and Leary (2001); the social psychological work cited in Chapter 2 (see Crocker and Quinn [2000]

for a synthesis); the formulation of Link and Phelan (2001a), updated in Link, Yang, Phelan, and Collins (2004); the syntheses of Corrigan and Kleinlen (2005) and Haghighat (2001); and the erudite work of Haslam (see Haslam [2000, 2005]; Haslam and Ernst [2002]; Haslam, Rothschild, and Ernst [2002]). Steele and Aronson (1995) and Major and O'Brien (2005) are particularly valuable with respect to stereotype threat and identity threat, respectively. Fife and Wright (2000) also provide important commentary on the multidimensional nature of stigma-related phenomena.

13. Davison, Neale, and Kring (2004); Murray and Lopez (1996).

14. Corrigan and Kleinlen (2005) argue that triggers of stigma include (a) symptoms of mental disorder, (b) social skills deficits associated with the symptoms, (c) deviant appearance that may be linked to the symptomatology, and (d) the label of mental illness, which is stereotypically associated with a number of negative features.

15. Solomon, Greenberg, and Pyszczynski (2000, p. 201). See also Pyszczynski, Greenberg, and Solomon (2005) for a recent review.

16. As Pyszczynski and colleagues (2005) have stated, they appear when the threats are "on the edge of consciousness." Despite the fascinating findings emanating from research on TMT, some of its core tenets are hard to disprove, rooted as they are in views of unconscious processing. Also, critiques have arisen that mortality salience may predict not only prejudice and stigma but also the desire to create new life or attain immortality. In other words, a host of effects may emerge from priming with death imagery or threatening images; TMT could become a "theory of everything," making it impossible to refute.

17. I thank Jeffrey Wyn Hinshaw for making this crucial point to me when he was 16 years of age. That is, when I asked him why mental illness is so threatening, he responded, without hesitation: "Dad, it's fear of the unknown."

18. Stangor and Crandall (2000).

19. Link et al. (2004); see also Link and Phelan (2001a).

20. Mendoza-Denton, Page-Gould, and Pietrzak (2006).

21. Goffman (1963). See also Frable, Platt, and Hoey (1998) and Quinn (2006). Note the intriguing finding of Frable and colleagues that college students with concealable stigmas (e.g., those who were gay, had eating disorders, or were from poor families) experienced temporary increases in self-esteem only when they were in the company of others with similar conditions.

22. See Smart and Wegner (2000), who also comment on the possibility for a form of projection to emerge, whereby the individuals with mental disorder who are suppressing behaviors and symptoms come to believe that interaction partners possess the attributes they are trying to conceal.

23. Corrigan and Kleinlen (2005); see also Gallow (1994) for discussion of the pejorative labeling of "self as garbage" that can accompany stigmatization.

24. For comprehensive reviews, see Corrigan and Watson (2002) and Watson and River (2005).

25. For example, see Aronson and Inzlicht (2004); Crocker, Cornwell, and Major (1993).

26. See Steele and Aronson (1995), Steele (1997), and Steele, Spencer, and Aronson (2002) regarding stereotype threat. See also the synthesis of Major and O'Brien (2005) regarding identity threat theories.

27. This focus on individual appraisals of threat and coping responses invokes classic theories related to stress, particularly those of Lazarus and Folkman (1984). Indeed, in their overview of identity threat theory, Major and O'Brien (2005) explicitly cite the seminal work of Lazarus and Folkman on cognitive appraisals and stress. In this view, during confrontation with stressors, people engage in primary appraisals (related to the severity of the stressor) and secondary appraisals (related to the adequacy of their coping resources). When the sum total of such appraisals is that the stressor outweighs the personal resources, intensification of stress responses takes place; however, when resources are appraised as adequate, a host of internally or externally focused coping strategies can be deployed, and stressors can be overcome.

28. See Mendoza-Denton and Mischel (in press) for a multifaceted model of coping with stigmatization that includes individual, relational, and institutional factors and synthesizes the dynamic nature of vulnerability and strength with respect to coping processes.

29. See evidence for greater stigma in Link, Phelan, Bresnahan, Stueve, and Pescosolido (1999) and Phelan Link, Stueve, and Pescosolido (2000). The points in the text borrow from and expand on the arguments made by Sartorius (1999) related to his reasoning about reasons for increased stigmatization in modern and Western societies.

30. However, in postmodern, postindustrial, pluralistic societies, it may be the case that pressures for behavioral conformity are somewhat relaxed. In addition, many fundamentalist cultures place a great premium on extreme conformity. Although the arguments of Sartorius are clearly speculative, the trends discussed here are still fascinating, if depressing, given their direct implication that stigma is enhanced rather than decreased in modern, Westernized cultures.

31. Lin and Kleinman (1988). Also, Littlewood (1998) contends that the worse prognosis for severe mental illness in Western nations may also relate to volitional perspectives in Western culture, which foster a more blameworthy set of attitudes toward deviant behavior.

32. Weiner (1985); Weiner, Perry, and Magnusson (1988).

33. Ekman (2003); Zajonc (1980).

34. S. Sontag (1978)/(1989). This may be particularly true in the case of substance abuse disorders.

35. For examples of the complexity of this issue, see Corrigan and Watson (2004); Dietrich, Beck, Bujantugs, Kenzine, Matschinger, and Angermeyer (2004); Mehta and Farina (1997); Morrison (1980); Phelan (2005); Phelan, Cruz-Rojas, and Reiff (2002); Read and Harre (2001); and Read and Law (1999). Whereas some investigations of attitudes do not reveal any major impact of biogenetic attributions on respondents' views of mental illness, others do. Moreover, recall that in the study of Mehta and Farina (1997), respondents in the biomedical/disease attributional condition gave their interaction partners higher levels of punitive electric shock. As Guimon et al. (1999) have stated, " 'Medicalizing' this particular form of deviancy [mental illness] has not led to an alleviation, or even a neutralization, of the negative responses it inspires" (Introduction, p. viii).

36. Wright, Gronfein, and Owens (2000).

37. Corrigan and Watson (2004); Read and Harre (1999).

38. I hasten to point out that each of these conditions exists on a continuum ranging from mild to quite serious, so it is a mistake to think that all learning disorders, for example, or all phobias, are mild. Rather, I am making the point that, on average, such conditions do not yield the devastation of schizophrenia or bipolar disorder—to take two extreme examples.

39. Link, Cullen, Frank, and Wozniak (1987).

40. See Kessler, Berglund, Demler, Jin, and Walters (2005), as well as Kessler, Chiu, Demler, and Walters (2005), for recent data on the prevalence of mental disorder in the United States. The current prevalence of the most serious forms of mental illness (those defined in the Kessler studies as involving psychosis, suicidality, or severe consequences such as job loss) is just under 6%, meaning that the majority of diagnosable conditions pertain to anxiety disorders and other more moderately impairing variants.

41. Moynihan and Cassels (2005). See also Critser (2005). Such conclusions, in fact, are difficult to escape with the emergence of direct-to-consumer advertisements for medication treatments for social anxiety, depression, and a number of other mental conditions, as well as sexual dysfunctions, borderline hypertension, and other more strictly "medical" problems.

Chapter 8

1. Link, Yang, Phelan, and Collins (2004).

2. See Ajzen and Fishbein (1980), who discuss the long-standing and thorny issue of attitudes and their relation to behavior. Struch and Schwartz (1989) found only weak associations between hostile intergroup attitudes and aggressive behavior, revealing that correspondence may not be strong even for major constructs like aggression. The meta-analytic review of Krauss (1995) has revealed an overall association of $r = .39$ for the linkage between attitudes and future behavior.

3. A good deal of more recent research also features excellent sampling strategies: The investigations of Link, Phelan, Bresnahan, Stueve, and Pescosolido (1999), Phelan, Cruz-Rojas, and Reiff (2002), and Martin, Pescosolido, and Tuch (2000), among others, have analyzed data from the General Social Survey. See also Crisp, Gelder, Rix, Meltzer, and Rowlands (2000) for British investigations of large and representative samples. Samples like those in Wahl (1999a, 1999b) are ample, but they have tended to utilize members of self-help or advocacy groups and may therefore not be fully representative.

4. Link and Cullen (1983).

5. See Gaertner and Dovidio (2000) for reports of such findings. These studies are important not only for separating bad from good adjectives but also for demonstrating that some forms of contemporary racism may reflect strong ingroup preferences rather than biases against the outgroup.

6. Brockman, D'Arcy, Edmonds (1979). See Link et al. (2004) for discussion of the potential yield from qualitative methods.

7. Greenwald, Nosek, and Banaji (2003).

8. See, for example, Dovidio, Kawakami, and Gaertner (2002); Greenwald and Banaji (1995).

9. Teachman, Gaspinski, Brownell, Rawlins, and Jeyeran (2003); see also Teachman, Gregg, and Woody (2001) and Teachman and Woody (2003) for the use of implicit associations in clinical treatment research on reducing fears and anxieties. In the first such investigation related to mental disorder, Teachman, Wilson, and Komarovskaya (2006) used the Implicit Association Test to reveal implicit bias against mental illness in both normative and mentally ill samples and found that, with the latter group, there was no ingroup protection against mental illness stigma by individuals who had themselves been diagnosed.

10. For example, Dasgupta and Greenwald (2001) reduced automatic, implicit racial bias—at least temporarily—by presenting pictures of admired Black individuals to research participants.

11. See, for example, Crisp et al. (2000), Link, Phelan, Bresnahan, Stueve, and Pescosolido (1999), and Phelan, Link, Stueve, and Pescosolido (2000).

12. Regarding schizophrenia, for example, Kraepelin's depiction of "dementia praecox" as a condition marked by progressive, inevitable deterioration set the stage for such views, which have continued nearly unabated (as highlighted by Neale and Oltmanns [1980]) despite evidence that many individuals with schizophrenia do show symptom remission over time.

13. Finzen and Hoffman-Richter (1999).

14. Riva (2005).

15. The film *Gattaca* (1997) portrayed a future in which children born through traditional mating (without genetic preprogramming for desired traits) are stigmatized as a permanent subclass.

16. Allport (1958); Crocker, Quinn, and Steele (1998).

17. See Link et al. (2004) and Watson and River (2005) for elucidation. See also O'Day and Killeen (2002) for the importance of qualitative, narrative research strategies.

18. Downey and Feldman (1996).

19. Major and O'Brien (2005).

20. See, for example, Hepworth and West (1988). Along these lines, a California proposition (Proposition 63, the so-called millionaire tax) was passed in the fall of 2004. Here, individuals with annual incomes of more than $1 million receive a 1% surcharge on their state tax debt, and counties use these proceeds to augment mental health services, particularly for individuals with serious forms of mental illness (see Feinberg [2005]). This proposition fueled passage of the Mental Health Services Act, designed to transform, county by county, mental health services in California.

21. Solomon, Greenberg, and Pyszczynski (1991).

22. Link, Yang, Phelan, and Collins (2004, p. 531).

23. Lefley (1989); Corrigan and Miller (2004).

24. Gottfredson (2004).

25. Wahl (2002). See discussion in Chapter 5.

26. Hinshaw (2005); Wahl (2002).

27. McKown and Weinstein (2003).

28. Hinshaw (2002b, 2006).

29. For reviews of such family mechanisms, see Corrigan and Miller (2004) and Hinshaw (2004, 2005). See also Goodman and Gotlib (2002).

30. Beardslee (2002); Hinshaw (2002b).

31. For extended discussion of resilience, see Cicchetti and Garmezy (1993); Luthar, Cicchetti, and Becker (2000); Masten, Best, and Garmezy (1990); and Rutter (1987).

32. Anthony (1974).

33. See, for example, Garmezy (1970); Elder (1974); Festinger (1983); Kandel, Mednick, Kirkegaard-Sorensen, Hutchings, Knop, Rosenberg, et al. (1988); Pavenstedt (1965); Werner and Smith (1992); Zigler and Glick (1986).

34. Luthar et al. (2000).

35. Kim-Cohen, Moffitt, Caspi, and Taylor (2004).

36. Luthar et al. (2000).

37. Cicchetti and Cannon (1999); Zigler and Glick (1986).

38. Lieberman, Perkins, Belger, Chakos, Jarskog, Boteva, et al. (2001).

39. Lieberman et al. (2001).

40. See, for example, Frese and Walker Davis (1997); see also Deegan (1988); Leete, (1992).

41. Hinshaw (2002b); see also Jamison (1995), who stated that she would not have traded her life with bipolar disorder.

42. See Sacks (1985, 1996). Jamison (1993) provides a lucid explication of the relationship between bipolar disorder and creativity.

43. Storr (1988).

44. It is understandable that many people would want to romanticize or glorify mental illness—but the common assumption that mental disorder fuels creativity is often erroneous. The Nobel prize–winning work of John Nash (the subject of the book and movie *A Beautiful Mind*) took place before he became overwhelmed by schizophrenia. See also Kramer (2005).

45. See Link et al. (2004) for emphasis on this point.

46. See U.S. Department of Health and Human Services (2001) for a supplement to the Surgeon General's report.

Chapter 9

1. Regarding the "rebound" of images that one attempts to suppress, see Wegner (1997); see also the discussion in Corrigan and Penn (1999) and Watson and Corrigan (2005).

2. Link and Phelan (2001a, p. 381).

3. For an impassioned presentation of the belief that stigma regarding mental illness is fundamentally a social injustice requiring political action and revamped social attitudes, see Corrigan (2005b). In addition, for a fine review of the kinds of programs that have been attempted around the world by the World Psychiatric Association's global program to fight stigma, see Sartorius and Schulze (2005). Such programs include media collaborations in Egypt and eastern Europe, the training of police in the United Kingdom and the United States, and the alteration of emergency room practices in Germany, to name a few.

4. Would the same level of federal involvement ever occur for enforcing nondiscrimination toward people of different sexual orientations—or people with mental illness? In the current political climate, such would be hard to imagine.

5. Additional strategies are required to transcend such deep bias and to increase empathy and compassion; see Gaertner and Dovidio (2000) and the material at the end of this chapter.

6. Separating group-level and individual-level efforts is ultimately an artificial distinction, as individual consciousness raising drives social change and altered policies can influence personal efforts. For discussion of issues related to fighting stigma, see Penn and Martin (1998).

7. New Freedom Commission on Mental Health (2003).

8. PatientView (2004a); see also website of the Campaign for Mental Health Reform, at http://www.mhreform.org. Along political lines, a new bipartisan mental health caucus in the United States Senate, composed of Senators Domenici, Kennedy, Smith, and Harkin, was formed in April, 2006. It features three priorities: mental health needs of returning veterans, suicide as a national priority, and mental health in the workplace (see http://www.mhreform/org/pdf/4-3-6-press release.pdf).

9. Wang, Berglund, Olfson, Pincus, Wells, and Kessler (2005).

10. Feldman, Bachman, and Bayer (2002); Pear (2000). Would hospitalization for recurrent cancer, for instance, be subject to lifetime caps?

11. Edward and John Kennedy's sister, Rosemary, suffered from mental retardation throughout her life. She was lobotomized. The legacy of their sister spurred the Kennedy family to become leaders in mental health reform and programs for mental retardation.

12. D. Sontag (2002).

13. PatientView (2004a). See also Feldman et al. (2002) and the news release from the Campaign for Mental Health Reform of April 3, 2006 at http://www .mhreform/org/pdf/4-3-6-pressrelease.pdf

14. Clinton (2004). As Chapter 6 notes, the recent switch from Medicaid to Medicare has produced a crisis in obtaining prescriptions for needed psychoactive medications for many people with mental illness, most notably those with few financial resources.

15. For a discussion, see Corrigan, Markowitz, and Watson (2004) and Corrigan and Kleinlen (2005). Legal *incompetency* may be validly applied to cases in which certain specified disabilities can be shown to interfere with the performance of certain functions or privileges, whereas global restrictions of rights on the basis of vague labels are inherently discriminatory.

16. Sturm, Gresenz, Pacula, and Wells (1999); Willis, Willis, Male, Henderson, and Manderscheid (1998). Of course, as discussed earlier, unemployment and underemployment may emanate from the disabilities related to mental illness, as well as from stigmatization per se. Still, it is clear that stereotypes about the label of mental disorder can bias employers and prevent them from granting adequate opportunities for those potential employees who disclose a psychiatric history (Farina and Felner, 1973). People with mental illness recall considerable bias on the part of employers, as noted in Wahl (1999b). The realities of serious mental illness combined with stigma produce a frustrating, negative state of affairs.

17. Corrigan and Kleinlen (2005); Mechanic (1998); Stefan (2001, 2002).

18. MacDonald-Wilson, Rogers, Massaro, Lyass, and Crean (2002). This survey was intended to address the kinds of accommodations mandated by Section 504 of the Rehabilitation Act of 1973, which has been on the books for a

longer period of time than ADA. See additional suggestions by Corrigan, Markowitz, and Watson (2004) and Goldberg, Killeen, and O'Day (2005). Another piece of relevant legislation is the Family Medical Leave Act of 1993, which allows for up to 12 weeks of unpaid leave for people with disabilities; see discussion in Goldberg et al. (2005).

19. Returning to ADA, Corrigan and Kleinlen (2005) comment on an interesting case brought before the U.S. Supreme Court, in which the state of Georgia was found to be in violation of this statute for lack of provision of community services to prevent institutionalization of persons with mental disorder. The scope of ADA is therefore quite broad, and such judicial rulings can be viewed as countering stigmatization.

20. For example, see Page (1995).

21. For commentary on housing, see Willis et al. (1998). Along with others, they document the hundreds of thousands or even millions of United States citizens with serious mental illness whose housing is substandard or nonexistent. For a review of this issue, see Corrigan and Kleinlen (2005). For documentation of the huge risk for people with mental illness to become victims of violent crime, see Teplin, McClelland, Abram, and Weiner (2005).

22. Sartorius (1998).

23. Murray and López (1996).

24. In addition, for decades NIMH has supported research on basic human processes, as well as mental disorders and their treatments per se. But because of strong advocacy, there has been a press for research to have direct relevance to easing the "burden of mental illness," meaning that much of the basic research mission is being phased out. See further discussion of this important issue in Chapter 12.

25. See Cicchetti and Cohen (2006).

26. Corrigan and Kleinlen (2005); see also Jemelka, Trupin, and Chiles (1989); Lamb and Weinberger (1998).

27. See, for example, Watson, Ottati, Lurigio, and Heyrman (2005).

28. Ibid. The scope of the problem regarding prisons and police is considerable; readers are strongly encouraged to consult this review.

29. A crucial question has to do with the conditions under which stigma is maximized: when children are placed outside the regular classroom for special services, removing them from typical peers, or when they are left in the regular classroom but then experience failure with school or social tasks in front of the peer group. Research is inconclusive on this topic. My belief is that, whereas regular-class inclusion is a worthy goal, it does not always lead to reduced stigma if the youth in fact requires more intensive instruction.

Also, the 1991 reauthorization of the Education for All Handicapped Children Act, in which the law was renamed as IDEA, allowed for ADHD to be included as one of the conditions that could trigger an IEP. This inclusion was a major reason for the large increases in diagnoses of ADHD immediately afterward; see Swanson, Lerner, and Williams (1995). The most recent reauthorization of IDEA (in 2004) added a paperwork reduction provision, reducing the frequency of mandated monitoring of progress. Parents and advocates are concerned that such provisions will weaken the ability of IDEA to provide adequate accommodations and could reduce educational gains.

30. Gillmore and Farina (1989).

31. New Freedom Commission on Mental Health (2003). For an example of screening for depression in New York City, see Santora and Carey (2005).

32. A major critique was initiated by U.S. Rep. Ron Paul, who misinterpreted the New Freedom Commission Report as advocating mandatory and involuntary mental health screening for every person in the United States. The Campaign for Mental Health Reform has clarified the rationale and goals for such a mission: to increase awareness of the reality and impact of child mental disorders and to emphasize the importance of early assessment (rather than an insistence on premature diagnoses). Indeed, monitoring at the level of primary care could result in important benefits for prevention, without the social control problems inherent in mandatory, school-based screening.

33. Kessler, Berglund, Demler, Jin, and Walters (2005); Kessler, Chiu, Demler, and Walters (2005); see also U.S. Department of Health and Human Services (1999). Several additional issues are relevant. First, children of poverty do not receive even basic, regular health care in far too many instances; hence, more basic health care reform is required. Second, a key problem is that early screening for most mental health problems tends to overpredict, as is always the case when an effort is made to detect relatively low-rate problems. Overzealous identification could lead to stigmatization, as well as the mandating of unneeded services. The point is not to brand a child as doomed to suffer from a mental disorder but to begin to detect early signs and prudently enlist help before problems have solidified. See Corcoran, Malaspina, and Hercher (2005), who present a picture of potential problems involved in the early identification of youth at risk for psychosis or schizophrenia.

34. See the fact sheet from the Campaign for Mental Health Reform, posted July 15, 2005, at http://www.mhreform.org/news/7-15-05roadmapfactsheet.htm. As noted earlier, California voters passed Proposition 63 in 2004, which taxes the state's wealthiest individuals an additional 1% to raise money for mental health services. It also mandates that families will not be required to relinquish custody of a child to obtain medically necessary mental health services; see Feinberg (2005).

35. This issue reflects the long-standing problem of separating aspects of child and adolescent care, on the one hand, from family preservation, on the other.

36. Campbell and Heginbotham (1991).

37. See Corrigan (2005b), who calls for parity, not pity, in terms of public views related to mental illness.

38. Corrigan and Penn (1999); see the review in Watson and Corrigan (2005).

39. See the groundbreaking discussion in Allport (1958) and the systematic review in Gaertner and Dovidio (2000).

40. Pettigrew and Tropp (2000). Their analysis included several investigations of the contact hypothesis in relation to mental disorder.

41. For evidence regarding mental health professionals, see Kolodziej and Johnson (1996). In a general review, Couture and Penn (2003) provide relevant evidence regarding contact; see also Corrigan, Edwards, Green, Diwan, and Penn (2001) for supportive findings. Methodologic issues regarding such work include potential sampling biases, specification of the types and lengths of contact that constitute the independent variable, and the choice of outcome measures that reflect reduced prejudice or discrimination.

42. For information on the conditions of contact, see Allport (1958), Gaertner and Dovidio (2000), and Watson and Corrigan (2005). The following paragraphs rely heavily on this material.

43. As a counterpoint, see Frable, Platt, and Hoey (1998) for provocative research about the increases in self-perceptions that emanate for people with concealable stigmas when they spend time with "similar others." In other words, total inclusion may need to be balanced by opportunities for contact with individuals perceived to be similar and sharing the same types of history. This approach may be particularly important for adolescents and adults, but sound developmental research in this area is lacking.

44. See Sarbin and Mancuso (1970) for a devastating critique of such public education programs in the 1960s. Their main contention was that medical model depictions did not ease stigma but may in fact have enhanced it.

45. See, for example, Pinfold, Huxley, Thornicroft, Farmer, Toulmin, and Graham (2003a); Pinfold, Toulmin, Thornicroft, Huxley, Farmer, and Graham (2003b).

46. Corrigan and Penn (1999); PatientView (2004a).

47. PatientView (2004a).

48. In the area of racial attitudes, Rudman, Ashmore, and Gary (2001) found that diversity education can reduce both explicit and implicit racial biases. See also the review in Watson and Corrigan (2005) for commentary.

49. For example, Watson, Otey, Westbrook, Gardner, Lamb, Corrigan, et al. (2004) provide preliminary evidence that a middle-school curriculum can increase knowledge and decrease stigmatizing attitudes among early adolescents. Better-controlled and longer-term interventions are needed.

50. See the review in Penn, Judge, Jamieson, Garczynski, Hennessy, and Romer (2005).

51. Estroff, Penn, and Toporek (2004).

52. PatientView (2004b).

53. For important discussion of this issue, see Batson, Polycarpou, Harmon-Jones, Imhoff, Mitchener, Bednar, et al. (1997).

54. Kunda and Oleson (1997). In all, educational information and personal contact that provide mild disconfirmation of stereotypes (rather than examples of persons with mental illness who are "superachievers") appear to be the best suited to changing attitudes; see Reinke, Corrigan, Leonhard, Lundin, and Kubiak (2004).

55. Monteith, Sherman, and Devine (1998); Penn and Corrigan (2002).

56. Rokeach (1971).

57. Bodenhausen, Schwarz, Bless, and Wanke (1995).

58. Blair, Ma, and Lenton (2001); Rudman et al. (2001).

59. Gaertner and Dovidio (2000).

60. Sherif and Sherif (1953).

61. Batson et al. (1997, p. 105).

62. Stephan and Finlay (1999); Finlay and Stephan (2000); Batson et al. (1997).

63. Read (2002).

Chapter 10

1. Corrigan and Penn (1999); Wahl (1995).

2. Wahl (1995, pp. 141–142).

3. Wahl (1995).

4. See http://www.nami.org/about_Stigmabusters.htm; see discussion in Watson and Corrigan (2005).

5. Wegner (1997); see also Macrae, Bodenhausen, Milne, and Jetten (1994).

6. Corrigan and Penn (1999); see also Watson and Corrigan (2005), who discuss another mechanism for rebound—that is, the "reactance" that builds when people are instructed by authorities to do something, which can lead individuals to do the opposite.

7. Social psychological research on rebound prompted the cautionary points of Corrigan and Penn (1999) about protest efforts. Yet for the reasons just noted, rebound phenomena may not be all that salient for public protests of stereotyped media images; this is an area ripe for additional research.

8. Sullivan, Hamilton, and Allen (2005). See also Ries and Ries (2002).

9. Sullivan et al. (2005).

10. Warner (2005).

11. Distantly related to buzz marketing, advocacy groups may promote awards for positive portrayals in the media. Indeed, as noted earlier, the Voice Awards, made during the summer of 2005 at a Hollywood banquet, honored a number of films, television programs, and authors for accurate, sensitive depictions of mental disorder in the media for the years 2003–2004. SAMSHA helped to initiate these awards as part of its Elimination of Barriers Initiative, which has fostered collaboration with the American Psychiatric Association, the American Psychological Association, the Mental Health Media Partnership, and State Mental Health Program Directors.

12. Sullivan et al. (2005, p. 299).

13. As discussed in Watson and Corrigan (2005); see http://www.notigma.org

14. For a provocative feature, see Bai (2005).

15. Lakoff (1996, 2004).

16. Bai (2005).

17. See http://www.neurodiversity.com; also see the apt discussion in Harrington (2005) and additional information on this topic in Chapter 12.

18. Indeed, Sullivan et al. (2005) lay out a framework for the kinds of detailed marketing plans that are needed to induce change in stigmatization through media outlets.

19. Penn, Judge, Jamieson, Garczynski, Hennessy, and Romer (2005).

20. HBO Home Video (2001).

21. Harrington (2005).

22. Sacks (1985, 1996). It is also the case that media portrayals that are simultaneously entertaining (i.e., promoting identification with the protagonist) and educational, along with after-presentation information sessions emphasizing counterstereotypic depictions of mental illness, can have noteworthy effects on public attitudes. See Ritterfeld and Jin (2006).

23. See Corrigan (2005a); see also Nairn and Coverdale (2005). Pennebaker and Seagal (1999) have shown via programmatic research that writing narratives about emotionally charged topics can provide important benefits for the writer.

24. Gabbard and Gabbard (1992).

25. M. Myers and Fine (2003).

26. Goode (2003). In the words of Jamison (2006, p. 534), "we need to start within our own clinical community and have more honest and open discussions."

27. See the material in Chapter 6, including Wahl (1999b).

28. Sullivan et al. (2005).

29. Kazdin (2000).

30. Chambless and Hollon (1998); Nathan and Gorman (2002).

31. For information on the distinction between efficacy (does therapy work under pristine conditions?) and effectiveness (does therapy work in the real world?), see Mintz, Drake, and Crits-Cristoph (1996).

32. See Hinshaw (2002a); Kazdin and Weisz (2003); Nathan and Gorman (2002).

33. For discussion, see Sue (2003).

34. See, for example, Lewis, Davis, Walker, and Jennings (1984).

35. For example, see Kazdin and Wassell (1998).

36. Corrigan and Lundin (2001).

37. See Hinshaw and Cicchetti (2000) for discussion.

Chapter 11

1. See, for example, Hinshaw, Owens, Wells, Kraemer, Abikoff, Arnold, et al. (2000), who showed that in a large-scale treatment study for ADHD—a condition with substantial heritability—improvements in parents' negative/ineffective discipline styles over the course of a year and a quarter's worth of treatment were associated with the child's *normalization* of disruptive behavior at school when the family and child received multimodal treatment (i.e., medication plus intensive behavior therapy). In other words, even though faulty parenting is not a primary cause of this condition, parenting practices can matter considerably for disorders, like ADHD, with substantial genetic liabilities. In other instances (most notably child abuse but also attachment disorders), insensitive or frankly harmful parenting is centrally related to the offspring's condition, but therapists must still engage the family in treatment to maximize understanding and responsibility, unless the child is placed outside the home.

2. Antipsychiatry pieces in the media and on the internet abound. Once again, actor Tom Cruise gained national attention in 2005 by claiming, on major media outlets, that psychotropic medications are poisons. His direct challenging of actress Brooke Shields, who was promoting her autobiographical account of her postpartum depression (Shields, 2005), was driven by his explicit links with the church of Scientology, a notorious antipsychiatry organization.

3. Butzloff and Hooley (1998).

4. For example, Anastopoulos and Farley (2003).

5. DeGrandpre and Hinshaw (2000); Hinshaw, Owens et al. (2000); Zito, Safer, dosReis, Gardner, Magder, Soeken, et al. (2000).

6. In fact, the offspring's risk of developing depression by early adulthood is more than 50% for families in which one or both parents has depression; see Beardslee, Versage, and Gladstone (1998) and Hinshaw (2004). As noted earlier, such risk may emerge because of shared genes, parental stress, discordant parent-child interactions, modeling of emotion dysregulation, or a combination

of such factors. For a comprehensive volume on children of depressed parents, including mechanisms of risk for pathology in offspring, see Goodman and Gotlib (2002). See also Zahn-Waxler, Duggal, and Gruber (2002).

7. For empirical evidence, see Beardslee, Gladstone, Wright, and Cooper (2003). However, when poverty and single-parent status are added to the mix, additional supports and alternative models may be needed.

8. Beardslee (2002, pp. 102, 104–105).

9. Wahl (1999b). Again, participants were selected from the rolls of a major self-help group, enhancing the chances for positive perceptions.

10. Corrigan and Miller (2004).

11. Dixon, Stewart, Burland, Delahanty, Lucksted, and Hoffman (2001); Dixon, Lucksted, Stewart, Burland, Brown, Postrado, et al. (2004).

12. Recall that it was not until the early 1970s that the American Psychiatric Association voted to eliminate homosexuality from the *DSM,* the official listing of mental disorders.

13. For advocacy of the position that societies must fundamentally accept mental illness, see Corrigan (2005b). This is a provocative position but one that I do not entirely share. That is, I agree that (a) societies must show some degree of flexibility in accepting diverse forms of behavior and (b) advocates for neurodiversity are correct in claiming that narrow conceptions of conformity are not helpful (see Chapter 12). Still, mental disorders should not be viewed as lifestyle choices or "differences." They require treatment, which can, once again, be of great personal benefit while simultaneously helping to reduce stigma. In all, stigma reduction should not rely solely on clinical treatment efforts to reduce symptoms, but at the same time, eliminating stigma should not be based exclusively on complete societal acceptance of mentally ill behavior patterns.

14. For material on effective treatments, see Nathan and Gorman (2002).

15. See ibid. For information specifically related to ADHD, see MTA Cooperative Group (1999a, 1999b); Conners, March, Frances, Wells, and Ross (2001); Hinshaw, Owens et al. (2000).

16. See, for example, Nathan and Gorman (2002).

17. For example, individuals with bipolar disorder may fear that their creativity and productivity may be lost if they receive treatment. Yet the vast majority of persons so treated feel more creative and productive *with* effective treatment—largely because the destructive elements of manias and depressions are now under control. Indeed, successful treatment of debilitating symptoms can make these persons feel more like themselves than previously. See also Kramer (2005), who discusses the invalidity of the often-made association between depression on the one hand and creativity, soulfullness, rebellion, etc., on the other hand.

18. Along these lines, treatments for both child and adult disorders show far greater benefits when tested in university-based laboratory settings with relatively uncomplicated patient populations than when evaluated in the "real world," where complex, multiply disordered individuals are typically treated through clinics in which overburdened therapists have large caseloads. In the parlance of psychotherapy and pharmacotherapy research, treatments typically show far greater evidence for *efficacy* than for *effectiveness;* see note 31 in Chapter 10 and Mintz, Drake, and Crits-Cristoph (1996).

19. Warner (1999) asks the crucial question as to whether people with mental disorders should accept their label. His response: The answer should be "yes" in order to obtain treatment—but a clear "no" with respect to any taking on of a disenfranchised, stigmatized societal role.

20. See http://www.nami.org.

21. Wang, Berglund, Olfson, Pincus, Wells, and Kessler (2005).

22. U. S. Department of Health and Human Services (1999); World Health Organization (2001).

23. See Corrigan and Watson (2002) and Corrigan and Calabrese (2005) for elaboration of the tripartite nature of response tendencies among persons with mental disorders: suffering because of stigma, ignoring it, or angrily and actively fighting it (see also Chapters 5 and 7). Major and O'Brien (2005) provide a review of the coping processes inherent in individuals' responses to threats to their identity that emanate from stigma. See also Holmes and Rivers (1998).

24. See, for example, Lazarus and Folkman (1984). The terminology is somewhat confusing in that some internal strategies (e.g., reappraising the stressor as a challenge) are typically branded as problem focused, even though they clearly involve emotion regulation. Furthermore, some of the strategies that are linked with emotion-focused coping (e.g., use of humor) may be more adaptive than others (e.g., "shutting down" or engaging in complete denial).

25. Although focused internally, such strategies would still be construed as a form of problem-focused coping in most accounts.

26. Corrigan (2005a); Goldberg, Killeen, and O'Day (2005); see also Corrigan and Lundin (2001).

27. Corrigan and Calabrese (2005).

Chapter 12

1. For example, see Kutchins and Kirk (1997) versus Hyman (2002). Once again, the developmental psychopathology perspective, which integrates psychobiological predispositions with psychosocial risks in terms of transactional processes, could serve as a more balanced antidote.

2. Beauchaine (2003). Still, the possibility exists that some variants of mental disorder may reflect qualitative differences, though these have been difficult to detect.

3. See S. Johnson (2005) regarding bipolar disorder in this regard.

4. Consider a parallel issue related to future societies' views of intelligence in children. Given the increasingly technological basis of Western cultures, it is easy to imagine that a child's academic potential, as measured by intelligence tests, will receive ever-greater scrutiny in future generations. The underlying model in this scenario is that intelligence is a single entity, with an individual's score on an IQ test predicting important life outcomes and determining much in the way of access to resources. An alternative perspective is that multiple forms of intelligent behavior exist, with differential predictive validity to key outcomes—and that motivation and drive may be more important for ultimate outcomes than a single IQ score (see, for example, Gardner, 1985). Could it be that a parallel conception of mentally healthy behavior will emerge to the extent that there is no single standard of conformity?

5. Such websites were quite prevalent several years ago but have tapered recently (in fact, some have been taken over by those who view eating disorders as forms of mental illness that require treatment). See, for example, http://www.Anorexic_Life.com and related links. Viewing the adoration of emaciated human figures on such sites is extremely disconcerting. I thank Andrea Stier for thoughtfully raising this important issue.

6. Such a stance clashes directly with evidence for the strong biological, psychological, and familial roots of serious eating pathology—see Wilson, Becker, and Heffernan (2003).

7. New Freedom Commission on Mental Health (2003).

8. See, for example, Corcoran, Malaspina, and Hercher (2005).

9. See, for example, "An out of control profession," the posting of April 3, 2006 at the Alliance for Human Research Protection website, http://www .ahrp.org.

10. See, for example, Zito, Safer, dosReis, Gardner, Boles, and Lynch (2000); Zito, Safer, dosReis, Gardner, Magder, Soeken, et al. (2003).

11. Far more aggressive medication treatment exists today for childhood asthma than was imagined only two decades ago; yet, because asthma is a disease of the lungs and not of the brain and mind, stigma is less of an issue in this regard. The analogy is intriguing, given that asthma—a biologically based and genetically linked condition—is highly exacerbated by living in smog-ridden, decrepit urban environments. Intervention for asthma therefore needs to be delivered at broad levels of policy and housing, as well as through individual pharmacology. Nonetheless, stigma regarding asthma exists, including its associations with frailty, weakness, and sickliness. See Beamer (2005).

12. Levenson (2005).

13. See, for example the report titled "A Federal Failure in Psychiatric Research: Continuing NIMH Negligence in Funding Sufficient Research on Serious Mental Illnesses" at http://www.psychlaws.org/nimhreport/federalfailure .htm. This report outlines the huge imbalance in spending between mental and physical disorders and also decries the lack of mandated funding for the serious forms of mental illness noted in the text. It recognizes the need for basic research but notes that other agencies, such as the National Science Foundation, might be more appropriate as funding sources toward these ends.

14. The goal of this initiative, announced in 1971, was to eliminate cancer in the United States within a 7-year period. With hindsight, the naive optimism of this objective is apparent.

15. In fact, it is too narrow to conceptualize only three means of effecting change in stigma—that is, the three empirically supported procedures of protest, education, and contact cited by Corrigan and Penn (1999). There may well be additional means of changing minds and behavior (see Chapter 9).

16. See Sullivan, Hamilton, and Allen (2005).

17. Lin and Kleinman (1988).

18. See http://www.neurodiversity.com.

19. Corrigan (2005b).

20. I raised a similar point in Chapter 4, citing the work of Grob (1994), who believes that overzealous promises and excessively high expectations were partly to blame for the failure of the deinstitutionalization movement of the 1960s and beyond.

References

Achenbach, T. M. (1974). *Developmental psychopathology*. New York: Ronald Press.

Adams, M. S., Robertson, C. T., Gray-Ray, P., & Ray, M. C. (2003). Labeling and delinquency. *Adolescence, 38*, 171–186.

Adorno, T., Frankel-Brunswik, E., Levinson, D., & Sanford, R. N. (1950). *The authoritarian personality*. New York: Harper.

Ajzen, I., & Fishbein, M. (1980). *Understanding attitudes and predicting social behavior*. Englewood Cliffs, NJ: Prentice-Hall.

Albrecht, G., Walker, V., & Levy, J. (1982). Social distance from the stigmatized: A test of two theories. *Social Science and Medicine, 16*, 1319–1327.

Alexander, F., & Selesnick, S. (1966). *The history of psychiatry*. New York: New American.

Al-Issa, I. (Ed.). (2000). *Al-Junun: Mental illness in the Islamic world*. Madison, CT: International Universities Press.

Allderidge, P. (1985). Bedlam: Fact or fantasy? In W. F. Bynum, R. Porter, & M. Shepherd (Eds.), *The anatomy of madness: Essays in the history of psychiatry: Vol. 2* (pp. 18–33). London: Tavistock.

Allen, L. (1943). A study of community attitudes toward mental hygiene. *Mental Hygiene, 27*, 248–254.

Alloy, L. B., Acocella, J., & Bootzin, R. R. (1996). *Abnormal psychology: Current perspectives* (7th ed.). New York: McGraw-Hill.

Allport, G. (1958). *The nature of prejudice*. Garden City, NJ: Doubleday.

American Psychiatric Association. (1952). *Diagnostic and statistical manual of mental disorders*. Washington, DC: Author.

American Psychiatric Association. (1980). *Diagnostic and statistical manual of mental disorders* (3rd ed.). Washington, DC: American Psychiatric Association.

American Psychiatric Association. (1994). *Diagnostic and statistical manual of mental disorders* (4th ed.). Washington, DC: American Psychiatric Association.

American Psychiatric Association. (2000). *Diagnostic and statistical manual of mental disorders* (4th ed., text revision). Washington, DC: American Psychiatric Association.

Anastopoulos, A. D. & Farley, S. D. (2003). A cognitive-behavioral training program for parents of children with attention-deficit/hyperactivity disorder. In A. E. Kazdin & J. R. Weisz (Eds.), *Evidence-based psychotherapies for children and adolescents* (pp. 187–203). New York: Guilford.

Angell, B., Cooke, A., & Kovac, K. (2005). First-person accounts of stigma. In P. W. Corrigan (Ed.), *On the stigma of mental illness: Practical strategies for research and social change* (pp. 69–98). Washington, DC: American Psychological Association.

Angermeyer, M. C., & Matschinger, H. (1997). Social distance towards the mentally ill: Results of representative surveys in the Federal Republic of Germany. *Psychological Medicine, 27,* 131–141.

Angermeyer, M. C., & Matschinger, H. (2004). Public attitudes to people with depression: Have there been any changes over the last decade? *Journal of Affective Disorders, 83,* 177–182.

Angermeyer, M. C., & Schulze, B. (2001). Reinforcing stereotypes: How the focus on forensic cases in reporting may influence public attitudes towards the mentally ill. *International Journal of Law and Psychiatry, 24,* 469–486.

Anthony, E. J. (1974). Introduction: The syndrome of the psychologically invulnerable child. In E. J. Anthony & C. Koupernik (Eds.), *The child in his family: Children at psychiatric risk: Vol. 3* (pp. 3–10). New York: Wiley.

Aries, P. (1962). *Centuries of childhood: A social history of family life.* New York: Knopf.

Aronson, J., & Inzlicht, M. (2004). The ups and downs of attributional ambiguity: Stereotype vulnerability and the academic self-knowledge of African American college students. *Psychological Science, 15,* 829–836.

Bai, M. (2005). The framing wars. *New York Times Sunday Magazine,* Sunday, July 17, 38.

Barkley, R. A. (2003). Attention-deficit/hyperactivity disorder. In E. J. Mash & R. A. Barkley (Eds.), *Child psychopathology* (pp. 75–143). New York: Guilford Press.

Barondes, S. H. (1998). *Mood genes: Hunting for the origins of mania and depression.* Oxford, England: Oxford University Press.

Batson, C. D., Polycarpou, M. P., Harmon-Jones, E., Imhoff, H. J., Mitchener, E. C., Bednar, et al. (1997). Empathy and attitudes: Can feeling for a member of a stigmatized group improve feelings toward the group? *Journal of Personality and Social Psychology, 72,* 105–118.

Beamer, L. (2005). Beyond the asthma stigma. Posted at http://geoparent.com.

Beard, J. J., & Gillespie, P. (Eds.) (2004). *Nothing to hide: Mental illness in the family.* New York: New Press.

Beardslee, W. R. (2002). *Out of the darkened room: When a parent is depressed: protecting the children and strengthening the family.* Boston: Little, Brown.

Beardslee, W. R., Gladstone, T. R., Wright, E. J., & Cooper, A. B. (2003). A family-based approach to the prevention of depressive symptoms in children at risk: Evidence of parental and child change. *Pediatrics, 112,* 119–131.

Beardslee, W. R., Versage, E. M., & Gladstone, T. G. (1998). Children of affectively ill parents: A review of the last 10 years. *Journal of the American Academy of Child and Adolescent Psychiatry, 37,* 1134–1141.

Beauchaine, T. P. (2003). Taxometrics and developmental psychopathology. *Development and Psychopathology, 15,* 501–527.

Becker, H. S. (1963). *Outsiders: Studies in the sociology of deviance.* New York: Free Press.

Beers, C. (1908/1945). *A mind that found itself.* Garden City, NY: Doubleday.

Belluck, P. (2005). Toy's message of affection draws anger and publicity. *New York Times,* Saturday January 22, A8.

Ben-Porath, D. D. (2002). Stigmatization of individuals who receive treatment: An interaction between help-seeking behavior and the presence of depression. *Journal of Social and Clinical Psychology, 21,* 400–413.

Bettelheim, B. (1967). *The empty fortress.* New York: Free Press.

Biernat, M., & Dovidio, J. F. (2000). Stigma and stereotypes. In T. F. Heatherton, R. E. Kleck, M. R. Hebl, & J. G. Hull (Eds.), *The social psychology of stigma* (pp. 88–125). New York: Guilford.

Black, E. (2003). *War against the weak: Eugenics and America's attempt to create a master race.* New York: Four Walls Eight Windows.

Blair, I. V., Ma, J. E., & Lenton, A. P. (2001). Imagining stereotypes away: The moderation of implicit stereotypes through mental imagery. *Journal of Personality and Social Psychology, 81,* 828–841.

Blashfield, R. (1984). *The classification of psychopathology: Neo-Kraepelinian and quantitative approaches.* New York: Plenum

Blasovich, J., Mendes, W. B., Hunter, S., & Lickel, B. (2000). Stigma, threat, and social interactions. In T. F. Heatherton, R. E. Kleck, M. R. Hebl, & J. G. Hull (Eds.), *The social psychology of stigma* (pp. 337–333). New York: Guilford.

Bloom, F. E., & Kupfer, D. J. (Eds.) (1995). *Psychopharmacology: The fourth generation of progress.* New York: Raven Press.

Bockoven, S. S. (1963). *Moral treatment in American psychiatry.* New York: Springer.

Bodenhausen, G. V., Schwarz, N., Bless, H., & Wanke, M. (1995). Effects of atypical exemplars on racial beliefs: Enlightened racism or generalized appraisals? *Journal of Experimental Social Psychology, 31,* 48–63.

Bogardus, E. S. (1925). Measuring social distances. *Journal of Applied Sociology, 9,* 299–308.

Bogardus, E. S. (1933). A social distance scale. *Social Research, 17,* 265–271.

Breakey, W. R., Fischer, P. J., Nestadt, G., & Romanoski, A. (1992). Stigma and stereotype: Homeless mentally ill persons. In P. J. Fink & A. J. Tasman (Eds.), *Stigma and mental illness* (pp. 97–112). Washington, DC: American Psychiatric Association.

Brewer, M. B. (1999). The psychology of prejudice: Ingroup love or outgroup hate? *Journal of Social Issues, 55,* 429–444.

Brizendine, L. (1992). The Devon Asylum: A brief history of the changing concept of mental illness and asylum treatment. In P. J. Fink & A. Tasman (Eds.), *Stigma and mental illness* (pp. 59–71). Washington, DC: American Psychiatric Press.

Brockman, J., D'Arcy, C., & Edmonds, L. (1979). Facts or artifacts? Changing public attitudes toward the mentally ill. *Social Science and Medicine, 13A,* 673–682.

Bronfenbrenner, U. (1979). *The ecology of human development: Experiments by nature and design.* Cambridge, MA: Harvard University Press.

Brown, R. P., & Pinel, E. C. (2003). Stigma on my mind: Individual differences in the experience of stereotype threat. *Journal of Experimental Social Psychology, 39,* 626–633.

Bruner, J. (1986). *Actual minds, possible worlds.* Cambridge, MA: Harvard University Press.

Bruner, J. (1990). *Acts of meaning.* Cambridge, MA: Harvard University Press.

Burt, R. A. (2001). Promises to keep, miles to go: Mental health law since 1972. In L. E. Frost & R. J. Bonnie (Ed.), *The evolution of mental health law* (pp. 11–30). Washington, DC: American Psychological Association.

Butzloff, R. L., & Hooley, J. M. (1998). Expressed emotion and psychiatric relapse: A meta-analysis. *Archives of General Psychiatry, 55,* 547–552.

Byrd, E. K., McDaniel, R. S., & Rhoden, R. B. (1980). Television programming and disability: A ten year span. *International Journal of Rehabilitation Research, 3,* 321–326.

Byrne, P. (1997). Psychiatric stigma: Past, passing, and to come. *Journal of the Royal Society of Medicine, 90,* 618–621.

Campbell, T., & Heginbotham, L. (1991). *Mental illness: Prejudice, discrimination and the law.* Aldershot, England: Dartmouth.

Carey, B. (2006, September 19). A psychologist is slain, and a sad debate deepens. *New York Times,* pp. D1, D6.

Carling, P. J. (1990). Major mental illness, housing, and supports: The promise of community integration. *American Psychologist, 45,* 969–975.

Cassata, M. B., Skill, T. D., & Boadu, S. O. (1979). In sickness and in health. *Journal of Communication, 29,* 73–77.

Chambless, D., & Hollon, S. D. (1998). Defining empirically supported treatments. *Journal of Consulting and Clinical Psychology, 66,* 7–18.

Cicchetti, D., & Cannon, T. D. (Eds.) (1999). Neurodevelopment and psychopathology [Special Issue]. *Development and Psychopathology, 11*(3), 375–654.

Cicchetti, D., & Cohen, D. (Eds.) (2006). *Developmental Psychopathology: Theory and Method: Vol. 1* (2nd ed.). New York: Wiley.

Cicchetti, D., & Garmezy, N. (Eds.) (1993). Milestones in the development of resilience [Special Issue]. *Development and Psychopathology, 5,* 497–774.

Cicchetti, D., & Rogosch, F. A. (1996). Developmental pathways: Diversity in process and outcome [Special Issue]. *Development and Psychopathology, 8*(4), 597–896.

Cioffi, D. (2000). The looking-glass self revisited: Behavior choice and self-perception in the social token. In T. F. Heatherton, R. E. Kleck, M. R. Hebl, & J. G. Hull (Eds.), *The social psychology of stigma* (pp. 184–219). New York: Guilford.

Clark, K. B., & Clark, M. P. (1950). Emotional factors in racial identification and preference in Negro children. *Journal of Negro Education, 19,* 341–350.

Clausen, J., & Yarrow, M. R. (Eds.) (1955). The impact of mental illness on the family. *Journal of Social Issues, 11*(4).

Clinton, H. (2004, April 18). Now can we talk about health care? *New York Times Sunday Magazine,* p. 26.

Cockeram, W. (1981). *Sociology of mental disorder.* Englewood Cliffs, NJ: Prentice-Hall.

Cohen, J., & Struening, E. L. (1962). Opinions about mental illness in the personnel of two large mental hospitals. *Journal of Abnormal and Social Psychology, 64,* 349–360.

Comer, R. J. (1999). *Foundations of abnormal psychology* (2nd ed.). New York: Worth/Freeman.

Conners, C. K., March, J. S., Frances, A., Wells, K. C., & Ross, R. (2001). Treatment of attention-deficit/hyperactivity disorder: Expert consensus guidelines. *Journal of Attention Disorders, 4*(Suppl. 1), S-1–S-128.

Cooper, E., & O'Hara, A. (2003, May). Priced out in 2002: Housing crisis worsens for people with disabilities. *Opening Doors, 21.* Retrieved from http://www.c-d-c.org/Issue21.pdf

Corcoran, C., Malaspina, D., & Hercher, L. (2005). Prodromal interventions for schizophrenia vulnerability: The risks of being "at risk." *Schizophrenia Research, 73,* 173–184.

Corrigan, P. W. (2000). Mental health stigma as social attribution: Implications for research methods and attitude change. *Clinical Psychology: Science and Practice, 7,* 48–67.

Corrigan, P. W. (2005a). Dealing with stigma through personal disclosure. In P. W. Corrigan (Ed.), *On the stigma of mental illness: Practical strategies for research and social change* (pp. 257–280). Washington, DC: American Psychological Association.

Corrigan, P. W. (2005b). Mental illness stigma as social injustice: Yet another dream to be achieved. In P. W. Corrigan (Ed.), *On the stigma of mental illness: Practical strategies for research and social change* (pp. 315–320). Washington, DC: American Psychological Association.

Corrigan, P. W. (Ed.). (2005c). *On the stigma of mental illness: Practical strategies for research and social change.* Washington, DC: American Psychological Association.

Corrigan, P. W., & Calabrese, J. D. (2005). Strategies for assessing and diminishing self-stigma. In P. W. Corrigan (Ed.), *On the stigma of mental illness: Practical strategies for research and social change* (pp. 239–256). Washington, DC: American Psychological Association.

Corrigan, P. W., & Cooper, A. E. (2005). Mental illness and dangerousness: Fact or misperception, and implications for stigma. In P. W. Corrigan (Ed.), *On the stigma of mental illness: Practical strategies for research and social change* (pp. 165–179). Washington, DC: American Psychological Association.

Corrigan, P. W., Edwards, A. B., Green, A., Diwan, S. L., & Penn, D. L. (2001). Prejudice, social distance, and familiarity with mental illness. *Schizophrenia Bulletin, 27,* 219–225.

Corrigan, P. W., & Kleinlen, P. (2005). The impact of mental illness stigma. In P. W. Corrigan (Ed.), *On the stigma of mental illness: Practical strategies for research and social change* (pp. 11–44). Washington, DC: American Psychological Association.

Corrigan, P. W., & Lundin, R. (2001). *Don't call me nuts: Coping with the stigma of mental illness.* Chicago: Recovery Press.

Corrigan, P. W., Markowitz, F. E., & Watson, A. (2004). Structural levels of mental illness stigma and discrimination. *Schizophrenia Bulletin, 30,* 481–491.

Corrigan, P. W., & Miller, F. E. (2004). Shame, blame, and contamination: A review of the impact of mental illness stigma on family members. *Journal of Mental Health, 13,* 537–548.

Corrigan, P. W., & Penn, D. L. (1999). Lessons from social psychology on discrediting psychiatric stigma. *American Psychologist, 54,* 765–776.

Corrigan, P. W., & Watson, A. C. (2002). The paradox of self-stigma and mental illness. *Clinical Psychology: Science and Practice, 9,* 35–53.

Corrigan, P. W., & Watson, A. C. (2004). At issue: Stop the stigma: Call mental illness a brain disease. *Schizophrenia Bulletin, 30,* 477–479.

Corrigan, P. W., Watson, A. C., Heyrman, M. L., Warpinski, A., Gracia, G., Slopen, N., et al. (2005). Structural stigma in state legislation. *Psychiatric Services, 56,* 557–563.

Coryell, W., Scheftner, W., Keller, B., Endicott, J., Maser, J., & Klerman, G. L. (1993). The enduring psychosocial consequences of mania and depression. *American Journal of Psychiatry, 150,* 720–727.

Cosmides, L., & Tooby, J. (1994). Origins of domain specificity: The evolution of functional organization. In L. Hirshfield & S. Gelman (Eds.), *Mapping the mind: Domain specificity in cognition and culture* (pp. 85–116). New York: Cambridge University Press.

Couture, S. M., & Penn, D. L. (2003). Interpersonal contact and the stigma of mental illness: A review of the literature. *Journal of Mental Health, 12,* 291–305.

Coverdale, J., Nairn, R., & Claasen, D. (2002). Depiction of mental illness in print media: A prospective national sample. *Australian and New Zealand Journal of Psychiatry, 36,* 697–700.

Crandall, C. S. (2000). Ideology and lay theories of stigma: The justification of stigmatization. In T. F. Heatherton, R. E. Kleck, M. R. Hebl, & J. H. Hull (Eds.), *The social psychology of stigma* (pp. 126–150). New York: Guilford.

Crisp, A. H. (1999). The stigmatization of sufferers with mental disorders. *British Journal of General Practice, 49,* 3–4.

Crisp, A. H. (2000). Changing minds: Every family in the land: An update on the College's campaign. *Psychiatric Bulletin, 24,* 267–268.

Crisp, A. H. (2005). Stigmatization of and discrimination against people with eating disorders including a report of two nationwide surveys. *European Eating Disorders Review, 13,* 147–152.

Crisp, A. H., Gelder, M. G., Rix, S., Meltzer, H. I., & Rowlands, G. J. (2000). Stigmatisation of people with mental illnesses. *British Journal of Psychiatry, 177,* 4–7.

Critser, G. (2005). *Generation Rx: How prescription drugs are altering American lives, minds, and bodies.* New York: Houghton Mifflin.

Crocetti, G., Spiro, H., & Siassi, I. (1971). Are the ranks closed? Attitudinal social distance and mental illness. *American Journal of Psychiatry, 127,* 1121–1127.

Crocetti, G., Spiro, H., & Siassi, I. (1974). *Contemporary attitudes toward mental illness.* Pittsburgh: University of Pittsburgh Press.

Crocker, J., Cornwell, B., & Major, B. (1993). The stigma of overweight: Affective consequences of attributional ambiguity. *Journal of Personality and Social Psychology, 64,* 60–70.

Crocker, J., & Major, B. (1989). Social stigma and self-esteem: The self-protective properties of stigma. *Psychological Review, 96,* 608–630.

Crocker, J., & Quinn, D. M. (2000). Social stigma and the self: Meanings, situations, and self-esteem. In T. F. Heatherton, R. E. Kleck, M. R. Hebl, & J. G. Hull (Eds.), *The social psychology of stigma* (pp. 153–183). New York: Guilford.

Crocker, J., Quinn, D. M. & Steele, C. (1998). Social stigma. In D. T. Gilbert, S. T. Fiske, & G. Lindzey (Eds.), *Handbook of social psychology: Vol. 2* (4th ed., pp. 504–553). Boston: McGraw-Hill.

Cronkite, K. (1994). *On the edge of darkness: Conversations about conquering depression.* New York: Delta.

Cumming, E., & Cumming, J. (1957). *Closed ranks: An experiment in mental health.* Cambridge, MA: Harvard University Press.

Dain, N. (1964). *Concepts of insanity in the United States, 1789–1865.* New Brunswick, NJ: Rutgers University Press.

Dasgupta, N., & Greenwald, A. G. (2001). On the malleability of automatic attitudes: Combating automatic prejudice with images of admired and disliked individuals. *Journal of Personality and Social Psychology, 81,* 800–814.

Davidson, L., Stayner, D., & Haglund, K. E. (1998). Phenomenological perspectives on the social functioning of people with schizophrenia. In K. T. Mueser & N. Torria (Eds.), *Handbook of social functioning in schizophrenia* (pp. 97–120). Needham Heights, MA: Allyn & Bacon.

Davison, G. C., & Neale, J. M. (1989). *Abnormal psychology* (6th ed.). New York: Wiley.

Davison, G. C., Neale, J. M. & Kring, A. M. (2004). *Abnormal psychology* (9th ed.). New York: Wiley.

Day, D. M., & Page, S. (1986). Portrayal of mental illness in Canadian newspapers. *Canadian Journal of Psychiatry, 31,* 813–816.

Deegan, P. E. (1988). Recovery: The lived experience of rehabilitation. *Psychosocial Rehabilitation Journal, 11,* 11–19.

Deegan, P. E. (1997). Spirit breaking: When helping professions hurt. *Humanistic Psychologist, 18,* 301–313.

DeGrandpre, R., & Hinshaw, S. P. (2000). Attention-deficit hyperactivity disorder: Psychiatric problem or American cop-out? *Cerebrum: The Dana Foundation Journal on Brain Sciences, 2,* 12–38.

deMause, L. (Ed.). (1974/1988). *The history of childhood: The untold story of child abuse.* New York: Peter Bedrick.

Desipriya, E. B. R., & Nobutada, I. (2002). Stigma of mental illness in Japan. *Lancet, 359,* 1866.

Deutsch, A. (1948). *The shame of the states.* Garden City, NY: Doubleday.

Devine, P. G. (1989). Stereotypes and prejudice: Their automatic and controlled components. *Journal of Personality and Social Psychology, 56,* 5–18.

deWaal, F. B. M. (2002). Evolutionary psychology: The wheat and the chaff. *Current Directions in Psychological Science, 11,* 187–191.

Dichter, H. (1992). The stigmatization of psychiatrists who work with chronically mentally ill persons. In P. J. Fink & A. Tasman (Eds.), *Stigma and mental illness* (pp. 203–215). Washington, DC: American Psychiatric Press.

Dickerson, F. B., Sommerville, J., Origoni, A. E., Ringel, N. B., & Parente, F. (2002). Experiences of stigma among outpatients with schizophrenia. *Schizophrenia Bulletin, 28,* 143–155.

Diefenbach, D. L. (1997). The portrayal of mental illness on prime-time television. *Journal of Community Psychology, 25,* 289–302.

Dietrich, S., Beck, M., Bujantugs, B., Kenzine, D., Matschinger, H., & Angermeyer, M. C. (2004). The relationship between public causal beliefs and social distance toward mentally ill people. *Australian and New Zealand Journal of Psychiatry, 38,* 348–354.

Dixon, L., Lucksted, A., Stewart, B., Burland, J., Brown, C. H., Postrado, L., et al. (2004). Outcomes of the peer-taught Family-to-Family Education Program for severe mental illness. *Acta Psychiatrica Scandinavia, 109,* 207–215.

Dixon, L., Stewart, B., Burland, J., Delahanty, J., Lucksted, A., & Hoffman, M. (2001). Pilot study of the effectiveness of the Family-to-Family Education Program. *Psychiatric Services, 52,* 965–967.

Donohue, B., Hersen, M., & Ammerman, R. T. (1995). Historical overview. In M. Hersen & R. T. Ammerman (Eds.), *Advanced abnormal child psychology* (pp. 3–19). Mahwah, NJ: Erlbaum.

Dovidio, J. F., Kawakami, K., & Gaertner, S. L. (2002). Implicit and explicit prejudice and interracial interactions. *Journal of Personality and Social Psychology, 82,* 62–68.

Dovidio, J. F., Major, B., & Crocker, J. (2000). Stigma: Introduction and overview. In T. F. Hetherton, R. E. Kleck, M. R. Hebl, & J. G. Hull (Eds.), *The social psychology of stigma* (pp. 1–28). New York: Guilford.

Downey, G., & Feldman, S. (1996). Implications of rejection sensitivity for intimate relationships. *Journal of Personality and Social Psychology, 70,* 1327–1343.

Doyle, A. B., & Aboud, F. E. (1995). A longitudinal study of White children's racial prejudice as a social-cognitive development. *Merrill-Palmer Quarterly, 41,* 209–228.

Doyle, J. (2005, July 28). Mental hospital probe shows major problems. *San Francisco Chronicle,* pp. A1, A4.

Druss, B. G., Bradford, D. W., Rosenheck, R. A., Radford, M. J., & Krumholtz, H. M. (2000). Mental disorders and use of cardiovascular procedures after myocardial infarction. *Journal of the American Medical Association, 283,* 506–511.

Dubin, W. R., & Fink, P. J. (1992). Effects of stigma on psychiatric treatment. In P. J. Fink & A. Tasman (Eds.), *Stigma and mental illness* (pp. 1–7). Washington, DC: American Psychiatric Press.

Dukakis, K., & Tye, L. (2006). *Shock: The healing power of electroconvulsive therapy.* New York: Penguin.

Eidelson, R. J., & Eidelson, J. I. (2003). Dangerous ideas: Five beliefs that propel groups toward conflict. *American Psychologist, 58,* 182–192.

Eisenberg, L. (2005). Violence and the mentally ill: Victims, not perpetrators. *Archives of General Psychiatry, 62,* 825–826.

Ekman, P. (2003). *Emotions revealed: Recognizing faces and feelings to improve communication and emotional life.* New York: Times Books.

Elder, G. H. (1974). *Children of the great depression.* Chicago: University of Chicago Press.

Engel, G. W. (1977). The need for a new medical model: A challenge for biomedicine. *Science, 196,* 125–135.

Erlich, E., Flexner, S. B., Carruth, G., & Hawkins, J. M. (1980). *Oxford American dictionary.* New York: Avon.

Estroff, S. E., Penn, D. L., & Toporek, J. R. (2004). From stigma to discrimination: An analysis of community efforts to reduce the negative consequences of having a psychiatric disorder and label. *Schizophrenia Bulletin, 30,* 293–509.

Fannon, D., Chitnis, X., Daku, V., & Tennakoon, L. (2000). Features of structural brain abnormalities detected in first-episode psychosis. *American Journal of Psychiatry, 157,* 1829–1834.

Farina, A., Allen, J. G., & Saul, B. B. (1968). The role of the stigmatized in affecting social relationships. *Journal of Personality, 36,* 169–182.

Farina, A., & Felner, R. D. (1973). Employment interviewer reactions to former mental patients. *Journal of Abnormal Psychology, 70,* 47–51.

Farina, A., Gliha, D., Boudreau, L. A., Allen, J. G., & Sherman, M. (1971). Mental illness and the impact of believing others know about it. *Journal of Abnormal Psychology, 77,* 1–5.

Farina, A., Holland, C. H., & Ring, K. (1966). The role of stigma and set in interpersonal interaction. *Journal of Abnormal Psychology, 71,* 421–428.

Farina, A., & Ring, K. (1965). The influence of perceived mental illness on interpersonal relations. *Journal of Abnormal Psychology, 70,* 47–51.

Farrington, D. P. (1977). The effects of public labeling. *British Journal of Criminology, 17,* 112–125.

Fein, S., & Spencer, S. J. (1997). Prejudice as self-image maintenance: Affirming the self through derogating others. *Journal of Personality and Social Psychology, 73,* 31–44.

Feinberg, D. T. (2005). Managed care: Dr. Robin Hood to cure California's mentally ill. *Journal of Child and Adolescent Psychopharmacology, 15,* 155–156.

Feldman, S., Bachman, J., & Bayer, J. (2002). Mental health parity: A review of research and a bibliography. *Administration and Policy in Mental Health, 29,* 215–228.

Festinger, T. (1983). *No one ever asked us.* New York: Columbia University Press.

Fife, B. L., & Wright, E. R. (2000). The dimensionality of stigma: A comparison of its impact on the self of persons with HIV/AIDS and cancer. *Journal of Health and Social Behavior,* 50–67.

Finlay, K., & Stephan, W. G. (2000). Improving intergroup relations: The effects of empathy on racial attitudes. *Journal of Applied Social Psychology, 30,* 1720–1737.

Finzen, A., & Hoffman-Richter, U. (1999). Mental illness as metaphor. In J. Guimon, W. Fischer, & N. Sartorius (Eds.), *The image of madness: The public facing mental illness and psychiatric treatment* (pp. 13–19). Basel, Switzerland: Karger.

Fishbein, H. D. (2002). *Peer prejudice and discrimination: The origins of prejudice* (2nd ed.). Mahwah, NJ: Erlbaum.

Fishbein, M., & Ajzen, I. (1975). *Belief, attitude, intention, and behavior.* Reading, MA: Addison-Wesley.

Fiske, S. T. (1998). Stereotyping, prejudice, and discrimination. In D. T. Gilbert, S. T. Fiske, & G. Lindzey (Eds.), *Handbook of social psychology: Vol. 2* (4th ed., pp. 357–411). Boston: McGraw-Hill.

Foucault, M. (1965). *Madness and civilization: A history of insanity in the age of reason.* New York: Random House.

Frable, D. E. S., Platt, L., & Hoey, S. (1998). Concealable stigmas and positive self-perceptions: Feeling better around similar others. *Journal of Personality and Social Psychology, 74,* 909–922.

French, H. W. (2002, August 10). Depression simmers in Japan's culture of stoicism. *New York Times,* p. A3.

Frese, F. J., & Walker Davis, W. (1997). The consumer-survivor movement, recovery, and consumer professionals. *Professional Psychology: Research and Practice, 28,* 243–245.

Frost, L. E., & Bonnie, R. J. (Eds.). (2001). *The evolution of mental health law.* Washington, DC: American Psychological Association.

Fryer, J. H., & Cohen, L. (1988). Effects of labeling patients "psychiatric" or "medical": Favorability of traits ascribed by hospital staff. *Psychological Reports, 62,* 779–793.

Gabbard, G. O., & Gabbard, K. (1992). Cinematic stereotypes contributing to the stigmatization of psychiatrists. In P. J. Fink & A. Tasman (Eds.), *Stigma and mental illness* (pp. 113–126). Washington, DC: American Psychiatric Association.

Gaertner, S. L., & Dovidio, J. F. (2000). *Reducing intergroup bias: The common ingroup identity model.* Philadelphia: Psychology Press.

Gallow, K. M. (1994). First-person account: Self-stigmatization. *Schizophrenia Bulletin, 20,* 407–410.

Gardner, H. (1985). *Frames of mind: The theory of multiple intelligences.* New York: Basic Books.

Garmezy, N. (1970). Process and reactive schizophrenia: Some conceptions and issues. *Schizophrenia Bulletin, 2,* 30–74.

Gerbner, G., Gross, L., Morgan, M., Signorelli, N, & Shanahan, J. (2002). Growing up with television: Cultivation processes. In J. Bryant & D. Zillmann (Eds.), *Media effects: Advances in theory and research* (pp. 43–68). Mahwah, NJ: Erlbaum.

Gillmore, J. L., & Farina, A. (1989). The social reception of mainstreamed children in the regular classroom. *Journal of Mental Deficiency Research, 33,* 301–311.

Goffman, E. (1961). *Asylums: Essays on the social situations of mental patients and other inmates.* New York: Doubleday.

Goffman, E. (1963). *Stigma: Notes on the management of spoiled identity.* Englewood Cliffs, NJ: Prentice Hall.

Goldberg, S. G., Killeen, M. B., & O'Day, B. (2005). The disclosure conundrum: How people with psychiatric disabilities navigate employment. *Psychology, Public Policy, and Law, 11,* 463–500.

Goldhagen, D. J. (1996). *Hitler's willing executioners: Ordinary Germans and the Holocaust.* New York: Vintage.

Goode, E. (2003, July 6). Doctors' toughest diagnosis: Own mental health. *New York Times,* pp. D5, D8.

Goodman, S. H., & Gotlib, I. H. (Eds.) (2002). *Children of depressed parents: Mechanisms of risk and implications for treatment.* Washington, DC: American Psychological Association.

Gottfredson, K. (2004). *Psychologists,' psychiatrists,' and other mental health professionals' use of psychoactive medication and therapy: The ongoing stigma connected to psychological problems and treatment.* Unpublished doctoral dissertation, Wright Institute, Berkeley, CA.

Gove, W. (1980). Labeling and mental illness: A critique. In W. Gove (Ed.), *Labeling deviant behavior* (pp. 53–109). Beverly Hills, CA: Sage.

Gove, W. (1982). The current status of the labeling theory of mental illness. In W. Gove (Ed.), *Deviance and mental illness: A critique* (pp. 273–300). Beverly Hills, CA: Sage.

Gove, W., & Fain, T. (1973). The stigma of mental hospitalization: An attempt to evaluate its consequences. *Archives of General Psychiatry, 28,* 494–500.

Grammer, K., & Thornhill, R. (1994). Human (homo sapiens) facial attractiveness and sexual selection: The role of symmetry and averageness. *Journal of Comparative Psychology, 108*, 233–242,

Granello, D. H., & Pauley, P. C. (2000). Television viewing habits and their relationship to tolerance toward people with mental illness. *Journal of Mental Health Counseling, 22*, 162–175.

Graves, R. E., Cassisi, J. E., & Penn, D. L. (2005). Psychophysiological evaluation of stigma toward schizophrenia. *Schizophrenia Research, 76*, 317–327.

Gray, D. E. (2002). Everybody just freezes. Everybody is just embarrassed: Felt and enacted stigma among parents of children with high functioning autism. *Sociology of Health and Illness, 24*, 734–750.

Green, D. P., Glaser, J., & Rich, A. (1998). From lynching to gay bashing: The elusive connection between economic conditions and hate crime. *Journal of Personality and Social Psychology, 75*, 82–92.

Greenberg, E., Kim, H. W., & Greenley, J. R. (1997). Factors associated with subjective burden in siblings of adults with severe mental illness. *American Journal of Orthopsychiatry, 67*, 231–241.

Greenwald, A. G., & Banaji, M. R. (1995). Implicit social cognition: Attitudes, self-esteem, and stereotypes. *Psychological Review, 102*, 4–27.

Greenwald, A. G., Nosek, B. A., & Banaji, M. R. (2003). Understanding and using the Implicit Association Test: An improved scoring algorithm. *Journal of Personality and Social Psychology, 85*, 197–216.

Griesinger, W. (1867). *Mental pathology and therapeutics* (C. L. Robertson & J. Rutherford, Trans.). London: New Sydenham Society.

Grob, G. N. (1994). *The mad among us: A history of care of America's mentally ill.* New York: Free Press.

Guimon, J., Fischer, W., & Sartorius, N. (Eds.). (1999). *The image of madness: The public facing mental illness and psychiatric treatment.* Basel, Switzerland: Karger.

Gupta, S., Mosnik, D., Black, D. W., Berry, S., & Masand, P. S. (1999). Tardive dyskinesia: Review of treatments past, present, and future. *Annuals of Clinical Psychiatry, 11*, 257–266.

Gussow, Z., & Tracy, G. S. (1968). Status, ideology, and adaptation to stigmatized illness: A study of leprosy. *Human Organization, 27*, 316–325.

Haghighat, R. (2001). A unitary theory of stigmatisation. *British Journal of Psychiatry, 178*, 207–215.

Hamre, P., Dahl, A., & Malt, U. (1994). Public attitudes to the quality of psychiatric treatment, psychiatric patients, and prevalence of mental disorders. *Norwegian Journal of Psychiatry, 4*, 275–281.

Hansen, T. E., Goetz, R. R., Bloom, J. D., & Fenn, D. S. (1997). Changes in questions about psychiatric illness asked on medical licensure applications between 1993 and 1996. *Psychiatric Services, 49*, 202–206.

Harrington, A. (2005). The inner lives of disordered brains. *Cerebrum: The Dana Forum on Brain Sciences, 7*(2), 23–36.

Harris, M. J., Milich, R., Corbitt, E. M., Hoover, D. W., & Brady, M. (1992). Self-fulfilling effects of stigmatizing information on children's social interactions. *Journal of Personality and Social Psychology, 63*, 41–50.

Hart, S., Field, T., Stern, M., & Jones, N. (1997). Depressed fathers' stereotyping of infants labeled "depressed." *Infant Mental Health Journal, 18*, 436–445.

Haslam, N. (2000). Psychiatric categories as natural kinds: Essentialist thinking about mental disorder. *Social Research, 67,* 1031–1058.

Haslam, N. (2005). Dimensions of folk psychiatry. *Review of General Psychology, 9,* 35–47.

Haslam, N., & Ernst, D. (2002). Essentialist beliefs about mental disorders. *Journal of Social and Clinical Psychology, 21,* 628–644.

Haslam, N., Rothschild, L., & Ernst, D. (2002). Are essentialist beliefs associated with prejudice? *British Journal of Social Psychology, 41,* 87–100.

Hatfield, A. B. (1978). Psychological costs of schizophrenia to the family. *Social Work, 23,* 355–359.

HBO Home Video. (2001). *Panic: A film about coping.* America Undercover series, VHS, Warner House Video.

Heatherton, T. F., Kleck, R. E., Hebl, M. R., & Hull, J. G. (Eds.) (2000). *The social psychology of stigma.* New York: Guilford.

Hebl, M. R., Tickle, J., & Heatherton, T. F. (2000). Awkward moments in interactions between nonstigmatized and stigmatized individuals. In T. F. Heatherton, R. E. Kleck, M. R. Hebl, & J. G. Hull (Eds.), *The social psychology of stigma* (pp. 275–306). New York: Guilford.

Helfer, R. E., & Kempe, C. H. (1968). *The battered child.* Chicago: University of Chicago Press.

Hemmens, C., Miller, M., Burton, V. S., & Milner, S. (2002). The consequences of official labels: An examination of the rights lost by the mentally ill and mentally incompetent ten years later. *Community Mental Health Journal, 38,* 129–140.

Henry, G. W. (1941). Mental hospitals. In G. Zilboorg (Ed.), *A history of medical psychology* (pp. 558–589). New York: Norton.

Hepworth, J. T., & West, S. G. (1988). Lynchings and the economy: A time-series reanalysis of Hovland and Sears (1940). *Journal of Personality and Social Psychology, 55,* 239–247.

Herman, E. (1995). *The romance of American psychology: Political culture in the age of experts.* Berkeley: University of California Press.

Hewstone, M., Rubin, M., & Willis, H. (2002). Intergroup bias. *Annual Review of Psychology, 53,* 575–604.

Hibbs, E. D., & Jensen, P. S. (Eds.). (2005). *Psychosocial treatment for child and adolescent disorders: Empirically based strategies for clinical practice* (2nd ed.). Washington, DC: American Psychological Association.

Hiday, V. A. (1995). The social context of mental illness and violence. *Journal of Health and Social Behavior, 36,* 122–137.

Hillert, A., Sandman, J., Ehmig, S. C., Weisbecker, H., Kepplinger, H. M., & Benkert, O. (1999). The general public's cognitive and emotional perception of mental illness: An alternative to attitude research. In J. Guimon, W. Fischer, & N. Sartorius (Eds.), *The image of madness: The public facing mental illness and psychiatric treatment* (pp. 96–104). Basel, Switzerland: Karger.

Hinshaw, S. P. (1999). Psychosocial intervention for childhood ADHD: Etiologic and developmental themes, comorbidity, and integration with pharmacotherapy. In D. Cicchetti & S. L. Toth (Eds.), *Rochester Symposium on Developmental Psychopathology: Vol. 9. Developmental approaches to prevention and intervention* (pp. 221–270). Rochester, NY: University of Rochester Press.

Hinshaw, S. P. (2002a). Intervention research, theoretical mechanisms, and causal processes related to externalizing behavior patterns. *Development and Psychopathology, 14,* 789–818.

Hinshaw, S. P. (2002b). *The years of silence are past: My father's life with bipolar disorder.* New York: Cambridge University Press.

Hinshaw, S. P. (2004). Parental mental disorder and children's functioning: Silence and communication, stigma, and resilience. *Journal of Clinical Child and Adolescent Psychology, 33,* 400–411.

Hinshaw, S. P. (2005). The stigmatization of mental illness in children and parents: Developmental issues, family concerns, and research needs. *Journal of Child Psychology and Psychiatry, 46,* 714–734.

Hinshaw, S. P. (2006). Stigma and mental illness: Developmental issues. In D. Cichetti & D. Cohen (Eds.), *Developmental psychopathology: Vol. 3. Risk and adaptation* (2nd ed., pp. 841–881). New York: Wiley.

Hinshaw, S. P., & Cicchetti, D. (2000). Stigma and mental disorder: Conceptions of illness, public attitudes, personal disclosure, and social policy. *Development and Psychopathology, 12,* 555–598.

Hinshaw, S. P., Owens, E. B., Wells, K.C., Kraemer, H.C., Abikoff, H.B., Arnold, L.E., et al. (2000). Family processes and treatment outcome in the MTA: Negative/ineffective parenting practices in relation to multimodal treatment. *Journal of Abnormal Child Psychology, 28,* 555–568.

Hoening, J., & Hamilton, M. (1966). The schizophrenic patient in the community and his effect on the household. *Journal of Social Psychiatry, 12,* 165–176.

Hoge, C. W., Castro, C. B., Messer, S. C., McGurk, D., Cotting, D. I., & Koffman, R. L. (2004). Combat duty in Iraq and Afghanistan, mental health problems, and barriers to care. *New England Journal of Medicine, 351,* 13–22

Holguin, G., & Hansen, D. J. (2003). The "sexually abused" child: Potential mechanisms of adverse influences of such a label. *Aggressive and Violent Behavior, 8,* 645–670.

Holmes, E. P., & Rivers, L. P. (1998). Individual strategies for dealing with the stigma of severe mental illness. *Cognitive and Behavioral Practice, 5,* 231–239.

Hovland, C., & Sears, R. R. (1940). Minor studies in aggression. VI: Correlation of lynchings with economic indices. *Journal of Psychology, 9,* 301–310.

Huffine, C., & Clausen, J. (1979). Madness and work: Short- and long-term effects of mental illness on occupational careers. *Social Forces, 57,* 1049–1062.

Hyman, S. E. (2002). Neuroscience, genetics, and the future of psychiatric diagnosis. *Psychopathology, 35,* 139–144.

Hyman, S. E. (2004). Introduction: The brain's special status. *Cerebrum: The Dana Forum on Brain Science, 6*(4), 9–12.

Jamison, K. R. (1993). *Touched with fire: Manic-depressive illness and the artistic temperament.* New York: Free Press.

Jamison, K. R. (1995). *An unquiet mind: A memoir of moods and madness.* New York: Free Press.

Jamison, K. R. (1998). Stigma of manic depression: A psychologist's experience. *Lancet, 352,* 1053.

Jamison, K. R. (2006). The many stigmas of mental illness. *Lancet, 367,* 533–534.

Jemelka, R., Trupin, E., & Chiles, J. A. (1989). The mentally ill in prisons: A review. *Hospital and Community Psychiatry, 40,* 481–491.

Johnson, D. L. (1989). Schizophrenia as a brain disease: Implications for psychologists and families. *American Psychologist, 44,* 553–555.

Johnson, M. (1999). Cortical plasticity in normal and abnormal cognitive development: Evidence and working hypotheses. *Development and Psychopathology, 11,* 419–437.

Johnson, S. L. (2005). Mania and dysregulation in goal pursuit: A review. *Clinical Psychology Review, 25,* 241–262.

Joint Commission on Mental Illness and Health. (1961). *Action for mental health: Final report of the Joint Commission on Mental Illness and Health.* New York: Basic Books.

Jones, E. E., Farina, A., Hastorf, A. H., Markus, H., Miller, D. T., & Scott, R. A. (1984). *Social stigma: The psychology of marked relationships.* New York: Freeman.

Jorm, A. F., Korten, A. E., Jacomb, P. A., Christensen, H., & Henderson, S. (1999). Attitudes toward people with a mental disorder: A survey of the Australian public and health professionals. *Australian and New Zealand Journal of Psychiatry, 33,* 77–83.

Josselson, R., Lieblich, A., & McAdams, D. P. (Eds.). (2003). *Up close and personal: The teaching and learning of narrative research.* Washington, DC: American Psychological Association.

Jost, J. T., & Banaji, M. R. (1994). The role of stereotyping in system justification and the production of false consciousness. *British Journal of Social Psychology, 33,* 1–27.

Jussim, L., Palumbo, P., Chatman, C., Madon, S., & Smith, A. (2000). Stigma and self-fulfilling prophecies. In T. F. Heatherton, R. E. Kleck, M. R. Hebl, & J. G. Hull (Eds.), *The social psychology of stigma* (pp. 374–418). New York: Guilford.

Kandel, E. R., Mednick, S. A., Kirkegaard-Sorensen, L., Hutchings, B., Knop, J., Rosenberg, R., et al. (1988). IQ as a protective factor for subjects at a high risk for antisocial behavior. *Journal of Consulting and Clinical Psychology, 56,* 224–226.

Kaplan, B. (Ed.) (1964). *The inner world of mental illness.* New York: Harper & Row.

Katz, I. (1981). *Stigma: A social psychological analysis.* Mahwah, NJ: Erlbaum.

Katz, I., Wackenhut, J., & Hass, R. G. (1986). Racial ambivalence, value duality, and behavior. In J. F. Dovidio & S. L. Gaertner (Eds.), *Prejudice, discrimination, and racism* (pp. 35–60). San Diego: Academic Press.

Kazdin, A. E. (2000). *Psychotherapy for children and adolescents: Directions for research and practice.* New York: Oxford University Press.

Kazdin, A. E., & Wassell, G. (1998). Treatment completion and therapeutic change among children referred for outpatient therapy. *Professional Psychology: Research and Practice, 29,* 332–340.

Kazdin, A. E., & Weisz, J. R. (Eds.) (2003). *Evidence-based psychotherapies for children and adolescents*. New York: Guilford.

Keane, M. (1990). Contemporary beliefs about mental illness among medical students. *Academic Psychiatry, 14*, 172–177.

Keane, M. (1991). Acceptance vs. rejection: Nursing students' attitudes about mental illness. *Perspectives in Psychiatric Care, 27*, 13–18.

Kessler, R. C., Berglund, P., Demler, O., Jin, R., & Walters, E. E. (2005). Lifetime prevalence and age-of-onset distributions of *DSM-IV* disorders in the National Comorbidity Survey replication. *Archives of General Psychiatry, 62*, 593–602.

Kessler, R. C., Chiu, W. T., Demler, O., & Walters, E. E. (2005). Prevalence, severity, and comoribidty of 12-month *DSM-IV* disorders in the National Comorbidity Survey replication. *Archives of General Psychiatry, 62*, 617–627.

Keusch, G. T., Wilentz, J., & Kleinman, A. (2006). Stigma and global health: Developing a research agenda. *Lancet, 367*, 525–527.

Kevles, D. J. (1985). *In the name of eugenics: Genetics and the uses of human heredity*. New York: Knopf.

Kim-Cohen, J., Moffitt, T. E., Caspi, A., & Taylor, A. (2004). Genetic and environmental processes in young children's resilience and vulnerability to socioeconomic deprivation. *Child Development, 75*, 651–668.

Kitayama, S. (2002). Culture and basic psychological processes—Toward a system view of culture: Comment on Oyserman et al. (2002). *Psychological Bulletin, 128*, 89–96.

Klasen, H. (2000). A name, what's in a name? The medicalization of hyperactivity, revisited. *Harvard Review of Psychiatry, 7*, 339–344.

Knapp, C. (1997). *Drinking: A love story*. New York: Dell.

Kolodziej, M. E., & Johnson, B. T. (1996). Interpersonal contact and acceptance of persons with psychiatric disorders: A research synthesis. *Journal of Consulting and Clinical Psychology, 64*, 1387–1396.

Kramer, P. D. (2005). *Against depression*. New York: Viking.

Krauss, S. J. (1995). Attitudes and the prediction of behavior: A meta-analysis of the empirical literature. *Personality and Social Psychology Bulletin, 21*, 58–75.

Kreisman, D. E., & Joy, V. D. (1974). Family response to the mental illness of a relative: A review of the literature. *Schizophrenia Bulletin, 1*(10), 34–57.

Kunda, Z., & Oleson, K. E. (1997). When exceptions prove the rule: How extremity of deviance determines the impact of deviant experiences on stereotypes. *Journal of Personality and Social Psychology, 72*, 965–979.

Kurzban, R., & Leary, M. R. (2001). Evolutionary origins of stigmatization: The functions of social exclusion. *Psychological Bulletin, 127*, 187–208.

Kutchins, H., & Kirk, S. A. (1997). *Making us crazy: DSM: The psychiatric bible and the creation of mental disorders*. New York: Free Press.

Lachenmeyer, N. (2000). *The outsider: A journey into my father's struggle with madness*. New York: Broadway Books.

Laing, R. D. (1965). *The divided self: A study in sanity and madness*. Baltimore: Penguin.

Lakoff, G. (1996). *Moral politics: What conservatives know that liberals don't*. Chicago: University of Chicago Press.

Lakoff, G. (2004). *Don't think of an elephant: Know your values and frame the debate: The essential guide for progressives.* White River Junction, VT: Chelsea Green.

Lamb, H. R., & Weinberger, L. E. (1998). Persons with severe mental illness in jails and prisons: A review. *Psychiatric Services, 49,* 483–492.

Lamy, R. E. (1966). Social consequences of mental illness. *Journal of Consulting Psychology, 30,* 450–455.

Langlois, J. H., Kalakonis, L., Rubenstein, A. J., Larson, A., Hallam, M., & Smart, M. (2000). Maxims or myths of beauty: A meta-analytic and theoretical review. *Psychological Bulletin, 126,* 390–423.

Lauber, C., Anthony, M., Ajdacic-Gross, V., & Rossler, W. (2004). What about psychiatrists' attitude to mentally ill people? *European Psychiatry, 19,* 423–427.

Lazarus, R. S., & Folkman, S. (1984). *Stress, appraisal, and coping.* New York: Springer.

Lee, S., Lee, M. T. Y., Ching, M. Y. L., & Kleinman, A. (2005). Experience of social stigma by people with schizophrenia in Hong Kong. *British Journal of Psychiatry, 186,* 153–157.

Leete, E. (1992). The stigmatized patient. In P. J. Fink & A. Tasman (Eds.), *Stigma and mental illness* (pp. 17–25). Washington, DC: American Psychiatric Press.

Lefley, H. P. (1989). Family burden and family stigma in major mental illness. *American Psychologist, 44,* 556–560.

Lefley, H. P. (1992). The stigmatized family. In P. J. Fink & A. Tasman (Eds.), *Stigma and mental illness* (pp. 127–138). Washington, DC: American Psychiatric Press.

Lehman, S., Joy, V., Kreisman, D., & Simmons, S. (1976). Responses to viewing symptomatic behaviors and labeling of prior mental illness. *Journal of Community Psychology, 4,* 327–334.

Lerner, R. (1980). *The belief in a just world: A fundamental delusion.* New York: Plenum.

Levenson, R. (2005, February). An exercise in NIH-ilism. *American Psychological Society Observer, 18(2),* 3.

Levy, C. J. (2002a, April 28). Broken homes: A final destination: For mentally ill, death, and misery. *New York Times,* p. A1.

Levy, C. J. (2002b, April 29). Broken homes: Where hope dies: Here is squalor and chaos. *New York Times,* p. A1.

Levy, C. J. (2002c, April 30). Broken homes: The operators: Voiceless, defenseless, and a source of cash. *New York Times,* p. A1.

Lewis, K. N., Davis, C. S., Walker, B. J., & Jennings, R. L. (1984). Attractive vs. unattractive clients: Mediating influences on counselors' perceptions. *Journal of Counseling Psychology, 28,* 309–314.

Lieberman, J. A., Perkins, D., Belger, A., Chakos, M., Jarskog, F., Boteva, K., et al. (2001). The early stages of schizophrenia: Speculations on pathogenesis, pathophysiology, and therapeutic approaches. *Biological Psychiatry, 50,* 884–897.

Lilienfeld, S. O., & Marino, L. (1999). Essentialism revisited: Evolutionary theory and the concept of mental disorder. *Journal of Abnormal Psychology, 108,* 400–411.

Lin, K., & Kleinman, A. (1988). Psychopathology and the clinical course of schizophrenia: A cross-cultural perspective. *Schizophrenia Bulletin, 14,* 555–567.

Lin, K., Kleinman, A., Andrews, H., & Cullen, F. T. (1994). The violent illegal behavior of mental patients reconsidered. *American Sociological Review, 57,* 275–292.

Link, B. G., & Cullen, F. T. (1983). Reconsidering the social rejection of ex-mental patients: Levels of attitudinal response. *American Journal of Community Psychology, 11,* 261–273.

Link, B. G., Cullen, F. T., Frank, J., & Wozniak, J. (1987). The social rejection of ex-mental patients: Understanding why labels matter. *American Journal of Sociology, 92,* 1461–1500.

Link, B. G., Monahan, J., Stueve, A., & Cullen, F. T. (1999). Real in their consequences: A social approach to understanding the association between psychiatric symptoms and violence. *American Sociological Review, 64,* 316–322.

Link, B. G., & Phelan, J. C. (2001a). Conceptualizing stigma. *Annual Review of Sociology, 27,* 363–385.

Link, B. G., & Phelan, J. C. (2001b, September). *On stigma and its public health implications.* Paper presented at Stigma and Global Health: Developing a Research Agenda. Bethesda, MD.

Link, B. G., Phelan, J. C., Bresnahan, M., Stueve, A., & Pescosolido, B. A. (1999). Public conceptions of mental illness: Labels, causes, dangerousness, and social distance. *American Journal of Public Health, 89,* 1328–1333.

Link, B. G., Struening, E. L., Rahav, M., Phelan, J., & Nuttbrock, L. (1997). On stigma and its consequences: Evidence from a longitudinal study of men with dual diagnoses of mental illness and substance abuse. *Journal of Health and Social Behavior, 38,* 177–190.

Link, B. G., Yang, L. H., Phelan, J. C., & Collins, P. Y. (2004). Measuring mental illness stigma. *Schizophrenia Bulletin, 30,* 511–541.

Littlewood, R. (1998). Cultural variation in the stigmatisation of mental illness. *Lancet, 352,* 1056–1057.

Luthar, S., Cicchetti, D., & Becker, B. (2000). The construct of resilience: A critical evaluation and guide for future work. *Child Development, 71,* 543–562.

Lynch, M., & Cicchetti, D. (1998). An ecological-transactional analysis of children and contexts: The longitudinal interplay among child maltreatment, community violence, and children's symptomatology. *Development and Psychopathology, 10,* 235–257.

MacDonald, J. D., & MacIntyre, P. D. (1999). A rose is a rose: Effects of label change, education, and sex on attitudes toward mental disabilities. *Journal of Developmental Disabilities, 6,* 15–31.

MacDonald-Wilson, K. L., Rogers, E. S., Massaro, J. M., Lyass, A., & Crean, T. (2002). An investigation of reasonable workplace accommodations for people with psychiatric disabilities: Quantitative findings from a multi-site study. *Community Mental Health Journal, 38,* 35–50.

Macrae, C. N., Bodenhausen, G. V., Milne, A. B., & Jetten, J. (1994). Out of mind but not out of sight: Stereotypes on the rebound. *Journal of Personality and Social Psychology, 67,* 808–817.

Macrae, C. N., Milne, A. B., & Bodenhausen, G. V. (1994). Stereotypes as energy-saving devices: A peek inside the cognitive toolbox. *Journal of Personality and Social Psychology, 66,* 34–47.

Maher, W. B., & Maher, B. A. (1985). Psychopathology: From ancient times to the eighteenth century. In G. A. Kimble & K. Schlesinger (Eds.), *Topics in the history of psychology: Vol. 2* (pp. 251–294). Mahwah, NJ: Erlbaum.

Major, B., Kaiser, C. R., & McCoy, S. K. (2003). It's not my fault: When and why attributions to prejudice protect self-esteem. *Personality and Social Psychology Bulletin, 29,* 772–781.

Major, B., & O'Brien, L. T. (2005). The social psychology of stigma. *Annual Review of Psychology, 56,* 393–421.

Mankowski, E., & Rappaport, J. (1995). Stories, identity, and the psychological sense of community. In R. S. Wyer (Ed.), *Advances in social cognition: Vol. 8* (pp. 211–226). Mahwah, NJ: Erlbaum.

Markowitz, F. E. (1998). The effects of stigma on the psychological well-being and life satisfaction of persons with mental illness. *Journal of Health and Social Behavior, 39,* 335–347.

Markowitz, F. E. (2005). Sociological models of mental illness stigma: Progress and prospects. In P. W. Corrigan (Ed.), *On the stigma of mental illness: Practical strategies for research and social change* (pp. 129–144). Washington, DC: American Psychological Association.

Marshall, C. (2005, August 20). Panel on prison rape hears victims' chilling accounts. *New York Times,* p. A9.

Martin, J., Pescosolido, B., & Tuch, S. (2000). Of fear and loathing: The role of "disturbing behavior," labels, and causal attributions in shaping public attitudes toward people with mental illness. *Journal of Health and Social Behavior, 41,* 208–223.

Masten, A., Best, K., & Garmezy, N. (1990). Resilience and development: Contributions from the study of children who overcome adversity. *Development and Psychopathology, 2,* 425–444.

Matas, M., el-Guebaly, N., Harper, D., Green, M., & Peterkin, A. (1986). Mental illness and the media: Part 2. Content analysis of press coverage on mental health topics. *Canadian Journal of Psychiatry, 31,* 431–433.

McConahay, J. B. (1986). Modern racism, ambivalence, and the Modern Racism Scale. In J. F. Dovidio & S. L. Gaertner (Eds.), *Prejudice, discrimination, and racism* (pp. 91–125). San Diego: Academic Press.

McGuffin, P., Riley, B., & Plomin, R. (2001). Toward behavioral genomics. *Science, 291,* 1232–1249.

McKown, C., & Weinstein, R. S. (2003). The development and consequences of stereotype consciousness in middle childhood. *Child Development, 74,* 498–515.

Mechanic, D. (1998). Cultural and organizational aspects of applications of the Americans with Disabilities Act to persons with psychiatric disabilities. *Millbank Quarterly, 76,* 5–23.

Mehta, S., & Farina, A. (1997). Is being "sick" really better? Effect of the disease view of mental disorder on stigma. *Journal of Social and Clinical Psychology, 16,* 405–419.

Mendoza-Denton, R., & Mischel, W. (in press). Integrating system approaches to culture and personality: The cultural cognitive-affective processing system

(C-CAPS). In S. Kitayama & D. Cohen (Eds.), *Handbook of cultural psychology*. New York: Guilford.

Mendoza-Denton, R., Page-Gould, E., & Pietrzak, J. (2006). Mechanisms for coping with race-based rejection expectations. In S. Levin & C. Van Laar (Eds.), *Stigma and group inequality: Social psychological approaches* (pp. 151–169). Mahwah, NJ: Erlbaum.

Merton, R. K. (1948). The self-fulfilling prophecy. *Antioch Review, 8,* 193–210.

Milgram, S. (1974). *Obedience to authority.* New York: Harper & Row.

Milich, R., McAninch, C. B., & Harris, M. (1992). Effects of stigmatizing information on children's peer relationships: Believing is seeing. *School Psychology Review, 21,* 400–409.

Miller, C. T., & Major, B. (2000). Coping with stigma and prejudice. In T. F. Heatherton, R. E. Kleck, M. R. Hebl, & J. G. Hull (Eds.), *The social psychology of stigma* (pp. 243–272). New York: Guilford.

Miller, G. (2006). The unseen: Mental illness's global toll. *Science, 311,* 458–461.

Mintz, J., Drake, K. E., & Crits-Cristoph, P. (1996). Efficacy and effectiveness of psychotherapy: Two paradigms, one science. *American Psychologist, 58,* 1084–1085.

Mirabi, M., Weinman, M. L., Magnetti, S. M., & Keppler, K. N. (1985). Professional attitudes toward the chronically mentally ill. *Hospital and Community Psychology, 36,* 404–405.

Monahan, J. (1992). Mental disorder and violent behavior: Perceptions and evidence. *American Psychologist, 47,* 511–521.

Monteith, M. J., Sherman, J. W., & Devine, P. G. (1998). Suppression as a stereotype control strategy. *Personality and Social Psychology Review, 2,* 63–82.

Moorman, M. (2002). *My sister's keeper: Learning to cope with a sibling's mental illness.* New York: Norton.

Mora, G. (1992). Stigma during the medieval and Renaissance periods. In P. J. Fink & A. Tasman (Eds.), *Stigma and mental illness* (pp. 41–57). Washington, DC: American Psychiatric Press.

Morrison, J. K. (1980). The public's current beliefs about mental illness: Serious obstacle to effective community psychology. *American Journal of Community Psychology, 8,* 697–707.

Moynihan, R., & Cassels, A. (2005). *Selling sickness: How the world's biggest pharmaceutical companies are turning us all into patients.* New York: Nation Books.

MTA Cooperative Group. (1999a). Fourteen-month randomized clinical trial of treatment strategies for attention-deficit hyperactivity disorder. *Archives of General Psychiatry, 56,* 1073–1086.

MTA Cooperative Group. (1999b). Moderators and mediators of treatment response for children with ADHD: The MTA Study. *Archives of General Psychiatry, 56,* 1088–1096.

Muhlbauer, S. (2002). Experiences of stigma by families with mentally ill family members. *Journal of the American Psychiatric Nurses Association, 8,* 76–83.

Mukherjee, R., Fialho, A., Wijetunge, A., Checinski, T., & Surgenor, T. (2002). The stigmatisation of psychiatric illness: The attitudes of medical students and doctors in a London teaching hospital. *Psychiatric Bulletin, 26,* 178–181.

Murray, C. J., & López, A. D. (Eds.). (1996). *The global burden of disease and injury series, Vol. 1. A comprehensive assessment of mortality and disability from diseases, injuries, and risk factors in 1990 and projected to 2020.* Cambridge, MA: Harvard University Press.

Myers, D. (1996). *Social psychology* (4th ed.). New York: McGraw-Hill.

Myers, M., & Fine, C. (2003). Suicide in physicians: Toward prevention. *Medscape General Medicine, 5.* Retrieved from http://www.medscape.com/viewarticle1462619

Nairn, R. G., & Coverdale, J. H. (2005). People never see us living this well: An appraisal of the personal stories about mental illness in a prospective print media sample. *Australian and New Zealand Journal of Psychology, 38,* 281–287.

Nathan, P. E., & Gorman, J. M. (Eds.). (2002). *A guide to treatments that work* (2nd ed.). New York: Oxford University Press.

Neale, J. M., & Oltmanns, T. (1980). *Schizophrenia.* New York: Wiley.

Neff, J. A., & Husaini, B. A. (1985). Lay images of mental illness: Social knowledge and tolerance of the mentally ill. *Journal of Community Psychology, 13,* 3–12.

Neuberg, S. L., Smith, D. M., & Asher, T. (2000). Why people stigmatize: Toward a biocultural framework. In T. F. Heatherton, R. E. Kleck, M. R. Hebl, & J. G. Hull (Eds.), *The social psychology of stigma* (pp. 31–61). New York: Guilford.

Neugebauer, R. (1979). Medieval and early modern theories of mental illness. *Archives of General Psychiatry, 36,* 477–483.

Neugeboren, J. (1998). *Imagining Robert: My brother, madness, and survival.* New York: Holt.

New Freedom Commission on Mental Health. (2003). *Achieving the promise: Transforming mental health care in America. Final Report.* DHHS Publication No. SMA-03–3832. Rockville, MD: SAMSHA. Retrieved from http://www.mentalhealthcommission.gov/reports

Nisbett, R. E., & Wilson, T. D. (1977). Telling more than we can know: Verbal reports on mental processes. *Psychological Review, 84,* 231–259.

Norvitilis, J. M., Scime, M., & Lee, J. S. (2002). Courtesy stigma in mothers of children with attention deficit/hyperactivity disorder: A preliminary investigation. *Journal of Attention Disorders, 6,* 61–68.

Nuland, S. P. (2005, August 11). Killing cures. *New York Review of Books,* pp. 23–25.

Nunnally, J. C. (1961). *Popular conceptions of mental health: Their development and change.* New York: Holt, Rinehart, and Winston.

Ochs, E., & Capps, L. (2001). *Living narrative: Creating lives in everyday storytelling.* Cambridge, MA: Harvard University Press.

O'Day, B., & Killeen, M. (2002). Research on the lives of people with disabilities: The emerging importance of qualitative research methodologies. *Journal of Disability Policy Studies, 13,* 9–15.

Oestman, M., & Kjellin, L. (2002). Stigma by association: Psychological factors in relatives of people with mental illness. *British Journal of Psychiatry, 181,* 494–498.

Ohaeri, J. U., & Abdullahi, A. (2001). The opinion of caregivers on aspects of schizophrenia and major affective disorders in a Nigerian setting. *Social Psychiatry and Psychiatric Epidemiology, 36,* 403–409.

Olmstead, D. W., & Durham, K. (1976). Stability of mental health attitudes: A semantic differential study. *Journal of Health and Social Behavior, 17,* 35–44.

Oltmanns, T. F., & Emery, R. E. (1998). *Abnormal psychology* (2nd ed.). Upper Saddle River, NJ: Prentice Hall.

Osgood, C. E., Suci, G. J., & Tannenbaum, P. H. (1957). *The measurement of meaning.* Urbana: University of Illinois Press.

Oskamp, S. (2000). Multiple paths to reducing prejudice and discrimination. In S. Oskamp (Ed.), *Reducing prejudice and discrimination: The Claremont Symposium on Applied Social Psychology* (pp. 1–19). Mahwah, NJ: Erlbaum.

Otey, E., & Fenton, W. S. (2004). Editors' introduction: Building mental illness stigma research. *Schizophrenia Bulletin, 30,* 473–475.

Ottati, V., Bodenhausen, G. V., & Newman, L. S. (2005). Social psychological models of mental illness stigma. In P. W. Corrigan (Ed.), *On the stigma of mental illness: Practical strategies for research and social change* (pp. 99–128). Washington, DC: American Psychological Association.

Page, S. (1995). Effects of the mental illness label in 1993: Acceptance and rejection in the community. *Journal of Health and Social Policy, 7,* 61–68.

PatientView. (2004a, February). Part 1: Campaigners fight to improve mental healthcare services: The social and policy battles. *HSC News International, 4,* 8–65.

PatientView. (2004b, February). Stamp Out Stigma. *HSC News International, 4,* 67–72.

Pauley, J. (2004). *Skywriting: A life out of the blue.* New York: Random House.

Pavenstedt, E. (1965). A comparison of the childrearing environment of upper-lower and very low-lower class families. *American Journal of Orthopsychiatry, 35,* 89–98.

Pear, R. (2000, April 18). Many employers found to violate law regarding parity for mental health coverage. *New York Times,* p. A18.

Pear, R. (2006, January 21). Medicare woes take high toll on mentally ill: Denied drugs, many face hospitalization. *New York Times,* pp. A1, A9.

Penn, D. J., & Corrigan, P. W. (2002). The effects of stigma suppression on psychiatric stigma. *Schizophrenia Research, 55,* 269–276.

Penn, D. L., Judge, A., Jamieson, P., Garczynski, J., Hennessy, M., & Romer, R. (2005). Stigma. In D. L. Evans, E. B. Foa, R. E. Gur, H. Hendin, C. P. O'Brien, M. E. P. Seligman, et al. (Eds.), *Treating and preventing adolescent mental health disorders: What we know and what we don't know: A research agenda for improving the mental health of our youth* (pp. 532–543). New York: Oxford University Press.

Penn, D. L., & Martin, J. (1998). The stigma of severe mental illness: Some potential solutions for a recalcitrant problem. *Psychiatric Quarterly, 69,* 235–247.

Penn, D., L., & Nowlin-Drummond, A. (2001). Politically correct labels and schizophrenia: A rose by any other name? *Schizophrenia Bulletin, 27,* 197–203.

Pennebaker, J. W., & Seagal, J. D. (1999). Forming a story: The health benefits of narrative. *Journal of Clinical Psychology, 55,* 1243–1254.

Perlick, D. A., Rosenheck, R. A., Clarkin, J. F., Maciejewski, P. K., Sirey, J., Struening, E., et al. (2004). Impact of family burden and affective response on clinical outcome among patients with bipolar disorder. *Psychiatric Services, 55*, 1029–1035.

Perlick, D. A., Rosenheck, R. A., Clarkin, J. F., Sirey, J. A., Salahi, J., Struening, E. L., et al. (2001). Stigma as a barrier to recovery: Adverse effects of perceived stigma and social adaptation of persons diagnosed with bipolar affective disorder. *Psychiatric Services, 52*, 1627–1632.

Pescosolido, B. A., Monahan, J., Link, B. G., Stueve, A., & Kikuzawa, S. (1999). The public's view of the competence, dangerousness, and need for legal coercion of persons with mental health problems. *American Journal of Public Health, 89*, 1339–1345.

Pettigrew, T. F., & Meertens, R. W. (1995). Subtle and blatant prejudice in Western Europe. *European Journal of Social Psychology, 25*, 57–76.

Pettigrew, T. F., & Tropp, L. R. (2000). Does intergroup contact reduce prejudice? Recent meta-analytic findings. In S. Oskamp (Ed.), *Reducing prejudice and discrimination: The Claremont Symposium on Applied Social Psychology* (pp. 93–114). Mahwah, NJ: Erlbaum.

Phares, V. (2003). *Understanding abnormal child psychology*. New York: Wiley.

Phelan, J. C. (2005). Geneticization of deviant behavior and consequences for stigma: The case of mental illness. *Journal of Health and Social Behavior, 46*, 307–322.

Phelan, J. C., Bromet, E., & Link, B. (1998). Psychiatric illness and family stigma. *Schizophrenia Bulletin, 24*, 115–126.

Phelan, J. C., Cruz-Rojas, R., & Reiff, M. (2002). Genes and stigma: The connection between perceived genetic etiology and attitudes and beliefs about mental illness. *Psychiatric Rehabilitation Skills, 6*, 159–185.

Phelan, J. C., & Link, B. G. (1998). The growing belief that people with mental illness are violent: The role of the dangerousness criterion for civil commitment. *Social Psychiatry and Psychiatric Epidemiology, 33*(Suppl. 1), S7–S12.

Phelan, J. C., Link, B. G., Stueve, A., & Pescosolido, B. A. (2000). Public conceptions of mental illness in 1950 and 1996: What is mental illness and is it to be feared? *Journal of Health and Social Behavior, 41*, 188–207.

Phillips, D. L. (1963). Rejection: A possible consequence of seeking help for mental disorders. *American Sociological Review, 28*, 963–972.

Phillips, D. L. (1966). Public identification and acceptance of the mentally ill. *American Sociological Review, 29*, 679–687.

Pickles, A., & Angold, A. (2003). Natural categories or fundamental dimensions: On carving nature at its joints and the rearticulation of psychopathology. *Development and Psychopathology, 15*, 529–555.

Pinel, E. C. (2002). Stigma consciousness in intergroup contexts: The power of conviction. *Journal of Experimental Social Psychology, 38*, 178–185.

Piner, K. E., & Kahle, L. R. (1984). Adapting to the stigmatizing label of mental illness: Gone but not forgotten. *Journal of Personality and Social Psychology, 47*, 805–811.

Pinfold, V., Huxley, P., Thornicroft, G., Farmer, P., Toulmin, H., & Graham, T. (2003a). Reducing psychiatric stigma and discrimination: Evaluating an educational intervention with the police force in England. *Social Psychiatry and Psychiatric Epidemiology, 38*, 337–344.

Pinfold, V., Toulmin, H., Thornicroft, G., Huxley, P., Farmer, P., & Graham, T. (2003b). Reducing psychiatric stigma and discrimination: Evaluation of educational interventions in UK secondary schools. *British Journal of Psychiatry, 182,* 342–346.

Polubinskaya, S. V. (2001). Law and psychiatry in Russia: Looking backward and forward. In L. E. Frost & R. J. Bonnie (Eds.), *The evolution of mental health law* (pp. 113–125). Washington, DC: American Psychological Association.

Pratto, F., Sidanius, J., Stalworth, L., & Malle, B. F. (1994). Social dominance orientation: A personality variable prediction social and political attitudes. *Journal of Personality and Social Psychology, 67,* 741–763.

Pyszczynski, T., Greenberg, J., & Solomon, S. (2005). The machine in the ghost: A dual-process model of defense against conscious and unconscious death-related thought. In I. P. Furgus, K. D. Williams, & S. M. Laham (Eds.), *Social motivation: Conscious and unconscious processes* (pp. 41–54). New York: Cambridge University Press.

Quinn, D. M. (2006). Concealable versus conspicuous stigmatized identities. In S. Levin & C. Van Laar (Eds.), *Stigma and group inequality: Social psychological approaches* (pp. 83–103). Mahwah, NJ: Erlbaum.

Quinn, D. M., Kahng, S. K., & Crocker, J. (2004). Discreditable: Stigma effects of revealing mental illness history on test performance. *Personality and Social Psychology Bulletin, 30,* 803–815.

Rabasca, L. (1999, July/August). White House Conference an important "first step." *American Psychological Association Monitor, 30,* 11.

Rabkin, J. G. (1972). Opinions about mental illness: A review of the literature. *Psychological Bulletin, 77,* 153–171.

Rabkin, J. G. (1974). Public attitudes toward mental illness: A review of the literature. *Schizophrenia Bulletin, 1*(10), 9–33.

Raguram, R., Raghu, T. M., Vounatsou, P., & Weiss, M. G. (2004). Schizophrenia and the cultural epidemiology of stigma in Bangalore, India. *Journal of Nervous and Mental Disease, 192,* 734–744.

Ramsey, G. V., & Seipp, M. (1948a). Attitudes and opinions concerning mental illness. *Psychiatric Quarterly, 22,* 428–444.

Ramsey, G. V., & Seipp, M. (1948b). Public opinions and information concerning mental health. *Journal of Clinical Psychology, 4,* 397–406.

Rappaport, J. (2000). Community narratives: Tales of terror and joy. *American Journal of Community Psychology, 28,* 1–24.

Ray, M. C., & Downs, W. R. (1986). An empirical test of labeling theory using longitudinal data. *Journal of Research in Crime and Delinquency, 23,* 169–194.

Read, J. (2002). The need for evidence-based destigmatization programmes. *Incite: The Mental Health Journal of New Zealand, 1,* 10–16.

Read, J., & Baker, S. (1996). *Not just sticks and stones: A survey of stigma, taboo, and discrimination experiences by people with mental health problems.* London: Mind.

Read, J., & Harre, N. (2001). The role of biological and genetic causal beliefs in the stigmatization of "mental patients." *Journal of Mental Health, 10,* 223–235.

Read, J., & Law, A. (1999). The relationship of causal beliefs and contact with users of mental health services to attitudes toward the "mentally ill." *International Journal of Social Psychiatry, 45,* 216–229.

Reinke, R. R., Corrigan, P. W., Leonhard, C., Lundin, R. K., & Kubiak, M. A. (2004). Examining two aspects of contact on the stigma of mental illness. *Journal of Social and Clinical Psychology, 23*, 377–389.

Rhodes, R. (1999). *Why they kill: The discoveries of a maverick criminologist*. New York: Vintage.

Ries, A., & Ries, L. (2002). *The fall of advertising and the rise of PR*. New York: Harper Business.

Rissmiller, D. J., & Rissmiller, J. H. (2006). Evolution of the antipsychiatry movement into mental health consumerism. *Psychiatric Services, 57*, 863–866.

Ritsher, J. B., & Phelan, J. C. (2004). Internalized stigma predicts erosion of morale among psychiatric outpatients. *Psychiatry Research, 129*, 257–265.

Ritterfield, U., & Jin, S. (2006). Addressing media stigma for people experiencing mental illness using an entertainment-education strategy. *Journal of Health Psychology, 11*, 247–267.

Riva, G. (2005). Virtual reality in psychotherapy: A review. *CyberPsychology and Behavior: Special Use of Virtual Environments in Training and Rehabilitation, 8*, 220–230.

Rokeach, M. (1971). Long-range experimental modification of values, attitudes, and behavior. *American Psychologist, 26*, 453–459.

Rootman, I., & Lafave, H. (1969). Are popular attitudes toward the mentally ill changing? *American Journal of Psychiatry, 126*, 261–265.

Rosenfeld, S. (1997). Labeling mental illness: The effects of services and perceived stigma on life satisfaction. *American Sociological Review, 62*, 660–672.

Rosenhan, D. (1973). On being sane in insane places. *Science, 179*, 250–258.

Rosenhan, D., & Seligman, M. E. P. (1994). *Abnormal psychology* (2nd ed.). New York: Norton.

Rudman, L. A., Ashmore, R. D., & Gary, M. L. (2001). "Unlearning" automatic biases: The malleability of implicit prejudice and stereotypes. *Journal of Personality and Social Psychology, 81*, 856–868.

Rutter, M. (1987). Psychosocial resilience and protective mechanisms. *American Journal of Orthopsychiatry, 57*, 316–331.

Rutter, M., & Silberg, J. (2002). Gene-environment interplay in relation to emotional and behavioral disturbance. *Annual Review of Psychology, 53*, 463–490.

Rutter, M., & Sroufe, L. A. (2000). Developmental psychopathology: Concepts and challenges. *Development and Psychopathology, 12*, 265–296.

Sackeim, H. A., Devanand, D. P., & Nobler, M. S. (1995). Electroconvulsive therapy. In F. E. Bloom & D. J. Kupfer (Eds.), *Psychopharmacology: The fourth generation of progress* (pp. 1123–1141). New York: Raven.

Sacks, O. (1985). *The man who mistook his wife for a hat*. London: Duckworth.

Sacks, O. (1996). *An anthropologist on Mars: Seven paradoxical tales*. New York: Vintage.

Sameroff, A. J., & Chandler, M. J. (1975). Reproductive risk and the continuum of caretaking casualty. In F. D. Horowitz (Ed.), *Review of child development research: Vol. 4* (pp. 187–244). Chicago: University of Chicago Press.

Santora, M., & Carey, B. (2005, April 13). Depressed? New York screens people at risk. *New York Times*, pp. A1, A13.

Sarbin, T. R., & Mancuso, J. G. (1970). Failure of a moral enterprise: Attitudes of the public toward mental illness. *Journal of Consulting and Clinical Psychology, 35,* 159–173.

Sartorius, N. (1998). Stigma: What can psychiatrists do about it? *Lancet, 352,* 1058–1059.

Sartorius, N. (1999). One of the last obstacles to better mental health care: The stigma of mental illness. In J. Guimon, W. Fischer, & N. Sartorius (Eds.), *The image of madness: The public facing mental illness and psychiatric treatment* (pp. 138–142). Basel, Switzerland: Karger.

Sartorius, N., & Schulze, H. (2005). *Reducing the stigma of mental illness: A report.* New York: Cambridge University Press.

Scambler, G., & Hopkins, A. (1990). Generating a model of epileptic stigma: The role of qualitative analysis. *Social Science and Medicine, 30,* 1187–1194.

Scheff, T. J. (1974). The labeling theory of mental illness. *American Sociological Review, 39,* 444–452.

Scheff, T. J. (1984). *Being mentally ill: A sociological theory* (2nd ed.). Chicago: Aldine.

Schnittker, J. (2000). Gender and reactions to psychological problems: An examination of social tolerance and perceived dangerousness. *Journal of Health and Social Behavior, 41,* 224–240.

Schulze, T. G., Fangerow, H., & Propping, P. (2004). From degeneration to genetic susceptibility, from eugenics to genethics, from Bezugziffer to LOD score: The history of psychiatric genetics. *International Review of Psychiatry, 16,* 246–259.

Scott, D. J., & Philip, A. E. (1985). Attitudes of psychiatric nurses to treatment and patients. *British Journal of Medical Psychology, 58,* 169–173.

Segal, S. (1978). Attitudes toward the mentally ill: A review. *Social Work, 23,* 211–217.

Shain, R., & Phillips, J. (1991). The stigma of mental illness: Labeling and stereotyping in the news. In L. Wilkins & P. Patterson (Eds.), *Risky business: Communicating issues of science, risk, and public policy* (pp. 61–74). Westport, CT: Greenwood.

Shannonhouse, R. (Ed.). (2000). *Out of her mind: Women writing on madness.* New York: Modern Library.

Shaw, F. (1998). Mistaken identity. *Lancet, 352,* 1050–1051.

Sherif, M., & Sherif, C. W. (1953). *Groups in harmony and tension.* New York: Harper & Row.

Shibre, T., Negash, A., Kullgren, G., Kebede, D., Alem, A., Fekadu, A., et al. (2001). Perceptions of stigma among family members of individuals with schizophrenia and major affective disorders in rural Ethiopia. *Social Psychiatry and Psychiatric Epidemiology, 36,* 299–303.

Shields, B. (2005). *Down came the rain.* New York: Hyperion.

Sibicky, M., & Dovidio, J. F. (1986). Stigma of psychological therapy: Stereotypes, interpersonal reactions, and self-fulfilling prophecies. *Journal of Counseling Psychology, 33,* 148–154.

Sidanius, J., & Pratto, F. (1999). *Social dominance: An intergroup theory of social hierarchy and oppression.* New York: Cambridge University Press.

Sirey, J. A., Bruce, M. L., Alexopoulos, G., Perlick, D., Raue, P., Friedman, S. J., et al. (2001). Perceived stigma as a predictor of treatment discontinuation in young and older outpatients with depression. *American Journal of Psychiatry, 158,* 479–481.

Smart, L., & Wegner, D. M. (2000). The hidden costs of hidden stigma. In T. F. Heatherton, R. E. Kleck, M. R. Hebl, & J. G. Hull (Eds.), *The social psychology of stigma* (pp. 220–242). New York: Guilford.

Smith, B. (Ed.). (2003). *John Searle: Contemporary philosophy in focus.* New York: Cambridge University Press.

Smith, C. S. (2005, September 29). Abuse of electroshock found in Turkish mental hospitals. *New York Times,* p. A3.

Snow, R. P. (1983). *Creating media culture.* Thousand Oaks, CA: Sage.

Solomon, S., Greenberg, J., & Pyszczynski, T. (1991). A terror management theory of social behavior: The psychological functions of self-esteem and cultural worldviews. In M. P. Zanna (Ed.), *Advances in experimental social psychology: Vol. 24* (pp. 93–159). San Diego: Academic Press.

Solomon, S., Greenberg, J., & Pyszczynski, T. (2000). Pride and prejudice: Fear of death and social behavior. *Current Directions in Psychological Science, 9,* 200–204.

Sommer, R., Clifford, J. S., & Norcross, J. C. (1998). A bibliography of mental patients' autobiographies: An update and classification system. *American Journal of Psychiatry, 155,* 1261–1264.

Sontag, D. (2002, September 15). When politics is personal. *New York Times Sunday Magazine,* pp. 90–93, 115.

Sontag, S. (1978/1989). *Illness as metaphor and AIDS and its metaphors.* New York: Doubleday.

Spitzer, A., & Cameron, C. (1995). School-age children's perceptions of mental illness. *Western Journal of Nursing Research, 17,* 398–415.

Spitzer, R. (1981). The diagnostic status of homosexuality in *DSM-III:* A reformulation of issues. *American Journal of Psychiatry, 138,* 210–125.

Sroufe, L. A. (1989). Pathways to adaptation and maladaptation: Psychopathology as developmental deviation. In D. Cicchetti (Ed.), *Rochester Symposium on Developmental Psychopathology: Vol. 1. The emergence of a discipline* (pp. 13–40). Hillsdale, NJ: Erlbaum.

Stangor, C., & Crandall, C. S. (2000). Threat and the social construction of stigma. In T. F. Heatherton, R. E. Kleck, M. R. Hebl, & J. G. Hull (Eds.), *The social psychology of stigma* (pp. 62–87). New York: Guilford.

Steadman, H. J., Mulvey, E. P., Monahan, J., Robbins, P. C., Appelbaum, P. S., Grisso, J., et al. (1998). Violence by people discharged from acute psychiatric inpatient facilities and by others in the same neighborhoods. *Archives of General Psychiatry, 55,* 393–401.

Steele, C. M. (1997). A threat in the air: How stereotypes shape intellectual identity and performance. *American Psychologist, 52,* 613–629.

Steele, C. M., & Aronson, J. (1995). Stereotype threat and the intellectual test performance of African Americans. *Journal of Personality and Social Psychology, 69,* 797–811.

Steele, C. M., Spencer, S. J., & Aronson, J. (2002). Contending with group image: The psychology of stereotype and social identity threat. In M. P. Zanna (Ed.), *Advances in experimental social psychology: Vol. 34* (pp. 379–440). San Diego: Academic.

Stefan, S. (2001). *Unequal rights: Discrimination against people with mental disabilities and the Americans with Disabilities Act*. Washington, DC: American Psychological Association.

Stefan, S. (2002). *Hollow promises: Employment discrimination against people with mental disabilities*. Washington, DC: American Psychological Association.

Stein, J., & Flexner, S. B. (Eds.) (2001). *Random House Roget's college thesaurus*. New York: Random House.

Stephan, W. G., & Finlay, K. (1999). The role of empathy in improving intergroup relations. *Journal of Social Issues, 55,* 729–743.

Stephan, W. G., & Stephan, C. W. (2000). An integrated threat theory of prejudice. In S. Oskamp (Ed.), *Reducing prejudice and discrimination: The Claremont Symposium on Applied Social Psychology* (pp. 23–45). Mahwah, NJ: Erlbaum.

Sternberg, R. J. (2003). A duplex theory of hate: Development and application to terrorism, massacres, and genocide. *Journal of General Psychology, 7,* 299–328.

Stoessner, I. J., & Mackie, D. M. (1993). Affect and perceived group variability: Implications for stereotyping and prejudice. In D. M. Mackie & D. L. Hamilton (Eds.), *Affect, cognition, and stereotyping: Interactive processes in group perception* (pp. 63–86). San Diego: Academic Press.

Storr, A. (1988). *Churchill's black dog, Kafka's mice, and other phenomena of the human mind*. New York: Grove.

Stout, P. A., Villegas, J., & Jennings, N. A. (2004). Images of mental illness in the media: Identifying gaps in the research. *Schizophrenia Bulletin, 30,* 543–561.

Strauss, J. S. (1989). Subjective experiences of schizophrenia: Toward a new dynamic psychiatry: II. *Schizophrenia Bulletin, 15,* 179–187.

Struch, N., & Schwartz, S. H. (1989). Intergroup aggression: Its predictors and distinctions from ingroup bias. *Journal of Personality and Social Psychology, 56,* 364–373.

Struening, E. L., Perlick, D. A., Link, B. G., Hellman, F. G., Herman, D., & Sirey, J. A. (2001). The extent to which caregivers believe most people devalue consumers and their families. *Psychiatric Services, 52,* 1633–1638.

Struening, E. L., Stueve, A., Vine, P., Kreisman, D. E., Link, B. G., & Herman, D. B. (1995). Factors associated with grief and depressive symptoms in caregivers of people with serious mental illness. In J. R. Greenley (Ed.), *Research in community and mental health: Vol. 8* (pp. 91–124). Greenwich, CT: JAI Press.

Sturm, R., Gresenz, C., Pacula, R., & Wells, K. (1999). Labor force participation by persons with mental illness. *Psychiatric Services, 50,* 1407.

Styron, W. (1990). *Darkness visible: A memoir of madness*. New York: Harper & Row.

Sue, S. (2003). In defense of cultural competency in psychotherapy and treatment. *American Psychologist, 58,* 964–970.

Sugiura, T., Sakamoto, S., Tanaka, E., Tomada, A., & Kitamura, T. (2001). Labeling effect of seishin-bunretsu-byou, the Japanese translation for schizophrenia: An argument for relabeling. *International Journal of Social Psychiatry, 47,* 43–51.

Sullivan, M., Hamilton, T., & Allen, H. (2005). Changing stigma through the media. In P. W. Corrigan (Ed.), *On the stigma of mental illness: Practical strategies for research and social change* (pp. 297–312). Washington, DC: American Psychological Association.

Swanson, J. M., Lerner, M., & Williams, L. (1995). More frequent diagnosis of attention-deficit hyperactivity disorder. *New England Journal of Medicine, 333,* 944.

Szasz, T. S. (1961). *The myth of mental illness: Foundations of a theory of personal conduct.* New York: Hoeber-Harper.

Szmulker, G. I., Burgess, P., Herrman, H., Benson, A., Colusa, S., & Bloch, S. (1996). Caring for relatives with serious mental illness: The development of the experience of caregiving industry. *Social Psychiatry and Psychiatric Epidemiology, 31,* 137–148.

Tajfel, H., & Turner, J. C. (1979). An integrative theory of intergroup conflict. In W. G. Austin & S. Worchel (Eds.), *The social psychology of intergroup relations* (pp. 33–47). Monterey, CA: Brooks/Cole.

Tayman, J. (2006). *The colony: The harrowing true story of the exiles of Molokai.* New York: Scribner.

Teachman, B. A., Gaspinski, K. D., Brownell, K. D., Rawlins, M., & Jeyeran, S. (2003). Demonstrations of implicit anti-fat bias: The impact of providing causal information and evoking empathy. *Health Psychology, 22,* 68–78.

Teachman, B. A., Gregg, A. P., & Woody, S. R. (2001). Implicit associations for fear-related stimuli among individuals with snake and spider fears. *Journal of Abnormal Psychology, 110,* 226–235.

Teachman, B. A., Wilson, J. G., & Komarovskaya, I. (2006). Implicit and explicit stigma of mental illness in diagnosed and healthy samples. *Journal of Social and Clinical Psychology, 25,* 75–95.

Teachman, B. A., & Woody, S. R. (2003). Automatic processing in spider phobia: Implicit fear associations over the course of treatment. *Journal of Abnormal Psychology, 112,* 100–109.

Teplin, L. A., McClelland, G. M., Abram, K. M., & Weiner, D. A. (2005). Crime victimization in adults with severe mental illness: Comparison with the National Crime Victimization Survey. *Archives of General Psychiatry, 62,* 911–921.

Tessler, R., & Gamache, G. (2000). *Family experiences with mental illness.* Westport, CT: Auburn House.

Thara, R., & Srinivasan, T. N. (2000). How stigmatising is schizophrenia in India? *International Journal of Social Psychiatry, 46,* 135–141.

Thompson, A. H., Stuart, H., Bland, R. C., Arbodele-Florez, J., Warner, R., & Dickson, R. A. (2002). Attitudes about schizophrenia from the pilot site of the WPA worldwide campaign against the stigma of schizophrenia. *Social Psychiatry and Psychiatric Epidemiology, 37,* 475–482.

Thompson, E. H., & Doll, W. (1982). The burden of families coping with the mentally ill: An invisible crisis. *Family Relations, 31,* 379–388.

Tooby, J., & Cosmides, L. (1992). The psychological foundations of culture. In J. H. Barkow, L. Cosmides, & J. Tooby (Eds.), *The adapted mind: Evolutionary psychology and the generation of culture* (pp. 19–136). New York: Oxford University Press.

Torrey, E. F. (1997). *Out of the shadows: Confronting America's mental illness crisis.* New York: Wiley.

Torrey, E. F., & Miller, J. (2001). *The invisible plague: The rise of mental illness from 1750 to the present*. New Brunswick, NJ: Rutgers University Press.

Tringo, J. L. (1970). The hierarchy of preference toward disability groups. *Journal of Special Education, 4*, 295–306.

Tsang, H. W. H., Tam, P. K. C., Chan, F., & Cheung, W. M. (2003). Stigmatizing attitudes toward individuals with mental illness in Hong Kong: Implications for their recovery. *Journal of Community Psychology, 31*, 338–396.

Twenge, J., & Crocker, J. (2002). Race, ethnicity, and self-esteem: Meta-analyses comparing whites, blacks, Hispanics, Asians, and Native Americans, including a commentary on Gray-Little and Hafdahl. *Psychological Bulletin, 128*, 371–408.

U.S. Department of Health and Human Services. (1999). *Mental health: A report of the surgeon general*. Rockville, MD: Author.

U.S. Department of Health and Human Services. (2001). *Mental health: Culture, race, and ethnicity, a supplement to mental health: A report of the Surgeon General*. Rockville, MD: Author.

Vanden Boom, D. C., & Lustig, D. C. (1997). The relationship between employment status and quality of life for individuals with severe and persistent mental illness. *Journal of Applied Rehabilitation Counseling, 28*, 4–8.

Wahl, O. F. (1992). Mass media images of mental illness: A review of the literature. *Journal of Community Psychology, 20*, 343–352.

Wahl, O. F. (1995). *Media madness: Public images of mental illness*. New Brunswick, NJ: Rutgers University Press.

Wahl, O. F. (1999a). Mental health consumers' experience of stigma. *Schizophrenia Bulletin, 25*, 467–478.

Wahl, O. F. (1999b). *Telling is risky business: Mental health consumers confront stigma*. New Brunswick, NJ: Rutgers University Press.

Wahl, O. F. (2002). Children's views of mental illness: A review of the literature. *Psychiatric Rehabilitation Services, 6*, 134–158.

Wahl, O. F. (2003). Depictions of mental illnesses in children's media. *Journal of Mental Health, 12*, 249–258.

Wahl, O. F., & Harman, C. R. (1989). Family views of stigma. *Schizophrenia Bulletin, 15*, 131–139.

Wahl, O. F., & Lefkowitz, J. Y. (1989). Impact of a television film on attitudes toward mental illness. *American Journal of Community Psychology, 17*, 521–528.

Wahl, O. F., & Roth, R. (1982). Television images of mental illness: Results of a metropolitan Washington media watch. *Journal of Broadcasting, 26*, 599–605.

Wahl, O. F., Ward, A., & Richards, R. (2002). Newspaper coverage of mental illness: Is it changing? *Psychiatric Rehabilitation Skills, 6*, 9–31.

Wakefield, J. C. (1992). Disorder as harmful dysfunction: A conceptual critique of *DSM-III-R*'s definition of mental disorder. *Psychological Review, 99*, 232–247.

Wakefield, J. C. (1999). Evolutionary vs. prototype analyses of the concept of disorder. *Journal of Abnormal Psychology, 108*, 374–399.

Walker, E. F., & Diforio, D. (1997). Schizophrenia: A neural diathesis-stress model. *Psychological Review, 104*, 667–685.

Walker, I., & Read, J. (2002). The differential effectiveness of psychosocial and biogenetic causal explanations in reducing negative attitudes toward "mental illness." *Psychiatry: Interpersonal and Biological Processes, 65,* 313–325.

Wang, P. S., Berglund, P., Olfson, M., Pincus, H. A., Wells, K. B., & Kessler, R. C. (2005). Failure and delay in initial treatment contact in the National Comorbidity Survey replication. *Archives of General Psychiatry, 62,* 603–613.

Ward, M. J. (1946). *The snake pit.* New York: Random House.

Warner, R. (1999). Combatting the alienation experienced by people with mental illness. In J. Guimon, W. Fischer, & N. Sartorius (Eds.), *The image of madness: The public facing mental illness and psychiatric treatment* (pp. 118–128). Basel, Switzerland: Karger.

Warner, R. (2005). Local projects of the World Psychiatric Association programme to reduce stigma and discrimination. *Psychiatric Services, 56,* 570–575.

Warner, R., Taylor, D., Wright, L., Sloat, A., Springett, G., Arnold, S., et al. (1994). Substance abuse among the mentally ill: Prevalence, reasons for use, and effects on illness. *American Journal of Orthopsychiatry, 64,* 30–39.

Watson, A. C., & Corrigan, P. W. (2005). Challenging public stigma: A targeted approach. In P. W. Corrigan (Ed.), *On the stigma of mental illness: Practical strategies for research and social change* (pp. 281–295). Washington, DC: American Psychological Association.

Watson, A. C., Otey, E., Westbrook, A. L., Gardner, A. L., Lamb, T. A., Corrigan, P. W., et al. (2004). Changing middle schoolers' attitudes about mental illness through education. *Schizophrenia Bulletin, 30,* 563–572.

Watson, A. C., Ottati, V., Lurigio, A., & Heyrman, M. (2005). Stigma and the police. In P. W. Corrigan (Ed.), *On the stigma of mental illness: Practical strategies for research and social change* (pp. 197–217). Washington, DC: American Psychological Association.

Watson, A. C., & River, P. (2005). A social-cognitive model of personal responses to stigma. In P. W. Corrigan (Ed.), *On the stigma of mental illness: Practical strategies for research and social change* (pp. 145–164). Washington, DC: American Psychological Association.

Wegner, D. M. (1997). When the antidote is worse than the poison: Ironic mental control processes. *Psychological Science, 8,* 148–150.

Weiner, B. (1985). An attributional theory of achievement motivation and emotion. *Psychological Review, 92,* 548–573.

Weiner, B., Perry, R. P., & Magnusson, J. (1988). An attributional analysis of reactions to stigmas. *Journal of Personality and Social Psychology, 55,* 738–748.

Weinstein, R. (1983). Labeling theory and the attitudes of mental patients: A review. *Journal of Health and Social Behavior, 24,* 70–84.

Weiss, M. F. (1994). Children's attitudes toward the mentally ill: An eight-year longitudinal follow-up. *Psychological Reports, 74*(1), 51–56.

Wekerle, C., & Wolfe, D. A. (2003). Child maltreatment. In E. J. Mash & R. A. Barkley (Eds.), *Child psychopathology* (2nd ed., pp. 632–684). New York: Guilford.

Werner, E., & Smith, R. (1992). *Overcoming the odds: High-risk children from birth to adulthood.* Ithaca, NJ: Cornell University Press.

Wertheim, L. J. (2003, September 8). Prisoners of depression. *Sports Illustrated*, 71–75.

Whatley, C. (1958). Social attitudes toward discharged mental patients. *Social Problems, 6*, 313–320.

Williams, G. C. (1966). *Adaptation and natural selection: A critique of some current evolutionary thought*. Princeton, NJ: Princeton University Press.

Willis, A. G., Willis, G. B., Male, A., Henderson, M., & Manderscheid, R. W. (1998). Mental illness and disability in the U.S. adult household population. In R. W. Manderscheid & M. J. Henderson (Eds.), *Mental health, United States, 1998* (pp. 113–123). Washington, DC: U.S. Government Printing Office.

Wills, T. A. (1981). Downward comparison principles in social psychology. *Psychological Bulletin, 90*, 245–271.

Wilson, C., Nairn, R., Coverdale, J., & Panapa, A. (2000). How mental illness is portrayed in children's television: A prospective study. *British Journal of Psychiatry, 176*, 440–443.

Wilson, E. O. (1975). *Sociobiology: The new synthesis*. Cambridge, MA: Harvard University Press.

Wilson, G. T., Becker, C. B., & Heffernan, K. (2003). Eating disorders. In E. J. Mash & R. A. Barkley (Eds.), *Child psychopathology* (2nd ed., pp. 687–715). New York: Guilford.

Woods, N. S., Eyler, F. D., Conlon, M., Behnke, M., & Webie, K. (1998). Pygmalion in the cradle: Observer bias against cocaine-exposed infants. *Journal of Developmental and Behavioral Pediatrics, 19*, 283–285.

World Health Organization. (2001). *Mental health: New understanding, new hope*. New York: Author.

Wright, E. R., Gronfein, W. P., & Owens, T. J. (2000). Deinstitutionalization, social rejection, and the self-esteem of former mental patients. *Journal of Health and Social Behavior, 44*, 68–90.

Yarrow, M. R., Clausen, J., & Robbins, P. (1955). The social meaning of mental illness. *Journal of Social Issues, 11*, 33–48.

Zahn-Waxler, C., Duggal, S., & Gruber, R. (2002). Parental psychopathology. In M. H. Bornstein (Ed.), *Handbook of parenting, Vol. 4. Social conditions and applied parenting* (2nd ed., pp. 295–327). Mahwah, NJ: Erlbaum.

Zajonc, R. B. (1980). Feeling and thinking: Preferences need no inferences. *American Psychologist, 35*, 151–175.

Zigler, E., & Glick, M. (1986). *A developmental approach to adult psychopathology*. New York: Wiley.

Zilboorg, G., with Henry, G. W. (1941). *A history of medical psychology*. New York: Norton.

Zito, J. M., Safer, D. J., dosReis, S., Gardner, J. F., Boles, M., & Lynch, F. (2000). Trends in the prescribing of psychotropic medications to preschoolers. *Journal of American Medical Association, 283*, 1025–1060.

Zito, J. M., Safer, D. J., dosReis, S., Gardner, J. F., Magder, L., Soeken, K., et al. (2003). Psychotropic practice patterns for youth: A 10-year perspective. *Archives of Pediatric and Adolescent Medicine, 157*, 17–25.

Index

"abominations of the body," 30, 50, 253n.37
active coping, 167, 230
ADHD. *See* attention-deficit/ hyperactivity disorder
adolescents, 40, 111, 138, 207, 239, 221. *See also* children
advertising, 202–203, 206–208
advocacy groups, 37, 149, 178, 184, 200
  community-based initiatives and, 196–197
  as coping mechanism, 230
  families and, 82, 167–168, 222–225
  media watches and, 202–204, 207
  websites of, 218
Aesculapius, 57
aesthetics, 31, 32, 49, 158
affective empathy, 200
Afghanistan war, 142
African Americans, 43, 45, 265n.6
aggressive concealment, 107
alcohol use, 101–102, 232–233
Ali, Muhammad, 120
Allderidge, P., 61
Allen, L., 94
Allport, G., 37
almshouses, 63, 65, 66, 67, 78

ambivalence, 34–35, 52, 251n.18
American Psychiatric Association, 82, 279n.11, 281n.12
American Psychological Association, 279n.11
Americans with Disabilities Act (1990), 124, 182, 190, 267n.34, 276n.19
America Undercover (television series), 210
ancient societies, 56–59, 69, 71, 91
anger, 50, 86, 144, 146
Annenberg Public Policy Center, 112
anorexia nervosa, 219, 234–235
antidepressants, 78
anti-immigrant sentiment, 67–68, 69, 76
antipsychiatry movement, 40, 84, 218, 233, 258nn.30, 31, 280n.2
antipsychotics, 78, 84, 227
anti-Semitism, 77, 115
anxiety, 35–36, 39, 43, 84, 147, 227
appraisal, 44, 150, 271n.27
Aristotle, 58
Asclepiades, 58
astronomical forces, 56, 60, 61
asylums, xii, 59, 61, 63–67, 77–78

attention-deficit/hyperactivity
    disorder, xiii, 7, 227
  child-rearing practices and, 280n.1
  family-oriented therapies and,
    219–220
  heritability of, 85, 249n.26
  increased diagnosis of, 276n.29
  personal impairment model and,
    12
  statistical model and, 9
attitudes
  behavior and, 272n.1
  implicit vs. explicit, 160–161, 273n.9
  stigma and, 93, 94–98, 102–104, 113,
    158–160
attributional ambiguity, 149
attributions, 7–8, 247n.3, 260nn.40, 41,
    271n.35
  biogenetic model and, 85, 86–90,
    104, 152–154, 163
  research and, 163–164, 168
  stigma dimensions and, 32–33
authoritarian personality, 42, 253n.48
autism, xiii, 174, 211, 227
  blaming of parents and, 82
  heritability of, 85
  stigmatization of parents and, 109,
    263n.56
aversive prejudice, 252n.20
avoidance, 86, 106, 146

banishment, xii, 60, 61, 64, 66, 144,
    146
Basinger, Kim, 210
Batson, C. D., 200
Bazelon Center for Mental Health
    Law, 178
Beardslee, William, 221–222
beatings, 61, 63, 64, 67
Beautiful Mind, A (film), 210
Bedlam (London), 61, 64, 256n.15
Beers, Clifford, 75, 81
behavioral responses, 93, 113, 158,
    251–252n.19
  evolutionary model and, 50, 144
  research and, 99–100, 104
behaviorism, 74
benevolence, 87, 190, 253n.49, 261n.29
Ben-Porath, D. D., 103

Bethlehem Hospital (London), 61, 64,
    256n.15
Bible, 53, 56
Bicetre (Paris hospital), 64, 65
biogenetic models, 84–91, 144, 155,
    232, 259n.37, 271n.35
  attributions and, 85, 86–90, 104,
    152–154, 163
  family stigma and, 167–168
biological models, 68, 107, 209
biological treatments, 78, 257n.11
bipolar disorder, 21, 85, 109, 174, 227,
    233, 281n.17
Black, E., 76
blame, 32, 33, 44, 85, 198, 234
  families and, 109–110, 154, 221
  parents and, 82, 154, 217, 242
  of self, 138, 171, 221
  stigma reduction and, 86, 87
blemishes of character, 30, 48, 50
bloodletting, 58, 61, 63, 64, 66, 91
"board and care" homes, 80
Bodenhausen, G. V., 198
Bradshaw, Terry, 120
brain, 13, 14, 15, 18, 54, 57
  disorders and diseases of, 85–89,
    113, 152, 153, 218, 223
brain imaging, 13, 14, 85
Brandeis, Louis, 76
Brockman, J., 159
Buchwald, Art, 120
Buck v. Bell (1927), 76
buzz marketing, 207, 209, 240
Byzantine scholars, 60

California, 79–80, 257n.15, 273n.20,
    277n.34
Campaign for Mental Health Reform,
    178, 184, 277n.32
Campbell, Earl, 210
Canada, 103
Carnegie Foundation, 76
Catholicism, 62–63
cause marketing, 206
Celsus, 58–59
censorship, 118, 265n.6
character blemishes, 30, 48, 50
cheating, 48, 50
Chiarugi (Italian physician), 65

child abuse, 83
child custody rights, 125, 126, 131, 181, 191
  relinquishment of, 189–190
child guidance movement, 75, 81
child-rearing style, 74, 75, 82, 154, 217, 280n.1
children, 69–71, 81–83
  academic and clinical interest in, 82–83
  delinquency and, 40, 71, 80, 111
  disclosure to, 138, 221–222
  educational campaigns and, 195–196
  family-oriented therapies and, 219
  historical views of, 69–70
  labeling and, 40, 111–112
  mental illness in, 40, 110, 138
  as mental illness perceivers, 112–113, 169–170
  overcoming of stigma and, 185–190, 191, 194
  parental mental illness and, 171, 221–222
  parental stigma and, 107, 109, 171
  pejorative language use and, 117
  preventive mental health orientation and, 83, 187–189, 191, 277nn.32, 33
  self-blame and, 138, 221
  special education for, 71, 83, 185–187, 191, 194, 276n.29
  stigma research and, 169–171
  stigma's effect on, 107, 111–112, 114, 170–171, 264n.67
  television programming for, 118
  See also family; parents
children's rights, 71
child welfare, 81, 83
China, xiii, 56, 103, 109
Christianity, 60, 62–63
chronicity, 31, 144, 158, 162
Churchill, Winston, 181
Church of Scientology, 188, 258n.30, 280n.2
civil rights, 79, 125, 177, 209, 241, 257n.15
Clark University, 74
client-centered therapy, 74

clinical psychology, xiv, 82, 266n.21
Clinton, Bill, ix
coalitional exploitation, 47, 49–50
cognitive-behavioral therapy, 74
cognitive empathy, 200
cognitive therapy, 231
collaboration, 193–194, 199–200, 215
commitment (institutional)
  criminal, 126–127
  involuntary, 103, 126, 152, 257n.15
  laws concerning, 103, 126, 152, 184–185, 257n.15
common ingroup identity model, 199
Community Mental Health Centers Construction Act (1963), 79, 179
community mental health movement, 79, 83
Community Mental Health Services Act (1954), 79
community residences, x, 183, 246n.7
community treatments, x, 60, 78–81, 83, 121
  overcoming of stigma and, 191–201
compassion, xiv, 32–33, 35, 91, 168, 200–201, 209
competition, 37–38, 44, 45
concealability, 30–31, 158
concealment, 26, 107, 147–148, 167, 169, 171, 270n.21
confinement. See institutionalization
Congress, U.S., 76, 125, 179
conscience, 63
consciousness, 54
"consumers," mentally ill patients as, 263n.47
contact hypothesis, 192, 260n.41
controllability factor, 32–33, 60, 88, 152–154, 162, 163
cooperative tasks, 193–194
coping strategies, 104, 105–106, 107, 147–151, 156
  appraisal and, 271n.27
  families and, 167, 218–225
  humor and, 204
  for mental health professionals, 215–216
  for the mentally ill, 229–231, 282n.24
  research on, 164–165

corporate sponsorships, 208
Corrigan, Patrick, 90, 109–110, 125,
    141, 191, 215, 230, 241
counterstereotypic imagery, 198–199,
    210
course (of stigmatized attribute). *See*
    chronicity
courtesy stigma, 24, 106, 114, 121, 211,
    264n.61
Crandall, C. S., 146
Crazy People (film), 203
creativity, 26, 57, 174, 255n.6, 274n.44,
    281n.17
criminal commitment, 126–127
criminalization, xiii, 76, 80, 83,
    184–185
crisis theory, 64
Crisp, A. H., 103
Crocetti, G., 96, 97
Cronkite, Kathy, 128
crucifixion stigmata, 23
Cruise, Tom, x, 258n.30, 280n.2
Cullen, F. T., 98, 159
cultural competency, 214–215
cultural perspectives, xiii, 26, 115–
    139
    discrimination and, 44–45
    mental illness definition and, 7
    research and, 175
    treatments/care and, 152, 240
cultural seeding, 207–208
Cumming, E. and J., 95–96

dangerousness
    as civil commitment criterion, 152
    media portrayals of, 118, 119
    perception of, 101–103, 113, 155,
        261n.29
    as stigma dimension, 31, 32, 144,
        158
D.C. Comics, 204, 204
death. *See* mortality
defensive avoidance, 201
deinstitutionalization, x, 78–81, 83,
    151, 184
demonologic models, 54–55, 56, 60,
    62–63, 73, 91, 153, 163
dependent variables, 162–163

depression, xiii, 7, 21, 142, 227, 255n.6,
    280–281n.6
    family-oriented therapies for,
        221–222
    melancholia as, 57, 58
    shame and, 36
    statistical model and, 9
    stigma research findings on, 102,
        103, 105
despair, 88, 105, 124, 153
determinism, 55
    genetic, 67, 68–69, 234
Deutsch, A., 78
developmental psychopathology
    model, 16–17, 18, 86, 90, 282n.1
devil, 62, 63
Devine, P. G., 42
diagnosis, 13, 111, 122, 155
    accuracy of, 84, 113
    disorder categorization and, 19–20
*Diagnostic and Statistical Manual
    of Mental Disorders,* 18–20, 82,
    84, 102, 122, 248–249n.24,
    281n.12
disability. *See* personal impairment
    model
disclosure, 167, 269n.59
    to children, 138, 221–222
    job-related concerns about,
        130–131, 182
    by medical/mental health
        professionals, 132–134, 169
    overcoming of stigma and, 210–211,
        221–222, 230
    stigma related to, 131–132
discrimination, x, xiv, 21–23, 249n.33,
    266–267nn.28, 29
    ambivalence and, 35
    behavioral research findings on,
        99, 100, 104
    coping strategies for, 229–231
    counterstereotypic imagery and,
        198–199
    employment and, 45, 124, 130–131,
        182–183, 191, 275n.16
    housing and, 123–124, 183, 191
    individual differences in, 42–43
    institutional supports for, 44–45

self-esteem enhancement and, 38, 145
stigma and, 24, 26, 146
structural, 38, 146–147, 166–167
system justification and, 39, 147
See also prejudice; stereotyping
disgust, 50, 144, 146
disruptiveness, 31, 158
Dix, Dorothea, 67, 68, 70, 78
Domenici, Pete, 179
Dovidio, J. F., 99–100, 199
downward comparison, 37, 38
draepetomania, 13
driving privileges, 126, 191
drugs. See psychotropic medications; substance abuse
DSM-IV. See Diagnostic and Statistical Manual of Mental Disorders
dualism, 54
Durham, K., 98
dyadic cooperation, 47–48, 50
Dympna (patron saint of "mad" people), 255–256n.14

Eagleton, Thomas, 264n.4
eating disorders, 219, 234–235
ecological view, 12, 17, 18
economics, 45, 48, 69–70, 182, 265n.7
    housing and, 123–124, 183
    parity costs and, 179
education
    attainment level of, 109, 151
    mainstreaming and, 186, 193, 194, 276n.29
    special provisions for, 71, 83, 185–187, 191, 194, 276n.29
educational programs, xiv, 238
    for families, 217–218, 222
    to overcome stigma, 191–192, 194–196, 199, 278nn.44, 48, 49
Education for All Handicapped Children Act (1975). See Individuals with Disabilities Education Act
egalitarianism, 34, 51
Egypt, ancient, 56
Einstein, Albert, 135

electroconvulsive treatment, 78, 257n.11
"Elimination of Barriers" initiative, 195, 279n.11
elitism, 234
e-mail alert networks, 204
embarrassment, 108, 109
emetics, 58, 66
emotional responses, stigmatization and, 50
emotion-focused coping, 230, 282n.24
empathy, xiv, 198, 200–201, 214
employment, 124, 151, 182, 193, 194, 275n.16
    discrimination in, 45, 124, 130–131, 182–183, 191, 275n.16
empowerment, 196, 215, 225, 268n.49
    group identification and, 149
    labeling and, 111, 113
    protest efforts and, 205
enacted stigma, 36
Engel, G. W., 90
England, 61, 64, 103
Enlightenment, 55–56, 63–66, 70, 71
entitlement programs, 123, 180
environmental factors, 78, 86, 143, 154, 218, 259n.37
equifinality, 19
Estroff, S. E., 196
Ethiopia, 109
ethnic cleansing, 77
ethnicity, 175
    prejudice and, 67–68, 69, 76
    stereotype threat and, 43–44
eugenics, xii, 75–77, 83, 89, 154, 234
    social Darwinism and, 46, 67, 76
Eugenic Sterilization Law (Nazi Germany), 76–77
evidence-based treatments, 213, 214, 227
evil spirits, 54–55, 56, 60
evolution, 15, 16, 28, 46, 247n.14
evolutionary psychology, xiv, 28, 45–51, 88, 255n.72
    behavioral response model and, 50, 144
existential fears, 145

exorcisms, 60
"extra break" phenomenon, 261n.29

Fair Housing Act (1988), 183, 190
family
    as environment, 78, 86, 143, 154,
        218–222, 259n.37
    narratives by, 134–139, 242
    overcoming of stigma and, 217–225
    preservation of, 189–190, 191, 277n.34
    shame and, 107, 108, 109, 130, 217
    stigma research and, 167–168
    stigma's impact on, xi, 106–110, 114,
        263n.56
    stigmatization of, 24, 75, 82, 87
    treatment responsibility of, 154
    See also children; parents
Family Opportunity Act (under
    debate, 2005), 189–190
family-oriented therapies, 218–222
family systems approaches, 74, 107
Family-to-Family Educational
    Program, 225
Farina, Amerigo, 86–87, 99, 104,
    111–112, 186
FBI, 196
fear, 7, 50, 87, 89, 109, 146
    of contamination, 110, 144
Federal Mental Health Act (1940),
    77–78
feedback legitimacy, 148–149
Fein, S., 38
felt stigma, 36, 108–109
film, 202–203, 205, 211
Folkman, S., 271n.27
folk psychiatry, 248n.18
folk psychology, 71
folk wisdom, 75
Foucault, M., 84
Fox, Michael J., 120
framing, 208–209, 240
France, 63, 64, 65
free will, 54, 55, 63, 74
Freud, Sigmund, 68, 74
fright, 59, 64, 66
funding
    community-based programs, 197
    government initiatives, 166,
        182–183, 273n.20, 277n.34

research, 181, 183–184, 191, 214, 237,
    283n.13
special education, 186, 191

Gabbard, G. O., 211
Gabbard, K., 211
Gaertner, S. L., 199
Galen, 59
Galton, Francis, 68, 75
Gamache, G., 109
Gattaca (film), 273n.15
General Social Survey, 102
genetic determinism, 67, 68–69, 234
genetics, 163, 173, 247n.12, 259n.37
    eugenics and, xii, 75–77, 83, 89, 154,
        234
    mental illness and, 14, 68–69,
        85–91, 143, 153–154, 167–168,
        217–218
    See also biogenetic models
genocide, xii, 77, 83, 89, 91, 154
George III, king of Great Britain, 64
Germany, xii, 61, 76–77, 103, 115, 154
Gheel (Belgium), 60, 71, 91,
    255–256n.14
Gillmore, J. L., 111–112, 186
Goffman, Erving, 23, 24, 25, 30, 48, 50,
    106, 121, 147–148, 253n.37
Goldberg, S. G., 230
Goldhagen, D. J., 115–116
Gore, Tipper, ix
Gove, W., 97–98
government initiatives, 78–80, 83, 123
    funding of, 166, 182–183, 273n.20,
        277n.34
    See also legislation
Graves, R. E., 104
Greece, ancient, 56–59, 69, 71, 91
Griesinger, Wilhelm, 68
Grob, G. N., 81
group homes, 183
group identification, 149, 198, 199–200
guardian appointment, 61
guilt, 63, 107, 218
gypsies, xii, 77

handicap See personal impairment
    model
Harman, C. R., 108

harmful dysfunction model, 14–16,
    18, 19
Harre, N., 90
Harrington, A., 211
Harris, M. J., 112
Harris Poll, 102
Harvey, William, 63
Haslam, N., 74, 89–90, 248n.18
hatred, 50, 257n.7
HBO, 120, 210
healers, 57
healing temples, 57, 59, 71, 91
health insurance, 124–125, 267n.37
    lack of, 179–180, 191
    parity in, 125, 178–181, 190, 191, 193,
        228, 267–268n.39
heredity. *See* genetics
heretics, 60, 62
Hindu cultures, 56, 58
Hinshaw, Virgil, Jr., 135–138, 174
Hippocrates, 13, 55, 57–58, 59, 66, 71,
    85, 152, 255n.9
Hitler, Adolf, xii, 76–77, 89, 115,
    252n.32
Hitler's Willing Executioners
    (Goldhagen), 115
Hoge, C. W., 142
Holmes, Oliver Wendell, 76
Holocaust, xii, 77
homelessness, x, xii–xiii, 11, 80, 123
Homer, 57
homosexuality, xii, 10, 11, 77, 281n.12
hopelessness, 105, 122, 124, 151, 212, 228
hospitals. *See* institutionalization
hostility, 33, 109
housing, 123–124, 183, 191, 193, 194
Hovland, C., 45
humanization, 26, 210–211
humor, 204
humors, imbalance of, 55, 58, 73
Hyman, Steven, 247n.12

IDEA. *See* Individuals with
    Disabilities Education Act
identity, 37–40, 43, 121
identity threat, 44, 150–151, 165
immigrant groups, 67–68, 69, 76
impairment, 11–12, 14–15
Implicit Association Test, 160, 273n.9

implicit stereotypes/prejudices, 34,
    160–161, 251n.16
incompetence, 61, 126, 275n.15
independent variables, 161–163
India, xiii, 103, 109
indirect stigma, 106
Individual Education Plan, 185–186,
    276n.29
individualism, 34
Individuals with Disabilities
    Education Act (1975, 1991, 2004),
    83, 185–186, 190, 191, 276n.29
infanticide, 69, 70
ingroups, xiv, 29–30, 42, 145
    coalitional exploitation and, 49–50
    enhancement of, 38, 43
    multiple memberships in, 252n.29
    outgroup personal contact with,
        192–194
    reconstruction of, 199–200
    social identity and, 37–38
Inquisition, 62
insanity defense, 127, 268n.44
institutional discrimination, 44–45
institutionalization, x, xii, xiii, 77–78,
    83, 91
    children and, 70–71
    history of, 59–69
    involuntary, 103, 126, 152, 257n.15
    stigma reduction and, 193
    See also commitment;
        deinstitutionalization
insulin shock treatment, 78
insurance. *See* health insurance
integrated marketing communication,
    208
intergroup bias, 252–253n.35
Internet, 120, 208, 218
intolerance. *See* discrimination;
    prejudice; stereotyping
involuntary commitment, 103, 126,
    152, 257n.15
Iraq war, 142
Islam, 60, 166
isolation, 58, 68, 77, 104, 148

jails. *See* penal systems
Jamison, Kay Redfield, 128–129, 131,
    137

Japan, xiii, 263n.47
Jews, xii, 77, 115
John Deere, 120
Joint Commission on Mental Illness
    and Health, 79, 95
Jones, Edward, 30–31, 144
Judd, Ashley, 120
jury service, 125, 126, 181, 191
"just world" hypothesis, 33, 38
juvenile delinquency, 40, 71, 80, 111
Juvenile Justice Delinquency
    Prevention Act (1974), 83

Kaplan, B., 128
Keeping Families Together Act (under
    debate, 2005), 189–190
Kennedy, Edward, 179, 275n.11
Kennedy, John, 79, 179, 275n.11
Kennedy, Rosemary, 275n.11
Kevles, D. J., 76
Kim-Cohen, J., 173
Knapp, Caroline, 129
Kramer, Heinrich, 62
Kurzban, R., 46–47, 48, 49–50, 51, 144

labeling, xiv, 10, 99, 100–102, 113, 155,
    253n.39
    children and, 40, 111–112
    as stigmatization factor, 30, 39–41,
        88, 97, 146, 162
Lachenmeyer, Nathaniel, 134
Lafave, H., 96
Laing, R. D., 84
Lakoff, George, 208
Lamy, R. E., 96–97
Lancet (journal), 141
language, 116–117
    reframing of terminology and,
        85–90, 113, 152, 223, 238–239
Lanterman-Petris-Short Act (Calif.),
    257n.15
Larry King Live (television program),
    120
law. See legal rights; legislation
Lazarus, R. S., 271n.27
Leary, M. R., 46–47, 48, 49–50, 51,
    144
"least restrictive alternative"
    principle, 186, 194

Lee, Carmen, 196
Leete, Esso, 129–130
Lefley, H. P., 108
legal rights, 125–127, 131, 181–182, 191,
    275n.15
legislation, xiv, 83
    commitment, 103, 126, 152, 184–185,
        257n.15
    overcoming of stigma via, 177,
        178–191
    parity, 125, 179, 181, 190
    sterilization, xii, 76–77, 89, 257n.5
    See also specific acts
legitimating myths, 38–39
leprosy, 32, 63
licensing, professional, 126
Lincoln, Abraham, 181
Link, B. G., 25, 98, 100–101, 102, 105,
    128, 141, 146, 147, 157, 159, 166,
    176–177
lobbying, 184, 225
lobotomies, 78, 91
Locke, John, 70
Los Angeles County Jail, 80
lunatic, origination of term, 60
Lundin, R., 215

MacDonald-Wilson, K. L., 182
mainstreaming, 186, 193, 194, 276n.29
Malleus Maleficarum (Sprenger and
    Kramer), xii, 62
marketing, 206–210, 239–240
marriage, 76, 125, 126, 181, 191
media, 113, 144, 264n.4, 265–266nn. 6,
    7, 17, 18
    future issues for, 239–240
    as information source, 218
    overcoming of stigma and, 202–211
    stereotypes portrayed by, x, xiii, 32,
        101, 102, 117–120, 146, 150,
        151–152, 166, 185, 202–205, 217
Media Madness (Wahl), 120
media-watch organizations, 202–204,
    207
Medicaid, 180, 189, 267n.37, 275n.14
medical models, 68, 84, 91, 167–168
    attributions and, 33, 152, 168
    mental disorder definition and,
        13–14, 18, 247n.10

medical professionals, 110–111,
    132–134, 169, 211–212
Medicare, 180, 267n.37, 275n.14
medications. *See* psychotropic
    medications
Mehta, S., 86–87, 104
melancholia, 57, 58
Mental Health Equitable Treatment
    Act (2001), 179
Mental Health Media Partnership,
    279n.11
Mental Health Parity Act (1996), 125,
    179
mental health professionals, 94, 108,
    110–111, 114
    attitudes and practices of, 120–123,
        168, 211–216, 240, 266n.26
    cultural competency and, 214–215
    disclosure by, 132–134, 169
    enhanced training for, 213–214
    family members and, 108, 110
    overcoming of stigma and, 211–216
    status elevation for, 212–213
    stigma research and, 168–169
    support and therapy for, 215–216
Mental Health Systems Act (1980),
    80
mental hygiene, 75, 77
mental illness, xii–xiii
    children and, 70–71, 81–83
    conceptions of, 18–21, 73–92,
        232–235
    definitions of, 7–18, 232–233
    deviance/dysfunction boundary
        and, 232–233
    future views of, 233–234
    historical views of, xii, xiv, 53–72,
        91
    impact of, 20–21, 48
    incidence/prevalence of, 6, 21, 155,
        238, 246–247n.1, 249n.29,
        272n.40
    independent variables of, 161–163
    integrative models of, 90
    knowledge levels about, 93, 94, 96,
        102–103, 104, 113, 158
    mild/moderate forms of, 154–156,
        162
    models for describing, 8–18

positive features of, 174–175
recovery from, 173–174, 227–228
research priorities and, 236–238
romanticizing of, 174, 241, 274n.44
screening for, 187–189, 191,
    235–236, 277nn.32, 33
stigma reduction and, 225–231
stigma research findings and,
    93–114
symptoms and signs of, 13, 18, 143
See also treatment and care
mental retardation, xii, 68, 77
meritocratic societies, 44–45
Meyer, Adolf, 81
middle-class values, 151
military, U.S., 142
Miller, F. E., 109–110
minority groups. *See* ethnicity;
    racism; stereotyping
M'Naughten Rule, 126–127
monasteries, 59, 60, 61, 91
mood disorders, 221–222
morality, 60, 71, 73, 91
moral transgression model, 10–11,
    17–18
moral treatment, 66–69, 70, 71, 79, 91
mortality
    anxiety about, 39, 145, 166,
        253n.37
    children's rates of, 69, 70
Morton (eighteenth-century author),
    65
MTV, 208, 239
mutual enhancement, 48
Myers, Michael, 211–212

NAMI Stigmabusters, 204
narratives, 127–131, 134–139, 164,
    210–211, 242, 268n.49
Nash, John, 274n.44
National Alliance on Mental Illness,
    106, 108, 178, 184, 203, 225
National Committee for Mental
    Hygiene, 81
National Institute of Mental Health,
    77, 98, 184, 236–237, 238, 276n.24
National Institutes of Health, 184
National Mental Health Association,
    178

National Mental Health Awareness
    Campaign, 208
National Stigma Clearinghouse, 203,
    204
natural functions, 15–16
natural selection. *See* evolution
Nazis, xii, 76–77, 115, 154
negative eugenics, 76–77, 154
neo-Krapelinian movement, 84
Netscape, 120
Neuberg, S. L., 46, 47
Neugeboren, Jay, 134
neurodiversity, 209, 227, 240–241,
    281n.13
neuroscience, 14, 84
New Freedom Commission on
    Mental Health, x, 142, 178, 188,
    235
newspapers, 118–120, 202–203, 218
Nigeria, 109
Norway, 103
Nunnally, J. C., 94, 110, 117–118
Nuremberg trials, 77

objective burden, 107–108, 109, 167,
    168
Olmstead, D. W., 98
optimal distinctiveness theory,
    252–253n.35
origin (of stigmatized trait), 31, 32, 158
orphanages, 70
Oskamp, S., 51
outgroups, xiv, 29–30, 145
    coalitional exploitation and, 49–50
    denigration of, 37–38, 43, 145
    homogeneity effect and, 41
    ingroup personal contact with,
        192–194
    reconstruing of, 199–200
    social identity and, 37–38
    stereotypes and, 34, 38, 251n.14
    terror management and, 39
outpatient therapy, 74–75, 83

Page, S., 100, 123, 183
parasite avoidance, 47, 48–49, 50, 88
parents
    blaming of, 82, 154, 217, 242
    child mental disorders and, 82

child-rearing style of, 74, 75, 82,
    154, 217, 280n.1
child's treatment by, 69–70, 71
with mental illness, 171, 221–222
relinquishing of custody by,
    189–190
as resilience factor, 173
stigma's effect on, 107, 109, 171
Paris, 63, 64, 65
parity, 125, 178–181, 190, 191, 193, 228,
    267–268n.39
Paul, Ron, 277n.32
Pauley, Jane, ix, 120
Pearson, Karl, 75
peer support programs, 225
penal systems, 66, 67, 78, 191
    as mental facilities, xiii, 80, 83, 126,
        185
Penn, David, 141, 191
Pennsylvania Hospital (Phila.), 64, 65
peril. *See* dangerousness
Perlick, D. A., 105, 109
personal accounts. *See* narratives
personal contact, 191–194, 198,
    278n.43
personal impairment model, 11–12,
    18, 30
personality disorders, 7
pervasiveness, 33–34, 117
pessimism, 55, 88, 153
Pettigrew, T. F., 192
Phaire (sixteenth-century author), 70
pharmaceutical industry, 155, 188,
    218, 272n.41. *See also*
    psychotropic medications
Phelan, J. C., 25, 87, 102, 105, 128, 141,
    176–177
Philadelphia State Hospital
    (Byberry), 78, 135, 269n.63
Phillips, D. L., 97
Pinel, Philippe, 65, 66, 256n.28
pity, 87, 88, 190, 212
plasticity, 86
Plato, 58
police, xiii, 185, 196, 268n.43
positive eugenics, 76
possession, 56–57, 60, 62, 63, 73, 153,
    163
posttraumatic stress disorder, 142

poverty, 123, 124, 175
prediction specificity, 50–51
prejudice, 21–23, 38, 145, 175, 249n.33
  ambivalence and, 35
  aversive, 252n.20
  behavioral research findings on, 99
  contact hypothesis and, 192
  dominant cultural beliefs and, 115
  ethnic, 67–68, 69, 76
  implicit, 34, 160–161
  individual differences in, 42–43
  stigma and, 24, 26, 29, 51–52, 88
  system justification and, 39, 44
  unconscious biases and, 160–161
  See also racism; stereotyping
preventive care and services, 78
  children and, 83, 187–189, 191,
    277nn.32, 33
  screening and, 235–236
primary appraisals, 271n.27
primary labeling theory, 40, 97
prisons. See penal systems
pro-anorexia movement, 234–235
problem-focused coping, 230,
  282n.24
productivity, 174, 281n.17
Proposition 63 (Calif., 2004), 273n.20,
  277n.34
protective factors, 173
Protestant ethic, 44
Protestantism, 62–63
protest efforts, 191, 197, 202–205
psychiatry, xiv, 67, 68, 84, 266n.21
  "branding" of, 213
  depictions of, 211
  developmental focus and, 82
  See also antipsychiatry movement
psychoanalytic theory, 68, 74, 82
psychodynamic models, 107
psychological testing, 75
psychology, 68, 71, 84, 213
  behavior models and, 73–75
  See also evolutionary psychology;
    social psychology
psychopharmacology. See
  psychotropic medications
psychotherapy, 78, 211, 214–215, 227,
  231
psychotic thoughts/behavior, 102

psychotropic medications, 78, 84, 215,
  227, 258n.31, 275n.14
  screening and, 236
  side effects of, 32, 227
public health, xiv, 14, 78
public hospitals, x, xiii, 59
public office, right to hold, 125, 181,
  191
public relations, xiv, 209, 213
public service announcements, 206,
  208, 209
punishment, 32, 144, 146, 154
  as treatment protocol, 58, 61, 91
purgatives, 66
Pussin, Jean-Baptiste, 65

Quakers, 65

Rabkin, J. G., 94
racism, 28, 35, 115, 177, 242, 272n.5
  aversive, 252n.20
  eugenics and, 76–77
  symbolic, 35, 160
radio, 208, 218
Razi, al-, 60
Read, J., 90
realistic group conflict theory, 37–38,
  44, 45
Real Sports (television program), 120
"rebound" mechanisms, 176, 204–205,
  279n.6
reciprocal altruism, 47
rejection, 32–33
  by family, 130
  sensitivity to, 36, 150, 165
  stigma and, xi, 34, 87, 99, 104, 105,
    109, 148, 165
religion, 56, 60, 62–63, 91
Religious Society of Friends, 65
Renaissance, 55–56, 62, 70, 71
reputation, 30
research, 93–114
  behavioral, 99–100, 104
  funding for, 181, 183–184, 191, 214,
    237, 283n.13
  future concerns for, 157–175,
    183–184
  priorities for, 236–238
residual deviance, 40

resilience, 168, 172–175, 210, 233
respect, 201, 209, 214
responsibility, 60, 88, 152, 163,
    260n.43
restraints, 58, 61, 64, 65, 66, 67
rights, 79, 125–127, 131, 181–182, 191,
    275n.15
Ritsher, J. B., 105
River, P., 148
Rockefeller Foundation, 76
Rodríguez, Alex, ix
Rogers, Carl, 74
Rokeach, M., 198
Roman Empire, 58–60, 69
Roosevelt, Theodore, 81
Rootman, I., 96
Rosenhan, D., 99
Rotary International, 195
Rousseau, Jean-Jacques, 70
Rush, Benjamin, 65–66
Russell, Bertrand, 135

Sacks, Oliver, 174, 211
Sartorius, Norman, 141–142
Satcher, David, ix, 142
schemas, 22, 41–42, 51, 156
schizophrenia, 21, 89–90, 227,
    259n.36, 263n.47
  blaming of parents and, 82
  cultural environment's influence
    on treatment outcome for, 152,
    246n.13
  heritability of, 85
  medication side effects and, 32
  onset of, 17
  recovery from, 173, 273n.12
  as social marketing program focus,
    207
  stigma research findings and, 95,
    102, 103, 109
Schizophrenia Bulletin (journal),
    129
schools. See education
screening, 187–189, 191, 235–236,
    277nn.32, 33
Sears, R. R., 45
secondary appraisals, 271n.27
secondary labeling theory, 40–41, 88,
    111, 162, 232

secrecy, 26, 104, 106, 107, 148, 167, 225
secularization, 73–75, 83
sedation, 67, 91
self-affirmation theories, 252n.33
self-blame, 138, 171, 221
self-denigration, 36–37
self-esteem, 252n.27
  concealment and, 148, 270n.21
  employment and, 124
  enhancement of, 38, 145
  stigma's effect on, 25, 36, 105, 164
self-fulfilling prophecies, 24, 43, 51,
    99, 150, 254n.51
self-help groups, 36–37, 149, 200, 218,
    230
  families and, 82, 167–168, 222–225
self-stigmatization, 26, 106, 125,
    147–151, 156
September 11 terrorist attack (2001),
    166
sexism, 35
shamans, 26, 56–57
shame, 57, 148, 151, 164
  family members and, 107, 108, 109,
    130, 217
  professionals' disclosure and,
    132–134
  as stigma feature, 36–37
Shame of the States, The (Deutsch),
    78
Shaw, Fiona, 132
Sherif, C. W. and M., 199
Shields, Brooke, ix, x, 120, 280n.2
shock treatment, 78, 257n.11
Short-Doyle Act (Calif.), 79
Sibicky, M., 99–100
siblings, 108, 109
slavery, 13, 77
Snake Pit, The (book and film), 78,
    135
social capital, 48, 50, 88
social Darwinism, 46, 67, 76
social desirability, 159, 161
social deviance models, 9–10, 17–18
social distance, xi, 88, 259n.38
  research on, 94–98, 100–104, 112
  threat and, 87, 153
social dominance orientation, 43
social exclusion adaptations, 47–51

social identity. *See* identity
social marketing, 206–207
social norms, 9–10, 14–15, 17–18
social policy, 123–127, 177, 178–191
social power
  equal status and, 192–193
  labeling and, 39–40
  stigma and, 25, 26, 29, 147
social psychology, xiv, 28, 29–45, 46, 51
  attribution theory and, 32–33, 152
social status, 26
social support, 148, 149, 218, 222–225
social threat, 44
social work, 71
Society for the Prevention of Cruelty to Children, 70
sociology, xiv, 9–10, 28, 29–45, 51
Sontag, Susan, 90
sorcerers, 62
speaker bureaus, 196–197, 207
special education, 71, 83, 185–187, 191, 194, 276n.29
Spencer, S. J., 38
Sprenger, Jakob, 62
SSI. *See* Supplemental Security Income
Stamp out Stigma, 196–197
Stangor, C., 146
Star, Shirley, 95, 96
Star vignettes, 95, 102
state institutions, 67–68, 76, 77–78, 79, 121
State Mental Health Program Directors, 279n.11
statistical model, 8–9, 17
stealth marketing, 207, 209, 240
Steele, C. M., 43
stereotyping, 19, 21–27, 51, 156, 249n.33
  children and, 34, 112–113
  imagery to counter, 198–199, 210
  implicit, 34
  individual differences in, 42–43
  labeling and, 155
  media portrayals and, x, xiii, 32, 101, 102, 117–120, 146, 150, 151–152, 166, 185, 202–205, 217
  pervasiveness of, 33–34

self-esteem enhancement and, 38, 145
stigma from, 24, 26, 29, 33–34, 41–42, 43, 88, 104, 146
suppression of, 35, 251n.15, 252n.22
threat of, 43–44, 51, 149–150, 165, 254n.53
violence and, 166
sterilization, forced, xii, 76–77, 89, 91, 154, 257n.5
stigma, xi–xiii, xiv
  children and, 82, 111–112
  concept's overview, 23–27
  concept's viability, 140–143
  contact hypothesis and, 192, 260n.41
  contemporary increase in, 151–152
  controllability factors and, 32–33, 60, 88, 152–154, 158, 162, 163
  coping strategies for, 229–231
  cultural perspectives on, xiii, 26, 115–139
  current social issues and, 165–167
  definition of, 23–24
  effects on mentally ill people of, 104–106, 164–165, 262n.46
  everyday life indicators of, 115–139
  family members and, xi, 24, 75, 82, 87, 106–110, 114, 263n.56
  future research needs and, 157–175, 183–184, 238
  history of, xi–xiii, 23–24, 53–72, 91
  indirect, 106
  integrative model of, 44, 140–156
  international focus on, 142
  issues and controversies about, 232–243
  key features of, 33–37
  measurement and appraisal of, 157–161
  mechanisms underlying, 37–39, 158
  mental health professionals and, 108, 110–111
  modern mental disorder conceptions and, 85–91
  overcoming of, 75, 176–231, 238–240
  research findings on, 93–114

stigma (*continued*)
  self-imposed, 26, 106, 125, 147–151,
    156
  terminology reframing and, 85–90,
    113, 152, 223, 238–239
  three-stage stigmatization model
    of, 146
  tolerance and, 91–92, 96, 151,
    260n.49
  triggers of, 270n.14
  trilevel conceptualization of, 41–45
  types and dimensions of, 30–33, 144
stigma consciousness, 36, 43, 150, 170,
  252n.24
*Stigma: Notes on the Management
  of Spoiled Identity* (Goffman),
  23
stigmata, 23–24, 62
Storr, A., 174
stress, 271n.27
structural discrimination, 38, 146–147,
  166–167
Struening, E. L., 108
"stubborn child laws," 70, 256n.41
Styron, William, ix, 129
subjective burden, 108, 109, 136, 167,
  168, 217
subjective uncertainty reduction
  theory, 252–253n.35
substance abuse, 101–102, 232–233,
  249n.26, 262n.34
Substance Abuse and Mental Health
  Services Administration, 184,
  195, 205, 279n.11
suicide, 6, 212
suicide prevention centers, 196
Sullivan, M., 206, 207, 208, 213
Superman comics, 203–204
Supplemental Security Income, 123,
  124, 183, 267n.32
Supreme Court, U.S., 76, 177, 276n.19
Sweden, 109
Switzerland, 62
symbolic racism, 35, 160
sympathy, 32–33, 34, 52, 85, 200–201
syndromes, 13, 247n.9
system justification, 38–39, 44, 51,
  146–147, 198
Szasz, T. S., 84

Taft, William H., 76
Teachman, B. A., 161
television, 118, 119, 120, 202–203, 205,
  218
terror management theory, 39, 44, 145,
  166, 270n.16
Tessler, R., 109
Thompson, A. H., 103
threat, 7, 37–38, 94, 117, 252n.32
  appraisal of, 44, 271n.27
  biogenetic model and, 89
  identity and, 44, 150–151, 165
  integrative model of stigma and, xv,
    44, 143–147
  social distance and, 87, 153
  stigma dimensions and, 31, 32, 144
  terror management and, 39
  See also stereotyping, threat of
threat control-override symptoms,
  261n.30
Time Warner, 204
tolerance, 91–92, 96, 151, 260n.49
Torrey, E. Fuller, 107
Tourette's disorder, 174, 211
transaction, 17
treatment and care
  biological, 78
  cultural environment's impact on,
    152, 240
  discrimination and, 124–125,
    267–268n.39
  family's role in, 218–225
  health insurance and, 124–125,
    178–181, 190, 191, 267–268nn.37,
    39
  historical, 56–71, 77–79
  moral, 66–69, 70, 71, 79, 91
  in penal system, xiii, 80, 126, 185
  punitive vs. humane, 55, 61, 65
  reform efforts, 66, 67–68, 70–71, 77,
    78, 81, 181
  responsibility for obtaining, 154
  rights related to, 79
  stigma reduction and, 226–229,
    281nn.17, 18, 282n.19
  stigmatization of persons receiving,
    103
  See also institutionalization;
    psychotropic medications

trephining, 56, 255n.4
tribal characteristics, 30, 50
Tringo, J. L., 97
Tropp, L. R., 192
Tuke, William, 65
Turkey, xiii

unconscious biases, 160–161
unemployment, 124, 151, 182, 275n.16
University of Pennsylvania, 81, 112
unpredictability, 31, 48, 94, 144
urbanization, 151, 262n.41

vapors, 58
violence
    media portrayals of, x, xiii, 32, 101,
        102, 113, 119, 150, 152, 166, 185
    mental illness linked with,
        101–102, 113, 150, 152, 155, 166,
        261n.30
    mentally ill people as victims of, x,
        102, 119, 183
    in penal system, xiii, 80
    stereotypes and, 166
    substance use and, 101–102
virtual reality simulations, 162
Vives, Juan Luis, 62
Voice Awards, 205, 279n.11
voting rights, 125, 126, 181, 191

Wages and Hours Act (1938), 81
Wahl, Otto, 106, 108, 110, 120, 121, 122,
    130, 140, 169, 222, 263n.47
Wakefield, Jerome, 14–15, 18
Wallace, Mike, 120

Watson, A. C., 90, 148, 164
Weiner, B., 32–33
Wellstone, Paul, 179
Westernized cultures, 151–152, 175,
    271nn.30, 31
Weyer, Johann, 62
Whatley, C., 94–95
White House Conference on Children
    (1910), 81
White House Conference on Mental
    Health (1999), ix, 142
will. See free will
Willis, Thomas, 63
Wilson, C., 118
witches, xii, 24, 62–63, 65, 70
withdrawal, 104, 106, 148
Witmer, Lightner, 81
women
    as parents, 75, 82
    perceptions of violence and,
        262n.35
    sexual exploitation of, 50
    stereotype threat and, 43–44
    witchcraft charges against, xii, 24,
        62–63, 65, 70
Wonderland (television program),
    204
World Psychiatric Association, 207
Wright, E. R., 105
Wundt, Wilhelm, 68

Yarrow, M. R., 106–107
York Retreat (England), 65, 66

Zilboorg, G., 59, 62